THE BOOK TRADE

& ITS CUSTOMERS

ROBIN MYERS

THE BOOK TRADE
& ITS CUSTOMERS
1450-1900

Historical Essays for Robin Myers

EDITED BY
Arnold Hunt, Giles Mandelbrote
& Alison Shell

INTRODUCTION BY
D. F. McKenzie

ST PAUL'S BIBLIOGRAPHIES
WINCHESTER

OAK KNOLL PRESS
NEW CASTLE, DELAWARE

1997

First published 1997 by
St Paul's Bibliographies
West End House
1 Step Terrace
Winchester
Hampshire SO22 5BW
UK

Published exclusively in the United States of America
and its dependencies,
the Philippines and Canada by
Oak Knoll Press
414 Delaware Street
New Castle
DE 19720
USA

Library of Congress Cataloging-in-Publication Data

The book trade and its customers, 1450-1900 : historical essays for Robin Myers /
edited by Giles Mandelbrote, Arnold Hunt, and Alison Shell : introduction by
D. F. McKenzie.
     p.   cm.
    Includes index.
    ISBN 1-873040-42-3 (UK). -- ISBN 1-884718-34-5 (USA)
    1. Book industries and trade--Great Britain--History. I. Myers, Robin.
II. Mandelbrote, Giles. III. Hunt, Arnold. IV. Shell, Alison.
Z325.B72 1997
381'.002'0941--DC21   97-8786
                                                         CIP

ISBN 1-873040-42-3 (UK)
ISBN 1-884718-34-5 (USA)

Typeset in Dutch Roman by Ella Whitehead, Munslow, Shropshire
Jacket designed by Iain Bain
Printed in England by St Edmundsbury Press, Bury St Edmunds

Contents

Part I: The Book Trade

Part II: The Customers

Acknowledgements

The editors are delighted to thank all the contributors for their hard work and for managing to keep our secret so well. We are also very grateful for the enthusiasm and patience of all those involved in the production of this book, especially Robert Cross, David Way and Ella Whitehead, and to Iain Bain for his work on the design. Many of Robin's friends were a source of welcome encouragement and support; we would especially like to thank three Stationers, Keith Fletcher, Christopher Rivington and the late George Mandl, and two Secretaries of the Bibliographical Society, Mirjam Foot and David Pearson. Particular assistance was also provided by Anna Greening and Seija Lappalainen, by Michael Harris (who suggested the jacket illustration) and by Nest Davies and David Hall (with additions to the bibliography). Bernard Middleton has kindly agreed to bind a special copy, with a list of subscribers in calligraphy by Mary Shelbourne, for presentation to Robin Myers at the Bibliographical Society's Homee Randeria Lecture on 20 May 1997.

Finally, we would like to thank the *raison d'être* for this book. Robin has been completely unaware of the progress of her festschrift — even while research for a number of the essays was proceeding around her at Stationers' Hall — and, while still giving assistance and advice, she accepted with good humour the contributors' evasions of her usual interest and questions. This volume is testimony to her enabling powers.

A. H.
G. M.
A. S.

March 1997

Contributors

T. A. BIRRELL is a retired teacher of English. His publications include *The library of John Morris* and *English monarchs and their books*.

CHRISTINE FERDINAND is the Fellow Librarian of Magdalen College, Oxford. She is engaged on work on newspaper history, and a history of the College library.

ANNA GREENING is Archivist at the Fawcett Library, London Guildhall University, and Parish Archivist at All Hallows by the Tower, London.

DAVID J. HALL is a Deputy Librarian at Cambridge University Library, and has written articles and reviews on varied bibliographical and Quaker themes.

MICHAEL HARRIS is Senior Lecturer at Birkbeck College, University of London. He has worked extensively on 18th-century London serials and is co-editor, with Robin Myers, of the series of annual volumes on book trade history.

ARNOLD HUNT is currently a Research Fellow at Trinity College, Cambridge.

ELISABETH LEEDHAM-GREEN is Deputy Keeper, Cambridge University Archives, and a Fellow of Darwin College, Cambridge.

D. F. MCKENZIE has recently retired as Professor of Bibliography and Textual Criticism at Oxford University. Current projects include editions of Congreve and of the Stationers' Company's Liber A.

GILES MANDELBROTE is a Curator in the English Antiquarian section of the British Library.

SCOTT MANDELBROTE is a Fellow of All Souls College, Oxford.

DAVID PEARSON is the Librarian of the Wellcome Institute for the History of Medicine. His research interests focus on book binding and the history of book ownership, and he is the Secretary of the Bibliographical Society (London).

ESTHER POTTER is a bookbinding historian who is working mainly on the trade binders of the 19th century.

JAMES RAVEN is the author of numerous studies of the 18th-century book trade, and is University Lecturer in Modern History and Tutorial Fellow of Mansfield College, Oxford.

EILUNED REES spent her working life on the staff of the British Museum and the National Library of Wales. Her catalogue of pre-1820 Welsh books was published in 1987 under the title *Libri Walliae*.

ALISON SHELL currently holds a British Academy Post-Doctoral Fellowship in the English Department of University College, London.

JAMES E. TIERNEY, Department of English, University of Missouri — St Louis, is the editor of *The Correspondence of Robert Dodsley 1733-1764* and is currently preparing a CD-ROM index to pre-1800 British periodicals.

MICHAEL TREADWELL is Professor of English Literature at Trent University, Peterborough, Ontario, Canada. He has written extensively on the English book trade, in particular on London printing in the 17th and 18th centuries.

MICHAEL L. TURNER is the Head of the Preservation and Conservation Division at the Bodleian Library. He is also a member of the English Faculty at Oxford and holds a part-time lectureship in the History of Printing.

Abbreviations

ABMR   *Antiquarian Book Monthly Review*

Arber   *A Transcript of the Registers of the Company of Stationers of London; 1554-1640*, ed. Edward Arber (London: privately printed, 4 vols, 1875-7; and Birmingham: 1894)

BL   British Library

CSPD   *Calendar of State Papers: Domestic Series*

DNB   *Dictionary of National Biography*

ESTC   Eighteenth-Century Short-Title Catalogue

Greg   W. W. Greg, *A Bibliography of the English Printed Drama to the Restoration* (London: The Bibliographical Society, 4 vols, 1939-59)

Jackson   *Records of the Court of the Stationers' Company 1602 to 1640*, ed. William A. Jackson (London: The Bibliographical Society, 4 vols, 1957)

N & S   *British Newspapers and Periodicals 1641-1700*, compiled by Carolyn Nelson and Matthew Seccombe (New York: Modern Language Association of America, 1987)

PBSA   *Papers of the Bibliographical Society of America*

PRO   Public Record Office

SR   Stationers' Register

STC   *A Short-Title Catalogue of Books printed in England, Scotland, & Ireland, and of English books printed abroad, 1475-1640*, compiled by A. W. Pollard and G. R. Redgrave, second edition revised by W. A. Jackson, F. S. Ferguson and Katharine F. Pantzer (London: The Bibliographical Society, 3 vols, 1976-91)

Wing   *Short-Title Catalogue of Books printed in England, Scotland, Ireland, Wales, and British America and of English books printed in other countries, 1641-1700*, compiled by Donald Wing, second edition revised and edited by John J. Morrison, Carolyn W. Nelson *et al.* (New York: Modern Language Association of America, 3 vols, 1982-94)

Introduction

LIKE THE HISTORY OF THE BOOK ITSELF as a field of study, or indeed of any practice of reading or writing, a collection like this presents a challenge to define its disciplinary centre: where in the fissiparous variety of its tributes lies its intellectual and human coherence? Where in the cornucopia of its offerings do we find the principle of its unity?

'*E pluribus* Una' is of course the implied answer, locating its absolute value in the friendship and scholarship shared with a dedicatee whose own rich experience and unifying power is a paradigm of the way in which texts themselves bring us together in our common concern for their meanings and their making, both mentally and materially. In paying homage to Robin Myers, the contributors to the present volume affirm a community of interest that unifies them all in their commitment to that most distinctive human achievement, the creation and communication of meaning and its histories.

'The Book Trade' on the one hand 'and its Customers' on the other suggests at least an elementary division between the mechanics of the book trades, their formal structures and informal accommodations, and their human ends in learning and in transmitting knowledge. The material resources of paper and type and the technical skills of printing make way here for broader economic and social questions: business connections, patents, copyrights and their transfer, London's relations with Ireland and America, the Stationers' Company, and that special moment when, out of those formative but ever-changing conditions, the bound books pass into the customers' hands.

It is a richly varied world whose recovery would have been impossible were it not for the archivist, and it is only fitting that, in a collection dedicated to the distinguished Archivist of the Stationers' Company, this collection should itself be so rich in archival evidence. Elisabeth Leedham-Green, expert in inventories and minder and miner of the archives of the University of Cambridge, has drawn from them both a mass of detail and some valuable general statements about trade disputes in Cambridge at the end of the 16th century. Here Whitgift is seen to recommend Manasses Vautrollier as one 'in forrein bookes verie sufficient' and able therefore to furnish 'outlandishe bookes at first hand'. But to propitiate the Londoners and yet to protect the University's interests, it is also said that he should sell only foreign books in quires at London prices, and (foreshadowing a much later reality) that he should not 'suffer him selfe to be bought out of this Towne by the Stacioners'. Most significant however was Vautrollier's role in offering expert testimony on the means of valuing books in a dispute between Thomas Bridges and Hugh Burwell, and his statement that 'the Merchantes at London doe usuallie allowe unto the stacioners there; and all those that buy bookes of them, to sell them ageine three shillings in every pownd'. It is a claim reaffirmed elsewhere in the documents as: 'when the Stacioners of Camebridge doe buye bookes at London unbound they are allowed iij^s in the pownd'. These are valuable nuggets indeed.

The cache of Tottell family documents now at Stationers' Hall, a direct product of the vigilance of the Company's Archivist in noting their relevance and of her skills in securing them, yields broader evidence of the fortunes of a leading member of the London trade. Richard Tottell, holder of a lucrative patent for the printing of common-law books, may be better known for his miscellany, *Songes and Sonettes*, but the records of Tottell and son buying into the landed gentry are a telling measure of the personal rewards of his success in business. Some 140 documents concerning the Tottell family give, as Anna Greening says in her description of them, 'a rare glimpse into the financial affairs of a leading Elizabethan stationer'.

Many other leading Elizabethan stationers enjoyed equally rewarding patents, but from the point of view of a Company seeking in the late 1570s and 1580s to consolidate its membership and powers, all privileges held outside the Company and competitively within it were a serious threat to its integrity. However contingently complex were the means by which it was achieved, the creation of an English Stock in 1603 largely reconciled the rival factions by pooling numerous copyrights for the good of all members of the Company. What Arnold Hunt's account of book trade patents granted between 1603 and 1640 shows, however, is that such privileges were not only still being sold by the Crown and in increasing numbers, but that over half of them were to persons outside the Company – any of whom could thereby act quite independently of the Company's rules or interests. In that sense the patentees, who could argue from a distinct 'legal platform', were a constant threat to the Company's monopoly and made it especially vulnerable to legal challenge.

Arnold Hunt's valuable calendar of patents granted up to 1640 makes it clear that for all the work of Arber, Greg, Jackson and others, there is still much evidence about the book trade to be uncovered for the STC period. It is nevertheless more truly the case that the trade has no comparable body of scholarship for the years after 1640. Extending his list of patents would be immediately useful. It can also be more readily achieved than that other desideratum, an account of the acquisition, division, and transfer of copyrights within the Company which delves below imprints and the bare entries in the Stationers' Register.

The intricacies of ownership and its descent, whether in the differing periods for which patents were held, the variety of forms which reversions might take, the troubling overlaps of patent and copyright, or the passage of copyrights themselves within the Company, all point to the long-standing practice of shared investment. Giles Mandelbrote's discussion of Richard

Bentley's copies presents us with a document crucial to such questions. In its scale and detail it gives proof that, for example, investment in reference works was routinely shared between booksellers from at least the first half of the 17th century, that the study of certain classes of text may be more revealing than of individual titles, that any text in its variant forms might have several copyright histories, that the entry of copies at the Hall was becoming an increasingly inadequate way of recording the realities of publishing, and that by the end of the century they had indeed become only the smallest tip of a massive iceberg: 'Bentley and Wells between them . . . owned shares in at least 800 copies, but the entry books record their names against a mere 11.' It is a dramatic statement which, while it must give us pause and induce a measure of modesty in drawing conclusions from limited evidence, is also a challenge to bring to light far more such documents in this later, post-Shakespearian period.

Transitions in the forms of ownership, whether by patent, individual copyright, or overtly shared investment, and the emergence of the joint-wholesaling partnerships of the 18th century, fundamentally affect our understanding of the trade at every level. It is a background which is further illuminated in Michael Turner's account of the *List of Stockholders in the Worshipful Company of Stationers*, so expertly dated here to 5 July 1785. This list of 229 members of the English Stock might have been inferred from other documents, but its quite distinctive geographical structure reveals more than we hitherto knew of the mere mechanics of keeping members informed, and its annotation from the *London Booktrades Database*, which gives unique identifiers for every name, demonstrates the great improvements in method and accuracy now possible when editing such documents.

Comparable evidence and rigour in handling it, however, are not often found in what book historians might see as the liminal areas of text production, newspaper history and 'the picture trade'. Michael Harris's important contributions to the former are well known, and following his example the role of the newspaper as a highly significant form of text is coming to be much better understood. But the punning title he has given his present essay remains true of the print trade. Artistic prints and maps have their own scholarship, of course, as do the techniques of woodcutting, engraving, etching, lithography, and other forms of reproduction. But their relationship to texts within books, their multiple roles as quite independent texts, the application of the common skills of designing, drawing, and engraving to a wide range of products other than verbal texts by a body of still largely anonymous craftsmen who moved in and out of the print trade, and the very structure of that work force in the 18th century, are not yet well understood. 'Scratching the Surface' is too modest a title for what is in effect a preliminary sketch of an increasingly important aspect of the 18th-century book trade and a cogent plea for its thorough study both in itself and as a complement to book history.

Although the 18th-century trade in books between London and Dublin has been far from neglected, James Tierney is doubtless right in thinking that the paucity of primary evidence from the period has left us still largely ignorant about the extent to which it was in truth a piratical or a collaborative one. It is therefore a special pleasure to see that the story unfolded by Scott Mandelbrote about Bible printing in Ireland is drawn from such a revealing collection of correspondence with the SPCK. The first critical document is the apparently unique *Proposals for Printing (by Subscription) an Octavo Bible in Dublin*, dated here to 1718/19. And thereby hangs a tale of idealistic proselytising, economic ingenuity, and David and Goliath struggles with the main patentee, John Baskett. Since Andrew Crooke, the King's Printer in Ireland, had done little to print Bibles locally, they were virtually all imported from London (and Oxford) and Edinburgh. But their low standard and high price begot a plot to produce in Dublin 20,000 octavo Bibles of which the subscribers would take half 'at the prime Cost of Twenty Pence a piece in Sheets'. The subscription raised, the edition was printed by Aaron Rhames and published in 1722. By pricing these Bibles at only 1s 8d in sheets, the Dublin booksellers undercut not only Baskett's octavo Bibles (3s in sheets) but the cheapest of his duodecimos. Yet when all is said and done, they could only do so by the generosity of the subscribers and the Dublin SPCK in meeting half the costs of the edition, and the expenses of new type and employing a corrector. All of which, so uncharacteristic of normal trading conditions, is explanation enough for Dublin's failure to produce further such editions. As Scott Mandelbrote says, however, 'the possibility of printing the Bible in Dublin was more useful to English readers as a way of attempting to keep Baskett up to the mark, than it was as a source of cheap Bibles themselves.' In the book trade, Davids rarely beat Goliaths.

For other books where copyright was not a matter of patent rights, the story of London–Dublin relations is of course much less clear-cut. As with the ownership of copies in earlier periods, imprints do not reveal all. While acknowledging that recent studies have done much to suggest that the trade was often based on consultation and fair dealing, James Tierney's account of George Faulkner's London connections and correspondence with Dodsley further supports Faulkner's claim that he obtained his texts 'in the fairest Manner from the different Authors and Proprietors'. To his earlier demonstration that Dodsley was one bookseller who supplied his own publications for Faulkner's reprints, he now adds a cordial letter from Faulkner to Edward Cave, publisher of the *Gentleman's Magazine*, which yields the clear inference that Faulkner could expect a similar service from Cave or, failing his timely help, from yet another London agent.

Much of that trade must have been in sheets, yet the *coup de grâce* in customizing books was not their printing but their binding. Even the simplest forms of stitching demanded a labour force, still largely anonymous even when their materials and distinctive tools permit their products to be identified. At one end of the spectrum, symbols of ownership may enable the reconstruction of whole libraries; at the other, uniform trade bindings point rather to the indiscriminate dispersal of copies to largely anonymous readers. David Pearson's account of a binding with the arms of the Stationers' Company, however, offers an exception to the general rule that armorial bindings indicate ownership and suggests that books bearing the Company's arms might have been given as gift books or prizes by the Company.

The history of collections receives extensively informative and in many ways kaleidoscopic discussion in the second half of the volume. The demands of institutions and individuals, their choice of titles in response to different needs, the role of intermediaries, and the strengths of particular collections are the ostensible subject matter, but as with almost every aspect of book history the details merge to create what is really a complex picture of intellectual and social exchange.

This is well brought out in Christine Ferdinand's preliminary study of Magdalen College and the book trade in Oxford from 1450 to 1550. The idealism of Waynflete's foundation and the interest he took personally in the architecture of the college was intellectually reinforced by the gift in 1481 of 800 volumes for the library. Although most, sadly, are now lost, the choice of other books and their acquisition from local printers and booksellers and the means by which they were shared (some were chained and accessible to all but more were out on loan to fellows) bear vital witness in this critical period to the shift from medievalism to humanism. Books printed by Theodoric Rood show the college actively building its collections from local sources. And although names like those of John Foxe the martyrologist and John Jewel may loom larger in history, the continuing association with Magdalen of the Oxford bookseller Garbrand Harkes and his sons and grandsons (several of whom became members and even fellows of the college) indicates a healthy and constructive relationship between college and trade.

Two other studies which relate to collections in this earlier period are the splendidly complementary accounts by T. A. Birrell and Michael Treadwell. In detailing the subject range of the 2,000 titles in the library of the long-lived Sir Edward Sherburne, friend and confidant of John Flamsteed, T. A. Birrell not only shows a library in development from an earlier (1670) catalogue and reconstructs from the pressmarks its physical arrangement, but he reveals in microcosm what is itself, in its immense subject range, a text of late Renaissance man. As he says, 'Sherburne's library was not a hobby, it was an essential part of his working life' and its constitution here images the intellectual being of the man himself.

Sherburne is likely to have used Robert Scott as his main library agent, probably the best-connected and most knowledgeable supplier of specialist books in his time. But as Scott faded from the scene, others took over. Michael Treadwell's analysis of the role of Richard Lapthorne as an agent in securing books for client-collectors shows him at work from at least as early as 1683 to sometime after 1697, attending auctions and acquiring books for his fellow Devonian Richard Coffin. He was clearly assiduous in tracking down specific copies but his hunt for a 'perfect' copy of Higden's *Polychronicon* and his consciousness of the desirability of preserving an old binding 'because of its Antiquity' show him aware too of some bibliographical niceties. Like Sherburne, who built up a valuable collection of auction catalogues for reference purposes and acquired the other main reference tools of his time, Lapthorne sought out the major bibliographies, and it is from him we learn that there was a manuscript Book Auction Records available for consultation by *bona fide* inquirers. There is a wealth of information here on individual titles, their rarity, desirability, and cost, and on Lapthorne's associations with his clients and with other members of the trade. In this account we get a glimpse of a man knowledgeable and solicitous, in a central but generally shadowy role, go-between for the trade and collectors, and yet also with an eye to building collections himself for resale. While the chance survival of these Lapthorne letters yields a great deal which is new to us, it is also salutary in showing us yet again how much we are bound to simplify and misrepresent the past in the absence of comparable records of the relationships between the makers, distributors, and readers of books.

James Raven's discussion of the Charleston Library Society exploits another happy survival. The Society's relations with its successive London agents, and in particular the role of Lackington, Allen & Co. in supplying stock for the collection, yields a great fund of illuminating anecdote. An unusually complete letter book for the years 1759-1811 records the exchanges between suppliers and customer, and gives a rare insight into the practicalities of selection, packing, delivery, and turnaround times, as well as the problems of securing prompt payment under conditions of extended and dangerous Atlantic transit. In such matters the Society was probably typical of others further north also dependent on the London trade and affected in much the same way by the practicalities of demand and supply. Yet fired by a kind of cultural idealism perhaps, and imperious in the manner in which they sought its realization, the officers of the Charleston Library Society of South Carolina here reveal their will to be independent and their intemperate assertion of rights in a continued context of their direct material and cultural dependence upon London.

Many of the threads evident in Lapthorne's concern to run down perfect copies, albeit mainly for his clients, recur in David Hall's account of the collecting of the Bristol Quaker Francis Fry and his concern to run up (as one might say) 'perfect' copies for his great collection of English Bibles, later to be acquired by public subscription for the British and Foreign Bible Society. Like so many before and after him, Fry could be described on his death as having been 'one of the pillars of English bibliography', his efforts receiving universal support and acclaim, only to suffer an eclipse as new knowledge and standards of scholarship brought his most cherished assumptions into question. Yet although Fry undoubtedly muddied the bibliographical waters of Bible printing, as both A. W. Pollard and B. J. McMullin have shown, the balance between enthusiasm and scepticism essential to all good scholarship has never been easy to attain. To catch here, as we do from David Hall's essay, the sense of Fry's mission and the conviction of his own rightness is to understand as much of the age itself and of fashions in scholarship as of fashions in collecting. What more positively emerges is the remarkable strength of the fraternity of both private and institutional collectors and Fry's role within it as reporter, facilitator and, however self-interested in improving his own collection, as one beneficently inclined in noting and making good the deficiencies of others.

To move to Eiluned Rees's discussion of bookbindings in the National Library of Wales is to move from the 19th to the 20th century since, for all its historic depth with the addition of some extremely interesting bindings from earlier periods, the tale to be told about the collection is essentially one of the last 30 years. In this it is an important expression of a policy which, in acquiring such magnificent items as the *Liber Landavensis* with its 'exquisite gilt-bronze figure of Christ', illustrates both a national history and, pedagogically and aesthetically, an art and a craft. (As with Fry's practice in perfecting Bibles, however, it also reveals the destructive force of a misplaced idealism: its rebinding by the British Museum in 1892 was virtually an act of vandalism.) The intelligence with which the collection has been brought together is evident in how extraordinarily well it serves to illustrate this brief history of binding styles. The Welsh, unlike the Irish and Scots, did not themselves develop a tradition of fine binding, although the Gregynog Press, inspired by the Arts and Crafts movement, was to make a distinctive contribution. It is fully represented now in the National Library of Wales where, under the direction of the distinguished binder Julian Thomas, the historical collections give force to the excellence of the library's current achievements in fine binding.

Fine bindings are more peripheral to the central argument of Esther Potter's survey of the changing role of the trade binder in the 19th century, and yet (harking back to David Pearson's suggestion that books bearing the arms of the Stationers' Company might be intended as gifts), we find gift books illustrating one of the first stages in the evolution of publishers' bindings. Whereas in the 18th century trade binding was usually 'an *ad hoc* business carried on in small units', with the emergence of large publishing houses bindings became 'as much part of the book as the text' and each house, each genre, each series, might command a recognizable style to distinguish its market niche. Embossed leather bindings, for the top end of the gift book market, could be mass-produced. They are also a further example of the interdependence of various trades, on the lines suggested by Michael Harris: in their use of blocks and dies they drew on the overlapping skills of designers, engravers, and die-cutters. Although, as is often the case, there were major time-lags in the exploitation of technical innovation, the arrival of book cloth about 1825 and the introduction of the iron-framed blocking press in 1832 opened the way to economies of scale. Large editions could be uniformly bound and firmly identified with their publishers. Instead of being a final grace in giving distinctive form to an individual copy, binding was pre-planned as part of its printing. Since the edition could not go on sale until a large part of it had been bound, binderies had to increase their capacity dramatically: Westley's bound 6,000 volumes a day of Macaulay's *History* in 1855, and in 1890 two firms together bound 40,000 copies of Stanley's *Darkest Africa* in a fortnight. It was a remarkable shift within the century from the individuality of bespoke binding to a mass workforce 'feeding books into the machines'.

The Joker in this gift pack is Alison Shell's juxtaposition of Philip Morant's *History of Colchester* (1748) and John Clubbe's *History and antiquities of Wheatfield* (1758) which satirized it. It is an instructive exposition of the different mind-sets brought to the past by the antiquarian on the one hand, assembling local minutiae in the largely unargued belief that it is all intrinsically interesting, and the historian determined to derive moral lessons from an essentially literary past and to universalize experience. In fact, it is usually the antiquarian who has the last laugh, and logically so. For whatever nonsense might have to be discounted, the mere passage of time expands our knowledge in ways which can invest the details with an unexpected relevance. The demonstration here that Clubbe's satire is not merely verbal, as in the play with etymologies, but visual too in choice of format, layout, typography, and illustration, reinforces a larger point about material bibliography. It shows that, as Alison Shell puts it, there is nothing neutral about any element of a book's physical and textual presentation. Everything bespeaks meaning and a history of meanings.

In reflecting the wide-ranging interests of its dedicatee, this collection of essays on the book trade and its customers presents us with much new information about topics as varied as patents and copyrights, library history and personal collecting, the trade between London and Dublin, the supply of books to North America, antiquarianism, engravers and printsellers, the role of trade binders, and many new details about the Stationers' Company and its leading members. These contributions will be warmly welcomed by the ever-expanding body of scholars now recognizing the central value of book history to our understanding of past mentalities.

D. F. McKenzie

A 16th-century stationer and his business connections: the Tottell family documents (1448-1719) at Stationers' Hall

ANNA GREENING

AS ARCHIVIST OF THE STATIONERS' COMPANY, Robin Myers has not only acted as the custodian of the Company's muniments but has also been able to augment them by the acquisition of other book trade documents through gift and purchase. In the early 1980s a group of approximately 140 documents concerning the Tottell (or Tothill) family, from the muniments of the Drake family of Buckinghamshire, was acquired at auction through the generosity of five Liverymen and the Friends of the National Libraries. They are briefly noted in the published catalogue of the Stationers' Company archive, but the present article will describe them in more detail, with the object of making their contents better known to book trade historians.

At first sight, the Tottell documents appear sparse and peripheral. However, they start to reveal their secrets when ranged round the family settlement of 1592 (Documents 122 and 138) property by property, with apparent business transactions arranged in chronological order. They were originally conceived by some of the most influential legal minds of the day to conceal as much as they might reveal by means of the blandest of all-purpose legal instruments. English common law is very good at this and real intentions behind deeds often have to be teased out. For example, among the Tottell documents can be found bonds and counterbonds used as quitclaims, as networking tools, as financial guarantees to raise capital, to lend money, to ensure peaceable possession and to strengthen all kinds of legal agreement. The transition from City to County is clearly shown, both family and business relationships being used to secure property or business deals. Sharp (or at least shrewd) practice does not seem to have been unknown, and the collection as a whole will reveal insights to those interested in the lives and careers of the individuals concerned, many of whom were active Stationers.

The title deeds and bonds forming this collection were amassed by Richard Tottell and his son William Tothill in their piecemeal acquisition of lands and subsequent consolidation of title, and through other partially related business activities. The properties, with their associated deeds, passed into the Drake estates through the marriage of William Tothill's eldest surviving daughter Joan into the Drake family.[1] The absence of personal letters or other informal documents is regrettable but not unusual in a collection of this nature, and the archive as it stands gives us a rare glimpse into the financial affairs of a leading Elizabethan stationer, Richard Tottell, from which it is possible to glean a good deal of information about his involvement with other members of the London book trade.

The life of Richard Tottell has been well researched and documented. H. J. Byrom's exhaustive article 'Richard Tottell – his life and work' appears to have left few stones unturned, and can be corroborated at many points by the evidence in the Tottell documents. Richard Tottell was born in about 1530 in Exeter, the third son of William Tothill, a prominent citizen and mayor in 1552. Richard served his apprenticeship under William Middleton, stationer and citizen of London, completing it under his widow Elizabeth. He worked for Henry Smith, also a renowned law printer, setting up on his own as a printer and bookseller after Smith's death.

In 1553, when he was still in his early twenties, Tottell was granted a seven-year patent giving him the exclusive right to print common-law books. This monopoly, which he may have acquired through his powerful legal and Catholic connections, was to prove extremely lucrative over the years. It attracted some opposition from less privileged printers and from some of Tottell's business rivals, notably Christopher Barker. Throughout his career Richard Tottell published about five or six books annually, his most famous non-legal text being perhaps the *Songes and Sonettes* ('Tottell's Miscellany') which was published in June 1557 and inspired many imitations.[2]

Richard Tottell was influential in the Stationers' Company. Active in the forerunner to the Company before 1557, his name was 67th on the list at incorporation. He was Renter Warden in 1559-60, Under Warden in 1561, Upper Warden in 1567, 1568 and 1574, and Master in 1578 and 1584. After 1585 Richard Tottell became much less active due to ill health and in about 1588 retired into the country at Wiston, Pembrokeshire. He died in 1593 or early 1594.[3]

Richard Tottell had married Joan, daughter of the printer Richard Grafton, and William, his eldest son, was born in 1560. William Tothill (as he preferred to spell his name) later entered the Middle Temple with Richard Grafton, second son of Richard Grafton the elder, and afterwards practised in partnership with Richard (assumed to be the younger); he was never a member of the Stationers' Company.[4] William Tothill married Catherine Denham, daughter of Sir John Denham, and it was their eldest surviving daughter Joan who married into the Drake family.

This collection falls neatly into several kinds of halves: about half the documents are property-related and about half probably business-related; about half date from before or during Richard Tottell's life-time and about half from after his death in 1593/4; about half are obviously title deeds and the other half bonds or counter-bonds with a much more opaque purpose. The documents range in date from 1448 to 1714 with the greatest con-centration in the second half of the 16th century, especially around the 1580s and 1590s.[5]

The pivotal document is dated 29 August 1592 (Document 138). It is a settlement to pay debts and secure the family's future, making properties and goods over to William Tothill in trust during Richard Tottell's lifetime, in return for various conditions. Both settlement and counterpart are present, the latter endorsed 'A deed of gift to my sonne William Tothill' and, in another hand, 'father and mothers will'.[6] H. R. Plomer was unable to trace any will of Richard Tottell, quoting only from the *inquisitio post mortem* held at Buckingham on 21 March 1594.[7] This mentions only freehold properties and corresponds so closely to the list in the family settlement that it is difficult not to believe that Document 138 was not in front of the jury at the time of the inquiry. However, no mention is made by Plomer of rights in any leasehold or copyhold property, goods, chattels or money, all mentioned in the family settlement.

As might be expected, the settlement gives no detailed description of Richard Tottell's business beyond 'all the books of laws of the realm and other printed books in the London house occupied by William Tothill and all paper, letter, presses and furniture for printing', although some facts may be inferred. There is a tantalizing reference to William Tothill's financial circumstances in the condition stating that, during Richard Tottell's lifetime, all income from the sale of books and all other specified goods is to be used towards the payment of £1,530 owed by William Tothill. From the specified annuities and other cash payments mentioned it is possible to augment the Tottell family tree. In particular, it appears that at this date William Tothill had a young son John, who seems not to have survived to inherit the family estates, although it is possible that he was a more distant relation.

Why did Richard Tottell choose to dispose of his property and goods by using a form of family settlement instead of the more usual will and testament? He may have wished for privacy – he is thought to have been a Roman Catholic and may have wished to be reticent about his faith in order to escape penalty. He may also have wished to be discreet about the ramifications of his business relationships or the exact extent of his wealth, and to avoid paying taxes or incidents.

The documents also reveal the extent of Richard Tottell's holdings of landed property. On 10 November 1572 he acquired a farm in Little Missenden from Alexander Denton, for the considerable sum of £360.[8] Similarly in 1596 William Tothill acquired for £400 'all that the Lordshippe and mannor of Agmondisham Woodrowe with all the rights members and appurtenances thereof'.[9] The Tottells, father and son, were buying into the landed gentry. They undertook the exercise slowly, discreetly and – as two further examples testify – ruthlessly. Document 141 is an assignment of a lease dated 14 May 1578 following distraint, and recites a writ of *fieri facias* brought by Richard Tottell. Document 139 is a bargain and sale of 3 July 1607 where William Tothill seems to have felt the need to impress – the second party to the deed is spelt out as 'John Clapham, esq. (one of the

Tentative Tothill Family Tree

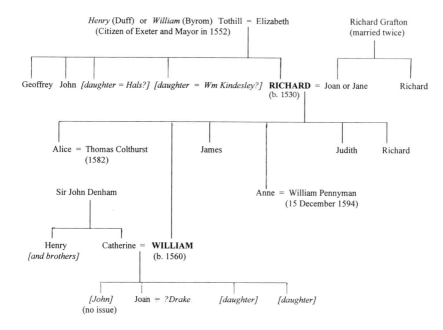

William Kindesley described by William Tothill as 'unkle Kindesley' (Document 114)
William Hals described by William Tothill as 'cosen' (Document 90)

Note: unconfirmed elements in italic

five clerks of Chancery), William Kyndesley, gent., and William Pennyman, gent. (cursitors of the Court of Chancery).' Both are examples of property transactions where perhaps all may not have been as it seemed. Both Tottells hedged round their property acquisitions with bonds, counterbonds, quitclaims and other legal constraints, for land tenure at this time was still theoretically feudal. Knowledgeable as they were in common law, they were able to use a variety of legal devices, such as the bargain and sale, leases for extraordinarily long periods of time such as 999 years, assignments of lease and, perhaps most sophisticated of all, a common recovery by triple vouchee (Document 125). Some such documents may also be concealed loans, since usury was still technically illegal at this period and it was relatively common for a loan at interest to be disguised as some other form of financial instrument, such as a lease or a bargain and sale; see Document 124 for a possible example.[10]

The documents in this collection which record title in property reveal a close family network. William Hals, for example, described in an endorsement to Document 40 as 'Cosen Hals', appears to have acted with

William Kindesley and William Tothill in family matters on some 11 occasions. He was part of the Devon branch of the family, living in Plymouth in 1600 and witness to a bond of 1597 (Document 33) relating to rights of inheritance at Queenlinch in the parish of Silberton, Devon. Similarly, there are six documents (4, 47, 68, 88, 112 and 134) relating to the Somerset Colthurst connection. Richard Tottell's daughter Alice had married Thomas Colthurst in 1582 (Document 134).

Perhaps of more interest in the context of the archives of the Worshipful Company of Stationers and Newspaper Makers are those deeds documenting relationships that combine family affairs with business, notably featuring the involvement of William Kindesley, Richard Grafton, Henry Denham and William Pennyman. William Kindesley (Kyndesley, Kingesley or Kingsley) described by William Tothill as 'unkle' (Document 114) must have been Richard Tottell's most trusted relative and friend. He was active on the Tothills' behalf from 1582, when he was a witness to the bond settling land in Somerset on Richard's daughter Alice on her marriage to Thomas Colthurst (Document 134), until 1607 (Document 139, mentioned above in connection with possibly questionable land deals). Most telling of all, he was trustee in the family settlement also discussed above (Documents 122 and 138). He acted with father and son (mostly son, as by 1587 Richard Tottell had retired) in complicated business deals secured and documented by an almost impenetrable system of bonds and counterbonds. He was party or co-party to no less than 25 such arrangements between 1583 and 1603, usually being co-bound with William Tothill.

One of the Richard Graftons was first witness to the family settlement of 1592. More palaeographical work needs to be undertaken on the Tottell documents to see which, if any, involved Richard Grafton senior, and which his son. Earlier documents in this collection feature also Edward, John and Robert Grafton as witnesses or parties. Edward Grafton is mentioned as the partner of Richard Tottell in a deed of 1575 (Document 41). Richard Grafton junior (Richard Tottell's brother-in-law and William Tothill's partner) appears to have been as actively involved in Tothill property and business arrangements as William Kindesley — though rarely if ever the same ones. He was the third named life in a lease (not in this collection) made on premises in Pembrokeshire — presumably the property in Wiston to which Richard Tottell retired in about 1588.[11]

Richard Grafton's business relationship with William Tothill appears to have been extremely close (always remembering that William Tothill was almost certainly acting as his father's agent, openly or otherwise, until very soon before Richard Tottell's death in 1593/4). In company with Henry Denham and Gerrard Dewes (Documents 1, 35, 66, 69, 130 and 154) Grafton was involved in several extremely complicated arrangements of bond and counterbond to raise and secure large amounts of money, especially between 1584 and 1586. In 1585 Richard Grafton mortgaged his house in Wood Street to William Tothill as security for several of these transactions (Document 124). William Tothill endorsed this document 'Unkle Grafton's ls [i.e. lease] to me for saving me harmless for div's bonds' – which might seem to argue an age difference of some years. It would appear that William (in his mid-twenties at the time) may have been a front-man or man of straw. The involvement of Gerrard Dewes in these transactions is particularly intriguing, as Dewes was, in McKerrow's words, 'a disorderly member of the Company, being frequently fined for such offences as keeping his shop open on Holy days and not attending the court', and it is unexpected to find him in partnership with such respectable pillars of the Company as Tottell, Grafton and Denham.[12]

Henry Denham, probably brother to Catherine Denham, William Tothill's wife, is seen in the context of this collection to have been active on William's (or his father's) behalf from 1584, mainly in a business connection when raising or lending funds. However, his Tothill family interest is made evident in that he was the second witness to the family settlement of 1592 (Documents 122 and 138).

Neither Richard Grafton (senior and/or junior) nor Henry Denham is represented in this collection after 1592 and certainly not after Richard Tottell's death. Incidentally, nor is Gerrard Dewes. By contrast, William Tothill's brother-in-law William Pennyman was active on William Tothill's behalf (or *vice versa*) from 1595 until 1609 (within the context of this collection in any case). He married William Tothill's sister Anne in 1594.[13] By 1607 he was a cursitor in the Court of Chancery (Document 133 discussed above). This appears to indicate a shift in William Tothill's associates after his father's death from law printers to the legal field itself. He was, after all, a 'gentleman of the Middle Temple'. Detailed examination of the deeds in this collection resulting from money-raising consortia might reveal their underlying purpose – perhaps to finance abortive ventures such as Richard Tottell's proposed paper-mill in 1585[14] – or perhaps just to raise publishing capital.

Robin Myers described her first impression of the Tottell collection, viewed in the auction-room, as a 'depressing cardboard boxful of dirty, damp-stained, twisted and illegible bits of vellum of the kind we all know so well.'[15] Only now that the documents have been conserved and catalogued has their significance begun to emerge, and Robin's far-sightedness in acquiring them for the Stationers' Company archive deserves to be applauded.

Archival note

The collection was calendared in 1989-90 by Anna Greening, with the assistance of Arnold Hunt and Alison Shell, using National Library of Wales deed listing conventions.[16] The resulting descriptive list (to which this article is intended as an introduction) has been arranged both chronologically and as structured round the key document of the series, the family settlement of 29 August 1592 (Documents 122 and 138).

Most of the documents are on parchment, in Latin and/or English. A small number of them are badly damaged and illegible. About 20 have undergone conservation treatment at Camberwell School of Art. Larger documents are stored flat in the plan-chest and the others in archival boxes in the muniment room at Stationers' Hall.

Some of the documents were microfilmed with the rest of the muniments before being catalogued, so their physical arrangement has not been changed. It is expected that researchers will study them on microfilm where possible.

References

1. H. J. Byrom, 'Richard Tottell—his life and work', *The Library*, 4th ser., vol.8, (1927-8), pp.199-232 (ref. p.217). On the Drake (latterly Tyrwhitt-Drake) family papers, see G. Eland, *Shardeloes Papers of the 17th and 18th Centuries* (London: Oxford University Press, 1947). Another group of manuscripts associated with William Tothill is described in Stuart Clark, 'Wisdom literature of the seventeenth century: a guide to the 'Bacon-Tottel' commonplace books', *Transactions of the Cambridge Bibliographical Society*, vol.6 (1976), pp.219-305, and vol.7 (1977), pp.46-73.

2. The standard modern edition is *Tottel's Miscellany (1557-1587)*, ed. Hyder Rollins, 2 vols, 2nd ed. (Cambridge, Mass.: Harvard University Press, 1927), which also contains a discussion of Tottell's activities as editor-publisher. A more recent account can be found in Arthur Marotti, *Manuscript, print and the English Renaissance lyric* (Ithaca: Cornell University Press, 1995), pp.212-19, 294-6.

3. See Byrom, p.212; *DNB*.

4. I am grateful to Peter Blayney for this information.

5. A more detailed breakdown of the distribution of documents by decade would run as follows: 1440s (1); 1460s (1); 1480s (1); 1500s (1); 1550s (1); 1560s (4); 1570s (22); 1580s (31); 1590s (49); 1600s (20); 1610s (3); 1620s (1); 1640s (1); 1710s (1).

6. These have been catalogued as Documents 122 and 138 in the list of Tottell documents held at Stationers' Hall (see Archival Note); all further references to documents will be given within the text.

7. H. R. Plomer, *Abstracts from the wills of English printers and stationers from 1492 to 1630* (London: The Bibliographical Society, 1903), preface and pp.33-5 (ref. p.33).

8. The title deeds augment Byrom's research earlier this century in the Close Rolls and Buckinghamshire Feet of Fines. For example, Byrom quotes Close Rolls, No.894, 14 Eliz., part 27, where he found the enrolment of Richard Tottell's purchase from Alexander Denton of a farm in Little Missenden for £360. Document 133 in this collection, dated 10 November 1572, gives the further information that the farm was called 'Mantells' (variants also given) and names the tenant. Document 98 throws further (though still murky) light on the transaction, being a bond dated 9 December 1571 in £100 between Leonard Buckenmaster (the tenant in question) and Alexander Denton, the condition being 'observance of a pair of indentures of even date' between the two—some sort of quitclaim, perhaps?

9. Close Rolls, No.1523, 38 Eliz., part 7: see Byrom, p.217. Documents in this collection include an adjunct (Document 50) to the actual deed of title which is only recited. This adjunct document is a counterbond in £500, the condition being that William Tothill is saved harmless from all claims respecting the manor and lands in Amersham Woodrow except for eight named leases ratified by several indentures dated 11 August. It recites a bond of 10 August recording the sale of the lordship of the manor and other pieces of land. Document 137 is one of the eight named leases dated 23 March 1595, and Document 126, a lease for 992 years dated 16 September 1601 to one Richard Smith of The Warren,

capital messuage at Amersham Woodrow, William Tothill to have egress to the hawk house for holding the manor court.
10. Arnold Hunt has suggested this interpretation of the evidence to me.
11. Reference to this lease is made in Documents 31 (bond in £2,000 of 6 March 1588), 51 (counterbond in £100 of 17 August 1588), and 135 (bond in £200 of 30 November 1588). All three were to secure payment and to strengthen title.
12. R. B. McKerrow *et al.*, *A dictionary of printers and booksellers . . . 1557-1640* (London: The Bibliographical Society, 1910), 'Garrat D'Ewes'.
13. See E. Gordon Duff, *A century of the English book trade (1457-1557)* (London: The Bibliographical Society, 1905), p.157; *DNB* (entry for Richard Tottell).
14. Byrom, p.215.
15. 'Maintaining a specialist archive in the location that engendered it', *Society of Archivists Specialist Repositories Group, Occasional Papers*, 1 (1983), 17-21.
16. I would like to thank Arnold Hunt and Alison Shell for help on a number of bibliographical points.

Manasses Vautrollier in Cambridge

Elisabeth Leedham-Green

. . . just now as I re-entered my room what should I see but a toad hopping across the floor. Fortunately it was a smallish toad. It has retired behind the curtains near the door. Will it clasp my legs as I go out? and what does it portend?[1]

So MONTY JAMES, writing from Eton on 11 November 1929. Similar misgivings must have stirred the breast of Dr Robert Some, Master of Peterhouse and Vice-Chancellor of Cambridge University, on receiving a letter from the Archbishop of Canterbury sent from Lambeth on 4 November 1590, with the following directive:

. . . Whereas this bearer Manasses Vautrovillier having bene brought up under his father Thomas Vautrovillier (latelie deceased) in the trade of printeing & bookeselling was lefte with diverse other Orphanes utterlie destitute of any releif, but onelie his fathers printeing stuffe & a fewe bookes, which lie on his hande, having no other meanes to live but upon the same, And is now desierouse to use the trade of bookeselling in that Universitie, I thought good at his earnest suite to commende him unto you, and to pray you that you would favour him there in what you may. He is an honest youngman, his skil in forrein bookes verie sufficient, & whereas you are now served at the thirde hand & at the highest price hee shall be able to furnishe you with outlandishe bookes at the first hand, and afford them also better cheape which would be a greate pleasure to the students of that Universitie. And therefore I pray you to lett him have your good freindshipp for obteyning this his suite, the rather for my sake.[2]

Why was Archbishop Whitgift, always abreast of affairs in his old university, now foisting on the university ostensibly as a bookseller a man equipped not only with his father's 'printing stuff' but also his father's knowledge both of the overseas book trade and of the Stationers' Company? When Thomas Thomas had set up his press in Cambridge the London stationers, predictably, had registered alarm, and the resident university authorities had been active participants in Thomas's manoeuvres in the face of the ensuing guerilla warfare,[3] while Whitgift's zeal for the establishment of a moderate Calvinist orthodoxy had made him sympathetic to the Stationers' vociferous warnings of the dangers of allowing printing outside the metropolis. The dangers had indeed been realized when Thomas proposed to print a new work by Burleigh's ex-chaplain, the presbyterian Walter Travers. On 30 June 1584 Whitgift had written to Burleigh, his frequent ally and the university's chancellor:

Ever sens I hard they had a printer in Chambridg I dyd greatlie feare that this and such like inconveniences wold followe, nether do I thingk that yt wyll so stay. for althowgh m' vicechancellor that now ys, be a verie carefull man and in all respectes greatlie to be commended, yet yf yt may fawle owt hereafter that some such as shal succeade hym wyll not be so well affected, nor have such care for the publike peace of the Church, and of the state . . .[4]

Dr Some was indeed inclined to espouse a more extreme form of Calvinism than was prudent but he had more sense, at least on this occasion, than lightly to dismiss any letter from Whitgift.

Thomas Thomas, the first Cambridge stationer privileged under the university's charter of 1534 to have actually exercised the right to print 'al maner bookes', had died on 9 August 1588. Among those charged with the valuation of his estate was a stranger, the London stationer John Legate, lately apprenticed to the Queen's printer, Christopher Barker, and perhaps sent on his recommendation to assist in the valuation.[5] By the time Vautrollier arrived in Cambridge Legate had been appointed printer to the university in succession to Thomas, but it had taken until 2 November 1589, fifteen months, for this to be achieved, and, even so, things were hardly settled. Legate and Thomas's widow, Anne, were fiercely embroiled in litigation in the Vice-Chancellor's court, Anne Thomas claiming that Legate had not paid her the £30 which he had promised her for her services, surely rashly promised, in securing him the place. Legate, meanwhile, was protesting that the £140 which he had paid for half of Thomas's premises and for his stock of books was a sum greatly in excess of their value.

Is it possible that Vautrollier, hearing of these altercations, had originally planned to come to Cambridge with an eye on the printer's place but had been overtaken by events while he waited for appropriate recommendations from those with influence in the University? The fact that his father Thomas, in making his will, had left to Manasses rather than any of his three other sons 'the printinge press which I brought back againe from Scotland furnished with all her appurtenances that is to saye with fower Chassis, and three Frisketts, two timpanes and a Copper plate. With a copper marbell and other smale tooles and instruments',[6] could be seen as suggesting that at that time he had appeared to his father to be the son most apt to trade as a printer, and Whitgift's mention of the press in his letter may well be a remnant of a previous plan. This is, however, the merest supposition and, if Thomas Vautrollier had indeed seen Manasses as his likeliest successor as a printer, his vision was defective. There is no evidence that Manasses ever worked as a printer; it was his brother, Thomas junior, who made a stab at it. A far likelier reading of the will is that of the four brothers the eldest, Simeon, to whom his father left 'That peece of golde of the kinge of Skotlande weyinge aboute ten crownes of the same', had already established himself in some other trade, leaving Manasses, the next oldest, and already four years into his apprenticeship with his father, as the obvious heir to his Edinburgh press.

The Vice-Chancellor, therefore, on receiving Whitgift's letter, although he may well have feared a Trojan horse, took it at face value. Vautrollier wished to set up as a bookseller, specializing in foreign books. Dr Some had the letter copied into the university's *Liber Rerum Memorabilium* (whence it is cited above) with the rider: 'Upon the receite of his Graces letters, Manasses Vautrouillier was pleasured accordinglie'. Or at least, if not actually upon receipt, for the letter can hardly have spent a month upon the road, then within a reasonable passage of time—after all, it does say 'accordinglie'. It was, in fact, on 10 December that it was recorded that the Vice-Chancellor and Heads

... did admitt and allow Manasses Vautrovillier to exercise the trade of booke sellinge within the Universitie of Cambr: soe that the said Manasses Vautrovillier doe enter bond with sufficient suerty for the performance of the Condicions followeinge

1° Inprimis that he sell noe bookes but suche only as have bene or shalbe printed beyond the Seas, whereby are understoode not only those bookes which have bene or shalbe originally printed beyond the Seas but allsoe suche bookes as beinge originally printed within this Realme of England shalbe afterwardes printed beyond the Seas

2° Item that \he/ shall sell noe bookes but only in quire, and unbound.

3° Item that he shall sell his bookes in quire unto the Stacioners and all other persons within this towne as good cheape as they are or shalbe bought or solde in London.

4° Item that he shall not suffer him selfe to be bought out of this Towne by the Stacioners or other persons for any Condicion or summe of monye

5° Item where as the said Vautrovillier hath certaine bookes left unto him by his Father that were printed in England it maye be lawfull for the said Vautrovillier to sell and utter the said bookes soe that he deliver unto Mr Vicechauncellour A true Inventary of them upon his oathe and doe not under Colour of them sell more then are now in his possession.[7]

The clear intention is to restrict the newcomer's activities and protect the position of the existing Cambridge stationers. Vautrollier shall sell only foreign books (none of those easy profits from ballads, almanacs and popular works of devotion), he shall not put the local binders out of business, he shall not make an excess profit, he shall not escape from these conditions but he may sell the stock remaining in his hands from the press of his father, Thomas Vautrollier—many of them, no doubt, the Ramist textbooks which had for some time been in demand in the university—so long as he buy no more in.

We get the distinct impression that Vautrollier was not welcomed with open arms, partly, no doubt, because the Cambridge stationers were no less anxious to defend their pitch than their London counterparts, and partly because he may well have been seen as what perhaps he was, a spy from the Company. It appears, small wonder, that he wriggled. We have also the draft of a later form of the agreement, drawn up at some time in 1591, perhaps in the light of loopholes perceived in the earlier form. The conditions imposed now were:

1° That the sayed vautrollier and his assignes doe at noe tyme hereafter sell or put to sale any bookes within this towne or the precinctes of the same but sutch only as have beene heretofore or shall hereafter be printed beyond the seas commonly called by the name of forren bookes.

2° That he shall not exercise or practise the byndinge of bookes for him selfe or other to make any benefite or commoditye thereby but shall sell and put to sale all and singuler his wares unbounde.

3° That he shall not refuse or deny to sell his wares [. . .] unbound as ys aforesayed unto the stationers and bookebynders of this towne and to all and singuler the studentes of this \town/ university at sutche prices and as good cheape from tyme to tyme as the sayed bookes may be afourded or bought of the printers stationers bookebynders or other artificers in London.

4° That he shall enter bond in the summ of xl^{tie} powndes of lawfull english money to the Chauncellor masters and schollers of this university for the trew performance of all and singuler the Conditions aforesayed and of all other orders heretofore established for and concerninge the trade and occupation of printers stationers and bookebynders within this university soe farr fourth as the sayed orders shall concerne \him/ the sayed Vautrolier.[8]

The inference is that, in order to make ends meet, young Vautrollier, whose name the authorities had at last mastered, had tried (1) to market English books in collaboration with one of the existing Cambridge stationers (his assigns), (2) to hire himself out as a binder (for himself *or other*) and (3) to negotiate prices above an absolute London minimum. The clauses concerning his being 'bought out of this town' and the sales of his father's stock have vanished, but the 'suerty' in which he is to be bound for the observance of the conditions on which he may trade is set at the substantial sum of £40.

What were Vautrollier's prospects of succeeding in Cambridge under these terms? Certainly the taste of students of that university for outlandish books was, then as ever, insatiable, but Cambridge was, on the face of it, adequately supplied with booksellers. Between 1580 and 1592 John Porter, Bennet Walker (died November 1588), Reignold (or Reginald or Renowde) Bridges, John Jones and Francis Macris were entered as booksellers in a list of those sworn as privileged by the university, along with Hugh Burwell, stationer, and a mysterious bookbinder, apparently French, Desiderius Rowyer.[9] Also listed as stationers in a list of privileged persons of 1591/2 are John Legate, a Mr Watson (perhaps the Simon Watson recorded as active in Cambridge in the late 1550s), Benjamin Prime, Thomas Bradshaw and John Cuthbert,[10] and to these we may add the names of William Knowsley and William Scarlet whom we shall see to have been active in the trade. Of these, Bradshaw, Walker, Porter, Knowsley and, probably, Cuthbert had all served their apprenticeships in London. Bradshaw and

Porter certainly had dealings with the London book trade; indeed, such dealings were obviously essential to their business.

As a bookseller Manasses Vautrollier has left relatively little trace in the surviving records. All stationers in Cambridge enjoyed the status of 'privileged persons', entitled to sue and be sued in the Vice-Chancellor's court, a court which had incessant business with bonds. Almost every bargain struck between two parties, however trivial, was embodied in a bond to perform the covenants of the agreement. Moreover, in an age when specie was in short supply, money lending was rife, and it was the practice for the borrower to enter into a bond to pay the lender twice the sum borrowed by a certain date.[11] Accordingly, there are few if any Cambridge tradesmen, especially among the more prosperous, who do not make frequent appearances in the records of the court. The relative invisibility of Vautrollier may well be significant.

He did, however, have a part to play, bringing his London experience to bear, in a case which arose shortly after his arrival in Cambridge, a case not unlike that which had originally brought Legate to the town, and one that sheds some light on the everyday troubles of the trade. The chief *dramatis personae* are Reignold Bridges, stationer, deceased, Susanna his widow, Thomas Bridges, of 'Sible Himmingham' [presumably Sible Hedingham], Essex, his father and executor, Thomas Holder of the nearby village of Orwell, his brother-in-law and the overseer of his will, and Hugh Burwell, stationer, of Cambridge. Bridges had died on 14 or 15 January 1590/1, and an inventory of his household goods was drawn up by George Sherwood and Thomas Howis, university appraisers, on 15 January of that year.[12] The total value assigned to his goods was £122 5s 4d to include plate, valued at £12 11s 4d, and his books, valued at £59 19s 8d. It was these last, of course, that were to cause the trouble.

Here is the version of events first propounded by Thomas Bridges exhibiting his allegations in the court on 27 January:[13]

1. That Renould Bridges left a valid will and named Thomas Bridges his executor.
2. That Thomas Bridges proved the Will and was granted administration.
3. That 'by reason of the said administration . . . there came certeyne bookes parchment and pastborde of the said Renould Bridges to the handes and possession of the said Thomas Bridges which bookes parchment and pastborde weare . . . the goods of the said Renould Bridges in his lifetime and at the hower of his death the value or price of which books [etc. amounted to] £60'.
4. 'That about a moneth or five weekes since . . . Hugo Burwell required and requested very earnestly of the said Thomas Bridges that the said Thomas Bridges would sell . . . him . . . all the said bookes parchment and pasteborde which he . . . had . . . to which request . . . the said Thomas Bridges did yeald and the said Hugo Burwell promised to the said Thomas Bridges to give soe muche money for them . . . as they . . . weare worth.'
5. 'That [Burwell] did knowe what the said bookes parchment and pasteborde weare worth for that he him selfe . . . did price or praise the same . . . by the

appointment or request of the university prisers or praisers of goods and that the said bookes parchment and pasteborde according to the pricers or praysers accompt or estimation were worth lx£ [£60] legal: . . . and soe were priced or praysed by [Burwell] and others'.

6. 'That after the premises [Burwell] desyred of the said Thomas Bridges that he Burwell might goe & peruse over the said bookes parchment and pasteborde where they laid the which the said Thomas Bridges granted unto and delivered to the said Burwell both the key of the shopp or roome in which the said bookes parchment and pasteborde were & also the Cattalogg of the said bookes & also the said Burwell required of the said Thomas Bridges that one Frauncis Mackeresse might help him Burwell to peruse over the said bookes . . . to all which requestes the said Thomas Bridges did yeald.'

7. 'That after the said Burwell had receaved the key of the roome or shopp wherein the said bookes [etc.] weare togither with the said Cattalogg & had perused them the said bookes [etc.] over the said Thomas Bridges asked him . . . how he . . . liked the said bookes . . . by the price they wear priced at in the said Cattalogg [and] the said Burwell answeared thus or the like in effect I . . . like them well / yett ther be some of them wanting[,] the said Thomas Bridges answeared the said Burwell thus or the like in effect looke what bookes or how many soe ever there be wanting you . . . shalbe allowed for them of me. Why then, said [Burwell], I doe like the said bookes parchment and pasteborde and the price & I will have them and I praye you deliver me the key of them meaning the key of the rooms . . . wheruppon the said Thomas Bridges did deliver to him Burwell the key . . . for and in the name of the possession of the said bookes parchment and pasteborde the which key . . . the said Burwell did accept and take of the said Thomas . . . or by his consent and wellikinge'.

8. 'That after the premises . . . the said Burwell did [at least once] goe into the shopp or roome . . . and did take some of the said bookes or on[e] of them and the said parchment and pasteborde or some of it out of the said shopp or roome wherein they lay & did carry it or them home to his . . . howse and did or might have converted it or them to his Burwells use or commodity or private profitte.'

9. That Burwell 'promised Thomas Bridges to pay to him . . . the on halfe of the price of the said bookes . . . viz. xxx£ [£30] legal . . . at or uppon a Satterday being a sennett more or lesse after such promise made by him . . . for the said payment . . . the which Satterday is past & the mony . . . is not payd'.

10. 'That the said Thomas Bridges might have sould the said bookes parchment and pasteborde for lx£ [£60] . . . since suche tyme as he Burwell had the possession of them delivered to him . . . yf soe be that Burwell had not had them'.

11. 'That the said Burwell by reason of the said bargaine had and made betwene him Burwell and the same Bridges is in quiett and peaceable possession of the said bookes parchment and pasteborde and doth or may convert them to his use ayther by him selfe or his assignes'.

12. 'That the bookes parchment and pasteborde . . . wear worth the sum of £60'.

13. That Burwell has failed to pay up.

14. That Burwell has admitted all the premises in the presence of credible witnesses.

15. That Burwell is a university stationer and so subject to the court.

Burwell's replies to these allegations, presented to the court with the usual promptness of legal processes on 26 April, add colour to his account. He claimed:

that the said bookes parchments and shoptooles were woorth fourtie five powndes and not above.

. . . that sithence the time of the death of the said Reignold Bridges and the administracion grauntinge the said Thomas Bridges came to this Respondent complaininge that he knew not well what to do with the bookes . . . both for the number and want of skill and fearinge that he should not make so mutch monie of them as they were praysed at in the inventarie this Respondent said unto the said Bridges that if they two could agree upon the prices he this Respondent woold by [buy] them of the said Bridges. And further [he] beleveth that at the time of the praysinge of the said bookes he this Respondent desired the said Bridges that he might have of him the said Bridges the parchments and pastbordes here articulate and on standige [standish] mencioned in the inventarie at such price as they were praysed at in the said inventarie . . . the which Bridges yealded and condescended unto.

. . . that he this Respondent knew the prices of the said bookes parchments and pastbordes and that he was at the priceing of the same and that they were eroniouslie priced by the Universitie praysers and this Respondent verie neere to the summe of iijxx£ [threescore pounds] thinkinge that that allowance should be made out of the same bookes which the stacioners of London doe usuallie make upon the sale of their bookes giveing the best choise to their Chapmen.

. . . that upon the speeches had betweene this Respondent and the said Bridges mencioned above he this Respondent desired the said Bridges that he might peruse the said books and not the parchments and pastbordes here mencioned for that they were delivered unto him before and that he might have the key of the shop or rome where the said bookes and allsoe the Catalogue of such bookes as were there and that Francis Macris might help him Burwell to peruse over the said bookes for that nothinge might be imbesiled or taken away to the prejudice of the said Bridges which the said Burwell would not be aunswerable for in case anie booke or bookes should be wanting whilest the said key should be in the custodie of the said Burwell.

. . . that after he this Respondent had received the key and perused the bookes soe as is aforesaid Bridges here articulate asked this Respondent how he liked the said bookes not mencioninge anie price and this Respondent aunswered the said Bridges that he liked the bookes well.

. . . that this Respondent did never after the time of the deliverie of the said key . . . take or carie away anie parchment or pastbordes or anie booke or bookes out of the shopp . . . which he did or purposed to commite to his owen use, but did at on time take out two of the said bookes from the place aforesaid and shew unto on that desired to see the same which booke he did againe sett into the place aforesaid.

. . . that he beleveth that the said Bridges pretendinge a simple bargain for the said bookes hath demanded of the said Burwell the summe of iij^{xx}£ which he this Respondent refused to pay unto him for that there was never anie bargaine passed betweene them.[14]

A number of interesting points arise, not least of them the question of why Burwell, assisting the appraisers, neither of them stationers, in the valuation of Bridges' goods, took no steps at the time to correct the alleged over-pricing of his stock. Needless to say, despite the copious documentation of this case, several crucial documents are missing including the original 'Catalogue' of the contents of Bridges' shop. The inventory drawn up on 15 January is of household goods only, with the value of the books added as a postscript. There may well have been a separate inventory of the trade stock, including the standish, which does not feature in the domestic inventory, but the term 'catalogue', rather than the appraisers' habitual 'inventory', may suggest a different class of document. Perhaps the valuation of the books was taken from Bridges' own 'catalogue' of his stock.

Corroboration of the facts of the case came on 20 September 1591 when Francis Macris (or Makaresse) made sworn depositions in reply both to Bridges' account of the case and to interrogatories submitted on behalf of Burwell. There are also some further details of fact and of the apparent motivation of the parties. The extracts below are taken out of order.

In his preliminary answers to the interrogatories Macris states that he himself is 'worth C£ legalis' [£100], and that he has known Thomas Bridges for six years and Hugh Burwell for seven years and favours the parties equally. He confirms that the university appraisers valued Reignold Bridges' books, parchments and pasteboards at £59 19s 4d, and that the verbal agreement on the sale of the stock to Burwell was as vague as it has appeared hitherto, saying that:

when the said Burwell had received the Catalogue and vewed the bookes the said Bridges asked the said Burwell howe he liked them and the said Burwell said he liked them well if he might be allowed for them which were wantinge and might have those bookes lower prized which were to deere to which speeches of the said Burwell the said Bridges did yeald \and/ the said Burwell therupon desired Bridges to give him the keye of the shopp where the said bookes were and the said Bridges did give him the keye and the said Burwell kept the said keye and went into the shop at his pleasure.

. . . that Burwell had the parchments and pastbordes and went into the shop divers times.

. . . that the parchments were carried out of the shop before Burwell had the key delivered unto him but at such times as they were prized they were valued at lxˢ [60s].

. . . that he thinketh that the said Burwell did buie the parchment and pastbordes of Bridges at such time as the said bookes were prized and the said parchments wer gone out of the shopp before the said Burwell received the key of the shopp.

. . . that the key was never delivered unto the said Bridges after the said Burwell had received it soe farr as this deponent knoweth and the woordes uttered by the said Burwell concerninge the buieing of the said bookes were these, viz. I like the bookes well if I may be allowed for them which be wantinge and have them sett lower which were to deere and ther wer certain bookes wantinge which were in the Catalogue And that the parchments were not in the shopp.

. . . that he this deponent did beleeve that the said Burwell would have given three score powndes for the said bookes at such time as he received the keye of the shopp

haveinge allowance made unto him for the bookes which were wantinge and the price of those abated which were to high prized and he belleveth that those bookes which were lefte were not worth lxf [£60].
. . . that when the Stacioners of Camebridge doe buye bookes at London unbound they are allowed iij^s in the pownd et *aliter nescit deponere* saveinge that he beeleveth that Burwell had noe intent to crave anie such allowance at such time as he received the key but he thinketh that the craveinge of allowance was put into his minde by some of the Stacioners of this universitie since that time.[15]

Which of the local stationers put the idea to Burwell of claiming three shillings in the pound off the purchase price of Bridges' books we have no way of telling. Legate's knowledge of London ways was almost as fresh as Vautrollier's; possibly fresher if Manasses had spent the years 1583 to 1587 in Edinburgh with his father, as seems likely. Nonetheless, Vautrollier must be a prime suspect. He too was examined by the court, on 18 February 1591/2, both on the *exceptatoria* entered by Burwell and on interrogatories on the part of Thomas Bridges without, regrettably, having to answer the standard questions about the date and place of his birth. In the first part of his examination he testified that:

the Merchantes at London doe usuallie allowe unto the stacioners there; and all those that buy bookes of them, to sell them ageine three shillings in every pownd, and soe this deponent doeth allowe unto Mr Legate and Burwell here in Camebridge when they doe buie bookes of this deponent three shillings in every pownd accordinge to the said custome.

In answer to the interrogatories, in addition to returning standard answers to the standard questions about his good faith, he returned negative answers to the enquiries as to whether he had ever heard Burwell admit to having let out any of the books in Bridges' shop and as to whether he had been given reason to believe that Burwell 'did bargaine and buie of the said Thomas Bridges the bookes of the said Reignold Bridges which be now in the shopp or house of one Mr Watson'. He claimed ignorance as to whether Burwell had offered any of Bridges' books for sale and expressed his belief in the trustworthiness of Macris as a witness. Finally, in reply to a standard question as to his financial relations with the litigants, he reported that Burwell was indebted to him, 'but he knoweth not in what summe untill he have cast over his bookes And likewise . . . [that he himself was] indebted to the said Burwell foure pence or theraboutes'.[16]

Among the records relating to this case there is one highly problematic document. The litigation dragged on until after 15 June 1592 when Thomas Bridges and Hugh Burwell were both bound in £60 by the mutual exchange of 6d 'to stand to, abide, performe, fulfill, observe and keep the award, order, doom, judgment and determinacion of the said Right worshipful Mr Vicechaunceller of in and upon this mater depending in sute betwixt them, soe that the sayd award, order, doom, judgment and determinacion be given up by him before the foure and twentith day of the presente moneth of June'.[17] Typically the Vice-Chancellor's arbitration is not recorded, but there is an inventory of Reignold Bridges' books, with their prices, taken by Manasses Vautrollier, William Scarlet and William Knowsley 'by Mr vic[echancellor's] apoyntment' – not the usual formula for a probate inventory. The trouble is that the endorsement dates the document as 1590, the year of Reignold Bridges' death. It seems overwhelmingly probable, however, that this date was added later and that what we have here is a new valuation drawn up as part of the exercise of arbitration.

This inventory is written in Manasses Vautrollier's hand, very neatly, and bears two prices for each book, one on the left and one, consistently lower, on the right.[18] It comprises 300 entries including four for 'Books wanting', all single items, while the last entry for the books found reads, exasperatingly, '14 Dozen of old bookes'. It cannot be the original inventory drawn up by the appraisers, partly because it was expressly drawn up by three stationers, none of them official appraisers, and partly because the totals shown are not £59 19s 4d but rather £32 16s 9d and £30 7s 2d respectively.

The significance of the double valuation is unclear. If the lower price were intended to represent a reduction on the lines of the three shillings in the pound allowed by the London stationers, then the discrepancy, on a total of around £30 would be of the order of £4 10s, not £2 9s 7d. Moreover, although the prices in the right-hand column show a fairly constant percentage reduction on those in the left-hand column, there are variations indicating that an element of judgement has entered into the exercise. Thus, two adjacent items valued in the left-hand column at 7s – an old edition of Lambinus' Plautus in folio and Johannes Jacobus Wecker's *Medicinae utriusque syntaxes*, also in folio – are valued in the right-hand column as 6s 8d and 6s 6d respectively. The variations can only be taken to reflect two separate valuations prepared for the court, with the likelihood that either they were prepared simultaneously, and effectively in collaboration, or that the second valuer had his colleague's valuation in his hand. It would be hard otherwise to account for the close correspondence in the values adjudged. In that case the 'London weighting' could be one element in the discrepancies in valuation.

After this brief flurry of excitement – if that is what it was – Vautrollier sinks into relative obscurity for a while. It would appear, however, that his standing as a stationer was later challenged since we find exhibited in the court on 25 February 1596/7 the following certificate:

These are to certifie you to whom thes presentes shall come, that Thomas Vautrollier of the precinct of the Blackfryers in London was a bookebinder, bookeseller, and printer, and that Manasses his sonne did serve his sayd father before his death the space of fowre yeres in maner of Apprentice, and after the death of his sayd father, did serve in maner aforesayd with francis Bovier over three \yeres/ residue of seven according to the order of the Citie of London, and that the printers, bookebinders, and bookesellers in London are all but one companie. And so fare ye well.

London, Febr. 12. Anno 1596

Richard Martyn

Richard Field

Peters dorange his marque

Romain De mainnemanes

Bovier[19]

Life was not without its ups and downs. In March 1598/9 Thomas Vautrollier junior, along with other apprentices of Legate's, went out on the town breaking the windows of Richard Metcalf and making 'rough music' outside the door of one of the Trott family, presumably on the basis of doubts as to Mistress Trott's virtue.[20] Delightfully the members of the orchestra are, for once, credited in detail: Anthony Harrison [later a successful notary], tongs and key; John Hall, capper, comb and paper; Henry Priest, cittern; Abel Hawkins, recorder; Thomas Redhead, servant to Croft, jew's trump, and Thomas Vautrollier, a cymbal. Two cymbals would probably have been even more satisfactory, but enough had been done to displease the authorities: Thomas Vautrollier, described as 'servant to John Legate', and Henry Priest, were imprisoned overnight and bound in £20 for their good behaviour, while Hall, Hawkins and Cross, all of them also servants to Legate, were obliged to pay the costs of their arrest and of the broken glass. Thomas's bond was never called in, so we cannot tell whether his big brother agreed to stand surety for him.

It would appear that, even without such irritants, Manasses Vautrollier was not having an easy time: on 3 March 1599/1600 a warrant was issued for his arrest to answer a suit against him brought by one Thomas Smith, 'gent'.[21] The debt was for the relatively modest sum of £3 10s, and the cause was first stated to the court on 29 February of that year. Vautrollier failed to make his appearance in court on that date, and on 7 and 14 March and 4 and 18 April. From allegations entered on 18 April we learn that the debt represented 'Rente of the howse wherein the said Vawtrollier nowe dwellethe in Cambridge, for three Quarters of a yeare ended at christmas last past'. The yeoman bedell, Benjamin Prime (sometime an employee of John Legate's) was ordered to make distraint of his goods and, as we hear no more of the issue, we may assume that Vautrollier finally paid up.[22]

It may have been to avoid a distraint on his goods that, on 8 October in a year eaten by rats but probably 1600, Manasses borrowed £10 from John Legate on a bond for £20,[23] a bond which remained unpaid until October 1604, when Vautrollier had perhaps already left Cambridge, and when Legate procured from the court permission to distrain on Vautrollier's goods, at that time in the custody of Thomas Hobson the carrier, to secure payment of the loan. This time the distraint was effected and the distrained goods duly inventoried on 8 October 1604 by John Warren and Thomas Bradshaw. The tools of Vautrollier's trade included:

Inprimis. ij. dossen & .a. half of calves skynnes	1 - 0 - 0
Item. a gilt service booke. 4°	0 - 5 - 0
Item. a dutch testament. 8°. &. english testament 12°	0 - 1 - 0
Item. ij. great. long. printes. ij. four square printes)	
—— ii. great. rownd printes. iij. smale ovals. and)	1 -10 - 0
—— .j. squar corner / .j. great pair of corners)	
—— j. smale pair of corners)	
Item .xij. smale. gilting knotes. x. flowers	0 - 4 - 0
Item .x. smaler. gilting. knotes. x. flowers	0 - 1 - 8
Item .xxij. smale letters	0 - 2 - 6
Item .ij. copper rowles	0 - 2 - 0
Item a beating hammer, a smale sawe, and other)	
—— fynyshing tooles)	0 - 3 - 4
an old plowe, & old knyves foure. and other trashe)	
and the box wherin the same tooles laye.)	0 - 2 - 0
a piece of lead	0 - 0 - 4
. . . .	
Item. a brussh, & a rubbinge brussh	0 - 1 - 0
Item. ij. rulers. iij. plainge hordes. cordes. & other trashe	0 - 3 - 4
Item. v. written. bookes. &. on box with letters & writinges	< blank >

In addition to these tools of the trade the Vautrollier family forfeited a substantial quantity of household goods and clothing including, intriguingly, two 'drinking clothes', one of diaper, valued at 5s; a remnant of scottish cloth, valued at 2s; three shirts for children, a smock, and a pair of 'old narrow shetes for a child to lie in'. The total value of the goods distrained was £13 4s 6d.[24] The tools listed are hardly those of one virtuously abiding by his agreement not to trade in Cambridge as a bookbinder, and it is as a binder that Manasses Vautrollier reappears in Edinburgh some years later, where, on 24 December 1617 he was made a Burgess, with the Dean of the Gild repaying his dues,[25] and where, on 4 October 1621 (perhaps), under the name of Vautroleis, he married Elizabeth Meldrum.[26] His last recorded appearance seems to be in 1633 when D. Robertson, bookbinder, complained to the Privy Council that Vautrollier had been guilty of illegal caption, but the distressing possibility remains that this may have been his ghost.[27]

References

1. M. R. James, *Letters to a friend*, ed. Gwendolen McBryde (London: Arnold, 1956), p.159.
2. Cambridge University Archives (henceforth CUA) Collect.Admin.5, f.206. I have, throughout, standardized the use of u/v and i/j but otherwise retained the spelling and capitalization of the originals, tacitly expanding contractions. Punctuation has been inserted and abbreviated terms expanded only where necessary to the sense.

3. See David McKitterick, *A history of Cambridge University Press*, vol.1 (Cambridge: Cambridge University Press, 1992), pp.80, 82, 93.

4. British Library, MS Lansdowne 42, f.109, cited in W. W. Greg, *A companion to Arber*, (Oxford: Clarendon Press, 1956), p.135 and McKitterick, *loc. cit.* p.93.

5. See McKitterick, *loc. cit.*, p.110, and pp.109-12 for further details of Legate's early months in Cambridge.

6. H. R. Plomer, *Abstracts from the wills of English printers and stationers, from 1492 to 1630* (London: The Bibliographical Society, 1903), p.27.

7. CUA: CUR 33.6 (3). Unfortunately the inventory mentioned in paragraph five seems not to have survived.

8. CUA: CUR 33.6 (4).

9. CUA: V.C.Ct.I.2, ff.344-7. Two superimposed attempts were made to give Rowyer's (?Rouillé's) birthplace: the text perhaps reads 'natus est bonini'.

10. Cambridge University Library (henceforth CUL) W. M. Palmer papers, bundle 9 (box 41).

11. This looks like 100% interest, but in practice the custom of the court was usually to award a sum, little if at all above the sum originally borrowed, along with legal expenses.

12. Bridges' will is dated 14 January 1590/1.

13. CUA: VCCt.III.2 (82).

14. CUA: VCCt.I.26, ff.151-151v and VCCt.III.2 (93 and 94).

15. CUA: VCCt.III.2 (131).

16. CUA: VCCt.III.2 (191).

17. CUA: VCCt.I.2, f.85. In fact the arbitration was clearly not promulgated on 24 June as further assignments for sentence are set for 13 July and 2 September 1592.

18. Printed in F. S. Leedham-Green, *Books in Cambridge inventories*, 2 vols (Cambridge: Cambridge University Press, 1986) i. 484-92.

19. CUA: VCCt.III.6 (25).

20. CUA: VCCt.III.8 (63).

21. CUA: VCCt.III.8 (174). The Thomas Smith in question was probably not the then Registrary of the University, so named, who would have been designated 'M.A.' nor yet the Secretary of State, Simpson's Smith, who was long dead.

22. CUA: VCCt.I.4, ff.292, 299v, 302v, 315, 324.

23. CUA: VCCt.III.9 (76).

24. CUA: VCCt.III.11 (29).

25. M. Wood (ed.), *Extracts from the records of the Burgh of Edinburgh, 1604-1626* (Edinburgh and London: Oliver and Boyd (for the Scottish Record Society), 1931), p.171.

26. H. Patton (ed.), *The register of marriages for the parish of Edinburgh, 1595-1700* (Edinburgh: Scottish Record Society, 1905), p.705. The children's clothes and bedding included among his distrained goods we must therefore suppose to have been either those of Manasses' youngest brother, James, or to some unrelated member of his household.

27. R. B. McKerrow, *A dictionary of printers and booksellers in England, Scotland and Ireland, and of foreign printers of English books 1557-1640* (London: The Bibliographical Society, 1910), p.272; *Privy Council Registers*, 2nd ser., 174, 177, 182, 572, 580. I am very greatly indebted to Richard Ovenden for pursuing, at the drop of a Tam o' Shanter, sources not available in Cambridge, including several that would never have occurred to me; I am, though I should not be, less grateful to him for finding in the Addenda to the *Canongate Register of Marriages*, ed. F. J. Grant (Edinburgh: Scottish Record Society, 1915) a reference to the same marriage dated 12 August, rather than 4 October, 1621 and, what is worse, reference in George Chalmers' manuscript *History of Scottish Printing* (National Library of Scotland Adv.MS.16.2.21, f.127v) to a note in Bagford's hand in Harleian MS 5905 (f.26v) recording the burial of a 'Manoseds Vatroler' at St Anne's, Blackfriars, on 6 November 1628. Giles Mandelbrote has most kindly confirmed for me the accuracy of Chalmers' note. Conceivably this was a nephew, but it is clear that work remains to be done.

A binding with the arms of the Stationers' Company

DAVID PEARSON

IT IS NOT UNUSUAL TO FIND late 16th and early 17th-century small-format books decorated with rectangular panel stamps.[1] They are usually gilt-tooled with quite an up-market look to them, and the use of the large single stamp covering a whole board at a time clearly offered a quick and simple way of making an appealing product. The patterns found on these stamps are usually derived from the contemporary ornamental grammar of centrepieces and cornerpieces, quite different from the blind-stamped panels which are associated with the early 16th century.

The National Art Library at the Victoria and Albert Museum has a copy of the third edition of Lewis Bayly's *The practise of pietie*, 12°, London, 1613 (STC 1602) which is attractively bound in this fashion, using a panel which incorporates at its centre the arms of the Stationers' Company (azure on a chevron or between three Bibles lying fessways on an eagle rising gules enclosed by two roses of the same in chief a demi-circle of glory edged with clouds therein a dove displayed argent). The binding is made of mid-brown calfskin over pasteboards, sewn on three alum-tawed thongs which are recessed in order to produce a smooth spine. The edges of the leaves are gilt and gauffered, the board edges have a narrow gilt roll run round (open diamonds), and the spine is decorated in gilt all along its length with six applications of a horizontal stamp, apart from a narrow strip of hatching at head and tail. The headbands of blue and pink thread are still largely intact. The book originally had reddish-pink cloth ties, which have been lost apart from the remaining stubs on the inner sides of the boards. There are no endleaves of any kind and no evidence to suggest that any pastedowns or flyleaves were once present and have been lost. The only mark of ownership is an inscription on the verso of the engraved title leaf, 'John Archer his booke 1662'; the book was purchased from Maggs in 1927 and there is no way of knowing where the book was between 1662 and 1921.[2]

An almost identical twin of this binding will be found on a copy of Joseph Hall's *Meditations and vowes*, 12°, London, imprinted by Humfrey Lownes for John Porter, 1606 (STC 12680), preserved in the archives of the Stationers' Company. This uses the same panel and has spine gilding and edge gauffering similar to, but not quite identical with, that found on the Bayly. It was acquired by the Company only recently: it was given to them by J. R. Abbey, and before that belonged to Hudson Gurney (early 19th-

L. Bayly, *The practise of pietie*, 12°, London, 1613, STC 1602. Gilt-tooled mid-brown calf. 132 x 74mm. National Art Library, Victoria and Albert Museum Dr.62. *Reproduced by kind permission of the Trustees of the Victoria and Albert Museum.*

century spade-shield bookplate) and one William Nuthall whose inscription in the book is dated 1679.[3]

Why does the panel incorporate the arms of the Stationers' Company? Armorial bindings commonly indicate ownership, but there is no reason to suspect that here. The armorial is a small part of the overall scheme and I believe that the purpose is essentially decorative, in much the same way that versions of the royal arms were regularly used to adorn bookbindings without any direct royal connection. The Maggs cataloguer, in 1921, suggested that this copy of *The practise of pietie* was bound for presentation to the Prince of Wales, the dedicatee of Bayly's text, but this is clearly nonsense. Neither Hall's *Meditations* nor Bayly's *Practise* formed part of the Company's stock, and the copyrights were owned by different people. The rights in *The practise of pietie* belonged to the bookseller John Hodgets and this third edition, like all the other editions produced down to 1625 (when Hodgets died) was 'printed for Iohn Hodgets' with no other bookseller or distributor mentioned in the imprint. It was a popular devotional manual with a puritan slant, and a runaway bestseller: 15 editions appeared between 1612 and 1624. Hodgets was evidently obliged to protect his copyright from piracy, as the Stationers' Company Court Books record an order in 1618 'that Thomas Iones should not ymprint . . . in the booke called the fathers blessinge any thinge that is in the booke called the Practice of pietye which belongeth to John Hodgetts'.[4] There is a well-documented group of late 16th and early 17th-century bookbindings decorated with the devices of booksellers and printers, which are generally believed to be books sold through their retail outlets, but there is no case for seeing these Stationers' Company bindings within that tradition.[5] Perhaps they were given as gift books or prizes by the Company — rewards for virtuous apprentices, or something like that? I do not have a clear answer to the question at the beginning of this paragraph and I offer it up to the dedicatee of this volume as a puzzle for her idle hours!

References

1. Cf. D. Pearson, 'An unusual panel-stamped binding of ca.1600-20', *The Book Collector*, 45 (1996), pp.218-21, and the references given there.
2. Its acquisition is reported in *Victoria & Albert Museum: review of the principal acquisitions during the year 1927* (London, 1928), and a small picture of the binding appears on plate 29. It is also illustrated in Maggs catalogue 407, 1921, as no.7/plate V.
3. The existence of the Hall binding is mentioned by A. N. L. Munby at the end of his note on 'Early trade bindings' in *The Book Collector*, 1 (1952), pp.128-9; the matching Bayly at the V&A is briefly described in a reply by J. P. Harthan, *The Book Collector*, 1 (1952), p.266. (I owe this reference to Arnold Hunt, to whom many thanks.) Hudson Gurney's bookplate is listed in E. R. J. Gambier Howe, *Franks bequest. Catalogue of British and American book plates bequeathed to the Trustees of the British Museum by Sir Augustus Wollaston Franks*, 3 vols (London: British Museum, 1903-4), no.13095.
4. W. A. Jackson (ed.), *Records of the Court of the Stationers' Company 1602 to 1640*, (London: The Bibliographical Society, 1957), p.105.
5. Most recently surveyed in G. Colin, 'Les marques de libraires et d'éditeurs dorées sur les reliures' in D. E. Rhodes (ed.), *Bookbindings and other bibliophily: essays in honour of Anthony Hobson* (Verona: Edizioni Valdonega, 1994), pp.77-115.

Book trade patents, 1603-1640

ARNOLD HUNT

DAVID FOXON HAS COMMENTED on the 'impression of omniscience and infallibility' created by a work such as Greg's *Bibliography of the English Printed Drama*, in which 'the final word appears to have been spoken'. 'I recollect my own sense of sacrilege when I discovered that E2 in Ben Jonson's *The Alchemist* 1612 was a cancel that Greg and Percy Simpson had missed in all the copies they had examined.'[1] In the same way, English printing before 1640 is so well documented—by STC, Arber, Greg's *Companion to Arber*, and Greg, Boswell and Jackson's editions of the Stationers' Company Court Books, to name only a few of the most important works—that it comes as a shock to discover that a great deal of significant documentary evidence still remains unpublished. This article will consider one source of such evidence: the patents for the printing and sale of books granted before 1603 and 1640 and recorded on the Patent Rolls in the Public Record Office. Some of these are well known to book trade historians, but it has not, I think, been appreciated just how many there were: Marjorie Plant, following Arber's list, counted 43 book trade patents in the period 1603-40, but in fact there were over 70, including reversions and renewals of existing patents.[2] There is much to be learned from them about the publishing history of particular books, including many of the bestselling religious and educational works of the period; but they also raise wider questions about the role of the Stationers' Company. Was the patent system always secondary to the Stationers' Register, or did it work to the Company's disadvantage by providing an alternative means of copyright protection over which the Stationers had no control? In an essay dedicated to Robin Myers there could be no more appropriate subject than the history of the Stationers' Company; and, in this brief introduction I want to argue for a new view of the early 17th century as a period when the Company's monopoly was seriously threatened.

Patents for the printing and sale of books had become a controversial feature of the English book trade in the late Elizabethan period, when, in the words of Sir Walter Greg, 'the struggle over privileges, or between what are rather misleadingly called the privileged and unprivileged printers, threatened to rend the Stationers' Company in two'.[3] The rights (or 'privileges') to print certain classes of book—lawbooks, schoolbooks, almanacs, and so forth—had been granted, by royal letters patent, to various members of the Stationers' Company, but in the late 1570s a small group of unprivileged stationers and booksellers started to pirate these books, on a

27

large scale, with the aim of breaking the patentees' monopoly. The dispute was referred to the Privy Council, and in 1583 a commission was set up to investigate the matter. The Council instructed the commissioners that 'if it shalbe found necessary', the patentees were to be 'drawne within the compasse of the Lawes, and thereby the poorer sort relieved', which Greg interpreted as a recommendation that the patents should be cancelled; but the final outcome was, predictably, a compromise: the commissioners upheld the legality of the patents, and the patentees surrendered some of their copyrights to the Company for the benefit of its poorer members.[4] The real winner was the Company itself, which, by reconciling its members, had succeeded in consolidating its own authority. The instrument of that authority was the English Stock: in effect, a company within the Stationers' Company, set up in 1603 to manage the Company's patents and divide the proceeds among its shareholders. Not only did it give the senior members of the Company a vested interest in maintaining the status quo, but there was enough money left over to provide charitable relief for its poorer members, and to buy off any malcontents who might try to break into the club.

The years 1603 to 1641 have thus tended to be seen as a period of stability between the disputes of the late 16th century and the great disruption of the Civil War. Edward Arber wrote that after the privilege disputes of the 1580s 'no such convulsion divided and disorganised the Company' for another 60 years. In Cyprian Blagden's picturesque simile, 'the Charter of 1557 was in the nature of a coming-of-age; the royal grant of 1603 was in the nature of a wedding, whose importance in the life of the Company was as much greater than a twenty-first birthday party as marriage is in the life of an ordinary citizen.'[5] Blagden's account of the period is entitled simply 'Growth, 1603 to 1641', by which he meant growth in the membership of the Stationers' Company, in the market for printed books and, last but not least, in the profitability of the English Stock.[6] Yet the problem of patents had not gone away. The commissioners had recommended in 1583 that no further privileges should be granted for 'any general title of bokes of any whole arte, nor any bokes extant in copie and at libertie for others to print before the preuilege', but patents of all kinds—for new books, for books 'extant in copie' and for whole classes of book—were still being granted, and in increasing numbers.[7] This was one growth area that was not wholly to the advantage of the Stationers' Company, for between 1603 and 1641 fewer than half of these patents went to the Company or its members. The old divide between the richer and poorer members of the trade was now, thanks to the unifying and stabilising influence of the English Stock, of considerably less importance, but there was the potential for a new conflict between Company insiders and outsiders.

Patents for printing were generally considered to fall within the royal prerogative: in 1602 Sir Edward Coke argued in *Darcy v. Allin* that the crown had the right to grant monopolies 'for the public good', in which category he included patents for printing; and it was probably for this reason that patents 'for or concerning printing' were exempted from the Statute of Monopolies in 1624, when most other forms of monopoly were outlawed.[8] Roger Wood and Thomas Symcock, holders of the controversial patent for printing on one side of paper, defended the legality of their patent by arguing in 1621 that 'the Kings Maiestie by vertue of his prerogatiue Royall, may graunt this . . . and all other priuiledges of printing at his pleasure, and is not restrained by any law to the contrary'.[9] A patent thus had several advantages over an entry in the Register. It was based on superior authority: while still recognizing an entry in the Stationers' Register as a legitimate form of copyright, the Commission on Privileges had declared in 1583 that 'we think her maiesties grauntes most meete to be mainteined aboue all other'. Consequently, it was rather better protected: faced with an unauthorized edition, the holder of a patent could prosecute his opponent in Star Chamber, without having to rely on the Stationers' Company to carry out disciplinary measures. Indeed, a patent usually contained provisions for its own enforcement, including the right to search the premises of anyone suspected of infringing the patent, to seize the offending books and to destroy the offender's presses and type. As William Barley discovered when he infringed the grammar patent in 1599, these measures were not merely theoretical.[10] Patents had teeth; and for this reason they were a useful way of safeguarding lucrative copyrights which would otherwise have been vulnerable to piracy.

However, it would be a mistake to suppose that the patent system was wholly independent of the Stationers' Register. Fynes Moryson's patent of 1617 to print his *Itinerary*, for example, did not preclude the printer John Beale, acting either on Moryson's behalf or as his assignee, from entering the book in the Register as an additional safeguard. Here, as in many cases, the patent system and the Stationers' Register worked in combination; indeed, many of the Company's own privileges were protected by patent, beginning with the 1603 patent for primers, metrical psalms and almanacs, the foundation of the English Stock. Over the next 40 years the Company added other major patents to its portfolio. In 1613 it acquired the schoolbooks patent, for which it paid £100 to secure the reversion in 1631; in 1614 it bought Verney Alley's psalm patent for £600; between 1619 and 1624 it controlled the patent for Greek and Latin grammars; and in 1631 it obtained the patent for Speed's *Genealogies* for £700. Other valuable patents belonged to members of the Company: the privileges for English Bibles, service books and official publications were attached to the office of King's Printer, and those for Latin Bibles and grammars to the office of King's Printer in Latin, Greek and Hebrew. In 1603 these offices were held by Robert Barker and John Norton respectively; by 1641, although they were still nominally owned by the Barker and Norton families, both offices had effectively passed into the hands of a syndicate led by Miles Flesher, who also acquired a share in the lawbook patent. By 1641, therefore, all the most important patents had ended up in the possession of the Stationers' Company or of its leading members. This meant, among other things, that it was no longer possible for Drapers and Haberdashers to gain a foothold in the book trade, as several had done in the late 16th century, by buying into a patent.[11] While the patent system was technically outside the control of the Company, in practice it helped to protect the Company's interests and to perpetuate the monopolistic character of the trade.

But the Stationers did not have the patent system sewn up quite as tightly as they would have liked. The snag was that while a patent provided adequate protection against piracy, it could not insure against subsequent patents overlapping or encroaching on the original privilege. When patent met patent, as in the clash between Thomas Morley's music patent and Richard Day's psalm patent in 1599, both parties 'standing peremptorily upon the validity of their several letters patent from her Highness' and claiming a right to print the psalms in metre, the result was likely to be stalemate unless one party was able to buy out the other.[12] Deliberate encroachment on an existing patent, with a view to a cash settlement with the patentee, could thus be a profitable speculation. In 1608 the courtier Sir William Woodhouse obtained a patent for all reports of Calvin's Case, an important test case concerning the civil rights of Scotsmen under English law. This was an infringement of the patent for common-law books, which at that time was held by the English Stock under assignment from Bonham Norton and Thomas Wight; and it is likely that Woodhouse's sole purpose in acquiring the patent was to sell it to the Stationers' Company.[13] The beauty of patents like these, from the crown's point of view – and the reason why the patentees tended to be courtiers or royal servants – was that they provided a way to settle debts, in kind, at no cost to the exchequer: Sir Richard Coningsby's patent to collect duty on playing-cards was in settlement of a debt of £1,800 owed to him by the crown.[14]

The King's Printing House was particularly vulnerable to encroachments of this sort, partly because its patent was of such a broad extent but largely because the financial difficulties of successive King's Printers left them unable to defend their privileges. It was in anticipation of such an encroachment that Robert Barker petitioned the King in 1615 for the right to print 'a treatise . . . concerning the proceedings of the Principalls & accessaries in the murther of Sir Tho. Overburye', a book which he might reasonably have expected to print by virtue of his patent for official publications.[15] The following year John Hebborne, a gentleman usher to the King, obtained a royal warrant for the printing of the King's *Speech in the Star Chamber*, which he was persuaded to assign to John Bill for a fee of £50. Bill, having by this time acquired a share in the King's Printing Office, then dug in his heels and refused to pay the full amount, claiming that the speech belonged to the King's Printer's patent, so that Hebborne's purported grant was invalid, and that in any case the printed edition had cleared less than £20. Hebborne declared that Bill's profit was closer to £500, but since he had been unwise enough to rely on a verbal agreement, with no witnesses, Hebborne had no means of redress.[16] This case was unusual in that it came to court; but it is probably typical of many others for which no documentary evidence survives.

The Stationers faced similar challenges from authors seeking the copyright of their own works, many of them attempting to break into the expanding and competitive market for educational books. Joseph Webb obviously had high hopes of his Latin textbooks, which he patented in 1626 after making an agreement to share future profits with the crown. Caleb Morley patented another Latin schoolbook the following year, with an ingenious, not to say cheeky proposal to pay the crown £50 a year if his book was officially endorsed as the best available method. Thomas Farnaby, one of the most prolific writers for the educational market, patented his series of editions of classical authors in 1631 in order to protect himself against a glut of foreign piracies. The enormous popularity of Farnaby's editions demonstrates that there were, potentially, large profits to be made from school textbooks; and one should not underestimate the threat that these authors posed to the Stationers' Company's command of the school-book market, a command that was based on the ownership of a handful of long-established texts which might easily be challenged by newcomers. Books were also frequently included in patents for inventions, though these naturally posed less of a threat to the Company: William Stallenge's *Instructions for the Planting and Increase of Mulberry Trees* was accompanied by a patent to import and plant mulberry seeds; Richard Delamaine's *Grammelogia, or the Mathematical Ring* was patented along with the logarithmic slide-rule it describes; and Gabriel Plattes obtained a patent for his *Certaine New Inventions and Profitable Experiments* in anticipation of a steady demand from farmers interested in his corn-setting machine.

Patents to authors were thus on the increase: Timothy Bright's patent of 1589 for his works on shorthand was described by Marjorie Plant as 'a rare grant of author's copyright' but by the 17th century such grants were far from rare.[17] There is some evidence to suggest that this increase may have been due to authorial dissatisfaction with the restrictions imposed by the system of publisher's copyright. Farnaby was driven to buy the copyrights of his classical texts from stationers who refused to reprint them; similarly, Paul Willet patented his father's *Synopsis Papismi* in 1630 because the stationer who owned the copy was 'not able or att least not willing to disburse or expend soe much moneys as the charge of reprinting the same will require'. John Minsheu's patent for his *Glosson Etymologicon* was part of an innovative scheme of self-financing, also involving a subscription list, which may have resulted from an inability to find a publisher willing to risk money on such an expensive and technically demanding work. Other authors may simply have felt that they could make more money by patenting their work than by selling it to a stationer. John Speed's *Theatre of the Empire of Great Britain* was patented by the stationer George Humble in 1608, but in

1610 Speed chose to retain the copyright of his *Genealogies of the Holy Scripture*, and patented it in his own name, with a scale of fixed prices at which copies were to be sold to the Stationers' Company. Viewed in this context, the most remarkable aspect of George Wither's patent for his *Hymns and Songs of the Church* in 1623 is not the fact of an author patenting his own work, nor even the requirement that the book was to be bound up with all copies of the Psalms in Metre—essentially no different from the requirement that Speed's *Genealogies* was to be bound with all copies of the Bible—but the exceptionally long duration of the patent: 51 years, a clear signal of Wither's intention to treat it as a long-term investment, rather than convert it into cash by selling it off to the Stationers' Company. Wither was not an isolated case, but one of a significant minority of authors who turned to the patent system as a means of reserving a measure of control over their works.

Books that were not patented by the author might still be patented by his descendants. In 1615 Alice, Cicely and Margaret Hooker, daughters of the theologian Richard Hooker, petitioned the King to grant them a patent for their father's magnum opus *The Laws of Ecclesiastical Polity*, first published in 1593.[18] The copyright of the *Laws* belonged to Hooker's friend and executor Sir Edwin Sandys, who had financed its publication, but Sandys would hardly have opposed Hooker's own daughters in their attempt to derive some financial benefit from their father's work. However, John Windet, Hooker's cousin and the printer of the first edition, had entered it in the Register on Sandys's behalf; and on the basis of that entry, Windet's successor William Stansby assumed that the copy belonged to him and proceeded to reprint it. The Hookers' patent application followed hard on the heels of a Chancery suit in which Stansby's claim to the copyright had been upheld.[19] Although the patent was never enrolled, the application appears to have had the desired effect of forcing Stansby to offer some financial compensation.[20] It may also have inspired Mrs Hester Ogden, daughter of another Elizabethan theologian, William Fulke, to submit a similar application in 1616 for a patent to print her father's *Confutation of the Romish Testament*. Here, again, the ownership of the copyright was a matter of dispute. Mrs Ogden declared that her father had bequeathed it to her, but the stationers Thomas Adams, John Bill and Bonham Norton claimed that it belonged to them, as the successors of Fulke's original publisher George Bishop. This time it was the outsider who won: Mrs Ogden finally obtained her patent in 1618, in the names of two assigns (neither of them Stationers), and took immediate steps to maximize its value, first by suing Adams, Bill and Norton for possession of existing stocks of the book, then by lobbying for a royal proclamation 'for the furnishinge of every parish Church with one of the said Bookes' to promote the sales of her own edition. 'If John Bill's statement is anywhere near the truth', commented Greg, 'the patent was grossly unfair.'[21] What the case demonstrates, however, is that a patent was a highly effective weapon in a copyright dispute, particularly for a private individual. The point was not lost on George Sandys, whose patent for his translation of Ovid's *Metamorphoses* enabled him to outgun the stationer Robert Young in 1628; sweet revenge, no doubt, for his brother Edwin's ignominious defeat at the hands of William Stansby 15 years earlier.

Another ingenious way to circumvent the Stationers' Register was to acquire a patent for an abridged edition of an existing work. In or around 1624 Gilbert Diglen, describing himself as a student of mathematics and a former servant to Prince Henry, applied for a 21-year patent for 'a smale booke, being the Epitomy of Mr Camdens Britannia . . . which is now fully finished, and all the severall Mappes of every sheere cut in Copper, to your petitioners greate Charge and expence'.[22] The patent was never enrolled, but the book is probably to be identified with *The Abridgment of Camden's Britannia with the maps* (STC 4527) published by John Bill in 1626, and Diglen presumably sold the sheets to Bill along with any privilege he may have obtained. A similar case occurred in 1621 when Mrs Helen Mason obtained a patent for her late husband Thomas Mason's abridgement of Foxe's Book of Martyrs. This was not the first time an abridged edition of Foxe had been mooted: Timothy Bright's abridgement of 1589, also published under patent, had proved a bestseller and severely damaged the sales of the unabridged edition. Mason's edition, however, never appeared, perhaps because the Stationers' Company bought the privilege in order to suppress it; although it may have been the abridgement that Robert Young proposed to publish some years later, for which Archbishop Laud refused to grant a licence on the grounds that 'abridgements, by their brevity and their cheapness, in short time work out the authors themselves'.[23]

A further problem for the Stationers was that many of their patents were only temporary. The patent for Latin schoolbooks, for example, ran for only 21 years; and in 1631, three years before it was due to expire, the reversion was granted to an outsider, George Rodolphe Weckherlin, one of the King's secretaries. As it turned out, Weckherlin was willing to sell the patent back to the English Stock; but it proved more difficult to retain the patent for common-law books, which the English Stock had bought in 1605 and which was granted by reversion to another outsider, John Moore, in 1618. In 1629, when the old patent expired, the Company had not succeeded in reaching an agreement with Moore, and the lawbook patent passed out of their control. Its loss evidently caused considerable ill-feeling, since the Privy Council had to order the Company to co-operate with Moore. Moore eventually assigned his patent to the Flesher syndicate, not to the English Stock, and the Company did not regain it until 1661. The patent for Greek and Latin grammars, granted to Bonham Norton in 1613 for 30 years, was captured in 1615 by yet another outsider, John Willie, under yet another reversionary patent.

These patents were certainly a nuisance to the Stationers' Company, but one might be forgiven for wondering whether they ever represented a serious threat. After all, the Star Chamber decree of 1637 strengthened the hand of what Blagden called 'the bookselling, copyright-owning, and English Stock-shareholding element among the Stationers', and the Company's monopoly lasted until the lapse of the Licensing Act in 1695. But simply because the Stationers won, one should not assume that they were bound to win. The Company's monopoly, as Graham Pollard pointed out, was essentially *de facto* rather than *de jure*: it was not the strength of its legal position which enabled it to defeat its competitors, but its control of book production and distribution which ensured that, as a rule, it had no competitors to defeat. The patent system, as Pollard was also well aware, was the great exception to that rule:

Copyright (*other than a grant of monopoly by patent*) was confined to members of the Stationers' Company. And was secured de facto and not de jure because the only people who could infringe the copyright were themselves members of the Stationers' Company and amenable to its regulations. It was because the Stationers' Company had a monopoly of book production that they could exclude any other claims than their own to property in copyright *except grants from the Crown*.[24]

In the early 1620s, as the Company came under attack from several different quarters, its monopoly began to look extremely vulnerable. Wood and Symcock's patent of 1619 for printing on one side of paper was intended to break the Company's monopoly of jobbing printing; and when the master-printers closed ranks against the patentees, refusing to print anything for them 'except they might have double the price that they usually had for printing the like', Symcock established his own press and hired journeyman printers to operate it. George Wither's patent of 1623 for his *Hymns and Songs of the Church* was an attempt to force an entry into the market for Bibles and metrical psalms; though ultimately unsuccessful, Wither gained the backing of the Privy Council and managed to force the Company into temporary compliance. Meanwhile, the University of Cambridge was asserting its own privilege to print almanacs, grammars and metrical psalms; and the University Printer, Cantrell Legge, declared that the Company's prices could be undercut by 50%.[25] As Pollard comments: 'There was a real danger that printers, lacking work and discontented with the policy of the Court of the Stationers' Company, might combine with a patentee to operate outside the Company's control.'[26]

This evidence has tended to be dismissed by book trade historians, often in a remarkably cavalier fashion: Sir Walter Greg's sole comment on Wood and Symcock's patent, for instance, was that 'the case is of interest for the fullness of the records and as showing the elaborate procedures necessary to expose a manifest racket'. Greg regarded printing patents as unnecessary, because copyright 'was already assured by the Company's own regulations and needed not the protection of the Crown'; since patents did not serve to protect copyright, Greg assumed that their sole purpose must have been the furtherance of 'vested interest' to the detriment of free trade.[27] He does not seem to have appreciated that the Stationers' Register protected the vested interests of the Company just as surely as the Patent Rolls protected the vested interests of the patentees. In the course of the Chancery case between Symcock and the Stationers' Company, it emerged that while the Company claimed to be opposing the patent in the interests of its poorer members, the printing of ballads and other single-sheet items had actually been monopolised by a group of master-printers, 'men of very good estate and sufficiency', who had formed a cartel in order to keep prices artificially high. The stationer John Hammond testified that 'all Ballads heretofore were usually printed & sold by the said Company in common, but of late yeares seaven Stationers or thereaboutes have ioyned themselves together in Company to print & sell Ballads'. The ballad partners were said to charge 13*s* 4*d* a ream, whereas Symcock 'hath sold Ballads a noble in the pounde better cheape then the said seaven Stationers have sold these ballads to any one whatsoever', and on better paper. Not surprisingly, the Company had tried to buy Symcock out, offering him an annuity of £200 or £300; when this failed, the master-printers were reduced to 'very scornefull & contemptuous speaches against the said Pattent', telling Symcock that they hoped to see him 'hanged and his Pattent about his necke'.[28] In the light of this evidence, it is difficult to regard Symcock's challenge to the Stationers' monopoly as merely a 'manifest rackct'. Pollard's *de facto* / *de jure* distinction reveals the fallacy of Greg's assumption that the Company's *de facto* control of book production gave it a legal or moral right to regulate the book trade.

With hindsight, one can argue that the Company's monopoly was bound to survive, since it formed part of the implicit bargain between the Stationers and the government, by which the Stationers co-operated with the government in enforcing the licensing system and the government protected copyright and guaranteed the Stationers' monopoly.[29] Contemporaries, however, simply assumed that the control of printing was a function of the royal prerogative – limited by law, certainly, but not limited by the terms of a contract with the Stationers' Company – and the controversy between the Stationers and their opponents was one in which both sides claimed to be championing the King's authority. The Stationers took their stand on the royal privileges that they themselves possessed, complaining that if Cantrell Legge continued to print grammars and metrical psalms in competition with the English Stock, 'he will . . . make his Maiesties prerogatiue in this kinde of no validitie'. Their opponents, like George Wither, declared that the Company's monopoly prejudiced the royal prerogative, since the Stationers were protected by their own ordinances 'better than any author can bee by the Kings grant'. Wither's argument was reiterated in a petition presented to the King in 1636 by one Mr Moore, which maintained that the Stationers' Register was in direct competition with the patent system:

The Stationers of London having set themselves in a way (by entring in their Hall Register all bookes for their owne printing that come within their reach) to preiudice his Maiesties present and future Graunts of priviledges for printing, being as absolute a right of his Maiesties prerogatiue as that of Coyning . . .[30]

This was not a controversy which the Stationers could be certain of winning, especially as the crown had a direct financial interest in the granting of patents. What swung the balance in their favour was the support of William Laud, who understood, with unusual clarity, the terms of the bargain between the Stationers' Company and the government. As Sheila Lambert has written, 'we do not know nearly enough about the effect of patronage on the Stationers' Company', but it is clear that Laud, as Bishop of London from 1628 and Archbishop of Canterbury from 1633, consistently supported the Company's interests and tried to clip the wings of rival patentees.[31] We have already encountered Laud protecting the English Stock by refusing to grant a licence for an abridgement of Foxe's Book of Martyrs, despite the existence of a patent. He sided with the Company in its dispute with Symcock, bluntly informing the latter that he would 'lay [him] by the heeles' if he continued to operate his press; and he discouraged the University of Oxford from competing with the Stationers, as Cambridge had done, in the market for Bibles, grammars and primers.[32] Lambert also shows that Laud, while restricting the number of master-printers, was cultivating the support of the journeyman printers in order to prevent a split within the Company.[33] To a large extent, therefore, the survival of the Company's monopoly down to 1641 should be put down to the political circumstances of the 1630s, and to good luck rather than manifest destiny.

The overlap between the Stationers' Register and the Patent Rolls is typical of the early modern period, when the boundaries between different jurisdictions were not always clearly defined and individuals were quick to take advantage of the resulting legal confusion. The two were not, as Wither would have us believe, necessarily in competition with each other; but they were, nevertheless, alternative methods of securing copyright. In observing that a printer who entered a book in the Register 'hath the same as seuerall to him self as any man hath any boke by her maiesties preuilege', the 1583 Commission on Privileges was not 'naively swallowing the whole of the patentees' case' by confusing privilege with copyright, as Greg suggests, but stating the sober truth.[34] In his history of the Cambridge University Press, which is also one of the best accounts of the London book trade in this period, David McKitterick has commented that 'the Stationers' Company's control of the printing trade was, so far as the University was concerned, all but absolute — not so much by the legal position which it claimed, as by the hold its principal members had over the wholesale and retail price structure.'[35] As a reiteration of Pollard's de facto / de jure distinction, this is fair enough; but it underestimates the importance of the patent system as a legal platform on which the University could challenge the Stationers' monopoly. At a time when the Net Book Agreement is on the verge of collapse it is, perhaps, easier to appreciate the fragility of any attempt to control the price structure of the book trade. It has been suggested that the

Stationers' Company was in decline by the middle of the 17th century: R. C. Bald, for example, has drawn attention to the number of occasions after the Restoration when the Company went to court to enforce its patents, which he interprets as a sign that the Company could no longer settle such disputes by its own authority.[36] There is, as yet, no consensus on the reasons for that decline, or on the underlying economic conditions of the book trade; my own opinion, however, based on a study of the Patent Rolls, is that the underlying weakness of the Company's monopoly was already apparent by the 1620s.

For the period 1603 to 1641, the following list of book trade patents largely supersedes the lists in Arber, Greg's *Companion to Arber*, STC volume 3 and the volume of *Printing Patents* published by the Printing Historical Society in 1969. It should be reasonably self-explanatory; but a brief outline of the mechanism by which patents were granted, and the documentary sources from which this list has been compiled, may prove helpful as an introduction.

Acquiring a patent was an arduous business. To begin with, the aspiring patentee addressed a petition to the King in person, to the Privy Council, or to one of the secretaries of state. The petition would be referred to the Attorney General or the Solicitor General for a legal opinion; and if it was approved, a bill would be prepared for the King's signature. This formed the authority for a Bill of Privy Signet, which in turn formed the authority for a Writ of Privy Seal, which in its turn formed the authority for Letters Patent under the Great Seal.[37] A copy was enrolled in Chancery, and the patent itself, with the Great Seal attached, was given to the patentee. Possession of this document gave its owner a presumptive claim to the privilege it embodied: thus in 1597, when John Battersby sold the grammar privilege to Thomas Dawson, Edward White and Cuthbert Burby, he handed over the patent to them; and when the privilege for Francis Holyoke's Latin dictionary passed into the hands of a syndicate, a certified copy of the patent was placed in the custody of the Wardens of the Stationers' Company 'for the ioynt use of all the said parties' on condition that it 'should not be delivered to any one of the parties, but unto the Maior parte of them'.[38]

Considering this lengthy process, it is hardly surprising that a patent tended to leave a paper trail behind it. The patentees' petition might be filed in the papers of the official who received it, and recorded in the letter-book of the official to whom it was referred, along with a note of the action taken. The bill would be docketed in the State Papers, and again as it passed through the Signet Office. Most of the patent-related documents printed in Greg's *Companion to Arber* fall into one of these categories: some are petitions, including several from the papers of Charles I's Attorney General Sir John Bankes; others are dockets from the State Papers in the Public Record Office. The fullest information, however, is to be found in the Patent Rolls themselves, a class of document which few book trade

historians, apart from the indefatigable Arber, have consulted. The Patent
Rolls list the terms and conditions of the privilege, often with important
details which are omitted in the documents printed by Greg; and they are
our only source of information on many patents for which no petition
happens to survive and no docket is calendared in the finding-aids to State
Papers Domestic. Consequently, I have chosen to rely on the Patent Rolls
as the basis of the following list.

However, acquiring a patent was expensive as well as arduous – it cost
Richard Field 20s 4d to have his patent for *Orlando Furioso* sealed in 1592
– and not all patentees went to the trouble and expense of having their
patent enrolled.[39] This could be risky if the patent was challenged:
Benjamin Fisher's privilege to print *The Attourneys Academy* (1623) was
rejected by the Privy Council in 1630 because he could only produce 'a Bill
signed from the King for the printing of the said booke', not a patent under
the Great Seal. Nevertheless, a good many patentees took the risk, and
some patents thus exist as royal warrants or Bills of Privy Signet without
ever having made it on to the Patent Rolls. Alternatively, a patent might be
blocked by opponents determined to prevent it reaching the legal high
ground of the Patent Rolls. Mrs Ogden's patent for Fulke's *Defence of the
Sincere and True Translation* was opposed by the Stationers' Company: it
eventually passed the Signet Office only to be 'stayed, by what meanes she
knoweth not', and she had to petition again 'to let it have the like passage
at the privy-seale'.[40] Mrs Ogden finally got her patent enrolled after a
year's delay, but Wood and Symcock's patent of 1619, which was also
opposed by the Stationers' Company, immediately became embroiled in
legal proceedings and does not seem to have been enrolled at all. In the
interests of completeness, all known printing privileges have been included
in the following list, whether or not they can be found in the Patent Rolls;
the term 'warrant' is used to denote a patent that was not enrolled.

For the majority of entries, however, the principal reference is to the
Patent Rolls (C66) in the Public Record Office.[41] If the patent is printed
in Thomas Rymer's *Foedera* (London, 1704-35), or if supporting documents
appear in Greg's *Companion to Arber*, then these references are given; and
if the patent was assigned, renewed or contested, then further information
is provided in the notes. In addition, anyone interested in the history of a
particular patent should not neglect the Signet Office docquet books (SO3)
in the Public Record Office, which identify the referring authority and thus
provide valuable information on patronage in the book trade. The list
includes patents for paper-making and playing-cards, but not Scottish and
Irish patents, which were enrolled separately and to which STC volume 3
remains the best available guide. Standard features of the patents have been
omitted from individual entries: thus the privilege to print a book can be
assumed to include the privilege to sell or import it, to appoint assigns, and
to search for and confiscate illicit copies. The list is in the nature of an
experiment, and I would welcome additions and corrections, as well as

suggestions for extending it to cover the largely uncharted terrain of late 17th and 18th-century patents.

References

1. David Foxon, *Thoughts on the History and Future of Bibliographical Description* (Los Angeles, 1970), p.21.
2. Marjorie Plant, *The English Book Trade* (2nd ed., 1965), p.110.
3. W. W. Greg, *Some Aspects and Problems of London Publishing between 1550 and 1650* (Oxford: Clarendon Press, 1956), p.89.
4. W. W. Greg, ed., *A Companion to Arber* (Oxford: Clarendon Press, 1967), pp.114-33.
5. Cyprian Blagden, *The Stationers' Company: a history, 1403-1959* (London: Allen & Unwin, 1960), p.92.
6. Blagden, *The Stationers' Company*, pp.110-29. However, Sheila Lambert paints a gloomier economic picture, suggesting that the Company had to cope with the problem of 'over-capacity in a period of economic recession': Lambert, 'The Printers and the Government, 1604-1637', in Robin Myers and Michael Harris, eds., *Aspects of Printing from 1600* (Oxford: Oxford Polytechnic Press, 1987), p.3.
7. Greg, *Companion to Arber*, p.129.
8. Sir Francis Moore, *Cases Collect & Report* (1663), pp.674-5. Harold G. Fox, *Monopolies and Patents* (Toronto, 1947), pp.319, 341.
9. Greg. *Companion to Arber*, p.170.
10. C. J. Sisson, 'The Laws of Elizabethan Copyright: the Stationers' View', *The Library*, 5th ser., vol.15 (1960), p.19.
11. Gerald D. Johnson, 'The Stationers versus the Drapers', *The Library*, 6th ser., vol.10 (1988), p.8, gives examples of Drapers buying into privileges in the late 16th century. It may also be significant that John Battersby's purchase of the grammar patent in 1597 was financed by a Haberdasher, Thomas Allen (PRO, C24/308/7).
12. Richard Bancroft to Robert Cecil, 18 Oct. 1597, quoted in D. W. Krummel, *English Music Printing 1553-1700* (London: The Bibliographical Society, 1975), p.24.
13. James G. MacManaway, 'Privilege to Print', *Studies in Bibliography*, vol.16 (1963), pp.201-3.
14. Joan Thirsk, *Economic Policy and Projects: the development of a consumer society in early modern England* (Oxford: Clarendon Press, 1978), p.59.
15. Paul Morgan, 'A King's Printer at Work: two documents of Robert Barker', *Bodleian Library Record*, vol.13, no.5 (Oct. 1990), pp.372-3.
16. PRO, REQ 2/398/54.
17. Marjorie Plant, *The English Book Trade*, p.109.
18. The patent application can be found in BL, Lansdowne MS 266, f.270.
19. C. J. Sisson, *The Judicious Marriage of Mr Hooker and the Birth of 'The Laws of Ecclesiastical Polity'* (Cambridge: Cambridge University Press, 1940) reconstructs the publication history of the book from the Chancery records.
20. Sisson concluded that 'it appears plainly enough that . . . his daughters were in no way benefited by the publication of the book' (*Judicious Marriage of Mr Hooker*, p.78), but Archbishop Abbot was ordered to confer with 'some of the chief stationers of London' to determine 'howe the petitioners may be conveniently relieved'.
21. Greg, *Aspects and Problems*, p.95.
22. BL, Add MS 69912, ff.88-9.
23. William Laud, *Works*, vol.4 (Oxford, 1854), p.265.
24. Graham Pollard to F. P. Wilson, 12 June 1942: Beinecke Library, Yale, F. P. Wilson papers box 8, folder 1. My italics.
25. David McKitterick, *A History of Cambridge University Press*, vol.1 (Cambridge: Cambridge University Press, 1992), p.149.

26. Graham Pollard, 'The English Market for Printed Books', *Publishing History*, vol.4 (1978), p.22.
27. Greg, *Aspects and Problems*, pp.91, 102.
28. PRO, C24/561/118.
29. This line of argument goes back to Arber, who argued that 'the concentration of the printing patents into fewer hands, chiefly those of the Stationers' Company and of the King's Printers' was the result of a deliberate royal policy (Arber III.15); for a more recent reiteration of the 'implicit bargain' argument, see D. M. Loades, 'Illicit Presses and Clandestine Printing', in A. C. Duke and C. A. Tamse, eds., *Too Mighty to be Free: Censorship and the press in Britain and the Netherlands* (Zutphen: De Walburg Pers, 1987), p.24.
30. Greg, *Companion*, p.339.
31. Sheila Lambert, 'The Printers and the Government, 1604-1637', in Myers and Harris, eds., *Aspects of Printing*, p.5.
32. PRO, C24/561/118, evidence of Laurence Norcott. McKitterick, *History of Cambridge University Press*, p.194.
33. Pollard believed that a split was averted by the 'considerable statesmanship' of the Stationers themselves; but it is clear that there was much resentment at the monopolistic activities of the Flesher syndicate, and one should not underestimate Laud's influence in holding the Company together. See Donald W. Rude and Lloyd E. Berry, 'Tanner Manuscript no.33: new light on the Stationers' Company in the early seventeenth century', *Papers of the Bibliographical Society of America*, vol.66 (1972), pp.129-31.
34. Greg, *Companion to Arber*, pp.122, 126.
35. McKitterick, *History of Cambridge University Press*, p.148; see also my review of McKitterick's book, in *Historical Journal*, vol.37 (1994), pp.996-9.
36. R. C. Bald, 'Early Copyright Litigation and its Bibliographical Interest', *Papers of the Bibliographical Society of America*, vol.36 (1942), p.85. McKitterick also suggests that the Company was in decline by mid-century (*History of Cambridge University Press*, p.113), though one should note Pollard's view that the English Stock was 'at the peak of its influence and prosperity' after the Restoration ('The English Market for Printed Books', p.25).
37. W. P. W. Phillimore, ed., *An Index to Bills of Privy Signet, commonly called Signet Bills, 1584 to 1596 and 1603 to 1624* (British Record Society, 1890), p.v. David Crankshaw has suggested to me that the Fine Rolls may contain records of expenses incurred in the granting of patents, and may thus provide information on patents that never reached the Patent Rolls.
38. PRO, C24/308/7, evidence of John Finch. W. A. Jackson, *Records of the Court of the Stationers' Company 1602 to 1640* (London: The Bibliographical Society, 1957), p.330.
39. Greg, *Companion*, p.151.
40. Folger Library, Washington, G.b.10, f.105.
41. Many of the contemporary calendars to the Chancery Patent Rolls have been published in facsimile by the List and Index Society.

Book Trade Patents, 1603-1640

1603, May 10. Patent to Christopher Barker junior, granting him the reversion of the office of King's Printer currently held by his father Robert Barker, with privilege to print statutes, acts of Parliament, proclamations, injunctions, the Bible in English, service books and other books wholly or partly in English, with the exception of Latin grammars. Barker is to receive an annual fee of £6 13s 4d. Length of grant: for life, or to his executors for four years if Christopher should predecease his father.
References: C66/1608/[25].
Notes: Robert Barker's patent, of which this is the reversion, is dated 9 July 1603.

1603, May 21. Patent to John Norton, printer and bookseller, granting him the office of printer to the King in the Latin, Greek and Hebrew languages, with privilege to print Tremellius' Latin Bible with or without notes, all Greek and Latin grammars (including the grammars of Lilly, Clenardus and Camden) and other books, and to provide any books required by the King in the said languages. Norton is to receive an annual fee of 26s 8d. Length of grant: for life.
References: C66/1608/[26].
Notes: This office was granted by letters patent dated 6 April 1597 to John Battersby, who assigned it to Thomas Dawson, Edward White and Cuthbert Burby for an annuity of £160. When Norton obtained his patent, this arrangement was disrupted: Dawson, White and Burby refused to pay the annuity, and were sued by Battersby. In the subsequent Chancery case (PRO, C24/308/7) Burby was alleged to have said that Norton 'must needes make them his farmers or deputyes of his new patent or els he should do litle good in regard that they had (as they sayde) so many thousande gramers allready printed in their handes that they could store England therwith for a good while'. For a full account of the dispute, see Nancy A. Mace, 'The History of the Grammar Patent, 1547-1620', *PBSA*, vol.87 (1993), pp.425-31.

1603, July 9. Patent to Robert Barker, confirming him in the office of King's Printer, with privilege to print statutes, acts of Parliament, proclamations, injunctions, the Bible in English, service books and other books wholly or partly in English, with the exception of Latin grammars. Barker is to receive an annual fee of £6 13s 4d. Length of grant: for life.
References: C66/1630/ memb. 22-23.
Notes: Confirmation of a patent of 8 August 1589 granting the office to Christopher Barker senior, and in reversion to his son Robert Barker. For this and subsequent patents, see H. R. Plomer, 'The King's Printing House under the Stuarts', *The Library*, new series, vol.2 (1901), pp.353-75.

1603, October 29. Patent to the Stationers' Company to print all primers, psalters, psalms in metre or prose, and licensed almanacs and prognostications, and to pass ordinances for the enforcement of these privileges. The Prayer Book and all books belonging to the King's Printer's privilege are excluded from this grant. Length of grant: in perpetuity.
References: C66/1619/ memb. 29-31. Arber III.42-44. Greg, *Companion,.* p.50.
Notes: The foundation of the English Stock: see Blagden, *Stationers' Company*, pp.92-3. The patent for almanacs had been granted to Richard Watkins and James Roberts for 21 years from 12 May 1588 (Arber II.16).

1604, February 8. Patent to Robert Barker, King's Printer, granting him the reversion of the office of printer to the King in the Latin, Greek and Hebrew languages, with privilege to print Tremellius' Latin Bible with or without notes, all Greek and Latin grammars, and all other books in these languages. Length of grant: 30 years from the death of John Norton.
References: C66/1611/ memb. 10-13.

1604, May 8. Patent to John Bateman, stationer, and his son Abraham Bateman, granting them the office of bookbinder to the King, for which they are to receive an annual fee of £6. Length of grant: for their lives.
References: C66/1631/10 (memb. 31-2).
Notes: On the Batemans and their bindings, see Mirjam Foot, *The Henry Davis Gift* (1978-83), vol.1, pp.40-3.

1605, July 17. Patent to James Ryme, bookseller, to print the works of Hieronymus Zanchius in Latin, 'very profitable for the Churche of England' and never before printed, and to import foreign editions. Length of grant: 14 years.
References: C66/1680/ memb. 35. Greg, *Companion*, p.153.
Notes: Ryme imported a number of foreign editions of works by Zanchius, and reissued them in 1605 with cancel title-pages (STC 26121 *et seq.*). He may subsequently have assigned his patent to John Bill, who published another work by Zanchius in 1608 (STC 26121a.3).

1605, July 19. Patent to Christopher Hunt, citizen and stationer, to print 'a small booke called the Househoulders practise', never before printed, which has been licensed by the Bishop of London and Dr William Hutchinson, and which is 'very profitable for the instruction of youthe in theire tender yeares in true religion and in the feare and knowledge of God Almighty'. Length of grant: 21 years.
References: C66/1682/ memb. 34.
Notes: The book is not recorded in STC and does not appear to have been published.

1606, April 15. Patent to John Legate, citizen and stationer of London and now printer to the University of Cambridge, to print Thomas Thomas's dictionary, which he has 'augmented' and printed in 'a more readie and exacte manner', and which is 'approved of the learned to be the best and afforded the better cheape unto our Subiects by more then one halfe that these have usuallie paid for other Dictionaries'. The patent does not extend to the dictionaries of Elliott, Cooper, Rider or any other, but solely to the dictionary of Thomas Thomas. Length of grant: 21 years.
References: C66/1696/5.
Notes: On 10 March 1606 Legate signed an agreement with the partners in Rider's Dictionary, by which he agreed to sell to them any edition of Thomas's Dictionary that he printed within the next three years, and the partners agreed not to reprint Rider's Dictionary 'to the preiudice of Mr Legatt' within the same period (Jackson p.18). See David McKitterick, *A History of Cambridge University Press*, vol.1 (Cambridge, 1992), p.119, for further information on what McKitterick calls 'this reprehensible agreement'. Editions of both dictionaries appeared in 1606 (STC 21032 and 24013).

1607, January 5. Patent to William Stallenge, gentleman, to print a book entitled *Instructions for the Planting and Increase of Mulberry Trees, Breeding of Silkworms and Making of Silk*. Length of grant: 21 years.
References: C66/1699/[10]. Greg, *Companion*, p.153.
Notes: Stallenge also acquired a seven-year patent to import and plant mulberry seeds: C66/1741/[6], dated 28 January 1608. The book was published in 1609 (STC 23138), apparently without being entered in SR, and is, according to STC, largely a translation of J. B. Le Tellier's *Mémoires et instructions pour l'establissement des meuriers* (Paris, 1603).

1607, May 19. Patent to Thomas Wilson, Esq., of London, and Percival Golding, gentleman, son of the late Arthur Golding, Esq., of Belchamp St Paul, Essex, to print 'manie workes of greate volume and importance' translated by Arthur Golding and Thomas Wilson, together with any other works which Wilson may in future translate, and any abridgements of the said works. These include Calvin's commentaries on the Psalms, his sermons on Galatians, Ephesians and Deuteronomy, Beza's *Certain Questions. . . concerning Matters of Divinity*, Hemmingsen's *Postills on the Gospels*, Chytraeus's *Disposements on the Epistles*, Philippe de Mornay's *The Truenesse of the Christian Religion*, Marlorat's *Exposition of the Apocalypse*, *The Testament of the Twelve Patriarchs*, the *Histories* of Justinus (Trogus Pompeius), Caesar's *Commentaries*, Seneca's *De Beneficiis*, 'a worke concerninge the duties of magistrates', Ovid's *Metamorphoses*, and the *History concerning the Wars of the Goths in Italy* by Leonard Aretine (Leonardo Bruni). Length of grant: 7 years.
References: C66/1731/ memb. 1-3.
Notes: A list of Golding's translations is given in STC (note following STC 11987) and includes all the above with the exception of *The testaments of the twelve patriarches* (STC 19465.7) which STC attributes to Anthony Gilby, and the 'worke concerninge the duties of magistrates' which cannot be identified. None of Golding's translations was reprinted after 1607, except for Ovid's *Metamorphoses* (STC 18962) which the Stationers' Company regarded as the property of the English Stock.

1608, March 22. Patent to Melchisedech Bradwood, stationer, to print John Jewel's *Defence of the Apology of the Church of England* and his *Book of Articles* (i.e. *A Replie unto M. Hardings Answer*). Length of grant: 10 years.

References: C66/1749/[5]. Greg, *Companion*, p.154.
Notes: Bradwood probably assigned his patent to John Norton, who published Jewel's *Works* in 1609 (STC 14579); indeed, he may have obtained the patent in anticipation of Norton's edition.

1608, April 30. Patent to George Humble to print John Speed's *Theatre of the Empire of Great Britain.* Length of grant: 21 years.
References: C66/1770/23. Greg, *Companion*, p.154.
Notes: The book was published in 1611 (STC 23041), apparently without being entered in SR.

1608, August 13. Patent to Sir William Woodhouse, gentleman of the Privy Chamber, to print all reports, abstracts, abridgements and collections of Calvin's case 'touching the postnati of Scotland', former patents to the contrary notwithstanding. Length of grant: 10 years.
References: C66/1769/6.
Notes: See James G. McManaway, 'Privilege to Print', *Studies in Bibliography*, vol.16 (1963), pp.201-3. The only published report of Calvin's case appears to be that in Sir Edward Coke's *La sept part des Reports* (1608), STC 5511. Woodhouse may have assigned his patent to the Stationers' Company, who held the patent for law books at that time.

1610, October 31. Patent to John Speed to print the *Genealogies of the Holy Scriptures* and the map of Canaan, which are to be inserted into every copy of the new translation of the Bible. Speed is to charge no more than 6*d* for every octavo copy, 12*d* for every quarto copy, 18*d* for every small folio copy and 2*s* for every large folio copy. Length of grant: 10 years.
References: C66/1868/9.
Notes: See the headnote to STC 23039 *et seq.* for details of the complex publishing history of this work. Speed's patent was renewed in 1617.

1611, February 20. Patent to John Minsheu, gentleman and professor of languages in the City of London, to print his *Glosson Etymologicon,* an etymological dictionary in twelve languages (English, Scottish, Welsh, High Dutch, Low Dutch, French, Italian, Spanish, Portuguese, Latin, Greek and Hebrew), which will lead to the advancement of learning and to the special advancement of the English, Scottish and Welsh languages among other nations, and which has received the approval of many learned men, including the general approval of the University of Oxford. Length of grant: 21 years.
References: C66/1868/20. Greg, *Companion*, p.157.
Notes: The book was published in 1617 (STC 17944) but was not entered in SR until 27 April 1635, when it was entered to Benjamin Fisher under licence from the Bishop of London (Arber IV.338). It was printed 'at the charges of J. Minsheu' and was one of the first English books to be published by subscription.

1611, August 1. Warrant to Arthur Standish, gentleman, to print a treatise concerning 'some proiects for the increasing of Woods; the decay whereof in this Realme is universally complained of'. Length of grant: not specified.
References: Not in the Patent Rolls. The warrant is printed in Standish's *The Commons Complaint* (1611) A2r, but does not appear to have passed the Signet Office.
Notes: The book was entered in SR on 17 May 1611, and published the same year (STC 23200.5 *et seq.*) under the title *The Commons Complaint.*

1612, February 29. Agreement between the King and Simon Sturtevant, gentleman, by which Sturtevant is granted the sole use of his invention for casting and working metal by means of sea-coal or pit-coal, as described in his *Treatise of Metallica*, which is to be printed and published before the end of Easter Term 1612. In return, Sturtevant is to pay shares of the annual profits to the King (30%), Prince Henry (15%), Prince Charles (6%) and Viscount Rochester (3%), dividing the remaining profits between himself and his investors. Length of grant: 31 years.
References: C54/2115/2.

Notes: See A. A. Gomme, *Patents of Invention* (1946), p.31. Sturtevant's treatise *Metallica* (STC 23411) bears the date 22 May 1612.

1612, October 22. Patent to Edward Allde (Alday), citizen and stationer, at the nomination of Susanna Hardanville, widow of Thomas Morley, to print set songs, sonnets and part songs in English, French, Italian and other languages, and to rule paper for the printing and pricking of songs. No printed songs or ruled paper may be imported from abroad except by Allde and his assigns. The grant does not extend to ballads. Length of grant: 21 years.
References: C66/1957/17.
Notes: A renewal of the patent granted to Thomas Morley in 1598, which would have expired on 27 September 1619. Krummel erroneously states that 'there is no record of a renewal' (*English Music Printing*, p.32).

1613, January 6. Patent to Bonham Norton, Esq., granting him the office of printer to the King in the Latin, Greek and Hebrew languages, with privilege to print Tremellius' Latin Bible with or without notes, all Greek and Latin grammars and other books, and to provide any books required by the King in the said languages. Norton to receive an annual fee of 26s 8d and any other allowances enjoyed by the former holders of the office. Length of grant: 30 years.
References: C66/1966/6.
Notes: John Norton, the previous holder of the office, had died in 1612, and Bonham Norton must have acquired the reversion from Robert Barker, to whom it had been granted in 1604. In December 1619 the Stationers' Company agreed to buy the grammar patent for a down-payment of £300 and an annuity of £300 during the life of Joyce Norton, £200 thereafter. In March 1624, however, it was 'agreed that Mr Norton shall take the grammer patent backe againe from the Companye', in return for which Norton was to hand over his stock of grammars and to pay the Company an annuity of £22 during the life of Joyce Norton (Jackson pp.117, 164).

1613, April 2. Patent to the Stationers' Company to print and import certain Latin schoolbooks (*Catonis disticha, Terentii comediae, Aesopi fabulae, Virgilii opera, Ciceronis opera, Ovidii opera, Corderii colloquia, Puerilis sententiae et confabulatiunculae*). Length of grant: 21 years.
References: C66/1992/10.
Notes: This patent had previously been granted to Henry Stringer in 1597 for 14 years (Arber II.16), and in 1631 the reversion was granted to George Rodolphe Weckherlin for 31 years.

1615, March 13. Patent to William Jorden of London, gentleman, and Nicholas Hooker of London, goldsmith, at the nomination of Lord Morley, to print *God and the King*, a defence of the Oath of Allegiance 'fitt for the instruction and capacity of youth to be taught both in Latin and English . . . as a meanes most requisit in theis tymes to preserve and season younge myndes against the pestilent doctrine of the Jesuites', together with any translation or epitome of the same. Length of grant: 21 years.
References: C66/2033/2. Greg, *Companion*, pp.157-61.
Notes: The book is attributed to Richard Mocket, and Latin (STC 14415 *et seq.*) and English (STC 14418.5 *et seq.*) editions were published simultaneously in 1615. The documents printed by Greg show that Lord Morley petitioned for the patent in return for the surrender of his right to the Marshalship of Ireland.

1615, July 21. Patent to Sir Richard Coningsby, gentleman usher to the King, granting him the office of 'viewer, searcher, settler and allower' of playing cards. Coningsby is to receive 5s per gross of playing cards manufactured in England, and 5s per gross of playing cards imported from abroad after 20 July 1616, this duty having been imposed for the relief of the playing-card-makers of London, who have complained that they are 'much decayed and impoverished in their said trade' by the importation of foreign cards. The grant is made in settlement of a debt of £1,800 owed to Coningsby by the crown, and Coningsby is to pay £200 annually into the Exchequer. Length of grant: 21 years.
References: C66/2069/19.

Notes: The community of foreign merchants in London strongly opposed this patent, and the Privy Council appointed a committee to consider the matter. The committee concluded that although the King had the right to create the office and to levy a duty on foreign playing cards, the levy on English playing cards was illegal 'for soe much as they maye doble, or treble the price of the Commoditye in the sale thereof' and the patent was accordingly rescinded by the Privy Council. (BL Lansdowne MS 160, ff.291-99.)

1615, August 28. Patent to John Willie to print all Greek and Latin grammars, including grammars partly in Greek or Latin and partly in English. Length of grant: 41 years from expiry of previous patent.
References: C66/2068/17.
Notes: A reversion of the 30-year patent granted to Bonham Norton in 1613, though no longer attached to the office of printer to the King in the Latin, Greek and Hebrew languages. Blagden incorrectly identifies the patentee as the stenographer John Willis (*Stationers' Company*, p.143, n.1).

1616, January 2. Patent to Simon Sturtevant, master of arts, and Abraham Williams, gentleman, for an invention called 'fortage and lineage', whereby all kinds of 'weake bibulous spongious and bad paper' may be strengthened 'and enabled to beare Inke on both sydes either for writing or printing or for drawinge of Inke lynes or mathemeticke lyneation', and paper and parchment may be ruled 'by meanes of impressinge of white lynes or by imprintinge of other coloured Inke lynes' in a manner suitable for account books or copy-books for 'young writing schollers'. The invention is described in detail in Sturtevant's treatise 'intytuled fower lynearie writinge bookes &c'. The patentees are to pay £4 annually into the Exchequer. Length of grant: 31 years.
References: C66/2059/3.
Notes: Sturtevant's treatise was published in 1616 under the title *The orthographiall declaration: containing, a briefe advertisement of two new inventions, called lineage and fortage* (STC 6455.5). An abstract of Sturtevant and Williams's petition of 1615, in which they promise to sell their paper 'as good cheape as any other paper is sould', can be found in BL Lansdowne MS 266, f.278.

1616, March 8. Patent to the Stationers' Company to print all primers, psalters, psalms in metre or prose, and licensed almanacs and prognostications, and to pass ordinances for the enforcement of these privileges. The Prayer Book and all books belonging to the King's Printer's privilege (other than the foregoing books) are excluded from this grant. Length of grant: in perpetuity.
References: C66/2072/1. Arber III.679-82. Greg, *Companion*, p.54.
Notes: This replaced the patent of 29 October 1603, which had been surrendered to the Court of Chancery, having proved (from the Company's point of view) defective in two respects. First, it granted the Company the right to print the psalms in metre, regardless of the fact that this was included in the 30-year reversionary patent granted to Verney Alley on 26 February 1592. The Company bought Alley's patent in 1614 (Jackson, p.68) and it is recited in the preamble to the present patent. Secondly, the 1603 patent specifically excluded the Bible and service books, as belonging to the King's Printer's privilege, and this gave Robert Barker the opportunity to compete with the Company by including the psalms in his editions of the Prayer Book. In 1615 the Company petitioned the King, complaining that the patent was defective because 'Mr Barker the kinges printer beinge putt in trust to followe the grante caused a clause to be inserted therein of purpose to preiudice their grante: & by colour thereof as also of a grante which he hath gotten to himselfe for printinge service bookes to the Church, he goeth about to prevent the said Company of the benefitt of their grante'. (BL Lansdowne MS 266, f.275.) Since 1609, it was claimed, Barker had printed 10,000 copies of the psalms every year, and had 'added and joyned them unto and with the bible and other bookes in small volumes which hath not byne used and accustomed to be done in former tymes' (Yale, Osborn MS fb 24, no.19). The new patent is worded so as to exclude the psalms from the King's Printer's privilege.

1616, April 4. Patent to John Harpur, William Pratt and Jeremy Drury to publish, teach and sell an 'instrument or table for cyfering and casting of accomptes' of their own invention. The patentees to pay £3 annually. Length of grant: 21 years.
References: C66/2107/5.
Notes: John Harpur, *The jewell of arithmeticke* (1617), STC 12796, appears to be covered by this patent.

1617, February 4. Patent to John Speed to print the *Genealogies of the Holy Scriptures* and the map of Canaan, which are to be inserted into every copy of the new translation of the Bible. Speed is to charge no more than 6*d* for every octavo copy, 12*d* for every quarto copy, 18*d* for every small folio copy and 2*s* for every large folio copy. Length of grant: 7 years from expiry of previous patent.
References: C66/2098/17.
Notes: Renewal of a previous 10-year patent, on account of Speed's 'great charges' in printing the work, and his inability to profit from it in the three years before the new translation was published. The patent was renewed again in 1623.

1617, February 11. Patent to Robert Barker junior, granting him the reversion of the office of King's Printer, with privilege to print statutes, acts of Parliament, proclamations, injunctions, the Bible in English, service books and other books wholly or partly in English, with the exception of Latin grammars. Barker is to receive an annual fee of £6 13*s* 4*d*. Length of grant: 30 years from the death of Robert Barker senior and Christopher Barker, or from the surrender of their grant.
References: C66/2098/9.

1617, March 13. Patent to John Bingham to print his translation of *The Tactics of Aelian*, for which he 'hath been at the charge not onely of graveing and cutting in copper the figures expressed in the saide booke but alsoe of the printing thereof'. Length of grant: 20 years.
References: C66/2096/14.
Notes: The book (STC 161) was entered in SR on 18 November 1616.

1617, April 29. Patent to Fynes Morison to print his *Itinerary*, written in Latin and translated into English, of which three parts are 'now finished and ready for the Presse' and one or two parts 'not yet fully finished'. Patent subject to licence. Length of grant: 21 years.
References: C66/2138/4. Rymer XVII: 10-11.
Notes: The book (STC 18205) was entered in SR on 5 April 1617.

1617, May 5. Patent to Nicholas Hilliard to 'make, grave and imprint' pictures of the King, Hilliard having previously refrained from publishing such pictures 'for feare his workes would be counterfeited by others'. Hilliard is to pay 13*s* 4*d* annually into the Exchequer. The patent does not prohibit the printing of the royal portrait from 'olde plates' not imitating Hilliard's work, or the publishing 'of any other new portrait'. Length of grant: 12 years.
References: C66/2138/15. Rymer XVII: 15-16.

1617, November 9. Patent to John Spilman, jeweller, to produce 'a newe kinde or sort of playinge cardes', Spilman having 'brought over men from beyond the seas' to manufacture paper for this purpose. The cards are to be sealed with the royal arms and the initials J. S. to prevent imitations. Spilman is to pay £3 6*s* 8*d* annually into the Exchequer. Length of grant: 21 years.
References: C66/2130/6.
Notes: This may be the John Spilman who obtained a 10-year patent for the manufacture of white writing paper on 7 February 1589 (Arber II.814-15).

1618, January 19. Patent to John Moore, Esq., in recognition of his 'good and faithfull service' to the King, to print all books concerning the common laws of England, the abridgements of the statutes commonly known as Rastell's and Poulton's Abridgements, and all 'amendments corrections allegations collections abstractes and additions' thereof. Length of grant: 40 years from expiry of previous patent.

References: C66/2133/7.

Notes: Moore's patent came into effect on 10 March 1629. On 29 July 1629 the Privy Council ordered the Stationers' Company to assist Moore and not to 'hinder or molest' him in the enjoyment of his patent. (*Acts of the Privy Council 1629-30* (London: HMSO, 1960), p.110.) By 1634 Moore had assigned the patent to Miles Flesher, John Haviland and Robert Young (Jackson, p.263).

1618, March 11. Patent to Samuel Daniel, one of the grooms of the Queen's Privy Chamber, to print *The Collection of the History of England* compiled by him. Patent subject to licence. Length of grant: 10 years.

References: C66/2152/13. Rymer XVII: 72-3.

Notes: The book (STC 6248) is an enlarged edition of *The first part of the historie of England* (1612) which was entered in SR on 20 April 1612. Daniel obtained his patent notwithstanding an earlier promise to the Stationers' Company 'that yf he mend or add any thing to the book hereafter. That then yt shalbe prynted according to thorders of the Companie' (Jackson, p.57).

1618, March 11. Patent to Aaron Rathburne, gentleman and mathematical practitioner, and Roger Burges to engrave and print maps of London, Westminster, York, Bristol, Norwich, Canterbury, Bath, Oxford, Cambridge and Windsor, with accompanying descriptions. Length of grant: 21 years.

References: C66/2152/12. Rymer XVII: 74-6.

Notes: The patent includes a long preamble, probably taken from the patentees' petition, stating that because no patent has previously been granted, all existing maps of London are 'false and meane draughtes cutt out in wood . . . to the greate disparagement and disgrace of soe famous and worthie a state'.

1618, March 20. Patent to John Marriott, stationer, to print *Pharmacopeia Londinensis*, newly compiled in Latin by the College of Physicians, on condition that the book is licensed. Length of grant: 21 years.

References: C66/2150/11. Greg, *Companion*, pp.162-3.

Notes: The book was entered in SR on 16 January 1618 and published the same year (STC 16772).

1618, April 4. Patent to Henry Sibdale, Esq., and Thomas Kenithorpe of Louth, Lincolnshire, Esq., at the nomination of Hester Ogden, daughter of the late William Fulke, to print Fulke's *Defence of the Sincere and True Translation of the Holy Scriptures* and his *Confutation* of the Popish translation. Length of grant: 21 years.

References: C66/2179/14. Rymer XVII: 80-2.

Notes: The letter-book of Sir Ralph Winwood, secretary of state to James I, contains a copy of a petition from Mrs Ogden complaining that although a warrant for the patent has been granted, 'one Adams a Stationer in London hath printed divers of the said bookes, having by sinister meanes, gotten a Copie of them from your Suppliantes father in law'. On 7 March 1617 Winwood referred the matter to the Bishop of London (Folger Library, Washington, G.b.10, ff.63, 105). Arber prints a statement by John Bill, dated 22 June 1619, claiming that the copyright belongs to himself, Bonham Norton and Thomas Adams, and complaining that 'because the words of the patent are doubtfull whether they looke backwards and forwards or only for the tyme to com' Mrs Ogden 'intends to tak away not only the copie but also those bookes which we have printed, before the said grant from his Maiestie' (Arber III.39-40). In May 1623 Mrs Ogden petitioned the King for an order that every parish church was to buy a copy of the book (BL, Add MS 69915, ff.1-2); her petition does not appear to have been granted. The 1633 editions of Fulke's works (STC 2947 and 11432, issued together) are 'Printed by Augustine Mathewes, one of the assignes of Hester Ogden'.

1618, August 7. Patent to William Alley, at the nomination of Thomas Middleton, to print Middleton's *The Peacemaker, or Britains Blessing* and any epitome or abridgement of it. The book is commended as necessary 'for the informing and well ordering of youth, preservation of Christian love and amitie and generall avoyding of all contention and bloodshedding' and

the Stationers' Company is ordered to assist Alley in making it widely available. Length of grant: 7 years.
References: C66/2169/114. Rymer XVII: 111-12. Greg, *Companion*, pp.163-4.
Notes: The book was first published in 1618 (STC 14387) and reprinted in 1619, 1620 and 1621.

1619, October 25. Warrant to George Wood to print in colours upon linen cloth in the manner invented by him and James Jenkinson. Wood is to pay £10 annually into the Exchequer. Length of grant: 21 years.
References: Not in the Patent Rolls. Entered in the Signet Office, June 1619 (PRO, SO 3/6) and summarized in STC 8614.
Notes: Wood was a journeyman printer who, having acquired this patent, began to employ his linen press for printing books, including primers and almanacs belonging to the English Stock: see Jackson, pp.xiv-xvi.

1619, October 30. Warrant to Roger Wood and Thomas Symcock, at the nomination of Marin de Boisloré, squire of the body to the King, to print all items on one side of one or more sheets of paper or parchment. The patentees are to pay £10 annually into the Exchequer. Length of grant: 31 years.
References: Not in the Patent Rolls. The warrant does not appear to have passed the Signet Office; and Symcock later petitioned to have the patent 'settled', which implies that it was never enrolled (see PRO, C24/561/118). However, it is not clear how Wood and Symcock managed to enforce their patent without having it enrolled, and its absence from the Patent Rolls is mysterious; it may, like Sturtevant's anomalous patent of 1612, have been enrolled in the Close Rolls (C54). It is recited in brief in the preamble to Symcock's 1628 patent, and printed at length in Greg, *Companion*, pp.165-7, from a printed broadside.
Notes: See Jackson, pp.xvi-xxii, for a full history of this patent, which was unsuccessfully contested by the Stationers' Company. A receipt for £5 paid into the Exchequer by Wood and Symcock on 6 November 1620 is now in the Houghton Library, Harvard, MS Eng 1319.

1621, February 13. Patent to John Legate, stationer, to print Thomas Thomas's *Dictionary*, Legate and his ten brothers and sisters, children of John Legate, late citizen and stationer of London, having petitioned for a renewal of the patent on the grounds that their father 'hath lefte little els amongst them towardes their education and advancement but the benefitt accrewing by the printing of that booke'. Legate junior, as his father's executor, has surrendered the old patent, which had not yet expired. The patent does not extend to the dictionaries of Elliott, Cooper, Rider or any other, but solely to the dictionary of Thomas Thomas. Length of grant: 21 years.
References: C66/2227/10. Greg, *Companion*, p.178.
Notes: A renewal of Legate senior's patent of 1606.

1621, April 13. Patent to Helen Mason to print the abridgement of the Book of Martyrs and other ecclesiastical histories compiled by her husband Thomas Mason, clerk, who 'at his great costes and charges caused some few bookes thereof to be imprinted' but died before the work could be completed, 'leaving his wife and children in necessitie and want'. Length of grant: 21 years.
References: C66/2258/1. Rymer XVII: 294-6.
Notes: The book is not recorded in STC, and the Stationers' Company may have bought the rights to it. The printer Robert Young later applied for the right to publish an abridgement, but was refused by Laud 'lest it should bring the larger book itself into disuse' (Laud, *Works*, vol.4 (Oxford, 1854), p.265).

1622, April 12. Warrant to Captain Richard Whitbourne, gentleman, to print his book *A Discourse and Discovery of New-found-land*, which is to be 'distributed to the seuerall Parishes of this Kingdome, for the incouragement of Aduenturers vnto the Plantation there'. Length of grant: 21 years.
References: Not in the Patent Rolls. The warrant is printed in Whitbourne's *Discourse*, but does not appear to have passed the Signet Office.

Notes: The book was first printed in 1620 (STC 25372) and reprinted in 1622.

1623, February 17. Patent to George Wither, gentleman, to print his *Hymns and Songs of the Church.* No copy of the Psalms in metre is to be bound up without the *Hymns,* 'the same being convenientlie imprinted in severall volumes to that purpose'. The price of the book is not to exceed the current rate per sheet charged by the Stationers' Company for the Psalms in metre. Length of grant: 51 years.
References: C66/2270/11. Rymer XVII: 454-5. Greg, *Companion*, pp.212-18.
Notes: Editions in folio, quarto, octavo, duodecimo and sextodecimo were published in 1623 (STC 25908 *et seq.*). In February 1627 the Stationers' Company agreed to sell as many copies of Wither's *Hymns* 'as shalbe agreed upon betwixt him and the Company' (Jackson, p.192). By 1634 Wither had assigned the patent for 21 years to Robert Crosse and Toby Knowles, two of the King's messengers, who petitioned to be released from their contract when they found that 'some disobedient Stationers' refused to comply with the patent (Greg, *Companion*, pp.216-17).

1623, April 24. Patent to John Speed to print the *Genealogies of the Holy Scriptures* and the map of Canaan, which are to be inserted into every copy of the new translation of the Bible. Speed is to charge no more than 6d for every octavo copy, 12d for every quarto copy, 18d for every small folio copy and 2s for every large folio copy. Length of grant: 21 years from expiry of previous patent.
References: C66/2313/18.
Notes: Renewal of a previous 7-year patent (1617), Speed having petitioned for the patent to be renewed 'for the better releife and comfort of himselfe being now aged and sicklie and of his wife and many children'. Speed died in 1629, and the ownership of the patent passed to his son, John Speed the younger. On 1 December 1637 Speed complained to the Privy Council that Michael Sparke and one Chetwynd, booksellers, refused to bind the *Genealogies* with the Bible (*Privy Council Registers*, new series, vol.2 (1967), p.422), and in 1638 he assigned the patent to the Stationers' Company for £700 (Greg, *Companion*, pp.301-4. Jackson, p.317).

1623, September 14. Warrant to Thomas Powell and Benjamin Fisher, stationer, to print Powell's books *Direction for Search of Records* and *The Attourneys Academy*, together with any future additions to these books. Length of grant: 31 years.
References: Not in the Patent Rolls. The warrant is printed by Greg (*Companion*, pp.218-19) and was entered in the Signet Office docquet book in October 1623 (PRO, SO 3/7).
Notes: Direction for Search of Records was entered in SR on 18 July 1622 and published the same year (STC 20166). *The Attourneys Academy* was published in 1623 (STC 20163) without apparently having been entered in SR. On 1 December 1630 the Privy Council declared that the latter book was an infringement of John Moore's law patent. Fisher produced 'a Bill signed from the King for the printing of the said booke', but this was rejected as being 'but a Bill signed' whereas Moore's patent was 'more auncient and under the great Seale'. Fisher declared he would reprint the book anyway, and on 31 January 1631 it was ordered 'that the said Booke should be suppressed as being not onely against the Patent of the said John More but also imperfect and false in diverse places'. (*Acts of the Privy Council 1630-31* (London: HMSO, 1964), pp.209-10.)

1626, April 24. Patent to George Sandys to print his translation of Ovid's *Metamorphoses* which 'to his great charge' he has caused to be printed. Length of grant: 21 years.
References: C66/2389/3.
Notes: Sandys's translation was first published in 1626 (STC 18964). However, the first five books had been entered to William Barrett and Matthew Lownes in 1621 (Arber IV.53) and on the strength of this entry an edition was published by Robert Young in 1628 (STC 18965). On 8 April 1628 Sandys's patent was produced at Stationers' Hall, and all entries and assignments of the book were ordered to be crossed out of the Register (Jackson p.201). On 30 November 1631, however, John Haviland and Robert Young petitioned the Privy Council in an attempt to regain ownership of the book. The Council ordered Haviland and Young to

hand over their stock of the book until the matter had been determined by two arbitrators (PRO, PC 2/41, pp.274-5).

1626, April 26. Patent to Joseph Webb, doctor of physic, to practise his new method of teaching languages and to print books concerning it. Webb has been 'often solicited to divulge his said invention in forraigne countries' but prefers to use it for the benefit of his own nation, and the patent is granted in view of the benefits that it may bring to the commonwealth, such as 'the concourse of forraine students'. Webb is to enjoy the full benefit of his invention for the first three years of the patent, after which he is to pay one fifth of the profit into the Exchequer, beginning on 26 March 1630 and at annual intervals thereafter. Length of grant: 31 years.
References: C66/2389/16. Rymer XVIII: 680-3.
Notes: Works covered by this patent include *Lessons and exercises out of Cicero ad Atticum* (1627), STC 5306.5, *Pueriles confabulatiunculae* (1627), STC 25170.5, *The first comedy of Pub. Terentius, called Andria* (1629), STC 23896, and *The second comedie of Pub. Terentius, called Eunuchus* (1629), STC 23898.

1627, March 9. Patent to Caleb Morley to print his book concerning 'a method for the firme and infallible helpe of memory and grownding of schollers in severall languages but chiefely in the English and Lattine tongues' which has been duly licensed, and any future books by him on the same subject. Morley is to pay £10 annually. If the book is approved by twelve grammarians as the best available method, it is to be mandatorily taught in all schools and Morley is to pay a further £40 annually. Length of grant: 21 years.
References: C66/2375/3. Greg, *Companion*, p.229.
Notes: Morley's book does not appear to have been published.

1627, April 18. Patent to Philip Burlamachi, merchant, to import Daniel Chamier's *Panstratia Catholica*, printed at Geneva in four volumes in folio. The book is to be sold for no more than 40s per copy in quires. Length of grant: 7 years.
References: C66/2437/7.
Notes: The preamble to the patent explains that Chamier died before the work could be printed, and that Lancelot Andrewes, late Bishop of Winchester, 'made meanes to have gotten those Coppies of his sent hither into this our Realme of England with purpose to have caused them to bee imprinted att his owne charge'. Chamier's widow and sons were 'loath to hazard a worke of that moment by sea' but were persuaded by Andrewes, James Ussher and others 'to imprinte the same att Geneva with promise to procure a convenient number of those bokes imprinted to be taken of theire handes'. The work has been printed, but 'nowe when they come to make sale of the bookes they find a combination amongst the buyers for theire owne private gaine refusing to take of the same bookes but att theire owne under rates and prices threatning that they will reprint the same by one of theire coppies in some other places att a cheaper rate as they have begunne already att Franckford'. Burlamachi therefore sought a patent on behalf of the undertakers of the Geneva edition, of whom he appears to have been one.

1627, July 20. Patent to John Bill and Bonham Norton, confirming them in the office of King's Printer, which had previously been assigned to them by Robert Barker senior, Christopher Barker and Robert Barker junior. Length of grant: for the lives of Robert Barker senior and Christopher Barker, and for 30 years thereafter, as specified in the Barkers' patents of 1603 and 1617.

1628, January 26. Patent to Sir William Alexander, secretary of state for Scotland, to print the Psalms of David translated by King James. Length of grant: 21 years.
References: C66/2413/9. Greg, *Companion*, p.237.
Notes: The work was not published until 1631 (STC 2732).

1628, August 20. Patent to Thomas Symcock, at the nomination of Roger Wood, to print all items on one side of one or more sheets of paper or parchment, including documents concerning letters patent granted by reason of any accident or loss, documents concerning the building and repair of churches, indentures for apprentices, bonds and recognizances for

alehouse-keepers, licences for collections, marriage licences, licences for the sale of wine, bills and acquittances for payment or receipt of money, visitation articles, bills for the instruction of scholars in foreign languages, bills concerning physicians, playbills, passports, epitaphs and inscriptions in prose or verse, ballads, portraits (except those bound in books) and decorative ornaments for domestic use. Symcock is to pay £10 annually into the Exchequer. Length of grant: 31 years.
References: C66/2455/3. Greg, *Companion*, p.175.
Notes: A renewal of Wood and Symcock's patent of 1619, with a few minor alterations; see Jackson, p.xix, n.8.

1629, September 9. Patent to Henry Cogan, goldsmith, granting him the duty of 2 shillings per gross of playing cards payable to the crown by the Company of Playing-Card Makers of London, in return for which he is to pay £50 annually into the Exchequer. Length of grant: 14 years.
References: C66/2520/3.

1630, April 16. Patent to Clement Cotton to print his *Brief Concordance* to the new translation of the Bible. No other concordance may be bound with the Bible without special authority from the Archbishops of Canterbury and York and the Bishop of London, or any two of them, or under the Great Seal. However, no person is to be 'constreyned to buy the saide concordance togeather with the Bible, but . . . with or without the said concordance as themselves shall please'. Length of grant: 21 years.
References: C66/2543/27. Rymer XIX: 153-5.
Notes: Cotton assigned the patent to Nicholas Bourne and Robert Young (Jackson, pp.271-2). Greg incorrectly states that the concordance was required to be bound up with all copies of the Bible (*Aspects and Problems*, p.94). This was one of the patents attacked in *Scintilla* (1641), where Michael Sparke complained that the patentees 'keep all others from Printing Concordances by their Patent, and these being Printed in another Volume beyond Sea, and brought over, and sold at half their prise, they seise and take them from others, and sel them again themselves' (A4r).

1630, April 26. Patent to Paul Willet, clerk, son of Andrew Willet, to print his father's book *Synopsis Papismi*, since 'the stationer who heretofore had the coppy thereof being not able or att least not willing to disburse or expend soe much moneys as the charge of reprinting the same will require, hath utterly relinquished the same', so that copies of the book are scarce and expensive, and the clergy are unable to purchase it. Length of grant: 21 years.
References: C66/2543/28. Rymer XIX: 161-3.
Notes: The work was assigned to the stationers Paul and Jonas Man in 1624, but no new edition appeared until 1634 (STC 25700a). This edition was still in print in 1691, when Dorman Newman remaindered it for 7s 6d in sheets or 10s bound (see Newman's catalogue printed with Wing B4670).

1631, January 4. Warrant to Richard Delamain, teacher of mathematics, to manufacture his mathematical ring 'together with a Booke so intituled, expressing the use thereof'. Length of grant: 10 years.
References: Not in the Patent Rolls. The warrant is printed in Delamain's *Grammelogia, or, the Mathematicall Ring* (1631), but does not appear to have passed the Signet Office.
Notes: Delamain's application for a patent was an attempt to establish priority over William Oughtred in a dispute over the invention of the logarithmic slide-rule: see D. J. Bryden, 'Richard Delamain's *Grammelogia* of 1631/3' in *Transactions of the Cambridge Bibliographical Society*, vol.6, pp.158-66.

1631, April 5. Patent to George Rodolphe Weckherlin, Esq., to print the Latin schoolbooks granted to the Stationers' Company in 1613 under a 21-year patent, with the addition of *Lud. Vivis Colloquia, Eclogae Mantuani* and *Epistolae Sturmii*, in recognition of his 'good and faithfull service' to the crown. Length of grant: 31 years from expiry of previous patent.
References: C66/2563/11. Rymer XIX: 269-72. Greg, *Companion*, pp.266-8.

Notes: Weckherlin's petition of 20 February 1631 states that he intends to 'get some small recompence . . . by letting the same grant to the Stationers' Company' (*CSPD 1629-31*, p.514). On 4 March 1631 the Stationers' Company paid Weckherlin £100 in return for the assignment of the patent to the English Stock (*The Trumbull Papers*, Sotheby's, 14 December 1989, p.111), and on 16 May 1631 the Company agreed 'that Mr Weckerlyn shall haue a peece of plate giuen him ouer & aboue the money agreed upon' (Jackson, p.228).

1632, April 6. Patent to Thomas Farnaby to print his editions of the satires of Juvenal and Persius, Seneca's tragedies, Martial's epigrams, Lucan's *Pharsalia, Florilegium epigrammatum graecorum, Index rhetoricus*, and *Phrases elegantiores oratoriae*, which he has already printed, together with his editions of Virgil's works, Petronius' *Satyricon* and Aristotle's *Ethics*, which are ready for the press. Length of grant: 21 years.
References: C66/2596/17. Greg, *Companion*, pp.275-6.
Notes: Farnaby's petition was referred to the Privy Council and approved by them on 25 January 1632. Farnaby stated that he had purchased the copyrights of his books 'from the Stationers, and printers, who formerly had interest in them', who had been unwilling to reprint them at their own charge 'by reason of so great store of them imprinted in divers places beyond the seas and brought thence into this Kingdome' (PRO, PC 2/41, pp.362-3. These unauthorized foreign editions are listed in M. A. Shaaber, *Checklist of Works of British Authors printed abroad, in languages other than English* (New York: Bibliographical Society of America, 1975), p.69.

1632, December 31. Patent to Patrick Young, librarian to the King, to print his edition of the epistles of Clement to the Corinthians, together with any translations. Length of grant: 10 years.
References: C66/2602/7.
Notes: This edition was published at Oxford in 1633 (STC 5398) with a copy of the privilege.

1633, March 4. Warrant to Richard Delamain to manufacture the improved version of his mathematical ring, and to print his book *Grammelogia, or the Mathematical Ring*. Length of grant: 14 years.
References: Not in the Patent Rolls. The warrant is printed by Greg (*Companion*, pp.252-3) and passed the Signet Office in March 1633 (PRO, SO 3/10).
Notes: This supersedes the grant of 1631 for the first version of the mathematical ring.

1633, March 13. Patent to the University of Oxford, granting it the privilege to appoint three printers and booksellers, either foreign or native, who may print any books licensed by the Vice-Chancellor and three doctors and not otherwise prohibited. Each printer may operate two presses and have two apprentices. They are to have a 10-year privilege for the printing of any book written by a member of the University, and a 21-year privilege for the printing of any manuscript in an Oxford library. Length of grant: in perpetuity.
References: C66/2602/3. Rymer XIX: 393-4.
Notes: See John Johnson and Strickland Gibson, *Print and Privilege at Oxford to the year 1700* (London: Oxford University Press, 1946), pp.10-11.

1633, November 9. Patent to John Harrison, stationer and bookbinder, and his son Richard Harrison, granting them the reversion of the office of bookbinder to the King, for which they are to receive an annual fee of £6. Length of grant: for their lives.
References: C66/2627/26.

1634, November 1. Patent to John Day, citizen, fishmonger and sworn broker of London, to print 'weekly billes of the severall rates and prices of all forraigne commodityes', for the advancement of trade, the benefit of merchants and the increase of customs. Length of grant: 14 years.
References: C66/2650/3. Rymer XIX: 577-9.
Notes: The preamble to the patent states that Day is the 'first and true inventor' of these bills, but that they have been discontinued for the past three years, to the hindrance of trade and the disgrace of the City of London. There appear to be no surviving examples of Day's bills.

1635, March 6. Patent to Alexander May and Thomas Matthew, gentlemen, to print bills of burials and christenings in London and Westminster, which, for the better safety of the inhabitants of London, are to list the 'streetes, lanes and frequent places of concourse' as well as the parishes of the deceased, and are to be arranged in 16 columns, four for the parishes and streets, four for burials, four for smallpox cases and four for plague cases. The Corporation of Parish Clerks is to continue to print the bills of burials and christenings as before, without imitating the style of May and Matthew's bills. The sextons of the parish churches are to make their returns to May and Matthew each week by six o'clock on Tuesday evenings, and to submit a list of burials and christenings scheduled for the following week by four o'clock the same afternoon, so that the weekly bills may be published on Fridays. May and Matthew are to pay £5 annually into the Exchequer, together with a fine of 40s if the patent is not enrolled within six months. Length of grant: 14 years.
References: C66/2678/14.
Notes: See James Christie, *Some Account of Parish Clerks* (1893) for an account of the bills of mortality printed for the Parish Clerks, who set up a press in their Hall in 1626. In 1630 Richard Hodgkinson, a journeyman printer, was appointed to print the bills, but by 1633 the Clerks were in dispute with him (see also BL Add MS 69914, ff.52-3), and this may have provided the opportunity for May and Matthew to obtain a rival patent.

1635, July 4. Patent to Francis Holyoke, alias Sacra Quercu, clerk, to print his *Dictionarium Etymologicum Latinum*. No other person is to print 'any other Dictionary of the same kind with English interpretation of wordes'. Length of grant. 14 years.
References: C66/2694/12. Rymer XIX: 642-3. Greg, *Companion*, pp.318-19.
Notes: Holyoke's dictionary, first published in 1627 (STC 13619.5), was a revised version of Rider's dictionary. For the early history of Rider's dictionary, see C. J. Sisson, 'The Laws of Elizabethan Copyright: the Stationers' View', *The Library*, 5th ser., vol.15 (1960). On 19 December 1639 the partners in Rider's dictionary agreed to deposit the patent with the Wardens of the Stationers' Company (Jackson, p.330).

1635, August 18. Patent to William Braithwaite, preacher and schoolmaster, to print his books 'for the more easie teaching and attayninge of musicke by voyce or instrumentes and for the furtherance of Poetry oratory and gracefull pronunciation of the Greeke and latyne tongues', according to the method invented by him, which involves the use of arithmetical figures to represent musical notes, 'comprehending tune and tyme in each Alphabeticall letter', and a means of expressing 'the long and shorte Sillables in the Greeke and latyne tongues by the letters themselves without the notes of length and shortnes'. Length of grant: 21 years.
References: C66/2694/9.
Notes: The only work of music printed according to this method was Georgius Victorinus' *Siren coelestis* (1638), STC 24715. No works on Greek or Latin pronunciation appear to have been published.

1635, September 26. Patent to Charles and Matthew Barker, sons of Robert Barker, granting them the office of King's Printer, with privilege to print statutes, acts of parliament, proclamations, injunctions, the Bible in English, service books and all other books wholly or partly in English. They are to receive an annual fee of £6 13s 4d. Length of grant: 30 years from surrender of previous patent.
References: C66/2714/18.
Notes: For a draft of this patent, see Bodleian Library MS Bankes 50/10. It was originally intended to be granted for the lives of Charles, Matthew and Matthew's son John Barker; and a clause in the first draft, later struck out, stated that illegally imported Bibles were to be forfeited to the patentees, for which they were to print proclamations without fee.

1635, December 4. Patent to George Sandys, Esq., to print his *Paraphrase upon the Psalms of David*. Length of grant: 14 years.
References: C66/2694/16. Rymer XIX: 708-10. Greg, *Companion*, pp.321-2.

Notes: This was technically an encroachment on the psalm patent held by the Stationers' Company, although Krummel comments that 'the Stationers found nothing at all menacing in Sandys's action: it was all quite harmless to their proprietary interests.' (*English Music Printing*, p.29.)

1635, December 13. Patent to William Stansby, Richard Hawkins and George Latham, citizens and stationers of London, to print set songs, sonnets and part songs in English, Latin, French, Italian and other languages, and to rule paper for the printing and pricking of songs. Length of grant: 21 years.
References: C66/2694/7.
Notes: A renewal of Edward Allde's patent of 1612, which had just expired.

1636, February 4. Patent to John Dibley, gentleman and clerk of the commission for exacted fees, to print 'all bookes and tables of such fees as nowe are and hereafter shall bee . . . authorized'. Length of grant: 31 years.
References: C66/2694/17. Greg, *Companion*, pp.319-20.
Notes: There appear to be no surviving examples of these 'bookes and tables'.

1637, April 29. Agreement between the King and the Company of Playing-Card Makers of London, specifying the number of cards to be made each week by each member of the Company (the following are named: Edward Fryer, Thomas Gate, Thomas Lynn, John Harlow, John Adams, William Finney, John Johnson, Richard Robinson and John Rolfe) and the prices to be paid for them by the King's agent. They are to receive 28s per gross (= 12 dozen sets) of the 'best and finest sort' of cards, and 28s per gross (= 18 dozen sets) of 'mattress' (i.e. inferior) cards. All cards are to carry the maker's name and mark.
References: C66/2777/2.
Notes: The purpose of the agreement, according to the preamble, is so that the cardmakers 'may be enabled competently to live and maynteyne themselves and famylies which for want of a constant sale and uttering thereof they are oft tymes now unable to doe'.

1637, July 1. Warrant to John Penkethman to print his new edition of *The Assize of Bread*. Length of grant: 21 years.
References: Not in the Patent Rolls. The warrant is printed by Greg (*Companion*, pp.350-1) but does not appear to have passed the Signet Office.
Notes: The book was entered in SR on 17 July 1638 and published under the title *Artachthos or a new book declaring the assise of bread* (STC 19598). It was recommended by a royal proclamation dated 19 November 1638: J. F. Larkin, *Stuart Royal Proclamations*, vol.2 (Oxford: Clarendon Press, 1983), pp.635-7.

1640, February 18. Patent to Gabriel Plattes, gentleman, to manufacture the machine invented by him for the speedy setting of corn, and to print his book of directions for the use of the said machine. Length of grant: 14 years.
References: C66/2842/1. Bodleian Library, MS Bankes 11/39.
Notes: The book was entered in SR on 11 April 1640 and published under the title *Certaine new inventions and profitable experiments necessary to be known of all farmers* (STC 19997.5).

1640, June 25. Warrant to Endymion Porter, Captain John Reade, Edward Reade and John Wakeman to manufacture white writing paper and to buy linen rags for that purpose. The patentees are to pay a yearly rent into the Exchequer. Length of grant: 14 years.
References: Not in the Patent Rolls. The warrant is printed by Greg (*Companion*, p.355) but does not appear to have passed the Signet Office.

Richard Bentley's copies:
the ownership of copyrights in the late 17th century

GILES MANDELBROTE

WRITING TWENTY YEARS AGO, in a festschrift with many themes in common with this volume, Terry Belanger traced the history of Jacob Tonson II's acquisition of the copyright of most of Shakespeare's plays and set out to explain how there came to be some fractions of these copyrights — and two whole plays — that eluded the firm of Tonson. In this he was building upon, and correcting, Giles Dawson's account of the booksellers who owned shares of the Shakespeare copyrights from the publication of the First Folio (1623) until the legal decision that ended perpetual copyright in 1774.[1] Dawson worked forwards, deriving his information for the earlier part of this period from the entries of copies recorded in the registers of the Stationers' Company and supplementing this by inference from the imprints of the various editions.[2] For the early 18th century, he was assisted by the survival of two important documents, in which the copies that had formerly belonged to Henry Herringman and George Wells were listed and assigned to Jacob Tonson II.[3] Belanger, on the other hand, worked backwards, using different sources, beginning with the evidence offered by the printed sale catalogue of Tonson copyrights (1767), and piecing together the ownership of the missing fractions by reference to other trade sale catalogues and to imprints.[4] Between them, these two scholars did much to unravel the tangled skein of the Shakespeare copyrights, but the different strands turned out not quite to join in the middle.

The key figure in the history of the 18th-century copyrights of Shakespeare, other than the Tonsons, seems to have been the bookseller Richard Wellington, whose death in 1715 marked the beginning of a series of divisions of his valuable literary estate.[5] The history of the copyrights immediately prior to their acquisition by Wellington, however, has proved much more difficult to reconstruct. The later 17th century saw a gradual loss of confidence in the ability of the Stationers' Company to provide an effective system of recognition and protection for the copyrights owned by its members. From 1679, the problem was made much worse by political uncertainty and the consequent lapsing of the statutory requirement to enter copies at Stationers' Hall. As is well known, the number of titles entered in the Stationers' registers — and the registers' usefulness as an historical source — falls away sharply in this period.[6] Using imprint evidence, Dawson and Belanger were able to identify several booksellers who appeared to have an interest in the Shakespeare copyrights during the 1680s and 1690s; they also inferred that it was one of these, Richard Bentley, whose copies had passed to Wellington. What shares of the copies were involved, or how Bentley came by them, they lacked the evidence even to speculate.

The document printed below, which was not known to Dawson or Belanger, is listed in the series of Chancery Masters' Exhibits as the 'sale of a bookseller's stock, London, 1698'. I have not been able to establish the case to which this document relates, though it may well have been exhibited in connection with the legal dispute over Wellington's estate between 1728 and 1730. What it records in fact is the sale to Wellington not only of Richard Bentley's stock, but also of his shares in the copyright of 380 titles.[7] Comparison with the lists printed in the trade sale catalogues makes plain that, with the exception of some later additions, most of the copyrights – and precise fractions of copyrights – known to the book trade during the 18th century as 'Wellington's copies' were Bentley's copies first.[8]

Richard Bentley was born in about 1645, the son of a Warwickshire gentleman (or so he was described), Thomas Bentley of Barton-on-the-Heath, on the southern border of the county. In March 1659, he was bound as an apprentice in the Merchant Taylors' Company, for a term of eight years, to James Magnes of Covent Garden.[9] The Merchant Taylors' records describe Magnes as a 'stationer'; at about this time, he was beginning to publish plays and novels from his shop at the Post House (or Post Office) in Russell Street, which ran east from the Covent Garden Piazza, giving access to Drury Lane. Russell Street had been part of the fashionable Bedford development of the 1630s, but after the Restoration this busy thoroughfare was given over mainly to shops and coffee-houses. Of the latter, the most famous was Will's, Dryden's habitual resort, where Pepys went to hear 'very witty and pleasant discourse' from 'all the wits of the town'.[10] Apart from shopkeepers, many of the inhabitants of Russell Street were actors, playwrights and others who earned their living from the nearby theatres in Drury Lane and Lincoln's Inn Fields. In 1720, it was described as 'a fine broad Street, well inhabited by Tradesmen'; it was in this street, in another bookshop, that Boswell first met Johnson in 1763. And it was here that 'NOVEL Bentley', as Dunton calls him, spent his entire career.[11]

Bentley appears to have worked for Magnes for the next 15 years. Although he presumably served out his apprenticeship, he seems never to have sought admission to the freedom of the Merchant Taylors' Company, perhaps because this conferred little advantage on someone working in the book trade. It was not until 1674 that his name began to appear in imprints, almost always in partnership with his former master at the same address. The death of James Magnes, in December 1678, provided the opportunity for Bentley to take control of the business, though still in partnership with Magnes's widow, Mary. She died less than four years later, however, leaving the stock and other assets relating to her 'Copartnership' with Bentley to her daughter Susanna, then aged about seventeen, and naming Bentley as one of the overseers of her will.[12]

Following the death of Mary Magnes, Bentley's business diversified markedly, both in terms of the range of his own list and the partnerships in which he became involved. He continued to publish literary works in the Magnes tradition; until 1689, the imprints of these usually link his name with that of 'S. Magnes'. Afterwards Bentley's name appears alone: Susanna Magnes had married in the previous year and he probably bought her out of her remaining share.[13] From 1683, however, Bentley also began to take part in what appear to have been mainly *ad hoc* partnerships, for particular books, with several other booksellers, notably Joseph Hindmarsh and Jacob Tonson I, as well as the leading literary bookseller of the day, Henry Herringman. At about the same time, as we shall see, Bentley had acquired a share in a block of copyrights which drew him into collaboration with a different group of booksellers altogether, with interests in a number of theological, political and scientific works. A year later he was admitted to the freedom of the Stationers' Company: the immediate reason for this change was pressure from the Company itself, as part of a drive to tighten control over non-Stationers in the book trade, but in the long term it probably helped him in his joint enterprises, as well as giving him the right to enter copies at Stationers' Hall.[14]

In the decades of the 1680s and 1690s, Bentley showed himself to be an energetic bookseller, imaginative in his use of marketing techniques. He advertised extensively in the *Term Catalogues* and had a hand in publishing a number of books by subscription, including the illustrated folio edition of *Paradise Lost* (1688), printed for Bentley and Tonson.[15] He also made notably full use of spare pages in the books he published, filling them up with lists of plays and novels, sometimes presented as a numbered series, at the uniform price of 12*d*. Advertisements and surviving volumes provide evidence of Bentley's practice of making up nonce collections of plays by authors such as John Dryden, Nathaniel Lee and Thomas Otway[16]. In 1692, he went further, publishing a series entitled *Modern Novels,* in no fewer than 12 thick duodecimo volumes, which seems to have been very largely a clever repackaging of the unsold sheets of some 50 novels printed — mostly, but not all, for Bentley or Magnes — in the 1670s and 1680s.

Plays, novels and light literature, including books in French or translated from the French, were always the staple of Bentley's business.[17] He aimed to cater principally for the leisure of customers (male and female) who lived in the wealthy and fashion-conscious residential districts of Soho, Leicester Square and St James's, on the fringes of the court, or who passed through Covent Garden on their way to the theatre or the coffee-house. Other local tradesmen and shopkeepers were trying to do the same, and they — together with craftsmen of luxury goods, portrait-painters and designers, entertainers, tutors and servants — formed a second group of potential customers. In addition to the location of his shop, two other factors seem to have given

Bentley some advantage. He was one of several booksellers who were able to benefit from Herringman's withdrawal from the publication of new plays and literature, both by filling the gap left in the market and by acting as distributors for Herringman's wholesale stock.[18] He also seems to have been adept at cultivating and managing a number of writers, particularly translators such as Peter Bellon and Ferrand Spence, who provided him with a regular supply of new copy. Relationships of this sort have usually been characterized as exploitative. Two of Bentley's authors, however, Thomas Otway and John Banks, took the unusual step of dedicating a play to their bookseller and both made a point of referring to his honesty in paying authors for their copy. Banks described 'my Friend the Stationer' with apparently genuine respect and affection: 'You never were closefisted to a good Poet, and your Generosity was always suitable to the Merit of the Author and his Book, and he is freely welcome to your Table too; if so, you are a Mecænas, and such I will stile you.' Writing from Charles Street, which ran into Russell Street, Banks apologized to Bentley for detaining him, 'for I know you to be a Man of Business', before signing himself 'your hearty Friend'.[19] Banks's expression of gratitude is also an exercise in self-justification: his play had been prohibited and never acted, and had taken ten years to find a publisher. This picture of the shrewd but hospitable bookseller is a lively one, nevertheless, and perhaps as close as we can come to the character of Richard Bentley.[20]

In August 1689, Bentley acquired the lease of a site in King Street, Covent Garden, adjoining the north side of St Paul's Church, for a new house of 'the best Second Rate'. A few months later, he married Katherine Davis, from the neighbouring parish of St Martin-in-the-Fields.[21] The 1690s appear to have been prosperous times for Bentley. He was publishing some 20 titles a year, had accumulated a backlist of perhaps as many as 200 different publications of his own, and the shop was busy enough for him to take on an apprentice, Edmund Rumball, in 1691.[22] His children were born in 1692 and 1693; the following year he invested in a share in the potentially profitable English Stock of the Stationers' Company.[23] Imprints also point to his increasing involvement with more complex and formal consortia of booksellers.[24] Richard Bentley died at the height of his career, in June 1697, having asked in his will to be buried in St Paul's, Covent Garden, 'with all the privacy imaginable', and leaving to his wife and children what appears to have been a flourishing business.[25]

Bentley's will gives no indication of his expectations for the business after his death. For a short period, Katherine Bentley's name appeared in a number of imprints, probably because earlier agreements were being honoured. After only 18 months, however, she assigned away her husband's copyrights. Perhaps she needed the 'Competent summe of money' to look after her surviving child, but the more likely explanation is that she lacked the experience and confidence to manage the copies and negotiate deals with printers and with other copy-owning booksellers. This was a masculine sphere of activity in which it was difficult for widows to participate except in protected circumstances, as in Bentley's partnership with Mary Magnes. A similar solution may have been proposed in this instance by the former apprentice Edmund Rumball, who had recently married the daughter of Robert Everingham. Everingham had been close to the business for years, had done much of the printing for Magnes and Bentley, had acted as Bentley's representative within the Stationers' Company and was also related by marriage to the Magnes family. He was a witness both to Bentley's will and to the assignment of his copies, but if his advice was to hand over the whole business to Rumball, it appears to have been ignored.[26]

Everingham's influence is apparent, however, in the clause asserting his own right to print 'The French Liturgie' (339), the only work which was made subject to specific conditions in the agreement with Wellington. This work was a special case in another respect too: the rights of its translator John Durel (1625-83) were protected under a royal privilege of 6 October 1662 and this presumably accounts for the contractual obligations that were passed on to the new proprietor. All of this perhaps made it more trouble than it was worth; Wellington reprinted it once, in 1702, but then sold the copy to the refugee bookseller Pierre Varenne, who printed it again in 1703. 'The French Liturgie' is the only copy noted on the list as having been sold.[27]

Women in the book trade were more often concerned with managing shops, and Mrs Bentley seems to have intended to continue the retail business herself, or to allow Rumball to run it for her: the books in the shop were specifically excluded from the assignment, which otherwise entitled Wellington to all Bentley's remaining stock of the titles named. This was an important aspect of the contract because a decision to reprint required accurate information about demand and about the availability of unsold stock. It is not clear how much of the stock was thus held back – possibly most of the books that would have had a ready sale. A list of 'Novells Printed for Richard Wellington', advertised a few months later, contains about 40 of Bentley's titles at what may have been a remainder price: 'Gentlemen may pick Novels at 6s. the Dozen.'[28]

In the event, Katherine Bentley did not carry on the business for much longer: she died in September 1699, followed soon afterwards by her remaining child, and the shop passed into the hands of Rumball, who promptly formed a partnership with Richard Wellington. Perhaps this had been in the air all along: some 20 titles were printed for Wellington and Rumball over the next three years before Rumball too died, ending nearly 50 years of bookselling from the Post House in Covent Garden.[29] A catalogue issued by Rumball in 1700 gives a good impression of the wide range of items on sale there, including nonce collections of plays, novels, historical memoirs, poetry, cookery, medical and devotional books, and 'all sorts of Writing Papers both plain and gilt, Pens, Ink, Wafers, &c.', but devoting most space to a list of almost 400 plays. Many of the titles are recognizable as Bentley's own publications, but there are also books printed for other booksellers, most notably Tonson, as well as Everingham's editions of the Bible in Gaelic and the liturgy in French.[30]

The document listing Bentley's copies may well have been compiled in hurried and confused circumstances, with consequent implications for its accuracy. Certainly it was dictated, as the phonetic spelling of some entries (1, 118, 261, 274) indicates, perhaps from the original assignments or other contracts. On the whole the arrangement of the list preserves blocks of copies with the same provenance, making it much easier to establish the process by which these 380 titles came into Bentley's possession. The list is by no means a complete record of all the copies that had been owned by Bentley, as we shall see, but it appears to include all those still owned by Mrs Bentley after 18 months. Some copies are listed as whole, while others are fractions; while it would have been possible for individual copies to have been sub-divided prior to this assignment, it seems to be consistent with the available evidence to assume (and I have) that the fractions listed represent Bentley's entire share in these particular titles.

The large group of copies (228-348) which Bentley owned in their entirety reflect the activity of a traditional copy-owning partnership between two booksellers occupying the same premises. The copies range over a long career, from the first book Bentley published (229) to one which seems to have not yet been published (281). Almost all would appear to have been acquired by Magnes or Bentley, or the two in partnership, directly from the authors, compilers or translators, some of whom are represented here several times. The exceptions, works which the partners set out to buy from competitors in the trade, are interesting ones. Their purchase (228) from the estate of the bookseller John Martyn seems to have been the precursor to a much larger transaction involving Martyn's copies, and was clearly a successful work, several times reprinted. The group of titles (288-9, 291) that had belonged to William Leake included the quarto edition of *Othello,* one of the plays that Tonson was always to lack. Most of the copies in this section were printed only once, as an independent venture by the partnership, sometimes with imaginative false imprints, and most were probably still in print in the 1690s — some were reissued then. On only five occasions did the partners think it worthwhile to register these copies at Stationers' Hall. This was difficult, of course, before Bentley became free in 1684, though not impossible (230).[31] Perhaps the ownership of the copies so entered was considered to be more than usually under threat or open to dispute (334).

Examples of the Magnes–Bentley partnership sharing copies with other booksellers (349-52, 354) are quite exceptional: most seem to result from a previous partnership between Magnes and Thomas Basset. By contrast, another group of titles, rather similar to those which Magnes or Bentley might once have owned outright, illustrates the changes that were taking place in the structure of the book trade in the 1680s and 1690s. After the end of his partnership with Magnes, Bentley became aware that there could be advantages in a more flexible approach, book by book, sharing the copy and stock—but also the costs and the distribution—with other literary booksellers. In the 1680s Bentley's shared copies seem, by choice, to have usually been halves, divided with one other bookseller (353, 355, 357-62); by the 1690s he was sometimes prepared to share with two or three (368-72, 380). In the case of a particularly desirable copy, such as Montaigne's essays (99), he settled for halving a third share with Joseph Hindmarsh, one of his frequent collaborators. These relationships are also observable from imprints, but the list establishes the fractions owned. While only a minority of Bentley's copies were shared in this way, their number (if the imprints are to be believed) was substantially more than is recorded here. Two (out of the three) copies, furthermore, that were entered at Stationers' Hall by Bentley jointly with other booksellers also fail to appear on this list.[32] One explanation might be that, prior to the assignment to Wellington, some other booksellers had already made arrangements to buy back Bentley's shares in their copies: as early as 1691, for instance, Jacob Tonson I had bought Bentley out of his third share in the reprint of *Seneca's morals*.[33] The string of desirable literary copies assigned to Wellington would seem to demonstrate, nevertheless, that Tonson signally failed to mop up Bentley's copies, and was perhaps even deliberately excluded from doing so. It is notable, certainly, that the names of Wellington and Tonson never appeared together in partnership in imprints before 1700.

Bentley probably had little choice regarding the fractions he owned of the largest block of copies listed here (1-227, excluding 99; 373-7). These had all belonged to John Martyn (d.1680) and, with a few exceptions, Bentley's share was a third of whatever Martyn's had been. The fractions varied because Martyn himself had acquired the copies in a variety of ways. Some of them had been in the book trade since the 16th century: the more hands they had passed through, the smaller the fraction was likely to have become. Thus Bentley owned a third of the impressive list of works, mainly scientific or theological, printed for Martyn or his partners James Allestry (d.1670) and Thomas Dicas (d.1669), mostly in the 1660s and 1670s (1-62). He owned a sixth of the copies which Martyn had shared on equal terms with one other bookseller, sometimes Walter Kettilby (65), or Nathaniel Brook (69, 71), or Richard Lambert at York (64), but most often Henry Herringman, with whom Martyn had divided a large group of literary and theological copies (68, 73-98) previously owned by Humphrey Robinson, Martyn's former master (d.1670). Many of Robinson's more valuable copies, particularly the literary ones, were themselves shared in partnership with Humphrey Moseley (d.1661), so that Martyn and Herringman had only a half share to split between them and Bentley owned a twelfth (173, 176-227).[34] Martyn appears to have owned relatively few shares of copies that had been split three ways, leaving Bentley with a ninth share (100-3).

The ownership history of the one remaining substantial group of Martyn's shares (104-67, 175, 374-6) is a little more complicated. Many of these were old books by Bentley's time, having been owned first by John Bill (d.1630), or his senior partner John Norton (d.1612), and then by Richard Whitaker (d.1648). When Whitaker's copies were reassigned in 1653, they were entered to Humphrey Robinson, Richard Thrale (d.1678), Joshua Kirton (d.1667) and Samuel Thompson (d.1668). It appears that the whole of these copies in fact passed into Kirton's ownership, for there is no trace of them in the assignments made by the executors of Thrale or Robinson (with one exception: 167). In 1673, Kirton's executor assigned them to Samuel Mearne, but again the entry books do not appear to tell the whole story. Mearne seems to have held these copies in partnership with Herringman and Martyn, as he did with other copies that he had purchased from the Kirton estate (175).[35] Martyn's share of these copies was a quarter, according to the assignment made by his widow, so Bentley's share was again a twelfth.

The vicissitudes of these copies must, however, be pursued a little further, since they shed light on the division of Martyn's literary estate and on the circumstances surrounding copy ownership in this period. John Martyn's widow had requested in July 1681 that her husband's copies be reassigned to Robert Scott, the most important bookseller in the learned, second-hand and import trade, and to Scott's brother-in-law George Wells. The copies were not entered at Stationers' Hall, however, until August 1683 and in the meanwhile they were the subject of no fewer than three separate disputes recorded in the minutes of the Company's Court. In November 1681, Scott presented to the Court his list of 361 copies bought from Mrs Martyn and complained that 'they were many of them Bookes of little or noe vallue & not above twenty of them worth the entring.' The solution, he suggested, was for the Company to allow him a special rate for entering this quantity, in which case he would be prepared to do so 'for Order & methods sake'. The Court consented to a reduced fee of 100 shillings (rather than 180 at the usual rate), but also made a special condition that 'Mr Mearne & Mr Herringman should be present at the entry of these Bookes & agree & consent to the entry of each Booke', presumably in recognition of their interest as former partners of Martyn. In March 1682, Mearne (who was Master of the Company) and Scott were in disagreement over the warehouse in which Martyn's stock was stored, the lease of which Scott wished to take over because he now owned the books inside. A month later, another dispute arose between Mearne, Herringman and 'Scott & partners concerning Severall Coppies . . . assigned by Mrs Kirton & entred the Register to the . . . Master in the yeare 1673.' Mearne appears to have dragged his heels over this matter, relying on the fact that he alone was the registered owner of Kirton's shares, and ignored the warnings to come to terms. After several months, and in Mearne's absence, an exasperated Court ruled his original entry null and void. On the same day, Herringman and Scott were authorized in the Company's name to prosecute at law anyone who infringed their copyrights.[36]

The crisis over Martyn's copies could hardly have come at a worse time for the Stationers' Company. In the summer of 1681 the Company had made desperate efforts to promote a number of by-laws relating to the entry of copies, in an attempt to fill the gap left by the lapsing of the Printing Act, to restore confidence and to establish a basis for common law protection for copyrights on the grounds of ancient custom. Blagden cites the Company's support for Herringman and Scott as an example of the book trade taking the law into its own hands, but he seems not to have recognized that these two booksellers were chiefly concerned to safeguard their copies not against outsiders but against the Master of the Stationers' Company itself. In such circumstances, it is not surprising that 'Scott & partners' did not trouble to make any further entries as they divided up Martyn's copies. Some of these copies, however, were soon reprinted and their imprints provide some evidence of the subsequent sub-divisions.

Between 1681 and 1683, Scott and Wells are briefly linked in these imprints to Robert Littlebury. The names of Bentley and Thomas Sawbridge appear from 1683 onwards, initially with both Scott and Wells, later with Wells alone. In 1685, they were joined by Richard Chiswell, who had already collaborated with Sawbridge on a number of other books, and it is the partnership of Chiswell, Sawbridge, Wells and Bentley that appears in the imprints of most of the reprinted Martyn copies.[37] Scott disappears from the title-pages of these copies for much of the 1680s, a period when he suffered financial difficulties; perhaps in any case his main interest had been in Martyn's stock. Following the death of George Wells in 1687, however, Scott reappears, having taken over the administration of Wells's share. Among these names, Bentley is the odd one out. Scott and Chiswell were both important and senior members of the trade, as was the Sawbridge family; Scott was married to Wells's sister.[38] Bentley, by contrast, was not even a member of the Stationers' Company by 1683 and had never participated before in a partnership of this type, nor owned shares in serious scientific and theological works. Yet there is further evidence to show not only Bentley's close involvement, from an early stage, with Martyn's copies, but also another instance of copyright apparently being infringed by a very senior member of the Stationers' Company. In November 1685, Bentley, Scott and Wells brought a joint complaint before the Court of the Stationers' Company against Richard Royston, accusing him of printing John Fell's biography of Henry Hammond (45). As the dispute dragged on, Wells and Bentley threatened legal action; but it is not clear how matters were finally resolved.[39]

Bentley's inclusion in this partnership was perhaps a measure of his success by the 1680s. A specific advantage may have been that it opened up new markets: Wells and Scott had their respective shops in St Paul's Churchyard and Little Britain, traditional centres of the scholarly book trade, so Bentley would not have offered direct competition. Bentley's own reasons for becoming involved call for some further explanation, however.

Mrs Bentley's assignment to Wellington included shares in 231 copies that had previously belonged to Martyn; many of these were old theological works, some presumably long out of print.[40] Martyn's own learned and scientific publications were undoubtedly valuable, but the stock seems to have passed to Scott and there is no clear evidence that Bentley had a share in it. A mere 20 or so of the copies listed were reprinted in the 1680s and 1690s, and of these no more than 15 name Bentley as one of the booksellers for whom they were printed. They included some literary and historical works (62, 70, 72, 76, 144, 156), language dictionaries and grammars (37, 38), and works of private devotion (12, 22, 64), all of which would have suited Bentley's customers. Less appropriate perhaps were more serious theological and reference works (36, 172).

Martyn's copies, as we have already seen, had originally numbered 361, of which Scott disingenuously protested that no more than 20 were of any value. The assignment to Wellington scrupulously excluded all Martyn's copies of works in Latin – and perhaps Bentley himself had taken no share in these. It also failed to include, however, several of the most important works of literary and general interest which had been reprinted – sometimes more than once – by the Chiswell–Sawbridge–Wells–Bentley partnership. Among these were Richard Allestree's *Forty sermons,* Edward Chamberlayne's *Angliæ notitia,* and John Evelyn's *Kalendarium hortense.* It is not altogether clear what happened to Bentley's shares in these copies: his name disappears from the imprint of *Angliæ notitia* after 1687, and presumably that share was sold separately, perhaps to Matthew Gillyflower, who is named in the imprint of the 1694 edition. Some of his other shares, notably those in works by Evelyn, seem to have passed to Benjamin Tooke in the year of Bentley's death. Evelyn himself, writing in 1697 to the scholar Dr Richard Bentley about the prospects for a new edition of *Sylva,* recorded that 'The Copy, wh[ich] I frankly gave about 30 years since to Allestry, is now in the hands of Chisswel & your Namesake Mr. Bentley; who have sold off 3 Impressions, & [are] now Impatient for the fourth; & it having be[e]n no unprofitable Copy to them, I had promis'd some considerable Improvements to it, upon Condition of Letting Ben: Took (for whom I have a particulur kindnesse) into a share: This, tho' with reluctancy, they at last Consented to.'[41]

The last section of titles assigned to Wellington (373-80) consists of copies which seem to have been grouped together at the end either because of their special importance and value, or because of the small fractions into which they had been divided. Reference works often used a large quantity of paper and sold relatively slowly, though offering a good return in the end; they required substantial capital investment and the copies of such works were routinely shared between booksellers from the first half of the 17th century onwards. By the time they were acquired by John Martyn, these shares (373, 374, 376) were already in small fractions; Bentley's shares, consequently, were as small as a twenty-fourth and a forty-eighth. In one instance (375), the imprints provide evidence of the way in which book-sellers had come to think differently about copy ownership in response to the problem of ever smaller shares. Instead of issuing *Plutarch's morals* with different title-pages (in proportionate quantities) each naming a bookseller, or group of booksellers, who were actively involved in the edition, the undertakers in 1694 simply referred to its wholesale distribution to 'most booksellers' — and did their division sums on the receipts.[42]

While it was known from the trade sales that Wellington had owned a third of *Paradise regained* (378) and a quarter share in *Paradise lost* (379), the evidence that these came through Bentley is at variance with the usual account of the ownership history of *Paradise lost*. The source most quoted (and misquoted) in modern accounts is Thomas Newton's life of Milton, which records that Jacob Tonson I bought the copy of *Paradise lost* from Brabazon Aylmer in two stages, half on 17 August 1683, and the other half on 24 March 1690 [i.e. 1691] 'and except one fourth of it which has been assign'd to several persons, his family have enjoyed the right of copy ever since.'[43] Newton's version follows closely that given in evidence by Jacob Tonson III in the suit he brought against Robert Walker in the Court of Chancery, which adds the further information that it was to Richard Wellington that Tonson assigned a quarter share on 19 October 1704.[44] This seems uncharacteristic for a man who made his fortune by accumu-lating literary monopolies: it is now clear that Wellington already had at least a claim to that share on the basis that the copy had earlier been divided between Tonson and Bentley (cf. 353-4, 357, 362, 367).

Of all Martyn's copies recorded in this assignment, only one breaks the general rule that Bentley's share was a third of Martyn's. This exceptional copy may also help to explain both how and why Bentley came to join the Scott partnership. Bentley's share in Shakespeare's plays (377) is noted as a third, rather than the sixth share that one would expect on the analogy of the other 230 copies with the same provenance. The imprints of the various issues of the Fourth Folio edition published in 1685 alert us to a change too: Edward Brewster appears where we might expect to find Wells and Sawbridge. Brewster, who was shortly to become Master of the Stationers' Company, was related by marriage to the Sawbridge family and appears with Chiswell in a few other imprints, including the works of Ben Jonson (1692).[45] Martyn's original share of Shakespeare's plays had been a half (the other half belonged to Herringman); it seems likely that Bentley bought Wells out of his sixth, thus owning two sixths, and the remaining sixth was split between Brewster and Chiswell.

If one of Bentley's main objectives had been the acquisition of a share in Shakespeare's plays, his success may well have owed something to the influence of Henry Herringman. Herringman owned the remaining share in many of these copies, with an interest in all those that had previously belonged to Kirton or Robinson, and it was with Herringman also that Bentley collaborated in the publication of quarto editions of Shakespeare:

Hamlet (1683), *Julius Caesar* (1684) and *Macbeth* (1687).[46] None of these plays is mentioned in the assignment, but the trade sale catalogues treat them as distinct copies and record that, in addition to a third of the copyright in Shakespeare's whole works, Wellington owned a third of the right of printing separately *Julius Caesar* and *Macbeth,* and the whole right in *Hamlet* and *Othello*. All of these presumably came from Bentley, and two indeed seem to have been entered at Stationers' Hall on Bentley's behalf, but only *Othello* is listed here (291).

The confusions that could arise over the ownership of copyright are well illustrated by the muddle over the ownership history of *Hamlet* in 1683 and — despite the best efforts of Sir Walter Greg — it remains confusing today. The play appears in the entry book of copies three times in the space of just over three months. In May 1683, Robert Everingham entered *Hamlet* at Stationers' Hall with the memorandum that 'This book is to be printed by me for Richard Bentley, he not being free of the Company it is entred in my name in trust for him.' Against this entry is a note made in December 1683 by John Garrett, the Company's Clerk, recording that 'a moyetie of this coppy belongs to Mr Henry Herringman . . . & was the whole entred to Mr Everingham by mistake.' Two months later Herringman, perhaps trying to clarify matters, entered *Hamlet* himself, jointly with 'the assignes of John Martin deceased' — just ahead of the third entry of *Hamlet,* in August 1683, as part of Scott's entry of Martyn's copies. According to Greg, the 'Hamlett' entered by Scott was not the play at all, but a prose version of the story that had been the property of Richard Cotes. Although the prose version may have been what Cotes was legally entitled to assign, it would appear from the context, a long list of Shakespeare's plays, that this had been forgotten by the time the collected plays were assigned to Martyn and Herringman in 1674 — and subsequently, in part, to Wellington (377).[47]

The first two entries of *Hamlet* are more problematic. It is possible that the same copy was entered twice because of Everingham's mistake. A more likely explanation, however, is that there were in fact two copies in circulation: the original version, which had belonged to Miles Flesher and was then also assigned to Martyn and Herringman, and an adaptation, probably by Sir William Davenant.[48] If so, this left Herringman in possession of three half shares in different copies with the same name: Bentley's share may have been a half and two (different) thirds. It is hardly surprising that this caused confusion at the time; certainly the mistake does not seem to have soured Bentley's collaboration with either Herringman or the Scott partners. In January 1684, Herringman and Everingham (again presumably acting for Bentley) entered the copy of *Julius Caesar;* quarto editions of both plays were reprinted for Herringman and Bentley jointly in the 1690s.

It appears from these entries that Mrs Bentley's assignment may not record all of her husband's copies that passed into Wellington's possession. It has certainly already become clear that the assignment gives an incomplete picture of the full range of copies that Bentley owned. By the time of Bentley's death, his name had appeared on the title-page of some 250 distinct works, as well as a further 200 or so reissues, reprintings, or works with which he was concerned as a distributor. By contrast, only some 160 out of the 380 copies listed here were actually printed for Bentley. The accuracy of the list, as far as it goes, however, seems to be confirmed by the printed sale catalogues of Wellington's copies. In time, the 'Chaste Seraglian' became the 'Chaste Seraphan' and the 'Golden mean' the 'Golden miner', but the copies continued to be sold in these fractions (and shares of fractions) for much of the 18th century, apparently without challenge. The trade sale catalogues also list some of Chiswell's copies and show that his share of Martyn's copies, like Bentley's, was consistently a third; presumably the other third was owned by Wells.[49]

One of the most remarkable features of Bentley's assignment is that it invites comparison not only with the trade sale catalogues but also with the two other documents, of slightly later date, assigning shares in many of the same copies to Jacob Tonson II. The Herringman copies, assigned for £140 in 1707, three years after Herringman's death, are more select than Bentley's: some 130 are named, concentrating on major literary properties and including no fractions smaller than a quarter. This may have represented a small proportion of the copies that Herringman had owned, even though phrases such as 'all that Moyety of Mr Humphrey Robinson's Copies and a Moyety of Mr Shakespiers plays bought of Mr Andrew Clarke' add over 100 copies at a stroke. Herringman's list lays claim not only to half the collected plays of Shakespeare (377), as might be expected, but also to the whole of *Hamlet* and *Julius Caesar*. Were it not for the fact that Wellington claimed a share in these too, one might assume that Herringman had bought Bentley out of his share. Confusion over *Hamlet* may perhaps have been caused by two plays with the same name, but in the case of *Julius Caesar* Herringman's assignment and the trade sale catalogues seem to contradict each other unequivocally. The Herringman and Bentley assignments themselves do not overlap greatly and appear broadly in line with each other; a few apparent contradictions may be explained on the basis that Herringman owned the copies of collected editions of authors such as Davenant and Killigrew whereas Bentley had a share in particular titles.[50]

Commenting on the 360 or so copies that had belonged to George Wells, assigned in 1709 for the sum of £100, Giles Dawson noticed the similarity to the list of Martyn's copies entered by Robert Scott and concluded that the two lists were 'substantially identical'. What he seems not to have observed was that although the titles are the same, the shares are not. In some instances, Wells was credited with a larger share of the copy than had been owned by Martyn in the first place: this should have been enough to raise further questions. Dawson, however, added Wells's putative half share of the Shakespeare copyrights to Herringman's half, and was then puzzled to find that Tonson did not claim ownership of the whole copy on the strength of the two assignments.[51]

The catalogue of Wells's copies is a more elaborate document than Bentley's. It was compiled some 20 years after George Wells died and it rearranges in alphabetical order information extracted from earlier documents. It would appear that the documents used had not been kept up to date, or that the compilers were too distant from the transactions to interpret them correctly. The compilers seem to have set down the list of Martyn's shares entered by Scott, taking no account of the subsequent divisions between the partners, and added half shares of the copies that had belonged to Mearne. Most obviously affected by this were the copies that had belonged to Kirton and had then been disputed between Herringman, Mearne and Scott: where Martyn had owned a quarter share (cf. 104-67, 175), Wells was credited with a half (sometimes expressed as 2/4 or 1/4 + 1/4).[52] It is not clear whether Wells had gained any direct advantage from the Stationers' Company ruling against Mearne; he seems to have purchased a half share in many of Mearne's copies in 1686 or 1687, for we happen to have information about them from another source, which also sheds some light on the obligations of copy ownership.

In 1692, the bookseller Abel Swalle brought a Chancery suit against Robert Scott, the executor of Wells's estate, in which he explained that he and Wells had had an equal share in Mearne's copies. Among these were 'Homilies of the Church of England', shared in partnership with George Pawlett, and 'Hoole's Orbis Pictus'. Swalle had reprinted these in 1687 and 1688 and expected Scott to contribute to the printing costs in return for a proportion of the books corresponding to Wells's share. Scott had refused to do this, despite — Swalle maintained — a long-standing custom among the booksellers of London that where two of them were joint owners of a copy, and one printed the book, the other could claim a share, paying his part of the charges. Wells's shares of these two copies were said to be a third and a half respectively; in his assignment they appear as a quarter and a half.[53]

It may be clear by now that documents from this period recording the ownership of copyrights should be compared wherever possible with other evidence, and that the most sensible approach is to trace the history of groups, rather than of individual copies. In some cases there is more than one history, relating not only to the copy's true ownership but also to what was mistakenly believed (or claimed opportunistically) on the basis of ambiguous or inaccurate records. By the late 17th century the Stationers' Company's system for registering the ownership of copies was becoming discredited. The entry books worked well enough for the entry of whole copies to named booksellers who were known to their fellow members of the Stationers' Company and bound by its rules. They had not been designed to cope with repeat entries of different shares of the same copy, in smaller and smaller fractions, often unspecified, over a longer span of time.[54] Bentley and Wells between them, as we have seen, owned shares in at least 800 copies, but the entry books record their names against a mere 11. The problem was not only the lapsing of the Printing Act and the difficulty of enforcement; it was a cumulative problem over decades, exacerbated by the widening membership of the book trade outside the Stationers' Company and sometimes exploited by those within it.

At the root of this problem, paradoxically, was continuity within the trade. As copies continued to be negotiable property over generations, their ownership history inevitably became more complex — while the memory of original agreements receded. There was no generally accepted manner of disposing of copyrights at this time. Ideally they were passed down from father to son, or at least from senior to junior partner, but even then the rules of inheritance might split up a group of copies if they were valuable enough, as in the case of Wellington himself. If they were sold, they might be offered individually (as with some of Moseley's copies) or in small groups (as with some of Bentley's). It became common practice with large and valuable collections of copies, however, to keep them all together, dividing the whole into fractions as necessary. The Norton and Bill assignment of 1632 is an early example; Bentley's copies were the product of no fewer than seven block assignments. This had the advantage of preserving a backlist that had proved successful, while depriving rival booksellers of monopoly control. It also achieved the best price by offering the copies in affordable units, while selling the worthless on the strength of the more desirable ones. It was this principle that ensured that Bill's copies eventually became Wellington's copies and that small fractions of them, carefully lotted, were still changing hands for money 150 years after their last publication.

In the absence of a reliable and authoritative record, accessible to all, of who owned what, the whole question of the proof of legal title to copyrights seemed confused and uncertain. By undermining proof of title, the fragmentation of copies threatened the few remaining opportunities for redress at law, in the common law courts or — in the case of partnership agreements — the courts of equity. It is hardly surprising, therefore, that copy-owning booksellers felt vulnerable. Blagden has drawn attention to changes in the structure of the trade in this period, emphasising the development of congers, groups of the most important copy-owning booksellers, as a self-conscious attempt to use trade pressure to protect copyrights.[55] Contemporary definitions of 'conger', on the other hand, tended to mention the sharing of the benefits of copyright ownership, particularly for wholesaling: 'a Set or Knot of Topping Book-sellers of London, who agree among themselves, that whoever of them Buys a good Copy, the rest are to take off such a particular number, as (it may be) Fifty, in Quires, on easy Terms.' In 1691, in the earliest known reference to book-trade congers, John Dunton complained that they were predatory ('an over-grown Eel') rather than defensive associations. By the early 18th century, the term seems to have acquired the more specific meaning of 'a particular

Society of Book-sellers, who put in Joynt Stocks for the Buying and Printing of Copies, and Trading for their common Advantage'.[56] Bailey's dictionary gives the derivation of 'conger' as '*congruere, L. i.e.* to agree together', but it seems most likely that the term was originally simply a corruption of 'conjuration'. Henry Oldenburg, the Secretary of the Royal Society, used this word in a book-trade context as early as 1665, when he complained to Robert Boyle of 'a kind of conjuration, and a very mysticall one, among Stationers'.[57] If congers, loosely defined, developed this early, then their origins must be found in the associations formed for printing reference books, in the English Stock and the Law Patent, and in the inexorable pressure, generation by generation, to sub-divide valuable accumulations of copies.[58]

One of the effects of this splintering process, which had begun to gain momentum in the middle of the century, was to propel booksellers — even the owners of literary copies which were less frequently divided — into a different sort of partnership. Various types of partnership existed side by side, as Richard Bentley's copies show; Bentley died, however, just as the congers were about to come of age. These were not traditional two-man partnerships, nor were they limited to collaboration on particular projects. They might involve several booksellers, unaccustomed to co-operating with each other and perhaps not members of the Stationers' Company, in a series of ventures over a long time; this in turn necessitated different, sometimes more formal, methods of agreement, record-keeping and doing business. If the books printed were much in demand, these partnerships effectively became groups of wholesalers. In this way, the fragmentation of copies prepared the ground for the joint-stock wholesaling partnerships of the 18th century.

References

1. Terry Belanger, 'Tonson, Wellington and the Shakespeare copyrights', in *Studies in the book trade in honour of Graham Pollard,* ed. R. W. Hunt, I. G. Philip and R. J. Roberts (Oxford: Oxford Bibliographical Society publications, new series vol.xviii, 1975), pp.195-209; Giles E. Dawson, 'The copyright of Shakespeare's dramatic works', in *Studies in honor of A. H. R. Fairchild,* ed. Charles T. Prouty (Columbia, Missouri: University of Missouri studies vol.xxi, no.1, 1946), pp.11-35. My version of events differs in some respects from both these studies, but I am nevertheless indebted to their authors, who have established the context for much of what follows.

    Booksellers in the 17th and early 18th century usually referred to copyrights, in the sense of the exclusive rights to publish and to benefit from the publication of particular works, as 'copies'; I have tended here to use the two terms interchangeably to refer to trade ownership of literary property.

2. All subsequent references to the entry books of the Stationers' Company are made here in the form SR followed by a date (New Style). The printed transcriptions are generally reliable: Edward Arber, *A transcript of the registers of the Company of Stationers of London; 1554-1640 A.D.* (London: privately printed, 5 vols, 1875-94); G. E. Briscoe Eyre and C. R. Rivington, *A transcript of the registers of the Worshipful Company of Stationers; from 1640-1708 A.D.* (London: privately printed, 3 vols, 1913-14); *Index to the Stationers' Register,*

1640-1708, ed. W. P. Williams (La Jolla, California: Laurence McGilvery, 1980). For the interpretation of imprints, see David Foxon, *Pope and the early eighteenth-century book trade* (Oxford: Clarendon Press, 1991), pp.1-8.

3. Dawson, pp.25-6; Herringman (11 September 1707): Bodleian Library, Oxford, MS Charters Surrey c. 1 (84); Wells (22 October 1709): Folger Shakespeare Library, Washington, MS S.a.160. I am grateful for the advice of Laetitia Yeandle of the Folger Library.

4. For a full account of the trade auctions and their catalogues, which survive from 1718, see Terry Belanger, 'Booksellers' trade sales, 1718-1768', *The Library*, 5th series, vol.xxx (1975), pp.281-301, and the same author's unpublished thesis, 'Booksellers' sales of copyright: aspects of the London book trade, 1718-1768' (New York: Columbia University, 1970). The latter includes a numerical system of reference to the catalogues, which I have followed below. See also Cyprian Blagden, 'Booksellers' trade sales 1718-1768', *The Library*, 5th series, vol.v (1950-1), pp.243-57.

5. Belanger explains the fragmentation, in the course of the 18th century, of the important group of literary copyrights known collectively as 'Wellington's copies'. Dawson, while noting Wellington's name in certain imprints, does not appear to have been aware of the full extent of his ownership of Shakespeare copyrights, perhaps because he was misled by the Wells assignment (see below).

6. For the background, see A. W. Pollard, 'Some notes on the history of copyright in England from 1662-1774', *The Library*, 4th series, vol.iii (1922-3), pp.97-114; R. C. Bald, 'Early copyright litigation and its bibliographical interest', *Papers of the Bibliographical Society of America*, vol.xxxvi (1942), pp.81-96; Cyprian Blagden, *The Stationers' Company: a history, 1403-1959* (London: George Allen & Unwin, 1960), pp.172-5; John Feather, *Publishing, piracy and politics* (London: Mansell, 1994), pp.42-50.

7. Public Record Office (hereafter PRO) C 108/406 14 December 1698. I am grateful for advice from Dr Amanda Bevan and Gervase Hood of the PRO, and to Arnold Hunt and Scott Mandelbrote for suggestions about the identification of some of the titles listed.

8. See, for example, the copies listed in Belanger 58: *A catalogue of books in quires, plays and copies, part of the stock of Mr. William Feales; which will be sold by auction . . . November 17, 1737,* lots (copies) i-lxxx. Lots lxxxii-lxxxiv and lxxxvi, not noted by Belanger as Wellington's copies and not advertised (as are the rest) as a ninth share, also appear to contain copies with a Bentley–Wellington provenance. Cf. Belanger 60: *A catalogue of books bound and in quires, and copies, which will be sold by auction . . . Dec. 22. 1737,* lots (copies) i-xli. There are some discrepancies between these two catalogues, e.g. the fractions owned by Wellington of 70 and 169 (all subsequent references in this form relate to the numbered list of Bentley's copies printed as an appendix).

9. Guildhall Library, London, Merchant Taylors' Company Apprentice Binding Books, vol.15, p.18, 22 June 1659. I am grateful to Michael Treadwell for encouraging me to look through these records a second time.

10. *Survey of London,* vol.xxxvi, *The parish of St. Paul Covent Garden* (London: Athlone Press, 1970), pp.192-5; *The diary of Samuel Pepys,* ed. Robert Latham and William Matthews, vol.v (London: G. Bell, 1971), p.37, 3 February 1664.

11. John Strype, *A survey of the Cities of London and Westminster* (1720), vol.ii, book vi, p.93; John Dunton, *The life and errors of John Dunton* (1705), p.364.

12. *The registers of St Paul's Church, Covent Garden, London,* ed. the Revd W. H. Hunt, vol.i, *Christenings, 1653-1752* (London: Harleian Society vol.xxxiii, 1906), p.24 (Susanna Magnes, 13 June 1665); vol.iv, *Burials, 1653-1752* (London: Harleian Society vol.xxxvi, 1908), pp.82 (James Magnes: 30 December 1678), 96 (Mary Magnes: 26 July 1682); PRO PROB 11/359/8 (will of James Magnes, proved 21 January 1679) and PROB 11/360/100 (will of Mary Magnes, proved 5 August 1682). Bentley, as overseer of Mary Magnes's will, probably took an interest in placing two of the younger Magnes children with his own associates in the book trade: Jane Magnes married the son of the printer Robert Everingham in 1689; James Magnes was apprenticed to Jacob Tonson I in 1686, but appears to have died before

he could be made free (*Stationers' Company apprentices, 1641-1700*, ed. D. F. McKenzie (Oxford: Oxford Bibliographical Society publications, new series vol.xvii, 1974), no.4523; *The registers of St Paul's Church, Covent Garden*, vol.iv, *Burials*, p.145, 16 February 1694). I am grateful to Michael Treadwell and Janelle Evans for information about the Magnes and Everingham families.

13. *Allegations for marriage licences issued by the Vicar-General of the Archbishop of Canterbury, July 1687 to June 1694*, ed. George J. Armytage (London: Harleian Society vol.xxxi, 1890), p.47, 15 February 1688 (marriage of Susanna Magnes to John Manley).

14. *Stationers' Company apprentices, 1641-1700*, no.2838, 25 June 1684; Blagden, *Stationers' Company*, p.169. Cf. note 26 below.

15. *The Term Catalogues, 1668-1709 A.D.*, ed. Edward Arber (London: privately printed, 3 vols, 1903-6): see, for example, vol.ii, pp.66, 185, 351.

16. Cf. W. W. Greg, *A bibliography of the English printed drama to the Restoration* (London: The Bibliographical Society, 4 vols, 1939-59), vol.iii, pp.1145-6.

17. See, for example, the list of French novels and memoirs advertised at the end of *Meroveus* (1682). Claude Mauger's *French grammar* (1688) contains an advertisement for 'French Bibles, French Common Prayers, French Testaments and French Psalms' sold by Bentley. The titles listed in the assignment to Wellington, and Rumball's catalogue of 1700 (see below), provide some further impression of the various types of books sold by Bentley. He also sold stationery, of course, and 'fortune-telling cards' (*Term Catalogues*, vol.ii, p.340).

18. From about 1678, Herringman concentrated on reprinting copies that he already owned and on various large-scale publishing projects. He turned over his retail business to Francis Saunders and Joseph Knight in 1684 and thereafter sold his books wholesale: see C. William Miller, 'Henry Herringman, Restoration bookseller-publisher', *Papers of the Bibliographical Society of America*, vol.xlii (1948), pp.292-306.

19. See the dedications in Thomas Otway, *The souldiers fortune* (1681; reprinted 1683, 1687, 1695) and John Banks, *The innocent usurper; or, the death of the Lady Jane Gray* (1694). Banks refers to the earlier dedication to Bentley by 'no mean Author, who before me, made you a Present of his best Comedy, with this Encomium, that you were a very good Patron'. Subsequent opinion regarding Banks's own merit offers little support for Bentley's literary judgment, if such it was. Edward Garnett, writing in the *DNB*, describes Banks as 'a dreary and illiterate writer, whose blank verse is execrable. It appears, however, that his scenes possessed a melodramatic pathos which appealed to vulgar hearers.'

20. Compare the account given by Henry R. Plomer *et al.*, *A dictionary of the printers and booksellers who were at work in England, Scotland and Ireland from 1668 to 1725* (London: The Bibliographical Society, 1922), pp.31-2. I have been unable to locate the letters from Bentley to which Plomer refers.

21. *Survey of London*, vol.xxxvi, p.95; *The marriage, baptismal, and burial registers of the Collegiate Church or Abbey of St Peter, Westminster*, ed. Joseph Lemuel Chester (London: Harleian Society vol.x, 1876), p.29, 13 February 1690.

22. *Stationers' Company apprentices, 1641-1700*, no.324, 6 April 1691; free 5 June 1699. It seems too much of a coincidence that Samuel Briscoe, the son of the rector of Barton-on-the-Heath, should have set up shop in Russell Street, Covent Garden, in 1691, seven years after being apprenticed to Richard Baldwin (*Stationers' Company apprentices, 1641-1700*, no.163; Paul Morgan, *Warwickshire apprentices in the Stationers' Company of London, 1563-1700* (Leeds: Dugdale Society occasional papers no.25, 1978), pp.22-3). One might speculate that perhaps Briscoe had acted as Bentley's assistant, before Rumball; subsequently, however, only one or two books seem to have been printed for Bentley and Briscoe in partnership.

23. *The registers of St Paul's Church, Covent Garden*, vol.i, *Christenings*, pp.87, 90; the English Stock dividend books record Bentley's ownership of a half yeomanry share (worth £40) from December 1694. Cf. Court Book F, 7 May 1694.

24. See, for example, Wing C 1817G, C 3720, H 1450, M 2253, S 4457; cf. no.375. See also Norma Hodgson and Cyprian Blagden, *The notebook of Thomas Bennet and Henry Clements* (Oxford: Oxford Bibliographical Society publications, new series vol.vi, 1956), appendix 12.

25. *The registers of St Paul's Church, Covent Garden*, vol.iv, *Burials*, p.160, 23 June 1697; PRO PROB 11/439/135 will of Richard Bentley, made 15 June, proved 16 July 1697.

26. Parish register of St Martin, Ludgate, 31 July 1698 (marriage of Edmund Rumball and Elizabeth Everingham): I am grateful to Michael Treadwell for this reference. For examples of Everingham entering copies on Bentley's behalf, see SR 16 July 1678, 19 May 1683, 12 January 1684; for Everingham's defence of his rights to print the French Bible see his caveat of 3 February 1686, Eyre and Rivington, vol.iii, p.468.

27. Five other titles are marked with a cross, but these still appear, unlike 339, in the trade sale lists of Wellington's copies.

28. Title-page and advertisement in Wing M 2949 Peter Motteux, *The island princess* (1699).

29. *The registers of St Paul's Church, Covent Garden*, vol.iv, *Burials*, pp.164 (Thomas Bentley: 20 March 1698), 171 (Katherine Bentley: 16 September 1699), 174 (Daubiny Bentley: 6 May 1700), 185 (Edmund Rumball: 8 January 1703). Rumball's partnership with Wellington remains obscure. The imprints suggest that these may have been joint publications, and Rumball's marriage may have provided him with money to invest. There is no evidence, however, that Wellington relinquished ownership of the copies concerned, which he had just bought, and Rumball's role was probably limited to that of a privileged distributor.

30. *Books sold by Edmund Rumball, at the Post-Office in Russel-Street in Covent-Garden. 1700.* This four-page, separately paginated catalogue is included in a volume of miscellaneous plays, British Library 841.c.5. It is not recorded by Wing, but has been partly printed in Greg, *Bibliography of the English printed drama*, vol.iii, pp.1186-8. Rumball advertised both quarto and duodecimo editions of the Irish Bible, cf. Wing B 2759A (1685) and B 2795B (1690).

31. Cf. note 26 above.

32. SR 12 June 1688 (half to Bentley; half to J. Knight and F. Saunders); SR 4 April 1691 (to Bentley and A. Roper).

33. See Bentley's assignment to Tonson of his third share in return for one guinea and a further 30 guineas to be paid on reprinting, 28 August 1691: Folger Shakespeare Library MS C.c.1(5). Sir Roger L'Estrange had assigned his translations of 'Senecas Moralls . . . Tullys Offices, and Bona's Guide to Eternity' to Bentley on 15 July 1687: see Stationers' Company 'Drafts of Court minutes 4 April 1687 to 5 March 1688'; I am grateful to Robin Myers for this reference. The translations were described in the Court minutes themselves as the joint property of Bentley, Tonson and Hindmarsh (Stationers' Company Court Book F, 1 August 1687). Cf. Wing S 2517A-2521.

34. Cf. SR 4 September 1646. Herringman also separately acquired a number of Moseley's copyrights (and half shares) piecemeal during the 1660s: see Miller, pp.299-300.

35. SR 11 April 1681 (Thrale assignment); SR 15 September and 15 November 1671. Imprints seem to confirm this version of events.

36. Stationers' Company Court Book E: 4 July 1681, 7 November 1681, 6 March 1682, 3 April 1682, 7 August 1682. Cf. Blagden, *Stationers' Company*, pp.174-5.

37. It is easiest to see this process in the imprints of those copies wholly owned by Martyn and subsequently by the partners: e.g. 12, 22, 37. Cf. Wing C 1830 (1682), E 3497 (1683), A 1114 (1684). Thomas Sawbridge died in 1692, when he was succeeded by his son, George Sawbridge (the younger).

38. PRO PROB 11/393/158 (will of George Wells, proved 22 November 1688) and PROB 11/341/13 (will of William Wells, proved 23 January 1673). George Wells's death was discussed by the Court of the Stationers' Company: Court Book F, 5 December 1687; I am grateful to Michael Treadwell for this reference.

39. Stationers' Company Court Book F, 2 November, 7 December 1685; 1 February 1686. Royston published most of Hammond's works, including a collected edition in 1684 which

contained Fell's life of Hammond (Wing H 508); he died in 1686. It is notable that
Chiswell and Sawbridge do not seem to have joined in this complaint: Chiswell was
Royston's son-in-law.

40. Some of the copies acquired by Bentley from Martyn had, however, remained in print for
much of the century, either through reprinting or as reissues (e.g. 74).

41. John Evelyn to Richard Bentley, 20 January 1697: British Library MS Evelyn 39b, letter
883. Cf. *The correspondence of Richard Bentley, D.D.*, ed. Christopher Wordsworth (London:
John Murray, 2 vols, 1842), p.135. The three previous editions of *Sylva* were all printed for
Allestry and Martyn between 1664 and 1679; the next did not appear until 1706, printed
for Scott, Chiswell, G. Sawbridge and Tooke.

42. Imprints referring to sale 'by the booksellers' began to occur in significant quantities in the
1650s and 1660s, but became much more common from the 1680s, at least partly because
of the growth of wholesaling.

43. John Milton, *Paradise lost,* ed. Thomas Newton (1749), pp.xxxviii-xxxix; this version, with
or without reference to the stray quarter share, is variously retailed by Masson and Parker
in their lives of Milton, and in the biographies of Tonson by Kathleen Lynch and Harry
Geduld. G. F. Papali, *Jacob Tonson, publisher* (Auckland: Tonson Publishing House, 1968),
p.111, asserts that Bentley bought the other half from Aylmer in 1683, and that Tonson
then bought Bentley's share in 1691. While this is plausible in itself (cf. note 33 above),
Papali cites no evidence other than imprints. His account is repeated in *A descriptive
catalogue of the Milton collection in the Alexander Turnbull Library, Wellington, New Zealand,*
compiled by K. A. Coleridge (Oxford: Oxford University Press, 1980), pp.133-4.

44. PRO C 12/1214/66 Tonson *et al.* v. Walker, 17 April 1739; cited by Bald, 'Early copyright
litigation', p. 94.

45. Cf. Wing J 1006. Brewster's sister, Hannah, was probably the aunt by marriage of the
Thomas Sawbridge mentioned here.

46. Herringman appears to have owned a share in (at least) 155 of the copies assigned to
Wellington: 39, 67-8, 70, 73-98, 103-67, 169, 173-227, 374-7.

47. SR 19 May, 27 July, 21 August 1683; Greg, *Bibliography of the English printed drama*, vol.i,
pp.312-15; Belanger, 'Shakespeare copyrights', p.203.

48. Cf. Hazelton Spencer, *Shakespeare improved* (Cambridge, Massachusetts: Harvard
University Press, 1927), pp.174 ff. *Macbeth* was also adapted by Davenant.

49. See note 8 above. The last sale of Wellington's copies noted by Belanger is *A catalogue of
books in quires, and copies; being the entire stock of Mr Tho. Woodward* (Belanger 122: 12
March 1752), lots i-ii. Chiswell's copies appear in the catalogues of copies belonging to
John Nicholson (Belanger 1: 3 April 1718) and Ranew Robinson (Belanger 82: 20 November 1740). Chiswell's shares listed there included a third of 4, 20 and 29; a sixth of 64 and
72; and a twelfth of 142, 169, 174 and 189. Comparison with the trade sale catalogues has
revealed only one likely mistake in the assignment, and that stems from a similar mistake
in the list of Martyn's copies: Blount's law dictionary (172) appears to have been divided
originally into thirds rather than quarters, and Bentley's share was probably a ninth, rather
than a twelfth. Wellington owned a ninth, as did Chiswell: Herringman had owned a third,
and so probably had Thomas Newcomb and John Martyn.

50. Herringman's copies included a third of 70 and 172 and a quarter share in 189. There are,
nevertheless, one or two anomalies: Herringman is credited with the whole of 182 and 238,
for instance.

51. Dawson, pp.25-6. Dawson's information about the Wells family is not correct: the George
and Mary Wells who made the assignment in 1709 were the children of the bookseller
George Wells (d.1687), whose sister married Robert Scott (see note 38 above). Scott
himself probably died in 1710, on the evidence of the English Stock dividend books, and
may have been too old or too ill to supervise this assignment.

52. If these fractions are reliable, Mearne's original share of the Kirton copies may therefore
have generally been a half. In a few instances where Martyn had owned an eighth (cf.

375-6), Wells was credited with 1/8 + 1/4; where Martyn had owned a sixteenth (cf. 374), Wells had 1/16 + 1/4.

53. PRO C 8/347/170 Swalle v. Scott, 13 April 1692. The two booksellers had also purchased some stock from Mearne's widow early in 1687. Cf. Wing C 4091I printed for G. Wells, A. Swalle & G. Pawlett, 1687; Wing C 5525A printed for A. Swalle, 1689. The sale catalogue of Samuel Keble's copies (Belanger 17: 18 June 1722), lot ix, refers to Swalle's purchase of copies from Charles Mearne.

54. For some earlier disputes relating to the recording of assignments of copies, and confusion over temporary assignments, see C. J. Sisson, 'The laws of Elizabethan copyright: the Stationers' view', *The Library*, 5th ser., vol.xv (1960), pp.8-20, which emphasizes (for the earlier period) the legitimizing role of the Stationers' Company Court and the final authority of the entry books. For a relatively early example of a small fraction that was recorded, somewhat hesitantly, as 'one sixteenth parte more or lesse', see SR 15 August 1656; cited by Feather, p.42.

55. See Hodgson and Blagden, pp.67-100, especially pp.76-7.

56. B. E., *A new dictionary of the terms ancient and modern of the canting crew* (1699); John Dunton, *A voyage round the world*, vol.ii (1691), p.77; E. Phillips, *A new world of words*, 6th edition (1706); N. Bailey, *Dictionarium Britannicum* (1730): these sources are cited by Hodgson and Blagden.

57. Oldenburg to Boyle, 19 December 1665: *The correspondence of Henry Oldenburg*, ed. A. R. and M. B. Hall, vol.ii (Madison, Milwaukee & London: University of Wisconsin Press, 1966), p.647.

58. Cf. Hodgson and Blagden, p.98; Cyprian Blagden, 'The English Stock of the Stationers' Company in the time of the Stuarts', *The Library*, 5th series, vol.xii (1957), pp.167-86.

Appendix

Introductory note

The document reproduced here (PRO C 108/406) consists of two pieces of vellum, one being the indenture between Katherine Bentley and Richard Wellington, signed, sealed and witnessed. Attached to this is a larger piece of vellum containing the 'Catalogue of all such Coppyes of Bookes . . . now in the possession of Catherine Bently', which lists the titles in four parallel columns, intended to be read downwards, with occasional marks or notes in the margins, including a number adjacent to each group of titles to record the fraction owned.

In the transcription below, the columns have been printed in sequence to allow space for editorial annotations, but the original layout is indicated. The notes recording the fractions owned have been transferred from beside the columns to the top of each page; each title has also been numbered. The original spelling, capitalization and punctuation have been retained. Abbreviations and contractions (where indicated by marks of contraction) have mostly been expanded, and the letters supplied are printed in italics. Interlinear insertions in the original document are enclosed within angled brackets; square brackets have been used for editorial insertions.

Six items in the list bear annotations of slightly later date, made in a different hand: nos.201, 210, 295, 297 and 315 have been marked with a cross; no.339 has been marked 'sold to mr. Varenne'.

My annotations have been guided more by principles of concision and clarity than by consistency. An attempt has been made to identify each title, giving the reference to STC or Wing for the latest edition published before the date of this document. In some cases, reference is also made to collected editions or reissues, including Bentley's series of *Modern novels* (*MN*), and to the list of 'lost plays' contained in W. W. Greg, *A bibliography of the English printed drama to the Restoration,* vol.ii (London: The Bibliographical Society, 1951). Where necessary, an attribution of authorship has been provided, usually separated from the imprint information by parentheses (or square brackets in the case of an anonymous work); in some instances, a fuller title has been supplied. Information derived from imprint statements is also included for each title, but only in so far as it may help to identify booksellers responsible for or interested in the edition concerned. Details relating to printers have generally been omitted, together with all addresses; the names of booksellers have been abbreviated and their spelling standardized, but they appear in the same order as in the imprint itself. Finally, I have attempted to record the previous ownership of the copies and shares of copies listed here by reference to the registers, or entry books, of the Stationers' Company (SR). The date when a copy was entered (ent.) is given here New Style; where the entry makes no mention of a fraction or part (pt) of a copy, it apparently (though not always reliably) refers to the whole. Time, and the available indexes, have not permitted an exhaustive search of the registers, nor the systematic tracing of other shares of the same copies; most references are to block entries, using the following abbreviations:

M   Assigned by the widow of John Martyn, 14 June 1681, to Robert Scott. Entered to Scott, 21 August 1683.

K   Assigned by the executor of William Kirton, executor of Joshua Kirton, 22 September 1671, to Samuel Mearne. Entered to Mearne, 17 September 1673.

R   Assigned by the executor of Humphrey Robinson, 13 May 1671, to John Martyn and Henry Herringman. Entered to Martyn and Herringman, 30 January 1673.

D   Assigned by John Dunmore, 24 August 1671, to Sir Thomas Davies. Entered to Davies, 29 December 1672. Reassigned by Davies to John Martyn and entered again to Martyn, 29 December 1672.

W   Copies formerly belonging to Thomas Whitaker, assigned by Alexander Broome, husband of Whitaker's widow. Entered to Humphrey Robinson, Richard Thrale, Joshua Kirton and Samuel Thompson, 7 March 1653.

Be   Assigned by John Beale to John Parker, and by Parker to Humphrey Robinson. Entered to Robinson, 16 March 1649.

B   Assigned by Bonham Norton and by the executors of John Bill. Entered to Joyce Norton and Richard Whitaker, 26 August 1632.

THIS INDENTURE made the Foureteenth day of December in the yeare of our Lord God One thousand Six-hundred Ninety and Eight Betweene Katherine Bentley Relict and Executrix of Richard Bentley late of the parish of St Pauls Covent Garden in the County of Middlesex Bookseller of the one part And Richard Wellington Cittizen & Bookseller of London of the other part Witnesseth That the said Katherine Bentley for and in Consideracion of a Competent summe of money to her in hand paid or secured to be paid by the said Richard Wellington att or before the enseling and delivery of these presents Hath granted bargained sold Aliened Assigned transferred and sett over And by these presents Doth grant bargaine sell Alien Assigne Transferr and sett over unto the said Richard Wellington his Executors Administrators and Assignes All and singular the Stocke of Bookes of her the said Katherine Bentley now in her possession <Except the bookes in the shopp:> And alsoe All and singular such Originall Coppyes of Bookes Parts and Shares and Proporcions of Coppyes of Bookes as shee the said Katherine Bently by vertue of her <said> Husbands last Will and Testament and att the date of these presents standeth possessed of or is Interested in or Entituled unto in such manner and according to such Shares partes and Proporcions as shee the said Katherine Bentley now standeth Entituled unto and possessed of them And as the said Coppyes are particularly mencioned and Expressed in a certaine Schedule or Catalogue to these presents annexed To have and To hold all and singular the said Stock of Bookes Coppyes & Shares parts and proporcions of Coppyes now of her the said Katherine Bentley unto him the said Richard Wellington his Executors Administrators and assignes To the sole use benefitt and behoost of him the said Richard Wellington his Executors Administrators and Assignes for ever And to and for noe other use intent or purpose whatsoever And the said Katherine Bentley doth further for herself her Executors Administrators and Assignes covenant promise and grant to and with the said Richard Wellington his Executors Adminstrators and Assignes That neither Richard Bentley her late husband nor shee the said Katherine Bentley nor either of them have att any time heretofore made done Comitted or suffered any Act or thing whatsoever whereby the said Richard Wellington or his Assignes may be Impeached disturbed or hind[e]red of the full quiet and peaceable Enjoyment of the said Coppyes Shares or partes of Coppyes above granted & Assigned or of any of them But that the said Coppyes Shares and parts of Coppyes shall and may att all times hereafter be held possessed or enjoyed by him the said Richard Wellington and his assignes free from all Claimes disturbances or Incumbrances whatsoever done by him the said Richard Bentley or by her the said Katherine Bentley or by either of them or by any person or persons claimeing or to claime from by or under them or either of them And the said Richard Wellington doth by these presents for himself his Executors and Assignes Covenant promise and grant to and with the said Katherine Bentley her Executors Adminstrators and Assignes That when and soe often as hee the said Richard Wellington shall cause an Impression to be made of that Booke or Coppy called The French Liturgie That then hee the said Richard Wellington his Executors Administrators and Assignes shall and will render give or pay to the First Compilers or Proprietors of the said Booke from whome the same was Originally bought [space] of the said Bookes bound according to and in performance of a certaine Agreement made by the said Richard Bentley at his first purchaseing of the said Coppy And alsoe That hee the said Richard Wellington and his Assignes shall and will att all times dureing the naturall life of Robert Everingham of the Citty of London Printer Employ and retaine him the said Robert Everingham to print the same:- In Witnesse whereof the partyes First above named to these present Indentures interchangeably have sett their hands and seales the day and yeare first above written.

[Sealed and signed:] Katherine Bentely

[Endorsed:] Sealed and delivered in the presence of Robert Everingham/ William Everingham/ William Guise

14th December 1698/ N°. 22

[Attached:] A True and perfect Catalogue of all such Coppyes of Bookes with the severall partes shares and proportions of them which are now in the possession of Catherine Bently or whereunto shee the said Katherine Bently is intituled and which are by her intended to be granted and sold to Richard Wellington by the Bargaine sale and Assignment hereunto Annexed.

[Column I:]
Of the Copyes of these bookes Following One Third parte or share
[1]   Prologium Imica   Wing W 3230 Robert Witty, *Pyrologia mimica,* for J. Martyn, 1669; M
[2]   Examen of Teaching the Latine tongue   Wing E 3707 for J. Martyn, 1669; M
[3]   Unexpected choice by Scarrone   Wing S 837 for J. Martyn, 1670 (included in Wing S 835 *Scarron's novels,* for R. Bentley, W. Hensman, F. Saunders, D. Browne & J. Knapton, 1694); M
[4]   Hooks Mycography   Wing H 2621/2621A Robert Hooke, *Micrographia,* By J. Martyn/for J. Allestry, 1667; M; D
[5]   —Attempt to prove the motion of the earth   Wing H 2613 for J. Martyn, 1674; M
[6]   —Animadversions on Hevelius   Wing H 2611 for J. Martyn, 1674; M
[7]   —Of Telescopes   Wing H 2614 *A description of helioscopes,* for J. Martyn, 1676; M
[8]   —Of Lamps   Wing H 2616 for J. Martyn, 1677; M
[9]   —Of Comets   included in Wing H 2618 *Lectures and collections,* for J. Martyn, 1678; M
[10] —Philosophicall Colleccions N°. one   N & S 537.1, for J. Martyn, 1679; M
[11] Towers [altered from 'Powers'] experimentall philosophy   Wing P 3099 for J. Martyn and J. Allestry, 1664; M
[12] Enter into thy Closett   Wing W 1500/1500B/1500C (by Edward Wetenhall) for T. Sawbridge, R. Bentley & G. Wells/for R. Bentley/for T. Sawbridge, 1684; M
[13] Remembrances of Tenn excellent men   Wing B 796 (by Clement Barksdale) for M. Pardoe, 1677 (a reissue of Wing B 806 for J. Martyn, 1670); M
[14] Laudes Summary of Devotions   Wing L 584 sold by J. Walthoe & R. Vincent, 1688 (cf. Wing L 592 for J. Martyn & J. Ridley, 1650); M
[15] Goddards discourse of the practice of physick   Wing G 914 for J. Martyn & J. Allestry, 1670; M
[16] Actons phisicall refleccions on Dewes Letteres   Wing A 450 for J. Martyn, 1668; M
[17] Englands wants   Wing C 1842 [by Edward Chamberlayne] for R. Baldwin, 1689 (cf. Wing C 1840 for J. Martyn, 1668); M
[18] Parkers Ecclesiasticall pollicy   Wing P 460 for J. Martyn, 1671; M

[1/3]

[19] —His defence and Continuation   Wing P 457 for J. Martyn, 1671; M

[20] Willoughby of birds English   Wing W 2280 for J. Martyn, 1678; M

[21] Towerson of the Lords Prayer   Wing T 1965A for J. Martyn, 1680; M

[22] —On the Creed   Wing T 1967 *et seq.* for R. Chiswell, T. Sawbridge, G. Wells & R. Bentley, 1685 (cf. Wing T 1966/1967D for J. Martyn, 1678-80; T 1967A-B for R. Littlebury, R. Scott & G. Wells, 1681; T 1969 for R. Chiswell, 1688); M

[23] —On the Decalogue   Wing T 1970A for R. Littlebury, R. Scott & G. Wells, 1681 (cf. Wing T 1970 for J. Martyn, 1676); M

[24] Greeves discourse of mixture   Wing G 1948 (by Nehemiah Grew) for J. Martyn, 1675; also included in Wing G 1950A for J. Martyn, 1678; M

[25] —Experiments in Consorts   Wing G 1950/1950A for J. Martyn, 1678; M

[26] Philosophicall essay on musick   Wing G 2216 (by Francis North, Baron Guilford) for J. Martyn, 1677; M

[27] Wallis discourse of gratiation   Wing W 574 John Wallis, *A discourse of gravity and gratiation,* for J. Martyn, 1675; M

[28] Bishopp Barlowes Lettere of the invocacion of Saints   Wing B 834 for J. Martyn, 1679; M

[29] Bishopp Taylour of the Sacrament   Wing T 424 Jeremy Taylor, *The worthy communicant,* for F. Wright, 1695 (cf. Wing T 420C for J. Martyn, 1678); M; D 2/3

[30] Philosophicall Discourse of Speech   Wing C 6282 (by Géraud de Cordemoy) for J. Martyn, 1668; M

[31] —Transaccions 4 Volume   N & S 539.01000/.02000/.03000/.04000 for J. Martyn & J. Allestry, [1667]/ for J. Martyn, [1668]/1669/1670; M

[32] Dailles right use of the Fathers   Wing D 119 for J. Martyn, sold by R. Boulter, 1675; M

[33] Holders Sermon on Navigacion   Wing H 2380 Richard Holden, *The improvement of navigation,* for J. Martyn, 1680; M

[34] Relacion of the River Nile   Wing L 2734 [by Jeronimo Lobo] for J. Martyn, 1673; M

[35] Holders Eliments of Speech   Wing H 2387 for M. Pardoe, 1677; M

[36] Bishopp Brownrilkes Sermons compleate   Wing B 5207/5207A (by Ralph Brownrig) vol. I, by R. Everingham/ for R. Chiswell, T. Sawbridge, G. Wells & R. Bentley, 1685; Wing B 5214 vol. II, by R. Everingham, 1685 (cf. Wing B 5211A/B by R.E., sold by John Salisbury/Thomas Salusbury, 1686); M; D vol. I 2/3 & vol. II all

[37] Torianos Dicionnary Italian and English   Wing F 1369/1369A for R. Chiswell, T. Sawbridge, G. Wells & R. Bentley, sold by S. Crouch, 1688/ for R.C. T.S. G.W. and R.B., sold by T. Sawbridge, S. Crouch, T. Horne & M. Gilliflower, 1690; M; D

[38] —Grammar   Wing T 1922 for R. Chiswell, T. Sawbridge & R. Bentley, 1689; M; D

[39] Hudibras 2^d. part   Wing B 6304A for H. Herringman, sold by R. Bentley, J. Tonson, F. Saunders & T. Bennet, 1694; M; D

[40] Consideracions concerning the west Church   Wing T 1050 (by Herbert Thorndike) for J. Martyn, J. Allestry & T. Dicas, 1662; M

[41] Taylors Sermon on Sir George Dalson   Wing T 392A for J. Martyn, J. Allestry & T. Dicas, 1658; M

[42] Pettys refleccon on Ireland   Wing P 1936 for J. Martyn, J. Allestry & T. Dicas, 1660; M

[43] —Discourse before the royall Society   Wing P 1919 for J. Martyn, 1674; M

[1/3]

[44] Fluellins Poem to King   Wing L 2628 [Martin Llewellyn], *To the Kings most excellent Majesty,* for J. Martyn, J. Allestry & T. Dicas, 1660; M
[45] Bishopp Fells life of Dʳ. Hammond   Wing F 617/618 for J. Martyn, J. Allestry & T. Dicas, 1661/1662; M
[46] Thorndikes Weight and measures   Wing T 1052 for J. Martyn, 1680; M
[47] —Epilogue of the Church of England   included in Wing T 1052; M
[48] Sandersons cases of conscience   Wing S 630 by T. Leach, sold by J. Martyn, J. Allestry & T. Dicas, 1660; M; D 2/3
[49] Rays Travells   Wing R 399 for J. Martyn, 1673; M
[50] Grants Observacion on the bills of mortality   Wing G 1602 for J. Martyn, 1676; M
[51] Bishopp Wards sermons against resistance   Wing W 812 for J. Martyn, J. Allestry & T. Dicas, 1661; M
[52] Bartons sermon before the Lord Mayor   Wing B 989 for J. Allestry, 1670; M
[53] Sharras of Vipers   Wing C 2039 Moise Charas, *New experiments upon vipers,* for M. Pardoe, 1677 (a reissue of Wing C 2038, for J. Martyn, 1673); M
[54] Discourse of Vipers   included in Wing C 2038/2039
[55] Discourse of [space] of Christian piety   Wing W 1522 [Edward Wetenhall], *Two discourses for the furtherance of Christian piety,* for J. Martyn, 1671; M
[56] Epictetus Life and Philosophy   Wing E 3152 for J. Martyn, 1670; M
[57] Liptius of Constancy   Wing L 2360 for J. Allestry, 1670; M; D
[58] Merrett against Lex Talionis   Wing M 1841 for J. Allestry, 1670; M
[59] —Apothecaryes abuses   Wing M 1844 for J. Allestry, 1670; M
[60] —View of Fraudes   included in Wing M 1844
[61] Lord Norths Observacions and Advices   Wing N 1286 for J. Martyn, 1669; M
[62] Miltons history of England   Wing M 2123/2124 for R. Chiswell, sold by N. Rolls/ for R. Scott, R. Chiswell, R. Bentley, G. Sawbridge, sold by A. Swall & T. Child, 1695; M; D

Of the Copyes of these bookes Following One sixth parte or share:
[63] The plaine mans pathway of Worshipp   Wing P 2365A for M. Pardoe, 1678 (cf. Wing P 2365 for R. White & J. Martyn, 1677); M; D
[64] Combes companion to the Alter   Wing C 5451 (by Thomas Comber) for R. Lambert, R. Chiswell, T. Sawbridge, R. Bentley & G. Wells, 1685; M 1/2
[65] More on the revelacions   Wing M 2641 (by Henry More) for J. Martyn & W. Kettilby, 1680; M 1/2
[66] Second door to the holy tongue   Wing R 1618 (by William Robertson) for H. Robinson & G. Sawbridge, [1655]; M 1/2; ent. to H. Robinson & G. Sawbridge, SR 21 Aug. 1654
[67] Doctrine and worship   Not identified; M 1/2; R 1/2
[68] Rival Freinds   STC 12935 (by Peter Hausted) for H. Robinson, 1632; M 1/2; R
[69] Method of prescribeing diseases   Wing M 2719 Pierre Morel, *The expert doctors dispensatory,* for N. Brook, 1657; M 1/2; part assigned to Brook by T. Dicas & T. Davies, SR 28 July 1656
[70] The history of Henry the Fourth of France   Wing P 1465gA/1465hA [by Hardouin de Beaumont de Péréfix] for H. Herringman/for R. Bentley, J. Tonson, F. Saunders & T. Bennet, 1692; M 1/2; also ent. to J. Martyn, J. Allestry & T. Dicas, SR 27 Nov. 1661, and to S. Speed, H. Herringman, J. Martyn 'and his partners', SR 15

[1/6]

Sept. 1662; (apparently different from 'The history of the death of Henry the fourth': K; W (pt); B (pt))

---

[71] French Pastry Cooke   Wing M 706A for O. Blagrave, 1686; M 1/2; part assigned to Brook by T. Dicas & T. Davies, SR 28 July 1656

[72] The rules of Civility   Wing C 6605 for R. Chiswell, T. Sawbridge, G. Wells & R. Bentley, 1685 (cf. Wing C 6604 for J. Martyn & J. Starkey, 1678); M 1/2

[73] Bacons Miscellanyes   Wing B 275 for H. R[obinson], sold by W. Lee, 1670; M 1/2; R

[74] Nortons Artillery   Wing N 1327A Robert Norton, *The gunner,* for H. Robinson, 1664 (a reissue of STC 18673 for H. Robinson, 1628); M 1/2; R

[75] Sermons by J. B.   STC 3468 (by John Boys) for H. Robinson, 1631; M 1/2; R

[76] Sidnams Sermons   STC 23573 (by Humphrey Sydenham) for H. Robinson, 1637; M 1/2; R

[77] Torianos Italian Tutor   STC 24137/24137.5 sold by H. Robinson, 1640; M 1/2; R

[78] Uniforme Articles for all the Visitacions   Cf. STC 10134, 10147.10 etc, Wing C 4009AB-AD etc.; M 1/2; R

[79] Halls contemplacions 3ᵈ. Vol.   STC 12654 for N. Butter & W. Butler, 1615 (cf. Wing H 376 sold by J. Tonson, 1679, and other collected editions); M 1/2; R; Be

[80] Perkins Duty of a Minister   STC 19733a for W. Welby, 1606 (cf. STC 19653a/19653b by J. Haviland/ by J. Haviland for J. Boler, 1631); M 1/2; R; Be

[81] Herns workes   STC 13384/13384.7 (by Samuel Hieron) vol. I by J. Beale, 1635/vol. II by W. Stansby, 1634; M 1/2; R; Be vol. I (pt), vol. II all

[82] Charltons remembrance   STC 4640 (by George Carleton) for R. Milbourne & H. Robinson, 1630; M 1/2; ent. to R. Milbourne & H. Robinson, SR 1 May 1624

[83] Edgertons Catechisme   Wing E 252 (44th edition) for H. Robinson, 1644 (cf. E 252A 'printed', 1671); M 1/2; R

[84] Gouges Catechisme   included in Wing G 1400 (see below); M 1/2; R; Be

[85] —Whole Armour   Wing G 1400 (a reissue of STC 12110.5 by J. Beale, 1639) for H. Robinson, 1647; M 1/2; R; Be

[86] Spellmans right of the Church   Wing S 4923 for A. Curteyn, 1676; M 1/2; R; Be

[87] Smith on Hoseah   STC 22847.3 for R. Woodroffe, 1616; M 1/2; R; Be

[88] Gouge on the Canticles   STC 12113 by J. Beale, 1615; M 1/2; R; Be

[89] Dike of repentance   STC 7409a Daniel Dyke, *Two treatises,* by J. Beale, 1635; M 1/2; R; Be

[90] Eltons Catechisme   STC 7618 by J. Beale, 1634; M 1/2; R; Be

[91] English Farrier   STC 10410 by J. Beale, 1639 (cf. Wing E 3083B for J. Wright, 1649); M 1/2; R

[92] Brinsleyes true watch 1 & 2ᵈ. part   Wing B 4733 for H. Robinson, 1648; M 1/2; R; Be

[93] Lloys Schoolemaster   Wing L 2672 [Richard Lloyd], *The school-masters auxiliaries,* by T. R[oycroft], 1659; M 1/2; R

[94] Saturny Ephemerides   STC 14269 (by Henry Isaacson) for H. Seile & H. Robinson, 1633; M 1/2; ent. to Robinson, SR 25 Feb. 1632

[95] Relacion of the Northerne Quakers   Wing H 1954 (by Francis Higginson) for H. R[obinson], 1653; M 1/2; R

[1/6]

[96]   Colleccion of papers   Wing S 4576A Giovanni Battista Stoppa, *A collection of the several papers sent to his Highness the Lord Protector . . . concerning the bloody and barbarous massacres . . . in the vallies of Piedmont,* for H. Robinson, 1655; M 1/2; R

[97]   Reasons for noe necessity of reformacon   Wing S 762/763 [Henry Savage], *Reasons shewing that there is no need of such a reformation,* for H. Robinson, 1660; M 1/2; R

[Column II:]

[98]   Satans Stratagems   Wing A 442 (by Giacomo Aconcio) by J. Macock, sold by W. Lee, 1651; M 1/2; R 1/2; ent. to J. Macock & J. Hancock, SR 4 March 1648

[99]   Montaignes Essayes 3 Vol.   Wing M 2480/2480A for T. Basset & M. Gilliflower & W. Hensman/ for M. Gilliflower & W. Hensman, R. Bentley & J. Hindmarsh, 1693; T. Basset's share (1/3) assigned to J. Hindmarsh, SR 15 July 1693; ent. to T. Basset, M. Gilliflower & W. Hensman, SR 10 Sept. 1684

Of the Copyes of these bookes Following One ninth parte or share:

[100]   Jacksons workes 3 vol.   Wing J 90 for J. Martyn, R. Chiswell & J. Clark, 1673; M 1/3

[101]   Woodfords psalms   Wing B 2529 for J. Martyn, J. Baker & H. Brome, 1678; M 1/3; D

[102]   Franks sermons   Wing F 2074/2074A/2074B for J. Martyn, H. Brome & R. Chiswell, sold by D. Newman & J. Edwin/ for J. Martyn, H. Brome & R. Chiswell/ for J. Martyn, H. Brome & R. Chiswell, sold by J. Edwin, 1672; M 1/3

[103]   Mulletts garden of pleasure   Wing M 2392 for J. Martyn & H. Herringman, 1670; M 1/3

Of the Copyes of these bookes Following One twelfth parte or share:

[104]   Gerrards Herball with Cutts   STC 11752 by A. Islip, J. Norton & R. Whitaker, 1636; M 1/4; K; W; B

[105]   Braithwaites natures   STC 3572 for R. Whitaker, 1623; M 1/4; K; W

[106]   —Essay of five Senses   STC 3567 sold by H. Shephard, 1635; M 1/4; K; W

[107]   Raboni or Mary Magdalen's teares   STC 24970 (by Thomas Walkington) for R. Whitaker, 1620; M 1/4; K; W

[108]   Translacion of certain psalms by Bacon   STC 1174/1174.5 for H. Barret & R. Whitaker, 1625; M 1/4; K (pt); W (pt)

[109]   History of Philip de Comines   Wing C 5542 for S. Mearne, J. Martyn & H. Herringman, 1674; M 1/4; K; W (pt); B

[110]   Mason's rustick or the Country Farmer   STC 10549 (by Charles Estienne & Jean Liebault) for J. Bill, 1616; M 1/4; K; W (pt); B

[111]   Riddles of Heraclitus and Demcritus   STC 13174 for J. Norton, 1598; M 1/4; K; W (pt); B

[112]   Catalogue of Colledges in Cambridge & Oxford   STC 14453 Thomas James, *Ecloga Oxonio-Cantabrigiensis,* impensis G. Bishop & J. Norton, 1600; M 1/4; K; W (pt); B

[113]   Basilicon Doron   Wing J 128/128A (by James I) for J. Hindmarsh/ for S. Mearne, 1682; M 1/4; K; W (pt); B (pt) (ent. to G. Bishop, T. Man, S. Waterson, J. Norton, C. Burby & F. Kingston, SR 28 March 1603)

[1/12]

[114]   Fabricks of the Church by Tooke   STC 24120 (by William Tooker) for J. Norton, 1604; M 1/4; K; W (pt); B

[115]   Willets Hexapla in Genesis   STC 25684-25685a.5 (5 issues) for the assigns of T. Man, P. Man & J. Man/sold by J. Boler/sold by J. Grismond/sold by W. Lee/sold by J. Parker, 1633; M 1/4; K; W (pt); B (pt)

[116]   Comparative Discourse of bodyes   STC 11188 (by Edward Forset) for J. Bill, 1606; M 1/4; K; W (pt); B

[117]   Bucanars institucions   Wing B 5269 for D. Pakeman, A. Roper & R. Tomlins, 1659; M 1/4; K; W (pt); B

[118]   The key of estates by R. Deluceing   STC 16897 René de Lucinge, *The beginning, continuance, and decay of estates,* for J. Bill, 1606; M 1/4; K; W (pt); B

[119]   Masons Authority of the Church   STC 17596 by J. Lichfield, 1634; M 1/4; K; W (pt); B

[120]   The poor mans preacher by Wakeman   STC 24951 for J. Bill, 1607; M 1/4; K; W (pt); B

[121]   Aphorismes or *the* Secret practices of the Jesuits   STC 14525 [for J. Bill], 1609 (cf. Wing J 709 (different translation of same text) by R. E[veringham] for J. Starkey, 1679); M 1/4; K; W (pt); B

[122]   Concordance or the Synonimns of the Bible   STC 13238 (by Robert Herrey) by J. Norton & J. Bill, 1622; M 1/4; K; W (pt); B

[123]   Charltons Jurisdiccion regar'   STC 4637 George Carleton, *Jurisdiction regall, epicopall, papall,* impensis J. Norton, 1610; M 1/4; K; W (pt); B

[124]   Poseing of the parts of Brinsley   Wing B 4704 for H. Herringman, T. Basset, N. Ranew, M. Wotton, R. Chiswell, J. Robinson, H. Sawbridge, G. Conyers, 1687; M 1/4; K; W (pt); B (pt)

[125]   —Of the Accidence and Grammar   included in Wing B 4704

[126]   Childs birth   STC 12497 (by Jacques Guillemeau) for J. Norton & R. Whitaker, 1635; M 1/4; K; W (pt); B

[127]   Mo<r>ton against Parsons   STC 18183 for J. Bill, 1610; M 1/4; K; W (pt); B

[128]   Golden mean   Not identified (ent. to Bill as 'The golden myne or the studentes storehouse by Thomas Draxey', SR 23 March 1613); cf. (though ent. separately in SR) Wing D 2144A Thomas Draxe, *Callipeia, or, a rich store-house . . . for the use and benefit of scholars,* for J. Kirton, 1662; M 1/4; K; W (pt); B

[129]   Biteing of a mad dog   STC 22977 (by Thomas Spackman) for J. Bill, 1613; M 1/4; K; W (pt); B

[130]   Breerwoods diversity of Languages   Wing B 4378/4379 for S. Mearne, J. Martyn & H. Herringman/ for S.M. J.M. H.H., sold by W. Kettilby, 1674; M 1/4; K; W (pt); B

[131]   True church by Charlton   STC 4632 George Carleton, *Directions to know the true church,* by J. Bill, 1615; M 1/4; K; W (pt); B

[132]   Vision of Balaams Ass by Hay   STC 12972 (by Peter Hay) for J. Bill, 1616; M 1/4; K; W (pt); B

[133]   Spalatos Sermons   STC 7004 (by Marco Antonio de Dominis) by J. Bill, 1617; M 1/4; K; W (pt); B

[134]   Necessity of Conformity by Sprint   STC 23108 by J. Bill, 1618; M 1/4; K; W (pt); B

[135]   Rock of Christian Shipwrack   STC 7005 (by Marco Antonio de Dominis) by J. Bill, 1618; M 1/4; K; W (pt); B

[1/12]

[136] Davids teares   STC 12994 (by Sir John Hayward) for R. Whitaker, 1636; M
1/4; K; W (pt); B

[137] Quarrles of Pope Paule with the Venetians   STC 21766 (by Paolo Sarpi)
for J. Bill, 1626; M 1/4; K; W (pt); B

[138] Almanzor   STC 354 (by Miguel de Luna) [by W. Stansby] for J. Parker, 1627;
M 1/4; K; W; B

[139] Christs Prayer   Probably STC 12990 (by Sir John Hayward) by J. Bill, 1624; M
1/4; K; W; B

[140] Councell of Trent   Wing S 696/696A (by Paolo Sarpi) for S. Mearne, J.
Martyn & H. Herringman/ for S. Mearne, 1676; M 1/4; K; W ; B

[141] Threefold resolucon   STC 6597.7 (by John Denison) for N. Bourne, 1630; M
1/4; K; W; B (pt)

[142] Vestegans Antiquityes   Wing V 271 Richard Verstegan, *A restitution of
decayed intelligence,* for S. Mearne, J. Martyn & H. Herringman, 1673; M 1/4; K;
W; B

[143] Camdens Epitomy of Mapps   STC 4527 *The abridgment of Camden's
Britania with the maps,* for J. Bill, 1626; M 1/4; K; W; B

[144] Bacons Wisdom of the Antients   included in Wing B 294-296 for G.
Sawbridge/sold by J. Newton/for A. Swalle & T. Childe/for S. Smith & B.
Walford/for H. Herringman, R. Scott, R. Chiswell, A. Swalle & R. Bentley, 1696;
M 1/4; K; W; B

[145] Bells Arithmatick   Possibly Wing P 1241A John Penkethman, *Accompts of
merchandise,* for S. Mearne, J. Martyn, H. Herringman, sold by G. Swinnock, 1676
(cf. STC 3059.6 with the dedication signed by John Bill); M 1/4; K; W; B

[146] —Manuall   Possibly included in Wing P 1241A; M 1/4; K; W; B

[147] Pallace of pleasure   STC 19823 (by George Pettie) by G. Eld, 1617 (cf. SR 11
March 1605); M 1/4; K; W; B

[148] Gardners devotions   STC 11574 for J. Bill, 1627; M 1/4; K; W; B

[149] Cluins institucons   STC 4425 Jean Calvin, *The institution of Christian religion,*
for J. Norton & R. Whitaker, 1634; M 1/4; K; W; B

[150] Cornelius tacitus with malvazzys   STC 23648 *The annales of Cornelius
Tacitus,* for R. Whitaker, 1640; Wing M 359 Virgilio Malvezzi, *Discourses upon
Cornelius Tacitus,* for R. Whitaker & T. Whitaker, 1642; M 1/4; K; W; B

[151] World of wonders   STC 10553 (by Henri Estienne) for J. Norton, 1607; M
1/4; K; W; B

[152] Free Schoole of Warr   STC 21758 (by Paolo Sarpi) by J. Bill, 1625; M 1/4;
K; W; B

[153] Hayward of Supremacy   STC 13003 by J. Bill, 1624; M 1/4; K; W; B

[154] Homers battle of Froggs   STC 13628 by J. Bill, [1624?]; M 1/4; K; W; B

[155] Mertons Appeal   STC 18177 (by Thomas Morton) impensis G. Bishop & J.
Norton, 1610; M 1/4; K; W; B (pt)

[156] Godfrey of Bulloigne   Wing T 174/174A/174B [by Torquato Tasso] for H.
Herringman, sold by J. Knight & F. Saunders/ for G. Wells & A. Swalle/ for R.
Chiswell, R. Bentley, T. Sawbridge & G. Wells, 1687; M 1/4; K; W; B

[157] Marchants Advice   STC 3908.9 (by J[ohn] B[rowne]) for R. Whitaker, 1640;
M 1/4; K; W; B

[158] Heaven of health   STC 5483.7/5484 Thomas Cogan, *The haven of health,* by
A. Griffin/ for R. Ball, 1636; M 1/4; K; W; B

[159] Gills philosophy of holy Scripture   STC 11878 for J. Norton & R.
Whitaker, 1635; M 1/4; K; W

[1/12]

[160]   Sure guide to the French tongue   Wing C 4893 (by Paul Cogneau) for J.
        Kirton, 1658; M 1/4; K; W
[161]   History of England by William Martin   STC 17529 by R. Young 'for
        himselfe & others', 1638 (cf. STC 17527 for J. Bill, W. Barrett & H. Featherstone,
        1615); M 1/4; K 1/3; W 1/3
[162]   Annotacons on the Old and new testament   Wing D 2064 (by John
        Downame et al.) by E. Tyler, 1657; M 1/4; K; W (ent. to T. Downes, N. Bourne,
        R. Mead, R. Whitaker, J. Legatt, E. Brewster, P. Stephens, R. Thrale & C.
        Meredith, SR 21 Oct. 1643)
[163]   Four Cardinall Virtues by E. Deering   Wing D 1110 for R. Whitaker,
        1641[2]; M 1/4; K; W
[164]   Declaracons of Prince Rupert   Wing R 2294 A declaration of His Highness
        Prince Rupert. With a narrative of the state and condition of the city and garrison of
        Bristol, by E. Griffin, 1645; M 1/4; K; W
[165]   A Small tract of the use of the Lords Supper   Not identified, possibly by
        John Downame (cf. SR 25 Nov. 1644); M 1/4; K; W
[166]   Despagne popular errors in religion   Wing E 3267 (by Jean d'Espagne) for
        T. Whitaker, 1648; M 1/4; K; W
[167]   Hackwell against Carrier   STC 12610 George Hakewill, An answere to a
        treatise written by Dr. Carier, by J. Bill, 1616; M 1/4; K; R ('all'); W (pt); B
[168]   King James Workes   STC 14344/14345 by R. Barker & J. Bill, 1616; M 1/4
        (cf. no. 113)
[169]   Dugdales Baronage 2 Volumes   Wing D 2480 for A. Roper, J. Martyn & H.
        Herringman, 1675-6; M 1/4
[170]   Broughtons View of Scripture   STC 12983 (an enlargement by Thomas
        Hayne of Hugh Broughton's Concent of scripture) by J. B[eale] & S. B[ulkley] for
        H. Ockould, 1640 (also included in Wing B 4997 for N. Ekins, 1662); M 1/4; R
        1/2; Be 1/2
[171]   Wilkins reall character   Wing W 2196 for S. Gellibrand & J. Martyn, 1668;
        M 1/4
[172]   Blounts Law Diccionary   Wing B 3341/3341A for H. Herringman, T.
        Newcomb, R. Chiswell & R. Bentley, sold by T. Salusbury/ for H. Herringman, T.
        Newcomb, R. Chiswell & R. Bentley, sold by J. Salusbury, 1691; M 1/4; ent. to J.
        Martyn, H. Herringman & T. Newcomb, SR 5 July 1670
[173]   Lord Newcastles Country Captaine   Wing N 877 (by William Cavendish,
        Duke of Newcastle) for H. Robinson & H. Moseley, 1649; M 1/4; R 1/2
[174]   Dugdales Origines Juredicialis   Wing D 2490 for C. Wilkinson, T. Dring &
        C. Harper, 1680 (cf. Wing D 2489 for A. Roper, J. Martyn & H. Herringman,
        1671); M 1/4
[175]   Herberts Henry the eight   Wing H 1507B (by Edward Herbert, Lord
        Herbert of Cherbury) for A. Mearne, sold by G. Sawbridge, 1693 (cf. Wing H
        1505B for J. Martyn, S. Mearne & H. Herringman, 1672 and Wing H 1506-
        1507AC (6 issues) for H. Herringman, 1682/ for A. Mearne, 1682/ for A. Mearne,
        sold by T. Sawbridge, 1683/ for R. Littlebury, R. Scott & G. Wells, 1683/ for H.
        Herringman, 1683/ for H. Herringman, sold by T. Passenger, 1683); M 1/4; K; also
        ent. to J. Martyn, S. Mearne & H. Herringman, SR 15 Sept. 1671
[176]   The Varietyes   included in Wing N 877 (by William Cavendish, Duke of
        Newcastle); M 1/4; R 1/2

[1/12]

[177]   Shirleyes doubtfull Heiress   Wing S 3466 *The doubtfull heir,* for H. Robinson
        & H. Moseley, 1652 (this and the next 4 items also issued as Wing S 3486 *Sixe
        new playes,* for H. Robinson & H. Moseley, 1653); M 1/4; R 1/2
[178]   —Impostures   Wing S 3476 for H. Robinson & H. Moseley, 1652; M 1/4;
        R 1/2
[179]   —Brothers   Wing S 3460 for H. Robinson & H. Moseley, 1652; M 1/4; R 1/2
[180]   —Sisters   Wing S 3485 for H. Robinson & H. Moseley, 1652; M 1/4; R 1/2
[181]   —Cardinall   Wing S 3461 for H. Robinson & H. Moseley, 1652; M 1/4; R 1/2
[182]   —Mayor of Quinborough   Wing M 1984/1984A (by Thomas Middleton) for
        H. Herringman, 1661; M 1/4; R 1/2 (also ent. as 'all'); also ent. to H. Herringman,
        SR 13 Feb. 1661 (ent. to H. Robinson & H. Moseley, SR 4 Sept. 1646)
[183]   —Passionate Lovers   Wing C 581/581A (by Lodowick Carlell) for H.
        Moseley, 1655; M 1/4; R 1/2
[184]   —Spartan Ladyes   Greg Θ 54: a 'lost play' by Lodowick Carlell; M 1/4; R 1/2
[185]   —Wilson of Switzer   Greg Θ 55: Arthur Wilson, *The Switzer,* a 'lost play'; M
        1/4; R 1/2
[186]   —The Corporall   Greg Θ 56: a 'lost play' by Arthur Wilson; M 1/4; R 1/2
[187]   —The Princes   included in Wing K 450 Thomas Killigrew, *Comedies and
        tragedies,* for H. Herringman, 1664 (ent. to H. Robinson & H. Moseley, SR 4
        Sept. 1646); M 1/4; R 1/2
[188]   —Fatall Friendship   Greg Θ 57: a 'lost play' by 'Burroughs'; M 1/4; R 1/2
[189]   Beaumonts and Fletchers mad Lover   Wing B 1582 *Fifty comedies and
        tragedies,* for J. Martyn, H. Herringman & R. Marriot, 1679, includes this and the
        next 34 items, together with nos. 288-290 below (cf. Wing B 1581 *Comedies and
        tragedies,* for H. Robinson & H. Moseley, 1647); M 1/4; R 1/2
[190]   —False One   included in Wing B 1582; M 1/4; R 1/2 (as 'safe one')
[191]   —Masque of Greyes Inn   included in Wing B 1582; M 1/4; R 1/2
[192]   —Nice Valour   included in Wing B 1582; M 1/4; R 1/2
[193]   —Witt at severall weapons   included in Wing B 1582; M 1/4; R 1/2
[194]   —Fair maid of the Inn   included in Wing B 1582; M 1/4; R 1/2
[195]   —Little French Lawyer   included in Wing B 1582; M 1/4; R 1/2
[196]   —Loyall Subject   included in Wing B 1582; M 1/4; R 1/2

[Column III:]
[197]   Beaumont and Fletchers Spanish Curat   included in Wing B 1582; M 1/4;
        R 1/2
[198]   —Custome of the Country   included in Wing B 1582; M 1/4; R 1/2
[199]   —Dubble Marriage   included in Wing B 1582; M 1/4; R 1/2
[200]   —Wife for a month   included in Wing B 1582; M 1/4; R 1/2
[201]   —Island princes   included in Wing B 1582; M 1/4; R 1/2
[202]   —Pilgrim   included in Wing B 1582; M 1/4; R 1/2
[203]   —Lawes of Candy   included in Wing B 1582; M 1/4; R 1/2
[204]   —Womans prise   included in Wing B 1582; M 1/4; R 1/2
[205]   —Knight of Malta   included in Wing B 1582; M 1/4; R 1/2
[206]   —The Captaine   included in Wing B 1582; M 1/4; R 1/2
[207]   —Noble Enemy   included (as *The humorous lieutenant, or generous enemies*) in
        Wing B 1582; M 1/4; R 1/2
[208]   —Woman pleased   included in Wing B 1582; M 1/4; R 1/2

[1/12]

[209] —Bonduca included in Wing B 1582; reprinted as Wing B 1584 for R. Bentley, 1696; M 1/4; R 1/2
[210] —Chances included in Wing B 1582; reprinted as Wing F 1339 for R. Bentley, 1692; M 1/4; R 1/2
[211] —Sea Voyage included in Wing B 1582; M 1/4; R 1/2
[212] —Maid of the Mill included in Wing B 1582; M 1/4; R 1/2
[213] —Queen of Corinth included in Wing B 1582; M 1/4; R 1/2
[214] —Coxcomb included in Wing B 1582; M 1/4; R 1/2
[215] —Noble gentleman included in Wing B 1582; M 1/4; R 1/2
[216] —Beggars bush included in Wing B 1582; M 1/4; R 1/2
[217] —Honest mans fortune included in Wing B 1582; M 1/4; R 1/2
[218] —Martiall Maid included (as *Love's cure, or the martiall maid*) in Wing B 1582; M 1/4; R 1/2
[219] —Valentinian included in Wing B 1582; M 1/4; R 1/2
[220] —The prophetesse included in Wing B 1582; M 1/4; R 1/2 (also ent. as 'all')
[221] —Loves pi[l]grimage included in Wing B 1582; M 1/4; R 1/2 (also ent. as 'all')
[222] —Loves progresse included (as *The lover's progress*) in Wing B 1582; (omitted from M entry); R 1/2 (also ent. as 'all')
[223] —Four plays or morall representacions in One included in Wing B 1582; M 1/4; R 1/2
[224] —Davenants Love and honour Wing D 320 *The works of Sr William D'Avenant,* for H. Herringman, 1673, includes this and the next 3 items; M 1/4; R 1/2
[225] —The Distresse included in Wing D 320; M 1/4; R 1/2
[226] —Fair Favourite included in Wing D 320; M 1/4; R 1/2
[227] —News from plymouth included in Wing D 320; M 1/4; R 1/2

All the entire Copyes of these Bookes following.
[228] Mauges French Grammar Wing M 1340C/1341/1341A (by Claude Mauger) for R. Bentley & S. Magnes, 1694/ for R. Bentley, 1694/ printed, 1696 (cf. Wing M 1340bA/1340dA for J. Martyn, 1679/for R. Bentley & M. Magnes, 1684 etc.); M 'sold' (assigned by T. Davies to J. Martyn, 24 Aug. 1671, and ent. to Martyn, SR 2 Dec. 1672)
[229] Andrewes Devocions and his Manuall for the Sick Wing A 3137/ 3137A/3138/3139 Lancelot Andrewes, *A manual of the private devotions* (including 'Directions for the sick') for R. Bentley, 1674/ for A. Churchill, 1682/ for W. Freeman, 1692; ent. to H. Moseley, SR 12 June 1649
[230] The Vanity of Arts and Sciences by Cornelius Agrippa Wing A 792 for R. Bentley & D. Brown, 1694; ent. to R. Everingham, SR 16 July 1678; ent. to S. Speed, SR 16 Nov. 1677
[231] D^r. Dentons Burnt Child dreads the fire Wing D 1064 for J. Magnes & R. Bentley, 1675
[232] Chamberlyns divine Poems possibly Wing C 1817 Sir James Chamberlayne, *A sacred poem,* for R. Bentley & M. Magnes, 1680
[233] Coppingers Poems Wing C 6108 for R. Bentley & M. Magnes, 1682

[all]

[234]   Chamberlains poem Mimeductum ad Cælum   Wing B 3552 Giovanni
Bona, *Manuductio ad coelum* (translated by Sir James Chamberlayne) for R.
Bentley & M. Magnes, 1681

[235]   The Offices of the Mouth   Wing R 1933 Giles Rose, *A perfect school of
instructions for the officers of the mouth,* for R. Bentley & M. Magnes, 1682

[236]   Prospect of humane Misery   Wing B 3366A Pierre Boaistuau, *The theatre of
the world: or, a prospect of humane misery,* for R. Bentley & M. Magnes, 1679

[237]   Vanity of honour wealth and pleasure   Wing H 468 [by James Halsey] for
J. Magnes & R. Bentley, 1678

[238]   The *natu*rall history of the passions   Wing C 3684A (by Walter Charleton)
for J. Magnes, 1674

[239]   Platoe's Apology of Socrates English   Wing P 2405 for J. Magnes & R.
Bentley, 1675

[240]   Patrick Fasts Sermon   Wing P 840 (by Simon Patrick) for J. Magnes & R.
Bentley, 1678

[241]   The earnest request of John Standish   Not identified among John
Standish's published sermons (cf. Wing S 5215-5219), but perhaps related to the
next item, a reply to Standish

[242]   Fallshood Unmaskt   Wing P 796 (by Simon Patrick) for J. Magnes & R.
Bentley, 1676

[243]   Happy Slave 3 parts   Wing B 4349/4349aA (by Sébastien Brémond) for R.
Bentley, sold by G. Cownley, 1685/ for G. Cownley, 1686; *MN* vol. 9

[244]   Count Brion   Wing B 4345 Sébastien Brémond, *The cheating gallant,* for J.
Magnes & R. Bentley, 1677; *MN* vol. 2

[245]   Triumphs of Love   Wing B 4357 (by Sébastien Brémond) for J. Magnes & R.
Bentley, 1678; *MN* vol. 4

[246]   Disorders of Love   Wing D 1188 [by Marie Desjardins, Madame de
Villedieu] for J. Magnes & R. Bentley, 1677

[247]   Essex and Elizabeth   Wing S 2345/2345A *The secret history of . . . Q.
Elizabeth, and the E. of Essex,* for Will with the Wisp, 1695/ Cologne, for Will with
the Wisp, [1695?] (cf. Wing S 2343 for R. Bentley & M. Magnes, 1681); *MN*
vol. 1

[248]   princesse of Cleeves   Wing L 170 [by Marie Motier, Countess de La Fayette]
for R. Bentley & S. Magnes, 1688

[249]   Hatige   Wing B 4352 (by Sébastien Brémond) Amsterdam, for Simon the
African, 1683; *MN* vol. 1

[250]   The Emperour and Empire betraid   Wing C 1672C (by Jean-Paul de
Cerdan) for B. M., 1682; *MN* vol. 12

[251]   The breaches and Controventions of France   Wing B 4336/4336A for R.
Bentley & S. Magnes/ for R. Baldwin, 1684

[252]   The memoirs of the Contabless of Colona   Wing B 4344 Sébastien
Brémond, *The apology: or, the genuine memoires of Madam Marie Manchini,
constabless of Colonna,* for J. Magnes & R. Bentley, 1679

[253]   The Oblidgeing *Mist*ress   Wing O 89 for J. Magnes & R. Bentley, 1678; *MN*
vol. 7

[254]   Fatall Prudence   Wing F 544 for R. Bentley & M. Magnes, 1679; *MN* vol. 6

[255]   The double Cuckhold   Wing B 4358 Sébastien Brémond, *The viceroy of
Catalonia, or the double cuckold,* for J. Magnes & R. Bentley, 1678

[256]   Almanzor and Almanzaide   Wing L 446 [by Mlle de La Roche-Guilhem] for
J. Magnes & R. Bentley, 1678

[all]

[257] The Pilgrim first and 2^d part   Wing B 4353A (by Sébastien Brémond) for R. Bentley, 1684

[258] The last efforts of afflicted Innocence   Wing J 1205 [by Pierre Jurieu] for M. Magnes & R. Bentley, 1682

[259] Idolatry of the Clergy of France   Wing J 1210 [Pierre Jurieu], *The policy of the clergy of France,* for R. Bentley & M. Magnes, 1681

[260] Barovius Prince of the Blood   Wing M 1834 *Meroveus, a prince of the blood-royal of France,* for R. Bentley & M. Magnes, 1682; *MN* vol. 11

[261] Narce Christianismus   Wing M 722 *Mars Christianissimus . . . or, an apology for the most Christian King's taking up arms against the Christians,* for R. Bentley & S. Magnes, 1684

[262] The Princess of Munferrat in 2 parts   Wing B 4355A/4356 (by Sébastien Brémond) for R. Bentley & M. Magnes, 1681; *MN* vol. 10

[263] Don Sebastians 3 parts   Wing D 1847 for R. Bentley & S. Magnes, 1683; *MN* vol. 5

[264] Life of the Duke of Guise   Wing V 44A (by Jean Baptiste du Trousset de Valincour) for R. Bentley & M. Magnes, 1681; *MN* vol. 6

[265] Instruccions for a young Noble Man   Wing T 2307 (by Joachim Trotti de La Chétardie) for R. Bentley & S. Magnes, 1683; *MN* vol. 12

[266] Neapolitan   Wing N 361 for R. Bentley, 1683

[267] Chat Seraglian   Wing P 3204 [Jean de Préchac], *The chaste seraglian,* for R. Bentley & S. Magnes, 1685; *MN* vol. 7

[268] History of the house of Medices   Wing V 111B/112 (by Antoine Varillas) for R. Bentley & S. Magnes, 1686

[269] Princesse of Fesse   Wing P 3207B [by Jean de Préchac] for R. Bentley & M. Magnes, 1682; *MN* vol. 7

[270] Zelinda   Wing V 684 [by Vincent de Voiture] for J. Magnes & R. Bentley, 1676; *MN* vol. 7

[271] Count Gabalis   Wing V 386/386A/386B (by Nicolas de Montfaucon de Villars) for B. M. 'Printer to the Cabalistical Society of the Sages'/for R. Harford, 1680; *MN* vol. 2

[272] Five Nuns Let*te*res to a Cavalier   Wing A 892 [attributed to Marianna Alcoforado], *Five love-letters from a nun,* for R. Bentley, 1693; ent. to R. Bentley, SR 11 Sept. 1686

[273] Five Cavaliers Let*te*res to a Nunn   Wing F 1111 for R. Bentley, 1694

[274] Madamant the Count of Guise   Wing A 3022 *The amours of Madame, and the Count of Guiche,* for B. C., 'Book-seller for the Kingdom of Love, at the Signe of the Three-Cupids', 1680; assigned by executors of W. Cademan to F. Saunders, SR 13 June 1689

[275] Extravagant poet   Wing O 571 (by César François Oudin) for B.M., 1681; *MN* vol. 8

[276] Queen of Polonia   Wing A 3021B *The amours of Bonne Sforza, queen of Polonia,* for R. Bentley, 1684; *MN* vol. 8

[277] Caracter of Love   Wing C 2020A for R. Bentley, 1692; *MN* vol. 4

[278] Don Henrique   Wing D 1844 [by Francisco Loubayssin de la Marca] for R. Bentley & S. Magnes, [1686]; *MN* vol. 6

[279] Count Teckley   Wing P 3203 [Jean de Préchac], *The amours of Count Teckeli,* for R. Bentley & S. Magnes, 1686

[all]

[280]   Great Alexande   Wing C 6596B [attributed to Gatien de Courtilz de Sandras], *The amorous conquests of the great Alcander,* for R. Bentley & S. Magnes, 1685; *MN* vol. 11

[281]   Victorious Lovers   Wing W 455 (by William Walker) for R. Smith, 1698

[282]   Agiates Queen of Sparta   Wing V 161 [by Pierre d'Ortigue de Vaumorière] for R. Bentley & S. Magnes, 1686

[283]   Amorous Abbess   Wing B 4343 (by Sébastien Brémond) for R. Bentley, 1684; *MN* vol. 5

[284]   Nisarotis [altered from Nisaritis]   Wing H 2128 *The history of Nicerotis. A pleasant novel,* for R. Bentley & S. Magnes, 1685; ent. to R. Bentley, SR 12 May 1685

[285]   Art of Poetry by Somes   Wing B 3464 (by Nicolas Boileau-Despréaux, translated by Sir William Soames) for R. Bentley & S. Magnes, 1683

[286]   Gallant Memoirs   Wing B 4347 (by Sébastien Brémond) for R. Bentley & M. Magnes, 1681; *MN* vol. 9

[287]   Turtuff   Wing M 2385 Jean Baptiste de Molière, *Tartuffe,* by H. L[loyd]. & R. B[attersby]. for J. Magnes, 1670 (ent. to R. Battersby, SR 28 June 1670)

[288]   Philaster   Wing B 1601 (by Francis Beaumont & John Fletcher, subsequently adapted by Elkanah Settle) for R. Bentley, 1695 (cf. Wing B 1600 for R. Bentley & S. Magnes, 1687); ent. to W. Leake, SR 25 Jan. 1639 (cf. no. 189 above)

[289]   The Maides Tragedy   Wing B 1597 (by Francis Beaumont & John Fletcher) for R. Bentley & S. Magnes, 1686; ent. to W. Leake, SR 25 Jan. 1639 (cf. no. 189 above)

[290]   Scornfull Lady   Wing B 1612 (by Francis Beaumont & John Fletcher) for D. Newman, 1691; assigned to H. Moseley by the widow of J. Raworth, SR 4 March 1647 (cf. no. 189 above)

[291]   Moore of Venice   Wing S 2942 William Shakespeare, *Othello,* for R. Bentley, 1695 (cf. Wing S 2940/2941 for W. Weak [i.e. Leake], sold by R. Bentley & M. Magnes, 1681/ for R. Bentley & S. Magnes, 1687); ent. to W. Leake, SR 25 Jan. 1639 (cf. also no. 377 below)

[292]   Force Marriage   Wing B 1736 Aphra Behn, *The forc'd marriage,* for J. Knapton, 1690 (cf. Wing B 1734 by H.L. & R.B. for J. Magnes, 1671)

[293]   Towne Fopp   Wing B 1769 (by Aphra Behn) for J. Magnes & R. Bentley, 1677

[294]   Abdelazer   Wing B 1716 (by Aphra Behn) for T. Chapman, 1693 (cf. Wing B 1715 for J. Magnes & R. Bentley, 1677)

[295]   Nero   Wing L 884 Nathaniel Lee, *The tragedy of Nero,* for R. Bentley, 1696 (also in Wing L 845A *The works of Mr. Nathaniel Lee,* for R. Bentley, 1694)

[296]   Gloriana   Wing L 849 (by Nathaniel Lee) for J. Magnes & R. Bentley, 1676 (also in Wing L 845A)

[297]   Rivall Queenes   Wing L 868 (by Nathaniel Lee) for R. Bentley, 1694 (also in Wing L 845A)

[Column IV:]

[298]   Methiridates   Wing L 856 Nathaniel Lee, *Mithridates King of Pontus,* for R. Bentley, 1693 (also in Wing L 845A)

[299]   Cæsar Borgia   Wing L 847 (by Nathaniel Lee) for R. Bentley, 1696 (also in Wing L 845A)

[300]   Theodosius   Wing L 880 (by Nathaniel Lee) for R. Bentley, 1697 (also in Wing L 845A)

[all]

[301] Oedipus   Wing D 2325/2326 (by John Dryden & Nathaniel Lee) for R. Bentley, 1692/ [reprinted] for T. Chapman, [1695?] (also in Wing L 845A)

[302] Kind Keeper   Wing D 2298 (by John Dryden) for R. Bentley & M. Magnes, 1690

[303] Mistaken Husband   Wing D 2318 [attributed to John Dryden] for J. Magnes & R. Bentley, 1675

[304] Calisto   Wing C 7377 (by John Crowne) for J. Magnes & R. Bentley, 1675

[305] Andromecha   Wing R 120 [Jean Racine, translated and adapted by John Crowne], *Andromache,* for R. Bentley, 1675

[306] Destruccion of Jerusalem 2 parts   Wing C 7386 (by John Crowne) for R. Bentley, 1693

[307] Country Witt   Wing C 7381 (by John Crowne) [reprinted] for T. Chapman, 1693 (cf. Wing C 7380 for J. Magnes & R. Bentley, 1675)

[308] Henry the 6th. 2 parts   Wing C 7388-9 (by John Crowne) for R. Bentley & M. Magnes, 1681

[309] Madam Fickle   Wing D 2745 (by Thomas D'Urfey) for R. Bentley, 1691

[310] Fond Husband   Wing D 2727 (by Thomas D'Urfey) for R. Bentley & S. Magnes, 1685

[311] Esquire Old Sap   Wing D 2786 Thomas D'Urfey, *Squire Oldsapp,* for J. Magnes & R. Bentley, 1679

[312] Fool turned Critique   Wing D 2728 Thomas D'Urfey, *The fool turn'd critick,* for J. Magnes & R. Bentley, 1678

[313] Virtuous wife   Wing D 2790 (by Thomas D'Urfey) for R. Bentley & M. Magnes, 1680

[314] Souldiers Fortune   Wing O 565 (by Thomas Otway) for R. Bentley, 1695

[315] Orphan   Wing O 555 (by Thomas Otway) for R. Bentley, 1696

[316] Earl of Essex   Wing B 665 John Banks, *The unhappy favourite: or, the Earl of Essex,* for R. Bentley, 1693

[317] Ann Bullen   Wing B 668 John Banks, *Vertue betray'd: or Anna Bullen,* for R. Bentley, 1692

[318] Mary Queen of Scotts   Wing B 659 John Banks, *The island queens: or, the death of Mary, Queen of Scotland,* for R. Bentley, 1684

[319] Plain Dealer   Wing W 3755 (by William Wycherley) for R. Bentley, 1694

[320] All mistaken or the Mad Cupple   Wing H 2979 (by James Howard) for J. Magnes, 1672

[321] The English Monsieur   Wing H 2980 (by James Howard) for J. Magnes, 1674; assigned by the executors of W. Cademan to F. Saunders, SR 13 June 1689

[322] Generous enemies   Wing C 6294 (by John Corye) for J. Magnes, 1672

[323] Tamberlaine the great   Wing S 741 (by Charles Saunders) for R. Bentley & M. Magnes, 1681

[324] King Lear   Wing S 2919 [by William Shakespeare, adapted by Nahum Tate], *The history of King Lear,* for R. Bentley & M. Magnes, 1689 (cf. no. 377 below)

[325] Plurality of worlds   Wing F 1417 [by Bernard Le Bovier de Fontenelle] for R. Bentley, 1695

[326] Count of Soizions   Wing C 4586 [Isaac Claude], *The Count d' Soissons,* for R. Bentley & S. Magnes, 1688; *MN* vol. 10

[327] New Disorders of Love   Wing G 666 (by Richard Gibbs) for R. Bentley & S. Magnes, 1687; *MN* vol. 4

[all]

[328] Bassa Buda   Wing O 536 [B. Berenclow], *Ottoman gallantries, or, the life of the Bassa of Buda,* for R. Bentley & S. Magnes, 1687; *MN* vol. 6

[329] Sir Thomas Pope Blunts remarks on poetry   Wing B 3347 for R. Bentley, 1694

[330] —his *natu*rall History   Wing B 3351 for R. Bentley, 1693

[331] —his Essayes on Severall Subjects   Wing B 3350 for R. Bentley, 1697

[332] Art of pleaseing in Conversac*i*on   Wing V 161A [Pierre d'Ortigue de Vaumorière] for R. Bentley, 1691

[333] Cardinall Mazarins Letters   Wing M 1540 for R. Bentley, 1691; ent. to R. Bentley, SR 19 Nov. 1690

[334] Monsieur Collerts Will   Wing C 6601 [Gatien de Courtilz de Sandras], *The political testament of M. Jean Baptist Colbert,* for R. Bentley, 1695; ent. to R. Bentley, SR 7 Aug. 1694 (cf. Wing C 6600B *The political last testament of Monsieur John Baptist Colbert,* for C. Brome, 1695; ent. to C. Brome, SR 3 March 1694)

[335] Loves Secretary   Wing L 3258 *The lover's secretary,* for R. Bentley, 1692

[336] Rivall Mother   Wing R 1546A for R. Bentley, 1694

[337] Unfortunate Lovers   included in Wing D 320 *The works of Sr William D'Avenant,* for H. Herringman, 1673 (cf. nos. 224-6 above)

[338] Irish Princess   Wing V 647 *Vertue rewarded: or, the Irish princess,* for R. Bentley, 1693; *MN* vol. 12

[339] The French Liturgye in 12°   Wing B 3691B (translated by John Durel) *La liturgie,* par R. Everingham et se vend chez R. Bentley, 1695 (cf. Wing B 3621A/3633AD/3649B/3651A/3672D/3683AB/3683AD par J. Bill, 1661/pour J. Dunmore & O. Pulleyn, 1667/pour R. Scott, 1677/ pour R. Scott et se vend chez G. Wells & S. Carr, 1678/par R. E[veringham] pour R. Bentley & S. Magnes, 1683/par R. Everingham et se vend chez R. Bentley & M. Magnes, 1688/par R. Everingham et se vend chez R. Bentley & M. Magnes, 1689); D

[340] The Art of knowing One's Selfe   Wing A 45/46-7 (by Jacques Abbadie) for H. Clements & J. Howell, 1695/ for R. Bentley, 1696

[341] Machiavals Letteres   Wing M 141 *A true copy of a letter written by N. Machiavill,* for R. Bentley, 1691

[342] Mundayes Muliebris   Wing E 3521-3 Mary Evelyn, *Mundus muliebris,* for R. Bentley, 1690

[343] The Innocent Usurper   Wing B 658 [John Banks], *The innocent usurper: or, the death of the Lady Jane Gray,* for R. Bentley, 1694

[344] Cyrus the great   Wing B 656 (by John Banks) for R. Bentley, 1696

[345] Revengefull m*istress*   Wing A 4313/4313A (by Philip Ayres) for R. Bentley & R. Wellington/ for R. Wellington, 1696

[346] Lord Cutts Poems   Wing C 7709 (by John Cutts, Baron Cutts) for R. Bentley & S. Magnes, 1687

[347] —his Poem on the death of the Queene   Wing C 7708A for R. Bentley, 1695

[348] The history of the intrigues and Gallantry of Christiana Queen of Sweden   Wing F 2076A [by Christian Gottfried Franckenstein] for R. Baldwin, 1697

[1/2]

Of the Copyes of these bookes Following One moiety or halfe parte

[349]   D^r. Whitbys Answer to Cressy   Wing W 1736 Daniel Whitby, *Romish*
doctrines not from the beginning, or a reply to . . . S. C. [Serenus Cressy], for T.
Basset & J. Magnes, 1664; ent. to T. Basset, SR 6 Nov. 1663

[350]   —Of host Worshipp   Wing W 1719 for H. Brome, R. Bentley & M. Magnes,
1679

[351]   —Of Idolatry   Wing W 1722 for T. Basset & J. Magnes, 1674

[352]   D^r. Dentons hora Subsessiva   Wing D 1065 for T. Basset & J. Magnes, 1664

[353]   Love given Over   Wing G 1426 [by Robert Gould] for R. Bentley & J.
Tonson, 1690

[354]   Heroine Musqueteer   Wing P 3206/3208/3208B [by Jean de Préchac] for J.
Magnes & R. Bentley, & R. Tonson, 1678/ for J. Magnes & R. Bentley, & J.
Tonson, 1678/ for J. Magnes & R. Bentley, & J. Tonson, 1679

[355]   Life of the Marshall Tureine   Wing C 6598 [attributed to Gatien de Courtilz
de Sandras], *The history of the life and actions of . . . the Viscount de Turenne*, for
D. Newman & R. Bentley, 1686

[356]   King of France and Madam Lavalier   Wing P 203A *The palace royal, or the*
amours of the French King and Madam Lavalier, for R. Bentley, 1696; assigned by
executors of W. Cademan to F. Saunders, SR 13 June 1689

[357]   Duke of Guise   Wing D 2265 (by John Dryden & Nathaniel Lee) for R.
Bentley & J. Tonson, 1687

[358]   City Politicks   Wing C 7379 (by John Crowne) for R. Bentley & J. Hindmarsh,
1688

[359]   Sir Courtly Nice   Wing C 7405 (by John Crowne) for R. Bentley & J.
Hindmarsh, 1693

[360]   Common Wealth of Woman   Wing D 2715 (by Thomas D'Urfey) for R.
Bentley & J. Hindmarsh, 1686

[361]   Banditti   Wing D 2700 (by Thomas D'Urfey) for R. Bentley & J. Hindmarsh,
1686

[362]   The Atheist   Wing O 541 (by Thomas Otway) for R. Bentley & J. Tonson,
1684

[363]   Breif hist. of monasticall Orders   Wing G 394/394A [attributed to Antonio
Gavin] for W. Bentley [*sic*]/ for R. Clavell, 1693

[364]   Memoirs of the Court of France   Wing A 4218A/4219 [attributed to Marie
Catherine de La Mothe, Countess d'Aulnoy] for R. Bentley & T. Bennet, 1692/
for E. Whitlock, 1697

[365]   Bee Yee alsoe ready   Wing W 1488 [by Edward Wetenhall] for R. Bentley &
T. Bennet, 1694

[366]   Marryed Beau   Wing C 7394 (by John Crowne) for R. Bentley, 1694

[367]   Maids last prayer   Wing S 4760 (by Thomas Southerne) for R. Bentley & J.
Tonson, 1693

Of the Copyes of these bookes Following one Third parte or share:-

[368]   Cardinall Richlieu's Will   Wing R 1418 *The compleat statesman*, for R.
Bentley, J. Phillips, & J. Taylor, 1695; ent. to R. Bentley, J. Phillips & J. Taylor,
SR 3 Aug. 1694

[369]   Marriage hater matched   Wing D 2750 (by Thomas D'Urfey) for R. Bentley,
R. Parker, & S. Briscoe, 1693

[1/3]

[370]   Royall Mischeife   Wing M 436 (by Mary de la Rivière, Mrs Manley) for R.
          Bentley, F. Saunders & J. Knapton, 1696
[371]   Rivall [altered from 'Royall'] Sisters   Wing G 1434 (by Robert Gould) for
          R. Bentley, F. Saunders & J. Knapton, 1696
[372]   Lost Lovers   Wing M 435 (by Mary de la Rivière, Mrs Manley) for R.
          Bentley, F. Saunders, J. Knapton & R. Wellington, 1696

Of these Copyes as Followeth:
[373]   One Fifteenth part of Wases Dictionary of [space]   Wing W 1017
          Christopher Wase, *Dictionarium minus: a compendious dictionary English-Latin &
          Latin-English,* for J. Good, 1675; M 1/5; assigned by C. Wase & D. Maxwell to S.
          Gellibrand, S. Thompson, G. Sawbridge, J. Martyn, J. Allestry, E. Brewster, T.
          Davies & T. Dicas, SR 23 April 1662
[374]   One fortye eight part of Riders Diccionary   Wing R 1443 for A. Crooke,
          1659; M 1/16; K; W (pt); B (pt); (earlier shares appear to have been assigned to
          printers by their owners on a temporary basis: cf. 1/6 share ent. to G. Sawbridge,
          SR 30 June 1655, and another 1/6 share ent. to J. Field, SR 7 Dec. 1660)
[375]   One Twenty Fourth part of plutarchs Moralls English   Wing P
          2642aA/2644C/2647/2649A/2651 second edition, 5 vols, for R. Bentley, 1690; Wing
          P 2642A/2645/2648/2650/2652 [reissued] for T. Sawbridge, M. Gilliflower, R.
          Bentley, S. Crouch, A. Churchill, W. Freeman, J. Taylor, T. Bennet, R. Parker, &
          S. Anson, 1691; Wing P 2643/2646/2649/2651/2653 [reprinted] by T. Braddyll, sold
          by most booksellers in London & Westminster, 1694: M 1/8; K; W (pt); B (pt);
          (also ent. to J. Gellibrand, SR 10 Nov. 1683)
[376]   One Twenty fourth part of Camdens Brit. English   Wing C 359 *Camden's
          Britannia newly translated into English,* for A. Swalle, & A. & J. Churchill, 1695; M
          1/8; K; W (pt); B (pt); (cf. pt assigned by Mrs A. Legatt to J. Field, SR 7 Dec.
          1660; pt sold by A. Hebb to J. Legatt, H. Hood, A. Roper & R. Tomlyn, SR 2
          July 1653; 1/12 share assigned by M. Sparke to A. Hebb, SR 2 Oct. 1641)
[377]   One third part of Shakespeeres playes   Wing S 2915/2916/2917 for H.
          Herringman, E. Brewster, & R. Bentley/ for H. Herringman, E. Brewster, R.
          Chiswell, & R. Bentley/ for H. Herringman, sold by J. Knight & F. Saunders,
          1685; M 1/2; assigned by the executor of E. Cotes, widow of R. Cotes, & ent. to J.
          Martyn & H. Herringman, SR 6 Aug. 1674
[378]   One third part of paradise regained with Sampsons Agonistes   Wing M
          2154 (including Wing M 2177) (by John Milton) sold by R. Taylor, 1688;
          [reprinted, but not in Wing, though included in Wing M 2163] sold by J.
          Whitlock, MDCCXV [i.e. 1695]; ent. to J. Starkey, SR 10 Sept. 1670
[379]   One Fourth part of Miltons paradise lost   Wing M 2149 for R. Bentley &
          J. Tonson, 1691 (cf. Wing M 2150/2150A [reissued] for J. Tonson, 1692/ for J.
          Tonson, 1693; Wing M 2151 (included in Wing M 2163) [reprinted] for J. Tonson,
          1695); ent. to B. Aylmer, SR 24 July 1683; ent. to S. Simmons, SR 20 Aug. 1667
[380]   One fourth part of Diogenes Laertius   Wing D 1517 *The lives, opinions,
          and remarkable sayings of the philosophers,* for R. Bentley, W. Hensman, J. Taylor
          & T. Chapman, 1696 (cf. Wing D 1516 for E. Brewster, 1688)

Finis

Scratching the surface:
engravers, printsellers and the London book trade in the mid-18th century

Michael Harris

ILLUSTRATION AND TEXT have merged and separated within the general environment of print since the first application of moveable type. Each was the product of a series of processes, distinct but closely related, which overlapped within the organization of the London print trades. This created intricate patterns through the work force as well as across the output in print. The tendency to separate out the different lines of material has fragmented the view, as text, pictures, maps and music have become part of distinct structures of research, buttressed by the publication of specialist journals and by the form of institutional collections. The process of splitting rather than lumping has its advantages but can also lead to some distortion and dislocation.

This is particularly the case in relation to the first half of the 18th century, a period of intense and dynamic commercial activity. Conventionally, the picture trade continues to be represented as either aspirational, its members striving towards a status in fine art, or as subordinate drudgery in a business entirely controlled by booksellers and printers. Both these views have some validity. However, the purpose of this essay is to problematize the picture and to explore some of the other relationships involving the picture and book trades in a commercial setting. The term 'picture trade' will be used inclusively to identify any of the activities in which engraving was applied to print. What follows can only scratch at the surface of a colossal subject. Even so, the attempt may suggest a modified way of looking at the organization of print in an under-researched period.

The skills involved in the picture trade were based on the techniques of writing and drawing and were therefore accessible to a broad range of individuals ranging from leisured amateurs to desperate professionals. Gentlemen, antiquaries, travellers, surveyors, writing-masters and actors as well as artists were among those who engaged with print through the variable forms of engraving and woodcutting. Within a commercial setting the skills were applied promiscuously and many of those who worked in the picture trade came to copper plates and wood blocks by way of other materials.[1] A number of the most successful started out cutting coats of arms on pewter or silver plate. Equally, the combination of engraving on brass or steel with work on other materials for print can be identified in the careers of a number of London craftsmen. Benjamin Cole, a mathematical instrument maker at the Orrery in Fleet Street, invented a quadrant for use at sea as well as dealing in prints and engraving the plates for a variety of publications.[2] Pewter, silver, brass and steel were all used in the making of plates for printing, and the cross-over between trades was probably common.

The range of activities which involved engraving and which lay along the frontiers of print was suggested in some of the trade cards which, like book-plates, themselves formed one of the jobbing specialities of the trade. About 1730, Thomas Oughtibridge at the Sun in Brooks Market, Holborn, offered a cross-section of services. As well as cutting arms, crests and cyphers on gold and silver plate he could supply 'Copper plates of all Sorts, Stamps Cutt in Brass or wood, for such as can't write. Inscriptions in Brass, Stone, or Marble for Monuments, Shopkeepers' bills, bills of Parcels, or Lading, allso Gentlemens seats neatly Drawn in Perspective, and Engraven if Required. &c.'[3] Engravers were employed on various kinds of high-class jobbing work which could involve print but which led across the frontiers of the print trade into a more generalized commercial setting. John Pine, a high-status English engraver on copper, followed a line of upward mobility: partly at least through his skill as a seal-cutter, which he continued by appointment.[4]

Such mixed activities were probably characteristic of the unknown work-force of engravers moving in and out of the print trades during the first half of the 18th century. None the less, a hierarchy existed among those working as designers or copyists in different sectors defined both by the levels of skill and the materials used. At the upper level were the continental immigrants moving for mixed reasons from the continent, mainly France and Holland, often to work in the first instance on fine-art picture projects. They formed an élite group of craftsmen which included a few individuals, like Michael Vandergucht, who came to be located firmly within the book trade. The native engravers were generally allotted a lower status, though individuals, particularly the mezzotinters of the late 17th century, achieved high levels of reputation and financial success. Those who worked mainly on cutting hardwood blocks, usually box or pear, were categorized by the cheapness of their materials. Employed within the book trade mainly in providing ornaments or head and tail pieces, they were also identified with such low-key activities as providing wrappers and labels for tobacconists or other London tradesmen. Between these upper and lower levels there seems to have been considerable fluidity, and some of those working on copper plate engraving did so to offset dire personal circumstances. 'Mr. Neckens', confined to the Westminster Gate House for debt, scratched out copies of portraits to be used in the extra-illustrated volumes of Clarendon's works offered for sale by John Bullfinch.[5]

Perhaps more characteristic of those moving through the book and picture trades was Francis Hoffman, elements of whose chequered career have been illuminated by David Stoker.[6] Hoffman had some claim to a classical education and had written whiggish pamphlets during Queen

Anne's reign. By the 1720s he was working as a woodcutter, providing the mastheads for several of the London newspapers and ornaments for several leading printers including Henry Woodfall, Charles Ackers and William Bowyer. In the mid-1730s, in correspondence with the Reverend Francis Blomefield who was looking for an experienced and cheap picture-cutter, he provided an optimistic view of his skills and activities. He claimed to be able to provide original drawings and to cut them in both wood and copper. He also described how he spent the summer working on surveys of country estates before returning to London in the winter to work for the printers.[7] This was a timetable followed by many with an interest in picture production. The Buck brothers travelled on regular summer circuits to accumulate the materials which were published through their business in topographical prints, and their tours coincided with the scholarly jaunts of the members of the Society of Antiquaries which could also lead to picture publication. Engraving was a transferable skill and mobility was probably a conventional element in the pattern of employment. When Hoffman claimed in his usual flamboyant way to have 'engraved for most of the printers in Europe', he may have signalled the existence of a pan-European movement of craftsmen which led out of London and balanced the influx of continental engravers.[8] This would have run in tandem with the flow of the engraved materials themselves. For those seeking to earn a living in the London picture trade, working for the booksellers represented one line of regular employment. The demand for their skills in the provision of illustration and ornament appeared clearly in the recurrent references to engravers and engraving in the records of such core members of the trade as the printer William Bowyer and the bookseller Robert Dodsley.[9] Hoffman appears in Bowyer's ledger in the 1720s as a resident employee.[10] However, there was more to life than working in the London book trade and many, if not most, members of the picture trade were independently involved in selling as well as cutting engraved material.

Most of those moving into dealing in prints, maps and music had a background in engraving and many continued to practise their skills on their own behalf or for others. Even so, the open-access character of engraving gave the picture trade a heterogeneous character as it recruited from artists like William Hogarth and Arthur Pond, surveyors like John Rocque, and writing-masters like George Bickham senior and junior, as well as specialists trained in the different areas of engraved material. Like most other trades in London, the picture trade was increasingly dominated by a small number of large-scale businesses dealing across the main categories of engraved print and organizing a wholesale and retail trade by catalogue.[11] In 1735 it was claimed that in 'the whole Extent of *London* and *Westminster*, there are not above Twelve Print-Shops of any note, and these are in the Power and Direction of a very few who are the Richest.'[12] These axe-grinding comments were probably aimed at such long-standing and proliferating dynasties as the Overtons and Bowles. Dealers at this level could achieve substantial financial benefits and in 1740, when the former printseller John Smith, styled 'Esquire', died at his house in Great Russell Street, he was said to be worth 'upwards of £20000'.[13]

In sketching the shape of the expanding picture trade into the mid-18th century, it is particularly difficult to arrive at any realistic estimate of the numbers of people involved. This is partly the result of the fluidity of the work force and the absence of any company focus for the picture trade. Generations of Overtons were routed through the Stationers' Company but, on the whole, apprentices destined for the picture trade were scattered around the City companies, with some concentrations in the Weavers, Merchant Taylors and Goldsmiths.[14] The problem of identification by function is indicated in James Alexander's analysis of the City tax returns of the early 1690s.[15] The names of 21 engravers working in the City are listed though there is no way of knowing which, if any, were associated with print. The same difficulty appears in relation to the 21 carvers listed. Only one printseller was included, 'Mr. Robert Prick', yet Sarah Tyacke has indicated that there were about 16 mapselling businesses, mostly in the City, at this time. Other problems relate to the contemporary estimates made by the artist-engraver George Vertue. He drew up a list of the names of 'all ye Engravers or impres-gravers, Burinators, Sculpture-Gravers Living in London, Ano 1713, as by a Memorial I then made'. It contained 33 names.[16] In 1744 he put together an updated list, more fully classified by interest, which by this time extended to 55 names.[17] Vertue did not include any dealers or engravers of music and did not record all the individuals working at the lower levels of the picture trade, who can sometimes be identified in other ways. His lists suggest an expansion of activity, but his omissions indicate an inclination to emphasize the artistic basis of engraving. In 1763 the compiler of Mortimer's *Universal Directory* followed this line when he included engravers among sculptors, mathematicians and portrait painters in his main category of 'Masters and Professors of the Polite and Liberal Arts and Sciences'.

The clearest sense of the structure of the picture trade emerges in relation to its geographical distribution, though, as usual, the lack of detail can blur the outlines. The picture trade had one geographical focus in the western suburbs of London, centred on Covent Garden. To some extent, it was geared to the presence of the general apparatus of the fine-art business. Painters, many living around the Piazzas, auctioneers, tapestry designers and manufacturers, among others, formed a fruitful environment for the engravers and printsellers whose premises can be identified across Soho, Seven Dials, Leicester Fields, Bloomsbury, Lincoln's Inn and Holborn.[18] This concentration on the western fringe had a modest counterbalance to the east of the City where a cluster of mapsellers were located adjacent to the busiest stretch of the River Thames. However, just as a book trade presence can be identified in all these areas, so the picture trade was also represented in the strongholds of the book trade itself. A few of the more important printsellers were located in and around the precincts of St Paul's Cathedral, as well as in the satellite centre of book printing in Clerkenwell, where the watch and clock trade probably offered an alternative line of employment for the pool of freelance engravers.

The physical overlap between sectors of the print trade was most highly developed within the hectic commercial environment provided by Fleet Street and the Strand. During the first half of the 18th century these thoroughfares, running between the City and Charing Cross, became the primary location for small-scale businesses concerned in the production and distribution of print. Clusters of individuals in the book and picture trades can be identified at the Fleet Bridge, Temple Bar, the Exeter Exchange in the Strand and at Charing Cross as well as further west in Westminster Hall.[19] This was in some sense neutral territory where all elements of the print business rubbed shoulders, using the networks of public houses as a shared means of identifying their premises on imprints and in advertisements.

Some sense of the density of this print-based community can be obtained through the work of Ian Maxted, one of the few historians to take an inclusive view of the London print trades and to construct a topographical account of their locations.[20] Maxted's work is focused in the last quarter of the 18th century, by which time an unquantified expansion seems to have taken place in most areas of the business. The lack of close and detailed research on the first half of the century, partly at least through a general tendency to view the period as either postscript or prelude, makes it impossible to get much beyond this. However, Maxted's analysis is at least suggestive of a build-up which probably began well before 1775. Taking the names identified only with the two main thoroughfares (a serious limitation given the dense occupancy of the surrounding streets, lanes and alleys) and including all separate entries for each address, whether identifiable with family sequences and partnerships or not, the numbers are impressive. Maxted lists 55 engravers and 53 printsellers on Fleet Street and the Strand as well as some 30 music businesses located in the Strand alone. Other entries relate to map and globe-sellers, paper-hangers, pencil-makers and pen-cutters. Clearly, a well-established and highly localized element of the picture trade was crammed into the neighbourhood. When the predominant booksellers and printers are added, the way in which the two thoroughfares became a primary artery in the general flow of all forms of print begins to take shape.

The rest of this essay will seek to track some of the ways in which the organization of the picture and book trades were intertwined, and to suggest how the patterns of overlap, visible in the physical environment of London, can be extended into the organization of the production and marketing of print. Like the printer-publishers who continued to operate on the fringes of the London book trades, members of the picture trade were closely involved in all the stages of production and distribution. The print, map and music sellers, as publishers, usually owned the plates and blocks on which the materials of their trade were cut. Hoffman was clearly in breach of convention, and the law, when he absconded with the wood blocks he had carved during his short stay with Blomefield, and such attempts to apply a sort of personal copyright were only possible *sub rosa*.[21] The smaller dealers, including Arthur Pond during the early stages of his career as a printseller, farmed out plates for both cutting and printing, though whenever possible the production was concentrated on the premises.[22] Pond, as Louise Lippincott has shown, acquired several presses from the late 1730s by way of the Knaptons; his house in Great Queen Street, Lincoln's Inn, subsequently became an active production centre as well as a show room and distribution point.[23]

The fragmented evidence suggests that dealers of all kinds had an interest in in-house production. At his death in 1700 the mapseller Philip Lea had a room in his house set aside for printing and had 16 hundredweight of copper plates in the shop area.[24] William Henry Toms 'rolled off' (printed) the plates for Blomefield's *History*, which he cut from drawings supplied by the subscribers and by Blomefield himself, while George Bickham junior was found to have a press on his premises when these were searched during legal proceedings in the mid-1740s.[25]

Printsellers were therefore likely to be the producers of a proportion of their own stock. To this extent, their commercial organization ran parallel to the apparently limited number of London printers who also acted as publishers on the fringes of the 'respectable', book-centred trade. One of the most durable businesses in which engraving formed part of an integrated system of production and distribution was established by John Cluer at his office in Bow Churchyard off Cheapside.[26] During the second decade of the century he was cutting and engraving fine prints as well as undertaking high-quality jobbing work for a range of London tradesmen. In 1715 a notice directed specifically at perfumers, apothecaries and distillers advertised his production of shop signs and labels 'either in Gold, Silver or other Colours. Done after an entire new Method, known to no other . . . nicely Cut or Engrav'd on Wood or Copper'.[27]

As an independent printer/publisher, Cluer was inevitably drawn towards the popular end of the market with its mainly non-book interests and street-based distribution system. Part of his picture output consisted of humorous, single-sheet prints which he advertised wholesale in 1718 in the newspaper produced by the Jacobite sympathizer Nathaniel Mist.[28] One of the main selling points was Cluer's oversight and control of each stage of production.

Advertisement concerning Prints cut in Wood.
* * At the Printing Office in Bow-Church Yard, London by John Cluer and Company, all Dealers in black and white, and coloured Prints, may now be supply'd with more Sorts than the whole Town can produce, better cut than others. And Country Chapmen are desired to take notice that as the aforesaid Company are both

the real Cutters and Printers of them, they may and shall be better served than by those who put out both the Cutting and Printing.[29]

This blunt statement was followed by a peculiar and rambling offer of the titles available including the 'Hieroglyphical Love Letters'.

During the 1720s and 1730s, Cluer moved into music printing and publishing, advertised from his 'Printing and Engraving Office' at the sign of the Maidenhead behind Bow Church. His output of this material, printed both from copper-plates and specially designed type, was substantial enough to challenge the well-established entrepreneur John Walsh.[30] Cluer died in 1728 and the Bow Churchyard office passed to his widow Elizabeth who married the foreman Thomas Cobb. Cobb inherited the office at Elizabeth's death in 1731 and in 1736 assigned it to his brother-in-law the printer William Dicey.[31] This reinforced the family overlap between the Cluers and the Diceys and may have brought the printing businesses located in Bow and Aldermary Churchyards under a single management. At all events, from these interlocking production centres engraved pictures flowed on to the market in huge numbers alongside the chapbooks and ballads that made up the bulk of the letterpress output.[32]

The existence of independent lines of production and distribution through which the members of the picture trade organized their work did not imply a separation of interest from other areas of print. A process of convergence between the picture and book trades, characterized by intricate forms of co-operation and conflict, are visible at all levels. Members of the picture trade became, during the first half of the century, deeply implicated in the publication of texts. Some of this material was based on a simple application of the skills of the engraver. Texts cut in metal and rolled off in individual sheets to be sold, like maps and music, individually or in sets became an increasingly diverse element in the pattern of publication. The main line of this material was formed by the educational interests of a string of writing-masters who combined various kinds of teaching with engraving and printselling within the London trade.[33] The decorative and didactic publications, designed for use as copy-books as an aid to learning, covered a range of subjects and rolled through the first half of the 18th century in serial form. During the 1730s and 1740s the market was dominated by the erratic but ever-present sequences engraved and published by George Bickham senior under the general titles of the *Universal penman* (1733-41) and the *British monarchy* (1743-49?).[34]

Engravers with a background in calligraphy used engraved texts to display their skills and persistence: John Sturt cut the *Book of common prayer* (1717) entirely on silver plates while John Pine published his elaborately designed Latin text of Horace (1733-7) in a fully engraved version running to two volumes. Like other forms of print, engraved texts diversified during the first half of the century, particularly through the publication of routine information which may have proved more saleable in this form. John Pine and Benjamin Cole, appointed successively as official

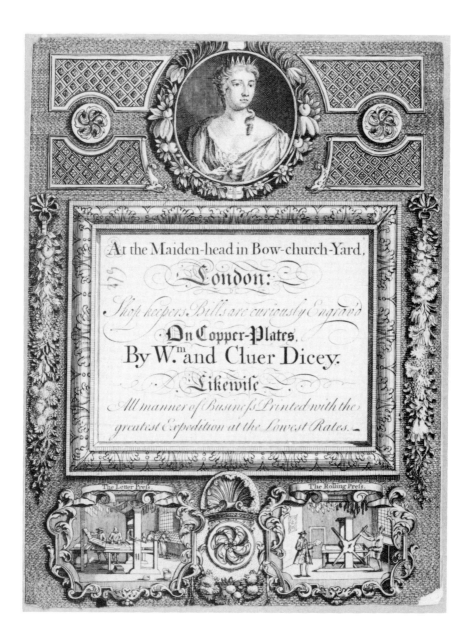

Fig. 1.   Shopbill for the Diceys indicating their mixed letterpress and rolling-press output, *c.*1736.
From the Ambrose Heal Collection of Tradecards and Shopbills. *Reproduced with the*
kind permission of the Department of Prints and Drawings, British Museum.

engravers to the Society of Freemasons, published their constitutions as engraved texts, and in the City various forms of tabular material designed for use in business appeared in increasingly bulky volumes engraved throughout.[35] Whether or how far this represented a means of evading book trade intervention is unclear. Engraving could certainly be used to create a high level of flexibility in publication. In 1740 John Millan offered at his premises opposite the Admiralty in Whitehall, a *Compleat list of the Royal Navy* 'curiously engrav'd by Mr. Child'. It was available bound in folio, quarto, octavo, ninemo, and twelvemo as well as in a single sheet of superfine paper for framing.[36]

As this suggests, even the publication of engraved texts could involve co-operation across the book and picture trades. Engraved texts were an eccentric and limited element in the output of the print trades. Forming common ground between the book and picture dealers were the letterpress texts on specialist topics or with a substantial element of illustration which could be initiated and published through either the book or picture trade. Print, map and music dealers could become involved in book publishing through works which related directly to their main area of specialization. Mount and Page, mapsellers on Tower Hill, had a substantial interest in books on such topics as navigation and gunnery, while a broad range of individuals in the picture trade published works on architecture, surveying, building and mathematics as well as on topography and history.[37] Such works could be organized through the picture trade by individuals or groups working on the same sort of shareholding basis as was usual among the London booksellers. Partnerships in this sector sometimes emerge in relation to the publication of prints and other forms of engraved material.[38] In book publishing, picture trade interest can sometimes be identified if not followed through.

One such project centred on the work of the antiquary and clergyman John Dart. The position of Dart as author is hard to pin down. He may, like Blomefield and a number of other literary and polemical clergymen in mid-century, have been struggling to follow a line of independent publication, working with members of the picture trade as an alternative to becoming a client of the booksellers.[39] At all events, the publication of Dart's text was apparently associated with another project initiated by the engraver James Cole of Hatton Garden. In 1721 Cole issued 'Proposals for engraving and printing by subscription, the monuments of Westminster-Abbey'. These engravings may have been the 142 plates issued about three years later in combination with a long introductory poem and descriptive text by Dart. This work, under the title *Westmonasterium*, appeared in two folio volumes, each with an engraved title and a subscription list followed by a long sequence of the engraved arms of subscribers, as requested in the initial proposals. The handsome appearance of the work was heightened by the inclusion in volume I of a mezzotint portrait of Dart by John Faber and in volume II of a detailed folding view of the interior of the Henry VII chapel by the Dutch engraver James Schynvoet.

The dedication was signed by 'The Proprietors' who were presumably those named on the imprint, led off by the undertaker James Cole.[40] They consisted of the printseller Joseph Smith at the Exeter Exchange, the two John Bowles at their shops in St Paul's Churchyard and at Stocks Market, the bookseller Jeremiah Batley in Paternoster Row and the unclassified Andrew Johnstone in Round Court off the Strand (a hotbed of printsellers and their associates). James Cole persisted in this line of publication and he may have been the sole proprietor of the heavily illustrated history of Canterbury Cathedral, the text also by Dart, which was published in 1726. Cole himself signed the dedication and was followed on the imprint by a modified group from the picture trade which did not include the main City names. In this case, 'J. Hoddle, Engraver, in Bridewell Percinct [sic], near Fleet-Bridge, J. Smith, at Inigo-Jones-Head, near the Fountain Tavern in the Strand; and A. Johnson on the Pav'd Stones in St. Martin's-Lane.' The Dart publications were evidently a product of co-operation mainly, if not entirely, within the picture trade, and were the sort of work which a few years later was more likely to appear in serial form.

It was usual for the lines of commercial co-operation to run across the frontiers of the book and picture trades. Most forms of engraved material were issued with some element of letterpress, printed on paper from the suppliers used by the book printers and booksellers, marketed through overlapping forms of advertisement, including newspapers and handbills, and distributed through many of the same outlets. The mutual interests which coincided at most points in the organization of publication prompted a wide range of joint activities. The partnerships involving members of the picture and book trades, not based on a system of clientage but arising from a combination of business interest and personal connection, are not easy to disentangle.

One of the more clearly defined lines of convergence appeared among the groups of continental immigrants. The localized clusters of mainly French and Dutch Protestants rapidly became associated with print through the import business. By the first decade of the 18th century the French booksellers on the Strand had become an identifiable sub-group within the London book trade, and by the 1720s continental booksellers were visible in the communities established further west in the neighbourhood of St Martin's Lane and Leicester Square.[41] This was fine-art territory where printsellers were dealing in high-quality engravings imported from Paris, Amsterdam and Rome. The import of texts and pictures could form part of the business of a mainstream bookseller such as John Nourse. Sometimes the strands of print came together through partnerships involving members of the picture and book trades.

This was the case with Claude Du Bosc and William Darres. Du Bosc was one of the first wave of skilled engravers to arrive in London during the early years of the 18th century.[42] Employed on a series of prestige projects, his success as an engraver in the French manner enabled him in 1729 to set up as a printseller, initially at the Golden Head in Charles Street, Covent Garden, and by 1740 in Whitcomb Street near Leicester Square.[43] He continued to work as an engraver while publishing several long-running serials, notably Jean Frédéric Bernard's *Religious ceremonies* (1733-7),[44] involving the translation and reworking of continental originals. One of Du Bosc's main commercial interests was the import of prints routed through his contacts in Paris, and in the late 1730s he moved into a partnership with the bookseller William Darres. Their association would repay investigation, but at this stage it is clear that they had a joint interest in the shop at the Three Flower-De-Luces at the corner of the Haymarket and Piccadilly. From this location Du Bosc and Darres were involved in the import of a substantial range of books in most continental languages, on topics which included history, antiquities, architecture and mathematics as well as classical texts.[45] They also published books in several languages which were printed in London by Godfrey Smith, Henry Woodfall and James Betterton, but were also printed abroad at The Hague and Geneva.[46]

Such combinations based on professional and personal interest can be tracked from the picture trade into the heart of the book-trade establishment. The work of Louise Lippincott has opened up one important area of linkage involving the Knaptons, a bookselling dynasty that figured prominently in the hierarchy of the Stationers' Company. The generation of James, John and Paul Knapton, who moved the book business to Ludgate Hill in the mid-1730s, became closely intertwined with the picture trade through their family connections with the fine arts. A long-term interest in publication in this field was developed through two members of the family who practised as artists, George who specialized in portraits and Charles in landscapes. The artist and printseller Arthur Pond moved into the picture trade in close association with the Knaptons and between 1738 and 1744 Charles and his wife organized the printing and sales of engravings at Pond's premises in Great Queen Street.[47] The Knaptons' interest in the publication of long-running and heavily illustrated serials from the 1720s to the 1750s was one manifestation of this personalized picture and book trade integration.[48]

To some extent, the picture trade shadowed the book trade. But with the forms of co-operation and overlap came the equal and opposite elements of ferocious competition and commercial conflict. Struggle occurred across the full spectrum of activities and at all levels as individuals and groups jockeyed for survival or financial advantage. However, as I have argued elsewhere, the London book trade was fractured.[49] Its structure, like that of other trades, was becoming polarized between respectable insiders and piratical outsiders represented by such printer-publishers as William Rayner and Robert Walker. One question arises: does this division manifest itself within the picture trade beyond the skirmishing between engravers and printsellers around the Engravers' Act?[50] Much more research needs to be done before the intricate internal relationships of the members of the picture and book trades can be sorted out. However, here and there, individual engravers and printsellers working in London in mid-century display the characteristics of anti-authoritarian, free-market dealing associated with the alternative trade.

This is most evident in the career of George Bickham junior. The Bickhams senior and junior have a sort of flickering half-life in the literature dealing with the period.[51] Both were writing-masters, engravers and printsellers and their publications are in many respects hard to disentangle without a clear publication statement. During the 1730s and 1740s both published work which fell into the uncontentious territory of routine engraved material. Bickham junior produced educational material and the long-running *Musical entertainer* (1737-9) as well as works on dancing.[52] He also cut trade cards and offered his services as a teacher of drawing. However, the main difference between the Bickhams lay in the move of Bickham junior into the orbit of the alternative trade. Working from two addresses in the Strand, one at the Exeter Exchange, and another at May's Buildings, Covent Garden (each identified by 'the Blackmoors Head'), he became involved in the publication of materials which would never have appeared under the imprint of Bickham senior.[53] His political satires, engraved on single sheets and also sold as fan mounts, identified him with the anti-Walpole grouping, a stance reinforced by his use of the *Champion* in the early 1740s as a medium for his advertisements.[54] He also displayed a willingness to engage with material which lay beyond the frontiers of respectable publishing. In 1741 he engraved the text of Pope's *Essay on Man* for publication and was caught up in the sweep of those involved in piratical letterpress versions. These included Jacob Ilive, a fully-fledged member of the alternative trade. Later in the 1740s Bickham junior was prosecuted for publishing pornography.[55] But perhaps the most significant way in which his career intersected with the printer-publishers of the alternative trade was through his association with the output of William Rayner. The printing office located within the Rules of the King's Bench Prison, south of the river, where Rayner was serving a term for seditious libel, became a dynamic centre for the publication of combinations of pictures and text in serial form.[56]

Rayner's links with the picture trade have yet to be explored. Whether he was engaged in the production of pictures or in the import business, or whether he formed partnerships with individual engravers or printsellers, may emerge from future research. What can be said is that his serials, which became the primary battleground between the alternative and respectable trade, were stuffed with engraved illustration and involved the skills of a range of individuals not easily identified elsewhere. In the mid-1730s he began to accumulate the pictures which were sprayed around in conjunction with a variety of mainly religious texts. His long-running publication of the

Bible in parts was a characteristically gung-ho enterprise in defiance of the Bible Patent,[57] and involved some very confusing variations of the standard model, some of which have been described in the work of R. M. Wiles. The pictures slotted into a long tradition of Biblical illustration and were said in some of the advertisements to be based on continental originals.[58] Many were not attributed, but, even so, the names that do appear on the plates suggest the existence of what might be described as a team of picture-cutters. Their work was initially issued in the mid-1730s with the *Compleat history of the Old and New Testament; or, a family Bible* annotated by the Reverend S. Smith D.D. and as new titles were published under his name the plates reappeared. Smith may have been a fiction and his portrait was said to have been a reworked version of the historian Rapin published by the Knaptons.[59]

Among the engravers working for Rayner was Francis Hoffman.[60] In 1735 he declined to become involved in a dispute over a second-hand press bought by Blomefield as he had 'already taken above 10li this winter' from Rayner and was anxious not to prejudice a valuable source of income.[61] Neither Hoffman's name nor initials appeared on any of Rayner's output, perhaps an indication that he did not wish to broadcast the association within the trade. Some of the names which did appear on the plates recurred in this and other projects. Bickham junior engraved the plate which appeared in the preliminaries of more than one Smith publication: characteristically based on a design by Sir James Thornhill, recently dead. A scatter of other plates also carried his name.

Most frequently present was the name of the engraver James Smith. Rayner was fond of Smiths and a James Smith witnessed his will in 1761.[62] The engraver James Smith cut the author's portrait and a number of the other plates in the religious sequence, as well as working on the *Universal musician; or, songster's delight* published by Rayner later in the 1730s.[63] This Smith also cut the elaborate engraved title for Robert Walker's edition of *The whole duty of man* published in 1735.[64] Another of those named in the religious sequences was John Carwitham, described variously in advertisements as painter, engraver and printseller, who published his own engravings from premises near St Giles, Covent Garden.[65] Others were named on the plates and folding maps and can, like Henry Roberts, be identified as engravers and printsellers working elsewhere in the London picture trade. The quality was mixed. Some plates stand up to scrutiny, others may reflect a rapid turn-around as well as limited skill. The series, which ran to about 150 pictures on completion, contains scenes in which lopsided figures engaged in dramatic but wooden action, and must have derived its appeal mainly from cheapness.

The sense of a division running through the print business generally, and separating out the linked sectors of the respectable and the alternative trades in books and pictures, can perhaps be identified in a clash, also in the mid-1730s, between Du Bosc and Rayner. As usual the conflict was focused on a serial, on this occasion concerned with an historical subject. During the early stages of his career in England Du Bosc had worked with others on a series of engraved plates showing the victories of the Duke of Marlborough.[66] It may have been a vestigial interest in this subject that prompted him in the mid-1730s to embark on the serial publication of *The military history of the late Prince Eugene of Savoy and of the late John Duke of Marlborough*, which described the course of the war between 1701 and 1706.[67] Du Bosc himself appeared as the engraver on most of the plates, maps and plans, while the French engravers he had brought over to work on the *Religious ceremonies* provided the head and tail pieces.[68] The work was to be issued in weekly parts at 1s each, the whole to be completed in just over a year at a total cost of about £2 16s. Both in design and execution, the project was a highly respectable one. Subscriptions were taken in by the Knaptons and Darres as well as eight printsellers, including two Bowles and an Overton, and local dealers in Norwich, Peterborough, Dublin and Exeter. The letterpress was to be printed by James Bettenham in the City.[69]

It was as this elaborate enterprise set sail into the market that Rayner launched his rival scheme. Using a virtually identical text and the same title, Rayner assembled his familiar team of engravers. The plates, fewer in number but larger in size, with a denser and more lively content than Du Bosc's rather enervated rococo material,[70] carried the usual names: Bickham junior, John Carwitham, a Smith and Henry Roberts among others. Following abruptly on the Engraving Act, both carried a publication statement on the plates, Du Bosc's 22 September 1735 and Rayner's 22 November 1735. Rayner's newspaper advertisements carried more user-friendly conditions, stating that the series would be complete in 40 numbers issued in weekly parts at 6d and would involve a total outlay of 10s. They also stated 'That for every whole Sheet Battle-Piece or Siege, done by the best Hands, no more shall be demanded than Three Pence; it shall be at the Option of the Subscriber whether they will have the Cuts or no.' At the same time the plates were issued together in sets under the general title of 'England's Glory'. Subscriptions were taken in by Rayner and three pamphlet sellers and the parts were 'sold by the Hawkers that carry the News'.[71] This was a characteristic Rayner enterprise. The two serials were announced in adjacent notices in the *Daily Advertiser*, the first number of the Du Bosc project to appear the following Thursday and the first of the Rayner version on the preceding Monday. Both ran their course and were subsequently published in book form.

What can be gleaned from this confrontation? It certainly reinforces the view that the book and picture trade were intertwined at all points and that the attempt to isolate the elements of organization and output may lead to difficulties of analysis. Specialists in the various sectors were probably more closely engaged with overlapping activities in the field of print than is usually supposed. Rayner has not received much attention either from book-

Fig.2. Second frontispiece to a reissue of *The military history of the late Prince Eugene of Savoy, and of the late John Duke of Marlborough* (1742). Published by William Rayner and engraved by James Smith. *Reproduced by permission of The British Library Board.*

trade or picture-trade historians, partly, at least, because he was working across both sectors. His interest in the picture trade was underlined in the advertisements for a subscription sale in which he probably had a dominant interest.[72] As well as the multiple copies of his illustrated and other serials in different formats, the final section of 'Copper-Plate Prints' listed:

1000 Sets of *England's Glory*: containing Nine Sheets in a Set of Copper-plate Cuts, representing the Sea-Fights, Bombardments &c. in the Reign of Queen Anne. 2s. each.
1000 Sets ditto of the Battles, Sieges, &c. in the said Reign. 2s. each.
1500 Sets of the Cartoons of Raphael Urbino, taken from the Original at Hampton Court. 2s. each.

The last of the entries contains an intriguing echo of Rayner's relationship to Du Bosc, who had first come to England in 1711 as one of a team employed to engrave the cartoons at Hampton Court. At all events, the numbers are large and Rayner's position in relation to the picture trade would repay closer investigation.

This essay has set out to explore some of the relationships within the print business which are often obscured by forms of specialization. The picture and book trades had their own spheres of influence. However, the areas of overlap were both more complex and far-reaching than is usually acknowledged. It is difficult to identify the configurations within the book trade without taking account of the intricate linkage involved in the publication of the full range of print. The products themselves flowed through the market, coalescing around areas of well-defined public interest such as the theatre and news. Texts, pictures, maps and music formed part of an integrated system which involved the London book trade but extended well beyond it. These remarks have only scratched a few faint lines on the plate. When it is inked up it may be possible to obtain a clearer impression.

References

1. William Hogarth and George Vertue were both apprenticed to London silversmiths, while the engraver Edward Kirkall learnt the skills in Sheffield where his father was a locksmith. Joseph Simpson senior was one of many who worked their way up from cutting arms on pewter and brass to engraving for print. Ronald Paulson, *Hogarth*, vol.i, The *'Modern Moral Subject', 1697-1732* (New Brunswick/London: Rutgers University Press, 1991), p.38 *et seq.*; *Vertue note books*, vol.iii (Oxford: Walpole Society, vol.22, 1933-4), pp.6, 20.
2. The name Benjamin Cole seems to have referred to more than one London tradesman of the period with an interest in engraving. A long and inconclusive correspondence on identification appears in the Ambrose Heal collection of tradecards and shopbills (Heal), British Museum Department of Prints and Drawings, 59 (Engravers). This Cole seems to have taken over the shop of Thomas Wright, globe-maker. An account of his invention appeared in *The description and use of a new quadrant* (London, 1749).
3. Heal, 59. A similar variety of services was offered by Sutton Nicholls in Tower Street, though his list, which included maps, charts and groundplots, was more artistic. He identified 'all Sorts of Pictures viz History, Perspective, Architect, Gardening & Landskips &c.' and stated that he 'also Cutts on Wood or Mettal for Book-printers or Book-sellers'.

4. In advertisements for his engraved edition of Horace, Pinc was described as 'Bluemantle Pursuivant at Arms, and Chief Engraver of Seals to His Majesty', *General Advertiser*, Friday 11 May 1750. A number of engravers specified work for jewellers on their trade-cards, including John Kirk of St Paul's Churchyard, Heal 59. Engravers on glass formed a related group, including Frans Greenwood (1680-1763), the Dutch poet and glass engraver.

5. John Bullfinch, 'Memorandum book' (1701-28), cited in Louise Lippincott, *Selling art in Georgian London: the rise of Arthur Pond* (New Haven/London: Yale University Press, 1983), p.15. Extra-illustrating Clarendon's *History* was a recurrent activity among the publishers of prints.

6. *The correspondence of the Reverend Francis Blomefield (1705-52)*, ed. David A. Stoker, Norfolk Record Society, lv (1990); also published by the Bibliographical Society (1992). The same author has published related material in 'Blomefield's History of Norfolk', *Factotum* (newsletter of the ESTC, British Library), 26 (July 1988), pp.17-22 and 'The peripatetic woodpecker: or, more tales from Hoffman', *Factotum*, 39 (February 1995), pp.14-18. See also R. J. Goulden, 'Further light on Francis Hoffman', *Factotum*, 37 (September 1993), pp.22-3.

7. Hoffman to Blomefield, 27 December 1735; 23 January 1736: *Blomefield*, pp.122, 137.

8. Hoffman referred to a 20-year period during which he had also worked 'for every printer in our own dominions' as well as being involved in selling letters between printers and printing his own cuts; 31 December 1735: *Blomefield*, p.123.

9. Entries under 'engraver' and 'engraving' in the topical index to *The Bowyer ledgers*, ed. Keith Maslen and John Lancaster (London: The Bibliographical Society; New York: The Bibliographical Society of America, 1991). *The correspondence of Robert Dodsley, 1733-64*, ed. James E. Tierney (Cambridge: Cambridge University Press, 1988), pp.48-9 *et seq*.

10. *Bowyer ledgers*, 1711 (2 October 1731), p.136.

11. Antony Griffiths, 'A checklist of catalogues of British print publishers c.1650-1830', *Print Quarterly*, 1 (1984), p.4.

12. *The case of designers, engravers, etchers &c. stated* (London: 1735), cited in David Hunter, 'Copyright protection for engravings and maps in eighteenth-century Britain', *The Library*, 6th ser., 9 (1987), p.134.

13. *London Evening Post*, Saturday 29 January 1740. John Smith was one of the most successful mezzotinters of the late 17th century, an activity he probably combined with printselling. Success of this sort was matched by the downward spirals of other engravers such as Robert White senior and junior and Marcellus Laroon. Vertue often identifies the shifting status of members of the picture trade.

14. The affiliations of engravers have not been worked out in any systematic way. The Painter-Stainers may have been one of the companies which provided a focus, even though artists had ceased to enrol by the early 18th century. Hogarth was apprenticed through the Merchant Taylors, and Sarah Tyacke listed this company, as well as the Weavers and Stationers, in relation to the London map-sellers. Paulson, *Hogarth*, vol.i, p.39; Sarah Tyacke, *London map-sellers, 1660-1720* (Tring: Map Collector Publications, 1978), p.xv.

15. J. M. B. Alexander, 'The economic and social structure of the City of London, c.1700', unpublished Ph.D. thesis, London School of Economics, 1989. 'Index to tax assessments arranged by occupations' (on a computer print-out) is available at the Corporation of London Record Office. The study is based on the Poll Tax (1692) and the '4s in the £' tax (1693).

16. *Vertue note books*, vol.ii, (Oxford: Walpole Society, vol.20, 1931-2), p.11.

17. *Vertue note books*, vol.vi, (Oxford: Walpole Society, vol.30. 1951-2), pp.197-8.

18. Vertue knew 11 artists living in the Piazzas at Covent Garden, Lippincott, *Selling art*, p.15. For the striking presence of the tapestry works in Soho see *Survey of London*, vol.xxxiv, *The parish of St Anne, Soho* (London: Athlone Press, 1966), pp.515-20. Engravers advertised their services for calico printers and were involved in wallpaper designing and printing and in the publication of a range of pattern books.

19. Pamphlet-sellers, working out of small-scale premises along this route, formed an important component of the infrastructure of print.
20. Ian Maxted, *The London book trades, 1775-1800* (Exeter: the author, Exeter Working Papers in British Book Trade History, 1985; revised introduction, 1991).
21. Nicholas Hussey to Doctor Gaylard, 127, 3 March 1736, *Blomefield*, p.147.
22. Until 1737 Arthur Pond made regular payments to 'Wyatt for printing', account books cited in Lippincott, *Selling art*, p.129.
23. *Ibid.*, p.132.
24. Tyacke, *Map-sellers*, pp.120-2.
25. Introduction, *Blomefield*, pp.39-40; David Hunter, 'Pope v. Bickham: an infringement of *An Essay on Man* alleged', *The Library*, 6th ser., 9 (1987), pp.268-73.
26. Cluer was apprenticed to Thomas Snowden in 1695 and freed by him in 1702, *Stationers' Company apprentices, 1701-1800*, ed. D. F. McKenzie (Oxford: Oxford Bibliographical Society, 1978), no.7631, p.326. He is shown here to have enrolled seven apprentices between 1718 and 1726, p.79. By 1713 the personal link between Cluer and the Northampton printer William Dicey, through his marriage to Dicey's sister Elizabeth, had been formed. The interchange of family names had begun by this time, Victor E. Neuburg, 'The Diceys and the chapbook trade', *The Library*, 5th ser., 24 (1969), p.220.
27. Advertisement in the *Weekly Journal*, 4 January 1718, cited in Charles Humphries and William C. Smith, *Music publishing in the British Isles* (Oxford: Basil Blackwell, 1970), p.21.
28. John Cluer was listed by Samuel Negus in 1723 among those 'Said to be High Flyers'. Negus should have known, as Cluer turned over an apprentice to him in July 1723, *Stationers' Company apprentices*, no.1830, p.79.
29. Advertisements in the *Weekly Journal; or, Saturday's Post*, Saturday 8 February 1718 *passim*.
30. Some elements of the music publishing carried out by Cluer, often in association with B. Creake at the Bible in Jermyn Street, can be followed in the materials collected in the data base compiled by Rosamond McGuiness at Royal Holloway College, London. The types for printing music in letterpress were said to have been invented by Cluer and his associate (foreman) Thomas Cobb, *London Journal*, Saturday 13 July 1728.
31. Neuburg, 'Diceys', p.221.
32. For some discussion of the Diceys and the print trade see Gilles Duval, 'The Diceys revisited', *Factotum*, 35 (August 1992), pp.9-11. Also follow-up comment by Mary Hollis and then by Duval again in 36 (February 1993), p.27; 40 (December 1995), pp.13-18. Two catalogues of the general output have survived for 1754 and 1764. In the latter, issued by Cluer Dicey and Richard Marshall, over 1,000 separate engravings were listed along with 150 chapbooks and nearly 3,000 ballads. Griffiths, 'Checklist'; Neuburg, 'Diceys', p.223.
33. Ambrose Heal, *The English writing-masters and their copy-books, 1570-1800; a biographical dictionary & a bibliography* (Cambridge: Cambridge University Press, 1931).
34. P. H. Muir, 'The Bickhams and their *Universal penman*', *The Library*, 4th ser., 25 (1945), pp.162-84. In 1731 Bickham junior was associated with Cobb and Dicey in the publication of copy-books, imprint of *Fables, and other short poems* (London: [1731]).
35. For Pine and Cole see Ambrose Heal, 'The trade cards of engravers', *Print Collectors' Quarterly*, July 1927, p.30. Among the engraved works aimed at the business market were those by John Smart and also by James Lostau whose second book of the *Manual mercantile* (London: 1735) ran to 446 engraved pages. This was one of the first publications to carry the copyright statement required by the Act: Hunter, 'Copyright', pp.128-47.
36. Advertisement in the *Daily Advertiser*, Thursday 2 April 1741.
37. Thomas R. Adams, *The non-cartographical, maritime works published by Mount and Page* (London: occasional papers of the Bibliographical Society, 1, 1985). Both the range and extent of the texts published by engravers and printsellers can be indicated by accessing imprints through the ESTC.
38. During the committee hearings leading up to the Engravers' Act evidence was given by Henry Fletcher that he was concerned with Mr Castles and Mr Furbour 'in Partnership in designing and engraving a Sett of Flower Prints, which cost about £500', *House of*

Commons Journals, 22, 14 February 1735, p.381. A string of printsellers were also concerned in the purchase and re-publication of the striking engravings of the gardens at Stowe in 1746: information from Michael Symes, Birkbeck College.

39. Among those who published through the picture trade was the antiquary William Maitland whose history of London (1739) was organized outside the conventional book-trade system.

40. In the mid-1720s James Cole was involved in competition with Cluer and Creake in the publication of music. He was one of those taking in subscriptions to a rival set of opera songs by Peter Fraser which were also collected at 'Mr. Tomm's great Glass Shop in Cheapside, over against Stocks-Market. Mr. Bristow, Harpsicod-maker [*sic*]; at the Anodyne Necklace near Temple-Bar. As also at most of the Musick Shops and great Coffee Houses in Town', *Daily Journal*, 5 November 1725.

41. Katherine Swift, '"The French Booksellers in the Strand": Huguenots in the London book trade, 1685-1730', *Proceedings of the Huguenot Society*, xxv, 2 (1990), pp.123-39.

42. Du Bosc (1682-1745?) came to England from Paris in 1711 and remained at work in London into the mid-1740s. Elements of his career can be reconstructed through the Vertue note books where he appears as a skilful but contentious member of the picture trade.

43. *Vertue note books*, vol.iii, p.41. Advertisement in the *Daily Advertiser*, Thursday 5 February 1741.

44. *The ceremonies and religious customs of the various nations of the known world*, published in French at Amsterdam between 1723 and 1743 with plates by Picart; R. M. Wiles, *Serial publication in England before 1750* (Cambridge: Cambridge University Press, 1957), p.288.

45. Advertisements for catalogues in the *Daily Advertiser*, Wednesday 18 March; Tuesday 24 November 1741.

46. The printers and locations were included in the imprints of the books in several languages printed for Du Bosc and Darres. For some comment on the work of Godfrey Smith see Michael Harris, 'Literature and commerce in eighteenth-century London: the making of the *Champion*' in *Telling people what to think: early eighteenth-century periodicals from The Review to The Rambler*, ed. J. A. Downie and Thomas N. Corns (London: Frank Cass, 1993), pp.100-1.

47. Lippincott, *Selling art*, p.8 *et seq.*

48. A focus for this activity was provided by the publication of a sequence of illustrated editions of the history of England by Rapin de Thoyras. In the 1720s the Knaptons published a small format edition in serial form, followed in the 1730s by a folio edition which provided work for George Vertue for over three years. In 1747 they published a three-volume abstract of the history re-using the plates from the 1720s. In the late 1740s the Knaptons also co-operated with Robert Dodsley in the publication of a picture series under the title *English history delineated*; subscription arrangements in *General Advertiser*, Monday 30 April 1750. For the Knaptons' and also for rival series of Rapin translations see Wiles, *Serial publication*, appendix B.

49. Michael Harris, 'Paper pirates: the alternative London book trade in the mid-eighteenth century' in *Fakes and frauds: varieties of deception in print and manuscript*, ed. Robin Myers and Michael Harris (Winchester/Detroit: St Paul's Bibliographies, 1989), pp.47-69.

50. The Act (8 Geo.II, cap.13) provided protection for the designers of engraved work threatened by piracy of various kinds. As David Hunter has pointed out, it fitted into a series of protective measures aimed at securing non-literary copyrights. During the 18th century legislation was applied to maps, music, linen and calico fabrics and sculpture, Hunter, 'Copyright'. p.128. The results of the Engravers' Act on the picture trade have yet to be examined in detail.

51. The Bickhams are usually described as father and son and their dates, as affirmed by Heal, given as senior (1684?-1758) and junior (1706-71). On the other hand, Heal comprehensively mixes up their careers as well as reasonably proposing that John Bickham, author of the *Fables* [1731], was brother of George junior.

52. Moira Goff, 'George Bickham junior and the Art of Dancing', *Factotum*, 36 (February 1993), pp.14-18.
53. Joint addresses in the *Champion*, 131, Saturday 13 September 1740. Other advertisements appeared between March and November 1740.
54. Bickham junior also had an interest in letterpress politics. In 1740 he appeared on the imprint as publisher of *The life and death of Pierce Gaveston, . . . by way of caution to all crowned heads and evil ministers* (1741), by 'a true patriot', with an engraved title and using some of the Woodfall (Hoffman?) ornaments.
55. Harris, 'Paper pirates', p.53; David Hunter, 'Pope v. Bickham'.
56. Harris, 'Paper pirates', p.52; the same author, *London newspapers in the age of Walpole* (Toronto/London: Associated University Presses, 1987), pp.90-8. Rayner used addresses at the Rising Sun in Angel Court, near the King's Bench, Southwark and Bird Cage Alley, near St George's Church, Southwark, before moving to Falcon Court in Southwark: advertisements in the *Daily Advertiser*, Monday 24 March 1735; Wednesday 9 July 1735.
57. In initial advertisements for the Family Bible Rayner displayed the phrase 'By Permission', while on the title-pages of both completed volumes the royal coat of arms (cut by Hoffman?) was prominently displayed. It seems unlikely that either was authorized. *Daily Advertiser*, Monday 24 March 1735.
58. Reference to 'French Originals' in *Daily Advertiser*, Wednesday 19 January 1737; Wiles, *Serial publication*, pp.71, 310.
59. *Grub Street Journal*, Thursday 20 May 1736, cited in Wiles, *Serial publication*, pp.215-16.
60. This emerges from the Blomefield correspondence. Hoffman was recruited through Doctor Gaylard, a journeyman printer with Jacobite leanings and a close association with Rayner: Harris, *London newspapers*, p.89 *et passim*.
61. Hoffman to Blomefield, 15 January 1736: *Blomefield*, p.134.
62. Will witnessed by George Walker, William Smith and James Smith, PROB 11/870(405), PRO (London).
63. Hans Hammelman, *Book illustration in eighteenth-century England*, ed. and completed by T. S. R. Boase (New Haven/London: Yale University Press for the Paul Mellon Centre, 1975), alphabetical entry J. Smith (wrongly suggested to be Jacob), p.68.
64. Author's copy, not in ESTC.
65. For example, *Daily Advertiser*, Wednesday 5 February 1735; Thursday 1 January 1741.
66. *Vertue note books*, vol.i (Oxford: Walpole Society, vol.18, 1929-30), p.43; vol.vi, pp.187-8.
67. The French original was written by Jean Dumont and Jean Rousset de Missy and was translated into English by John Campbell.
68. Louis Gerard Scotin, his brother and Henri Gravelot, *Vertue note books*, vol.iii, p.67.
69. *Daily Advertiser*, Friday 21 November 1735.
70. *The rococo in England: a symposium*, ed. Charles Hind (London: Victoria and Albert Museum, 1986), p.49 *et seq*.
71. *Daily Advertiser*, Friday 21 November 1735. No holding of the volume completed in 1736 is listed for a British library in the ESTC. The earliest version in the British Library, part of the Grenville collection, is a re-issue of the sheets 'Printed for J. Rowlands, in Exeter Exchange; and Benjamin Stitchall, at the Bible in Clare Court, Drury-Lane. MDCCXLII.' The plates carry the Rayner publication statement of 1735. See illustration.
72. 8,000 tickets were issued at 2s 6d each to be drawn by 'Mr. Foubert's Mathematical Machine'. The purchaser of the first to be drawn would receive a special prize and tickets were available from Mr Bly's in Russell Court, Drury Lane, Mrs Dodd's at Temple Bar and Mr Cook's and Mrs Nutt's at the Royal Exchange, *Universal Weekly Journal*, Saturday 5 May 1739.

John Baskett, the Dublin booksellers, and the printing of the Bible, 1710-1724

SCOTT MANDELBROTE

AMONG THE BOOKS AND PAPERS bequeathed to Christ Church, Oxford, by William Wake, Archbishop of Canterbury, at his death in 1737 are several volumes of letters dealing with affairs in Ireland during the early 18th century.[1] One of these volumes also contains an apparently unique copy of *Proposals For Printing (by Subscription) an Octavo Bible in Dublin*.[2] This consists of half a sheet, which has been folded to give two leaves. The first is printed on both sides with the text of the proposals.[3] The second has a specimen page from an octavo Bible or Testament, containing the text of Matthew 1.1-2.3, according to the Authorized Version, printed at right angles to the fold, and occupying slightly more than half of the recto of the leaf; it is otherwise blank. ESTC dates the *Proposals* to around 1750, and presumes that it was printed in Dublin. The booksellers named in the *Proposals*, Eliphal Dobson, John Hyde, Richard Gunne, Robert Owen, and Eliphal Dobson, junior, were all active in the Irish book trade in the first half of the 18th century, operating out of Dublin.[4]

The date given by ESTC cannot be correct, however. Eliphal Dobson, senior, disappears from view by about 1720, but the other undertakers were responsible for an edition of the Bible in octavo, printed in Dublin in 1722.[5] This was printed by Aaron Rhames, who also printed a number of other works for the same booksellers at around the same time.[6] The only ornament in the *Proposals* is a device enclosing the initial 'I' of the first line of the text, which depicts Moses and Aaron, standing beneath parting clouds, and supporting the tables of the law, which rest on a pedestal, containing the initial letter, which itself stands on a chequered floor. The same device, this time enclosing an initial letter 'E', appears at the start of the second part of Humphrey Prideaux's *The Old and New Testament Connected* (Dublin, 1719), which Rhames printed for John Gill, John Hyde, George Grierson, Richard Gunne, Robert Owen, and Eliphal Dobson, junior. This work was also supported by subscriptions. The copy of the *Proposals* which survives in the Wake manuscripts is bound among letters dating from 1721, but it was probably printed before then, either in 1718 or early in 1719. The presence of Eliphal Dobson, senior, among the undertakers argues for an earlier date, as does a letter from John Evans, Bishop of Meath, to Wake, dated 25 January [1719], in which Evans says that he has sent Wake a copy of some proposals for printing a Bible in Ireland. A further letter from Evans, dated 2 March [1719], refers to the raising of subscriptions for editions of the Bible consisting of 20,000 copies (as in the printed *Proposals*) and of 40,000 copies (as undertaken by the Chancellor of Meath, Evans's diocese).[7]

Although the names which appeared on the *Proposals* were those of Dublin booksellers, the market which they hoped to exploit was provided by the newly-established 'Society for Promoting Christian Knowledge in Ireland by the Method of Charity Schools', which had met for the first time in October 1717. The leading advocate for this voluntary association was the Cork clergyman, Henry Maule, who later became Dean and then Bishop of Cloyne, and who took a close interest in the progress of the Dublin edition of the Bible, and in its distribution to 'every house' and 'every school', and among the 'poor Tenants' of Protestant landowners.[8] The purpose of the Society was to establish Charity Schools to provide a basic education for poor children across Ireland. The primary recipients of charity were to be the children of poor Protestants, who, it was hoped, would be prevented by education from moral back-sliding and from any temptation to convert to Catholicism. Charity Schools would also help to spread the orthodox teachings of the Church of Ireland among the dissenting Protestant communities in both the north and the south of the island. Concentrating on providing an education through the medium of the English language alone, the Charity Schools were not really intended to be vehicles for the conversion of native Irish Catholics, although one or two did open their doors to Catholic pupils. In part because of its commitment to anglicization, the Charity School movement was somewhat less controversial than the schemes mooted by John Richardson, rector of Belturbet, between 1711 and 1713, for the conversion of the native Irish, through the provision of Charter Schools which would teach English, and the distribution of Irish translations of the liturgy and the Bible. Richardson had been heavily dependent on the patronage of William King, Archbishop of Dublin, and of other Whig clergymen.[9] King was relatively hostile to the Charity School movement, perhaps because of the extent of Jacobite links with some of the Charity Schools in England, sponsored by the London Society for Promoting Christian Knowledge.[10] Nevertheless, a number of other Whig clergymen, notably Edward Synge, Archbishop of Tuam, and Edward Nicholson, from Sligo, actively supported the establishment of Charity Schools in Ireland.[11] The association which these men drew between the Charity School movement, moral reformation, and the prevention of Catholic rebellion, might also have appealed to many Dublin dissenters.[12] The bookseller Eliphal Dobson was one of these, who was sympathetic to those who were 'sound in the main points, wherein all good men are agreed', irrespective of sectarian allegiance.[13] Aaron Rhames may also have held ideals in common with Synge or Nicholson; certainly he printed a large number of their works.[14]

Copies of the New Testament, and possibly of the whole Bible, had been printed in Dublin and Belfast by 1700, and in 1714 Rhames himself had printed an edition of the Bible in folio, for the booksellers William Binauld and Eliphal Dobson, which is the earliest Irish edition known to survive.[15] These ventures were made possible by the fact that the King's Printer in Ireland, Andrew Crooke (who died in 1732), made little attempt either to exercise or to enforce his theoretical monopoly on the trade in Bibles in Ireland.[16] Nevertheless, the demand for Bibles in Ireland, just as for most other books, had generally to be satisfied by imports. In the case of Bibles, the main sources of imports were the presses of the King's Printers, both in London and in Edinburgh. Bibles printed in Scotland were especially popular among the Presbyterian communities of the north of Ireland, who were keen to avoid doctrinal contamination either through the addition of the Book of Common Prayer or through the provision of the Apocrypha, both of which were regularly supplied with Bibles printed in England. There was also said to be 'a Presse att Carrig Fergus [Carrick-fergus] for Printing Bibles att a cheap rate wth out C:[Common] Prayer & Apocrypha'.[17] The deficiencies of this import trade provided the incentive for Dublin booksellers to back Rhames in a further edition of the Bible in 1722, aimed specifically at the market promised by the Charity Schools. They were doubtless buoyed up by encouragement from Maule and other clergymen, and by the success of their advertisements for an edition of Prideaux's *Old and New Testament Connected*, for which 646 copies were subscribed.[18]

On 3 July 1716, Evans had written to Wake, complaining about the dearth of Bibles for sale in Ireland; he followed this up with a further letter, three days later, in which he suggested that the relative lack of demand for Bibles in Ireland was due to their high price. He asserted that every good Christian man had a copy of the Book of Common Prayer, which was available far more cheaply, and begged Wake to organize the dispatch to Ireland of a thousand duodecimo copies of the Bible, to be supplied in quires at the cheapest rate by the King's Printer in London, John Baskett. The books were to be sent to John Afflick (or Afleck), in Damask Street, Dublin.[19] The London Society for Promoting Christian Knowledge at this time offered its members a choice of Bibles for charitable distribution. The cheapest of these was the duodecimo edition of 1717 that Baskett printed in 'old' or 'coarse' nonpareil type, which the SPCK sold at 1s 9d a copy in quires, supplying it with a uniform Book of Common Prayer and Psalter at a total price of 2s 4d.[20] This was presumably the edition from which Wake fulfilled Evans's request; the Bishop of Meath duly acknowledged the safe delivery of the Bibles in a letter dated 15 November [1718].[21] By then, however, a number of complications had arisen with this apparently simple transaction.

Firstly, there was the opposition of several of the Irish bishops to the distribution of English books. This opposition derived from two sources – a desire to promote local manufactures, and an awareness that English Bibles, bound up with the Book of Common Prayer, might be hard to distribute among the Scots-Irish Presbyterians. Suspicion of the motives of the newly-appointed Bishop of Meath, and of other bishops who had recently been sent over from England, such as William Nicolson, who had just taken up the see of Derry, exaggerated these concerns. As a result, Evans was incapable of disposing of all the Bibles which he had ordered, although it appears that Wake had only sent him 300 copies on this occasion, and he was forced to ask Nicolson and others to take some of them off his hands.[22] Bound up with these concerns, however, was a much more serious objection to Evans's efforts, which would be used to promote a new Dublin edition of the Bible, and to justify Irish clergymen in preferring it to alternatives supplied from England. As Archbishop Synge remarked, 'when small Bibles are printed; great care ought to be taken that the *Letter* be good and clear. In which respect I think the London Edition, w[ch] I have lately seen, is a litle defective.'[23]

By October 1712, the printer, bookseller, and publisher, John Baskett, had concluded a series of agreements giving him virtual control of the printing of Bibles in Great Britain. In 1710, he had bought a sixth share in the reversion to the patent of the King's Printer, and, through agreement with the other parties, had become Queen's Printer in 1712. In 1711, he had similarly bought his way into the Queen's Printing Office in Scotland, taking a share in the patent granted to Robert Freebairn. By the beginning of 1712, he had successfully expanded his contacts with Oxford University, and had won the lease of the University's right to print Bibles; in October 1712, he concluded an agreement with the Stationers' Company, to the effect that the Company would not print editions of the Bible at the University Press in Cambridge, over which it held a lease, provided that Baskett would buy copies of the metrical psalms, to be bound with his Oxford Bibles, from the English Stock, controlled by the Company. Baskett thus held a share in three of the presses entitled to print Bibles legally in Great Britain, and had an agreement with the fourth not to trespass on his monopoly.[24]

Within the borders of England, Baskett's monopoly did not constitute a significant change in the nature of Bible publishing. No Bibles had been issued from the Cambridge University Press since the early 1680s, while the King's Printers and the London Stationers had successfully seen off the worst of the challenge mounted to their various privileges by the Oxford University Press, and its allies among London booksellers, during the 1670s and 1680s. By the time that Baskett took over the right of Oxford University to print Bibles, the cut-throat competition provided by the Oxford Bible Press during the 1680s was already a thing of the past.[25] What was new was Baskett's control of the printing of Bibles throughout the recently-formed union of England and Scotland. Although the importation into England of Bibles printed in Scotland had been prohibited under the terms of the Bible patent, Scottish printers had traditionally been an alternative source of cheap Bibles for booksellers both in London and the provinces, who also infringed the patent from time to time by trading in imported Dutch Bibles. Baskett's rival for the title of King's Printer in Scotland, James Watson, defended his right to export Bibles to England, under the terms of the Act of Union, and argued that Baskett's attempt to win control of the printing of the Bible throughout Britain was resulting in an increase in the price of Bibles, and a fall in the quality of their production. Watson suggested that the only way by which quality could be improved would be if British printers emulated the methods of the Dutch; in turn, Baskett accused him of simply importing Dutch goods, under cover of his claim to a share in the Scottish Bible patent.[26] Baskett's lengthy dispute with Watson highlighted a number of problems with the printing of Bibles, several of which were relevant to the decision to try to print an octavo edition of the Bible in Dublin.[27]

Baskett's case against Watson brought out the uncertainties relating to the King's Printers' right to regulate the movement of Bibles between the various kingdoms of England, Scotland, and Ireland. The debate between the two printers helped to make public anxieties about the cost, and the quality, of contemporary printed Bibles, and raised doubts about Baskett's motives in acquiring a monopoly, which might otherwise have been justified in terms of economies of scale, and uniformity of product. Watson argued that competition guaranteed both higher quality of materials, and greater accuracy in printing, as well as cheaper prices. Similar points had been made by the University of Oxford, during its negotiations with various stationers in the early 1690s. However, as was sanguinely noted at that time, the real effect of competition to the death was a lowering of standards, so that 'no Ballad-letter was ever to that degree so bad' as that used to print the Bible, and the paper used was so poor and closely-cropped that it would not survive rebinding.[28] These problems were exacerbated by the reluctance of printers of the Bible to spend money on employing proof-readers. The show-piece of Baskett's new venture at the Oxford University Press, an otherwise magnificent folio Bible, for use in churches, which was completed in 1717, became known as 'the Vinegar Bible', a byword for inaccuracy and inadequate proof-reading.[29] Notwithstanding this example, Baskett's defence against accusations of profiteering and bad workmanship was that rising paper prices helped to determine his costs, and, presumably, to excuse corners cut elsewhere in an effort to keep the price of cheaper Bibles as low as possible. New duties on paper had been raised in 1712, and were increased by 50% in 1714; these rates on English and imported paper were confirmed in 1719.[30]

Baskett's near-monopoly over the printing of the Bible in Britain did bring some economies of scale. In particular, the printing of octavo Bibles, which Baskett sold for 3s each in quires, was divided between the presses of the King's Printing Office in London, and the Oxford Bible Press. This probably allowed for the continuous reprinting of the sections assigned to each printing house; certainly the numbers of cheaper Bibles held in stock by Baskett at the King's Printing Office at any one time were impressively large.[31] Despite this, Watson's criticisms of the production and cost of Baskett's Bibles seem to have been legitimate. The charade of 'the Vinegar

Bible' no doubt alerted some of Baskett's potential critics; certainly Archbishop Synge was far from alone in noticing faults in subsequent editions printed by Baskett. Henry Maule had informed the London Society for Promoting Christian Knowledge, which distributed many of Baskett's cheaper Bibles to its members, about the Dublin booksellers' plans in a letter of 19 December 1718.[32] Throughout the period 1719-22, the SPCK received complaints from its correspondents about the quality of Bibles supplied by Baskett.[33] Writing on 10 November 1719, Maurice Wheeler, who, almost fifty years before, had been tutor to William Wake, now Archbishop of Canterbury, bemoaned 'the Letters whereon the Bibles and prayer Books are printed', arguing that they would 'need to be decipher'd even to some of the Learned, except Printers or Scholars that have been conversant with the Press'.[34] In February 1720, Henry Darby argued that 'the badness of Paper together with the Blindness & Falsities in print occasioned by the Duties have been in his Opinion the greatest cause of Ignorance among the meaner sort.'[35] Initially, in November 1719, the SPCK responded by asking Baskett to provide specimens of his printing for evaluation.[36] When this failed to resolve the problem, however, the Society began to inquire after the alternatives available to it. In March 1722, the SPCK sought to discover whether Bibles could be printed at Cambridge, Dublin, or Edinburgh, and distributed without infringing Baskett's privilege. On 29 May 1722, it was reported that 'comparing the Specimen of the Impression of the Bible now making at Dublin for the Benefit of the Charity Schools in Ireland at Twenty pence a copy in Quires, with a Copy of the New Nonparel Bible printed by Mr Basket at Oxford in 1721 and sold at 2 Shillings a Copy in Quires, the Committee are of the Opinion that the Impression at Dublin is far better than that at London as well as much cheaper'.[37]

The correspondents of the SPCK in Dublin did their best to ram home the advantage which had been gained. Benjamin Everard dispatched several letters to London, reiterating the superiority of the Dublin Bible, to which he had subscribed, over those printed by Baskett.[38] But how had the Dublin undertakers been able to produce a cheaper, and better edition of the Bible than Baskett? One part of the answer lies in the use of subscription. The Dublin booksellers' *Proposals* required money to be raised to meet the cost of half of the edition, or 10,000 copies, before the work of printing began. It is therefore reasonable to suppose that between 1718 and 1722, more than £800 had been raised towards the costs of the edition. Yet, by pitching the price of their new, octavo Bible at 1s 8d in sheets, the Dublin booksellers were undercutting not only octavo Bibles printed in London or Oxford, and sold there at 3s in sheets (which sold in Dublin for 5s bound), but also the very cheapest of Baskett's duodecimo editions.[39] The costs of labour for the Dublin press might help to explain how Bibles could be printed so cheaply there, but it is more plausible to suppose that the real saving which the Dublin booksellers were able to make was on imported paper. In keeping his costs down, following the rise in duties on paper imported into England, Baskett had begun to print on inferior, English paper. This helps to explain the poor quality of some of his Bibles; at the same time, the duties on paper provided Baskett with an excuse for maintaining high prices for his Bibles. Duties on imported paper, set in 1662, were lower in Ireland than in England, a factor which helped to encourage Irish printers and booksellers into the reprint trade more generally.[40] The Dublin undertakers were able to guarantee a lower price for their octavo Bible despite having to import new type from Holland, at a cost of £272, with which to print it.[41] Although the Dublin octavo Bible of 1722 was closely modelled on similar Bibles which had been printed in London or in Oxford, both in terms of layout and of typography, its undertakers were no doubt eager to avoid the charge of using poor quality type that was levelled so frequently against Baskett.[42] Similarly, the Dublin booksellers engaged a corrector for their edition of the Bible, to try to ensure that it escaped the typographical errors which beset Baskett's editions. Here, the costs were eventually met by the Dublin Society for Promoting Christian Knowledge, which found £40 to pay the corrector, John Owen, a Dublin curate and acquaintance of Bishop Evans of Meath.[43]

Through the expedient of raising money in advance, and by taking advantage of lower local costs, the Dublin booksellers had produced their Bible for sale at a low price; by using fresh type, and employing a competent corrector, they had ensured that their edition would be, at least comparatively, accurate and clear. The Dublin Society for Promoting Christian Knowledge was pleased at the success of the undertaking which they had supported, and the London SPCK showed interest in distributing the products of the Dublin press, in preference to the Bibles with which Baskett had been supplying it. Yet no further edition of the Bible was printed in Dublin during a period of more than 15 years.[44] In Britain, Baskett enjoyed a monopoly over the production of Bibles made more certain by James Watson's death in September 1722.[45] This was despite the fact that complaints continued to be made about the quality of the Bibles which Baskett printed, leading the SPCK in 1726 to consider trying to persuade the University of Cambridge not to renew its lease to the Stationers' Company, and to resume printing the Bible at Cambridge.[46] Why, then, was the experiment of printing the Bible at Dublin, which appeared to be so fruitful, not repeated?

Part of the answer, at least, must lie in local circumstances. In 1716, John Evans had warned Wake that demand for the Bible in Ireland was not as great as he might have wished, and that there was little encouragement to venture on an impression of the Bible there.[47] At this time, Evans believed that the reason for low demand was the high price (4s 6d, simply bound) for which Bibles sold in Dublin, an opinion which was echoed in the *Proposals* of the Dublin booksellers.[48] Yet, apart from the Bibles which they mortgaged in exchanged for the capital provided by their subscribers, the Dublin booksellers proposed to sell the remainder of their edition, unless it was subsequently bought up by the same subscribers, at the rate of 3s a copy in sheets, or 3s 8d, simply bound in calf. Although the price of the Bibles available in Dublin may have fallen as a result of the undertaking, the new octavo edition remained a relatively expensive book. It also seems likely that few of those who had subscribed for half or more of the edition, at least 10,000 Bibles, would have been willing to renew their charitable endeavours for future undertakings.[49] One edition may simply have exhausted the Irish market, for a time, whilst still costing enough to make longer-term competition with English, or Dutch, printers seem risky. Only the extended charity of the Dublin Society for Promoting Christian Knowledge ensured that there was money to pay the corrector of the 1722 octavo Bible, whose services were one of the edition's selling points. If the Dublin Society and its subscribers really did buy up and disperse the entire edition of the octavo Bible, as Henry Maule indicated, then their charity in the years around 1722 amounted to 20,000 copies of the Bible. For comparison, it may be worth noting that the SPCK in London at this time tended to disperse approximately 1,000 Bibles a year.[50] Whereas it appears that the Dublin booksellers had to rely almost entirely on subscription and on charitable causes for the sale of their Bible, Baskett could clearly produce and sell frequent reprints, irrespective of charitable purchases. This had the additional consequence that it was Baskett himself who was able, in large measure, to dictate terms to the SPCK in London.

It is doubtful whether the London SPCK could have provided a sufficient market, by itself, to encourage Dublin booksellers and printers to continue to produce editions of the Bible at this time. But, in the early 1720s, the SPCK did seem to be lobbying to have Baskett's monopoly broken, and to allow some measure of freedom in the importation of Bibles, from Scotland or Ireland, into the market in England and Wales. In practice, however, restrictions remained in force, and, during the 1730s, were even strengthened, which made the sale of Irish books in England and Wales difficult, and which imposed heavy duties on those books which did get through.[51] Baskett's response to the displeasure of the SPCK, and to the threat posed by other printers to his monopoly, was also shrewd. Throughout the previous decade, he had argued that his prices were in part due to high paper costs, a fact which was acknowledged by a number of those who otherwise complained to the SPCK about the quality of Baskett's Bibles.[52] He now stressed that much of the poor presswork of which he was accused was in fact the fault of his agent, John Williams, and that, since Williams' death, he had expended money and effort to improve the quality of work done at the King's Printing House, buying new type and destroying the fount which had occasioned most criticism.[53] Although maintaining that he already kept two correctors for Bibles printed at his presses, Baskett prudently offered to employ a third, and to provide £50 as his pay each year, for which he hoped for support from the SPCK.[54] Perhaps most shrewdly of all, Baskett agreed to the sale of Bibles printed in a newer nonpareil fount at the lower price that he had previously reserved for those printed in coarse nonpareil, the type whose quality had helped to provoke complaints, and which he now claimed to have destroyed.[55] Criticism of Baskett's monopoly continued despite these assurances, and culminated in the issuing of an order by King George I on 24 April 1724 to regulate the quality and price of Bibles printed by the King's Printers.[56] Despite subsequent praise of the SPCK, and its clerical allies, especially Edmund Gibson, Bishop of London, for their work in securing this order, it really changed little.[57] Apart from specifying that a price should in future be printed on the title-pages of Bibles, the order represented not much more than a codification of the offers which Baskett had already made to the SPCK and its patrons.

The order accepted Baskett's right to continue to control the production of Bibles in England; it recognized that high prices might not be entirely Baskett's fault, and it agreed with his proposals to remedy errors in printing by appointing further correctors. Specimens from Baskett's own presses were to be taken as the standard for comparison with Bibles produced in the future, and were agreed to be competently printed. The order was to be enforced by the Secretaries of State, the Archbishop of Canterbury, and the Bishop of London, and it represented the fruit of Baskett's discussions with them over the preceding years.[58] However, it did not prevent further complaints about the quality of Baskett's Bibles, although it did ensure that some were published bearing an agreed price.[59] Baskett's concessions, minor though they were, pacified the most influential of his critics because they accepted his rights over the Bible patent. They realized that, without Baskett's efforts to enforce his monopoly, Bibles printed in Holland, which contained even more errors than those printed by Baskett, would enter the country in large numbers.[60] They accepted Baskett's contention that Watson and others were in fact importing their books from Holland, and agreed that greater widening of the scope of the Bible patent would further prejudice the quality of printing.[61] They trusted Baskett when he explained that he was himself subject to financial constraints, and to limitations imposed by agreements with other booksellers.[62] Not to accept Baskett's terms would have led the SPCK and its allies into expensive attempts to secure fresh legislation to govern the Bible patent, or to alleviate duties on imported Bibles; such a course would have represented a challenge to contemporary ideas of property, whilst doing little to guarantee the propriety of Bible printing.[63] It was suggested that poor people would always be tempted to buy what was cheapest, yet objections would continue to be made by them to even the finest small Bibles because 'Country People have such an Aversion to a Small Print, that neither Goodness of Paper, nor Binding, nor any other Excellency can reconcile them to it'.[64]

Thus, circumstances in London help to explain why the Dublin booksellers did not continue with their venture of printing the Bible. It is also worth recording that, once the decision to come to terms with Baskett had been made, the SPCK became significantly more critical of the products of the Dublin press.[65] The possibility of printing the Bible in Dublin was more useful to English readers as a way of attempting to keep Baskett up to the mark, than it was as a source of cheap Bibles themselves. There was neither the financial capital nor the intellectual strength of purpose to make things otherwise. Within Ireland itself, however, the 1722 octavo Bible did provide an answer to the demands of the Charity Schools, and other benefactors, for a home-grown product which would be acceptable to the hierarchy of the Church of Ireland. When it was initially proposed in 1718-19, the Dublin octavo Bible was a result of enthusiasm for a new, reforming scheme; by the mid-1720s, many of the Charity Schools founded at that time were themselves in trouble.[66] Ideologically, the project of printing a cheap edition of the Bible in Dublin appeared sound. It may even have come to seem essential once Cornelius Nary had published his own edition of the New Testament, intended for use by Catholics, and openly critical of existing translations.[67] Financially, the case for the Dublin Bible was less secure, depending as it did on subscriptions which would be hard to raise again, and on a new, and uncertain, market in the Charity Schools. Other projects for the reprinting of English books seemed to guarantee a safer income to Irish booksellers, with more secure markets both at home and abroad.[68] Coupled with the tenacity of John Baskett, these factors helped to ensure that the venture embarked on in the Dublin booksellers' *Proposals* proved short-lived.

References

1. For details of Wake's gift, see W. G. Hiscock, *A Christ Church Miscellany* (Oxford: for the author, 1946), pp.66-7, 72-3; Norman Sykes, *William Wake*, 2 vols (Cambridge: Cambridge University Press, 1957), I, 3 4.
2. Christ Church, Oxford, MS Wake Letters 13 (Ireland 1717-1721), ff.280-1; listed with a single location in ESTC (n39900).
3. A facsimile of the proposals is printed as an appendix to this article.
4. For the Dobsons, see Henry R. Plomer *et al.*, *A Dictionary of the Printers and Booksellers who were at work in England, Scotland and Ireland from 1668 to 1725*, ed. Arundell Esdaile (London: The Bibliographical Society, 1922; repr. 1968), pp.104-5; for the others, see ESTC; further information on all five undertakers can be found in Robert Munter, *A Dictionary of the Print Trade in Ireland 1550-1775* (New York: Fordham University Press, 1988), pp.80-1, 122, 142-3, 202-3.
5. *The Holy Bible, Containing the Old Testament and the New: Newly Translated out of the Original Tongues* (Dublin, 1722); T. H. Darlow and H. F. Moule, *Historical Catalogue of Printed Editions of the English Bible 1525-1961*, revised and expanded by A. S. Herbert (London: British and Foreign Bible Society, 1968), p.247 (number 962).
6. On Rhames, see Plomer, p.252; Munter, p.231.
7. MS Wake Letters 13, numbers 39, 45; information also derived from number 41 (Evans to Wake, 5 February [1719]), and from an entry, dated 16 January 1719, and mentioning the proposals, in the Assembly Roll of the City of Dublin, printed in *Calendar of Ancient Records of Dublin*, ed. John T. Gilbert *et al.*, 18 vols (Dublin, 1889-1922), VII, 85. Unlike the other undertakers for the Bible, Dobson senior was not listed among the booksellers

who organized the publication of Prideaux in 1719; Munter, p.80, states that he died in 1720.

8. MS Wake Letters 14 (Ireland 1722-25), numbers 195 (Maule to Wake, 29 April 1724) and 202 (Maule to Wake, 9 June 1724) (quotations from number 195); David Hayton, 'Did Protestantism fail in early eighteenth-century Ireland? Charity schools and the enterprise of religious and social reformation, c.1690-1730', in *As by Law Established: The Church of Ireland Since the Reformation*, ed. Alan Ford, James McGuire, and Kenneth Milne (Dublin: The Lilliput Press, 1995), pp.166-86.

9. See T. C. Barnard, 'Protestants and the Irish Language, c.1675-1725', *Journal of Ecclesiastical History*, 44 (1993), 243-72; Hayton, 'Did Protestantism fail?'; S. J. Connolly, *Religion, Law, and Power: The Making of Protestant Ireland 1660-1760* (Oxford: Clarendon Press, 1992), pp.297-307; John Richardson, *A Short History of the Attempts that have been made to Convert the Popish Natives of Ireland to the Established Religion*, 2nd edn. (London, 1713); Richardson, *A Proposal for the Conversion of the Popish Natives of Ireland* (Dublin, 1711); *The Correspondence of Jonathan Swift*, ed. Harold Williams, 5 vols (Oxford: Clarendon Press, 1963-5), I, 219-21, 242-4; Swift, *Journal to Stella*, ed. Williams, 2 vols (Oxford: Clarendon Press, 1948), I, 207, 229, 271; on the general problem of language in Ireland, see Joseph Theodoor Leerssen, *Mere Irish and Fíor-Ghael* (Amsterdam: John Benjamins, 1986).

10. Craig Rose, '"Seminarys of Faction and Rebellion": Jacobites, Whigs and the London Charity Schools, 1716-1724', *The Historical Journal*, 34 (1991), 831-55.

11. Hayton, 'Did Protestantism fail?', pp.177-82.

12. Cf. T. C. Barnard, 'Reforming Irish Manners: The Religious Societies in Dublin during the 1690s', *The Historical Journal*, 35 (1992), 805-38.

13. *The Life and Errors of John Dunton*, ed. J. B. Nichols, 2 vols (London, 1818; repr. New York: Burt Franklin, 1969), I, 238.

14. See ESTC.

15. R. W. Jackson, *The Bible and Ireland* (Dublin: The Hibernian Bible Society, 1950), p.16; Darlow and Moule, revised by Herbert, p.242 (number 928); Wesley McCann, 'Patrick Neill and the Origins of Belfast Printing', in *Six Centuries of the Provincial Book Trade in Britain*, ed. Peter Isaac (Winchester: St Paul's Bibliographies, 1990), pp.125-38; Munter, pp.181-2, 256; *The Holy Bible* (Dublin, 1714).

16. M. Pollard, *Dublin's Trade in Books 1550-1800* (Oxford: Clarendon Press, 1989), pp.10-11.

17. MS Wake Letters 13, number 45; information on imports can be found in Raymond Gillespie, 'The book trade in southern Ireland, 1590-1640', in *Books Beyond the Pale*, ed. Gerard Long (Dublin: Rare Books Group of the Library Association of Ireland, 1996), pp.1-17; Pollard, p.220, also notes the importation of Bibles printed in Holland.

18. For the advertising of Prideaux, see Pollard, p.132; a list of subscribers is printed before the first part of Prideaux; they were in the main resident in Ireland, and gave addresses from all over the island.

19. MS Wake Letters 12 (Ireland 1715-18), ff.61r-63v. For Afleck, see Pollard, p.157; Munter, p.14.

20. *The Holy Bible* (London, 1717); Darlow and Moule, revised by Herbert, p.245 (number 944); prices and descriptions are found in MS Wake Letters 27 (Charities etc.), number 165, and Archives of the Society for Promoting Christian Knowledge, London (SPCK), Minute Books, vol.8 (1717-19), pp.124-5.

21. MS Wake Letters 13, number 26; cf. SPCK, Minute Books, vol.8, p.169; it is possible that Wake sent copies of a similar edition of the Bible that Baskett had printed in 1718, for which see Darlow and Moule, revised by Herbert, p.245 (number 946).

22. MS Wake Letters 13, numbers 26 and 40 (Nicolson to Wake, 9 February 1719); British Library, London, Additional MS 6116 (letters of Nicolson to Wake), f.77r-v; on hostility to Englishmen appointed to Irish sees, see Louis A. Landa, *Swift and the Church of Ireland* (Oxford: Clarendon Press, 1954), pp.169-77; Patrick McNally, '"Irish and English interests": national conflict within the Church of Ireland episcopate in the reign of George I', *Irish*

Historical Studies, 29 (1995), 295-314, but compare the more positive assessment of such appointees in Connolly, p.184.

23. MS Wake Letters 13, number 25 (Synge to Wake, 13 November 1718).

24. Harry Carter, *A History of Oxford University Press, Volume I: To the Year 1780* (Oxford: Clarendon Press, 1975), pp.168-9; Robert L. Haig, 'New Light on the King's Printing Office 1680-1730', *Studies in Bibliography*, 8 (1956), 157-67; A. F. Johnson, *Selected Essays on Books and Printing*, ed. Percy H. Muir (Amsterdam: Van Gendt, 1970), pp.381-5; Archives of the Stationers' Company, London, Court Book G, f.204r; Bodleian Library, Oxford, MS Gough Gen. Top. 28, ff.305-6; [John Lee], *Memorial for the Bible Societies in Scotland* (Edinburgh, 1824), pp.179-81, and appendix, pp.67-9; S. C. Roberts, *A History of the Cambridge University Press 1521-1921* (Cambridge: Cambridge University Press, 1921), p.95.

25. David McKitterick, *A History of Cambridge University Press, Volume I: Printing and the Book Trade in Cambridge, 1594-1698* (Cambridge: Cambridge University Press, 1992), p.347; Carter, pp.93-109, 157-66; John Johnson and Strickland Gibson, *Print and Privilege at Oxford to the year 1700* (London: Oxford University Press, 1946).

26. On the use of Dutch methods, see James Watson, *The History of the Art of Printing* (Edinburgh, 1713), pp.20-2; for seizures of Bibles imported from Holland at this time, see Stationers' Company, Court Book G, f.146r.

27. For details of Baskett's dispute with Watson, see Bodleian, MS Ballard 7, f.64; MS Gough Gen. Top. 28, ff.305-8; MS Top. Middlesex c. 1, ff.23-34; *John Baskett His Majesty's Printer in London, and the Representatives of Andrew Anderson, Printer to K. Charl. II. in Scotland, Appellants; James Watson, One of His Majesty's Printers, Respondent* ([n.p.], [n.d.]); *A Previous View of the Case between John Baskett, Esq; One of His Majesty's Printers, Plaintiff, and Henry Parson, Stationer, Defendant* (Edinburgh, 1720); John A. Fairley, *Agnes Campbell, Lady Roseburn: Relict of Andrew Anderson the King's Printer, A Contribution to the History of Printing in Scotland* (Aberdeen: D. Wyllie & Sons, 1925); John S. Gibb, 'James Watson, Printer: Notes of His Life and Work', *Papers of the Edinburgh Bibliographical Society*, 1 (1890-5), 1-8; W. J. Couper, 'James Watson, King's Printer', *Scottish Historical Review*, 7 (1909-10), 244-62; D. Wyn Evans, 'James Watson of Edinburgh: a Bibliography of Works from his Press 1695-1722', *Edinburgh Bibliographical Society Transactions*, 5.2 (1976-80).

28. *Previous View*, pp.3-10; Joyce Helene Brodowski, 'Literary Piracy in England from the Restoration to the Early Eighteenth Century' (unpublished doctoral thesis, Columbia University, 1973), pp.205-6; cf. Bodleian, MS Ballard 49, ff.190r-v, 195r-7v; Johnson and Gibson, p.126; [Lee], pp.160-7, discusses the quality of Bibles printed in Scotland.

29. See Bodleian, MS Ballard 4, ff.111-12, MS Ballard 32, f.13; MS Ballard 34, ff.109-10; B. J. McMullin, 'The Vinegar Bible', *The Book Collector*, 33 (1984), 53-65; Percy Simpson, *Proof-Reading in the Sixteenth, Seventeenth, and Eighteenth Centuries* (Oxford: Oxford University Press, 1935; repr. 1970), pp.194-7; the faults mar even the splendid copy which Baskett presented to the University, now held at Bodleian, Bib. Eng. 1717 b. 1-2.

30. *Previous View*, pp.6-8, 21; *The Statutes at Large*, ed. Danby Pickering, 24 vols (Cambridge, 1762-9), XII, 327-93, XIII, 80-90, XIV, 135; D. C. Coleman, *The British Paper Industry 1495-1860* (Oxford: Clarendon Press, 1958), pp.64-8,124-6.

31. This division of labour is not made entirely plain by Darlow and Moule, revised by Herbert, p.245 (number 947); but cf. *The Holy Bible* (London and Oxford, 1718-19), of which there is a copy at Bodleian, Bib. Eng. 1718 e. 1, and Haig, pp.165-6, describing an inventory of the King's Printing Office from 2 March 1720, which records 10,000 octavo Bibles, in sheets, from an edition printed both in London and in Oxford.

32. SPCK, Abstract Letter Book 9 (1718-19), number 5857; the SPCK later offered its congratulations on the plans for a Dublin edition of the Bible, see SPCK, Society Letters, CS2/9, p.35.

33. SPCK, Abstract Letter Book 9, numbers 6151, 6171; Abstract Letter Book 10 (1719-21), numbers 6298, 6421, 6615; Abstract Letter Book 11 (1721-3), number 7262; cf. the SPCK's own complaints, CS2/12, pp.72-5.

34. SPCK, Abstract Letter Book 9, number 6171; on Wheeler, see Sykes, I, 9.

35. SPCK, Abstract Letter Book 10, number 6298.
36. SPCK, Minute Books, vol.9 (1719-21), p.62.
37. SPCK, Minute Books, vol.10 (1722-4), pp.19, 22, quotation at 46-7; see Darlow and Moule, revised by Herbert, p.246 (number 957), for the Oxford Bible used in this comparison.
38. SPCK, Abstract Letter Book 11, numbers 7262 and 7313; Minute Books, vol.10, p.129; cf. SPCK, CS2/14, p.85, for a further request for Everard to send a copy of the completed Dublin Bible; Everard's own comparison refers to Baskett's 'coarse nonpareil' edition of 1718, for which see note 20 above.
39. The Dublin undertakers seem also to have considered producing a duodecimo edition of their own, see the surviving fragment listed in Darlow and Moule, revised by Herbert, p.247 (number 961).
40. See Pollard, pp.9, 111-15, 130-3; cf. Coleman, 124-6; Carter, p.167, records Baskett's use of English paper. The exact difference between the duties payable in England and in Ireland varied according to paper size and quality, but, at approximately 10% in total, Irish duties had been no more than half those levied in England even before the new, higher duties of 1712 and 1714 were imposed.
41. Pollard, p.122.
42. The design of the Dublin octavo Bible may be compared with that of the Bibles printed by Baskett and described in note 31 above.
43. MS Wake Letters 14, number 202.
44. See Darlow and Moule, revised by Herbert, p.260 (number 1044).
45. Couper, p.259.
46. SPCK, Abstract Letter Book 13 (1725-7), numbers 8939-40, 8966(b), 8993, 9005, 9026; SPCK, CS2/17, pp.22-5, 33-4, 37-8.
47. MS Wake Letters 12, ff.61-2.
48. MS Wake Letters 12, f.63r-v.
49. Munter, p.81, wrongly suggests that the edition consisted of only 10,000 Bibles; for an example of a single, bulk subscription which was unlikely to be repeated, see *Calendar of Ancient Records of Dublin*, VII, 85, which records a decision that the Lord Mayor of Dublin should subscribe for a thousand Bibles 'for the use of the city'.
50. Comparative figures based on MS Wake 14, number 195; MS Wake 27, number 166; and cf. note 49 above. The SPCK sought advice from Dublin on the best method of correcting for the press, see SPCK, Minute Books, vol.10, pp.182, 186.
51. See Pollard, pp.67-87, 135-9; cf. SPCK, CS2/13, p.3.
52. *Previous View*; see also SPCK, Abstract Letter Book 10, number 6298; Abstract Letter Book 12 (1723-5), number 7341; SPCK, CS2/13, pp.3, 49-51.
53. MS Wake Letters 22 (Miscellaneous Letters 1721-4), number 276 (Baskett to Wake, 9 March 1724); SPCK, Minute Books, vol.10, p.102.
54. SPCK, Minute Books, vol.10, p.140; this proposal won the backing even of the SPCK's correspondent in Dublin, Thomas Prior, see Abstract Letter Book 12, number 7511.
55. SPCK, Minute Books, vol.10, p.202; this implied a fall in price from 2s a copy in quires to 1s 9d (see MS Wake Letters 27, number 165), but was not as large a concession as it seemed, since Baskett had already sold out of copies of the cheaper edition.
56. *The London Gazette*, 21 April to 25 April 1724; cf. John Lewis, *A Complete History of the several Translations of the Holy Bible and New Testament into English*, 2nd edn. (London, 1739), pp.350-1.
57. Congratulations can be found in Lambeth Palace Library, MS 1741 (Gibson Papers), ff.28-9, 38-9.
58. See MS Wake Letters 22, number 276; SPCK, Minute Books, vol.10, p.140; cf. Lambeth Palace Library, MS 1770 (Diary of William Wake, 7 March 1705 to 25 January 1725), f.247v.
59. Darlow and Moule, revised by Herbert, pp.249-51; the prices printed on the title-pages of these Bibles were at least as high as those which Baskett had been charging before the order (2s for an unbound duodecimo Bible; 3s for an unbound octavo); see also note 46

above, and the continued criticism of Bibles printed by the King's Printers in *The Flying Post or Post Master*, 25 August to 27 August 1724.

60. SPCK, CS2/13, pp.49-51.
61. SPCK, CS2/12, p.86; CS2/13, p.2; cf. *Previous View*.
62. SPCK, CS2/13, p.4; CS2/14, p.85.
63. SPCK, CS2/13, p.41.
64. SPCK, CS2/15, pp.66-7; quotation from SPCK, Abstract Letter Book 10, number 6421 (Thomas Allen to the SPCK, Kettering, 28 May 1720).
65. SPCK, CS2/17, p.378, where the use of Dutch type is blamed for errors; cf. the earlier criticisms of Irish printing by Bishop Evans, MS Wake Letters 13, numbers 30 and 39.
66. Hayton, 'Did Protestantism fail?', especially p.182.
67. *The New Testament of our Lord and Saviour Jesus Christ*, trans. C[ornelius] N[ary] ([Dublin], 1718); Darlow and Moule, revised by Herbert, pp.245-6 (number 951); cf. Lewis, pp.356-63; Patrick Fagan, *Dublin's Turbulent Priest: Cornelius Nary (1658-1738)* (Dublin: Royal Irish Academy, 1991), pp.79-91; Nary's work failed to win him the approval of the Catholic hierarchy.
68. See Pollard, pp.66-109.

Acknowledgements

I am grateful to Raymond Gillespie, Giles Mandelbrote, and William St Clair for their help with the writing of this paper; I would also like to thank the librarians and archivists of the collections from which I have cited, in particular, the late Gordon Huelin, and, of course, Robin Myers.

Appendix

The following illustrations are reproduced from MS Wake Letters 13 (Ireland 1717-1721), ff.280-1, and printed with the permission of the Dean of Christ Church, Oxford, and of the Wake Trustees.

PROPOSALS

For Printing (by Subfcription) an

Octavo Bible in Dublin.

IT having pleafed Almighty GOD to raife up a Spirit of Piety and Charity in this Kingdom, whereupon many well-difpofed Perfons, in divers Parts of it, have been excited to lay to Heart the Intereft of *Religion* and the Welfare of the *Publick*, and to exert their utmoft Endeavours for the furtherance of both, by erecting CHARITY-SCHOOLS for the Education of *Poor Children* in *Vertue* and *Induftry*, and furnifhing *Poor Families* with *Pious* and *Practical Books*, for the promotion of *Chriftian Knowledge* and *Devotion*.

And it having been intimated by feveral of the faid Perfons, that they lye under great Difficulties in purfuing thofe good Ends, by reafon of the Scarcenefs and Dearnefs of fmall BIBLES : It has therefore been thought Advifable to propofe the Printing a good Octavo Edition of the HOLY BIBLE in *Dublin*, in fuch a manner that *Families* and *Schools* may be furnifhed therewith at eafy Rates.

Upon a Prefumption, therefore, that this good Defign (which has been efpoufed and Recommended by divers Perfons of the moft eminent Stations in *Church* and *State*) will be generally approved of, and meet with all proper Encouragement : The Society in *Dublin* for promoting CHARITY-SCHOOLS throughout the Kingdom, have engaged certain Bookfellers to undertake the Printing 20000 fuch BIBLES, and the delivering to Subfcribers 10000 of them at the prime Coft of Twenty Pence a piece in Sheets; *By reafon of which very low Price, and it's being an uncommon Encouragment to Subfcribers, as alfo upon account of the great Expence (as well as Hazard) the Undertakers muft be at*, they defire that 10000 be Subfcribed for, and the whole Subfcription-Money paid down, before they begin the Work.

They are to be Printed in a fair Letter on a good Paper (according to the annex'd Specimen) after the beft Englifh Edition ; and will be Corrected with the utmoft Care and Exactnefs. So that thefe BIBLES, thô fold at 1 s. 8 d. a piece Unbound, will become as valuable as the beft Englifh BIBLES which now coft in *London* 3 s. a piece in Sheets, and are fold in *Dublin* for 5 s. Bound.

The

280

The Advantages of this Undertaking will be very great ; for, befides that by this means, a confiderable Sum of Money will be kept in the Kingdom, *Houfe-keepers* and *Benefactors* to CHARITY-SCHOOLS, may hereby be better enabled to provide BIBLES for their *Families* and *Schools*; and the *Reverend Clergy*, and *Gentlemen of Fortune*, may alfo be encouraged to Buy Numbers of them to Diftribute among their *Poor Parifhioners*, *Tenants* and *Neighbours* ; whereby, many of the *Roman-Catholick Natives*, may (in all probability) be brought over to the ESTABLISH'D CHURCH: So that (by GOD's Blefling) it may prove a Publick National Good, and ftrike at the Root of *Immorality*, *Ignorance* and *Error*.

The UNDERTAKERS.

Mefs[rs.] *Eliphal Dobfon*, *John Hyde*, *Richard Gunne*, *Robert Owen*, and *Eliphal Dobfon*, Junior, propofe as follows, *viz.*

Firft, That they will Print 20000 BIBLES, according to the annexed Specimen, which at the prime Coft of Paper and Printing, will amount to 1666 *l.* 13 *s.* 4 *d.*

Secondly, That 10000 be Subfcribed for at the prime Coft of Twenty Pence a piece, which for the 10000 will be 833 *l.* 6 *s.* 8 *d.*

Thirdly, That the faid Sum of 833 *l.* 6 *s.* 8 *d.* be advanced to them, before the Work be begun.

Fourthly, That after the faid Subfcriptions are compleated, and the Money paid in, they will immediately fend the Work to the Prefs, and get it finifhed with all poffible Care and Expedition.

Fifthly, That as foon as the Impreffion is finifhed, they will deliver to the Subfcribers (or Order) their refpective Shares of the 10000 BIBLES in Sheets.

Sixthly, That all Perfons fhall be furnifhed (for charitable Ufes) with any Number of the remaining 10000 BIBLES, at the fame Rate they are fold (for the time being) to Bookfellers.

Seventhly, That they cannot afford to fell to any other Perfons, any of the faid BIBLES, under 3 *s.* a piece in Sheets.

Eighthly, That they will (if defired) procure any Number of the faid BIBLES to be well Bound in Calves-Leather, for a Sum not exceeding 8 *d.* a piece.

Note, The above mentioned Undertakers have given their Bond, jointly and feverally, for the Sum of 1600 *l.* to his Grace the Lord Arch-Bifhop of *Dublin*, for delivering the Books according to thefe Propofals ; or elfe (in cafe the Subfcriptions are not compleated) for returning what Money they fhall receive to the refpective Subfcribers upon demand.

It is therefore moft humbly recommended to all *Pious* and *Charitable Perfons*, to Subfcribe liberally to fo generous and ufeful a Work ; and to pay in their Subfcription Money to the above Undertakers, with all convenient fpeed.

PROPOSALS will be given, and alfo Printed Receipts for the Subfcription Money, at any of the Undertakers Shops in *Dublin*.

Note, The Undertakers will take no Subfcription for lefs than Twenty Books ; nor will any Perfon be deem'd a Subfcriber till his Subfcription Money is paid to fome one of the Undertakers.

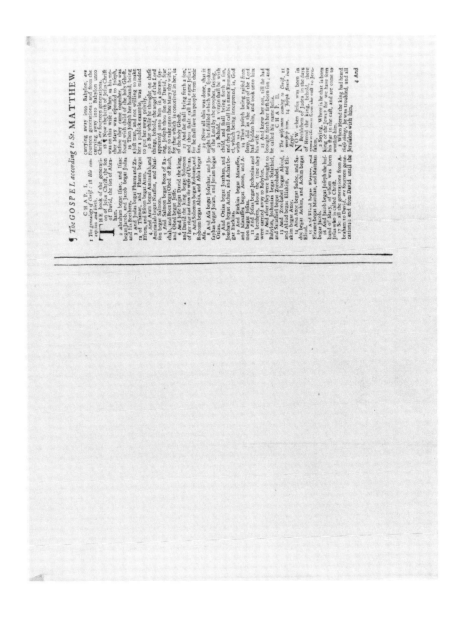

Dublin–London publishing relations in the 18th century: the case of George Faulkner

JAMES E. TIERNEY

A DEFINITIVE STUDY of the publishing relations between 18th-century Dublin and London booksellers has yet to be written, and probably the loss of essential primary materials will never allow the production of such a history. Most notably missing are the business records and correspondence of Irish booksellers and printers. Contributing to this grim circumstance was the destruction of the country's Public Record Office in 1922, a disaster for historians of all fields.

From the Irish perspective, this situation is indeed unfortunate since the annals of publishing have traditionally taken their colour from the celebrated charges of piracy levelled at Dublin booksellers by their historically more influential London counterparts, leaving the positive side of Dublin–London trade relations during the 18th century largely neglected. Better known than any other documents emanating from this conflict are Samuel Richardson's bitter attacks on the Irish trade for their unauthorized reprints of his novels *Pamela*, *Clarissa*, and *Sir Charles Grandison*. Regarding the last, he issued on 14 September 1753 *The Case of Samuel Richardson, of London, Printer; with Regard to the Invasion of his Property*, a pamphlet he distributed *gratis* in London. Then the following February, he included at the end of Volume VII of the first edition of *Grandison* his hostile *Address to the Public*. The *Case* summarized the actions of *Grandison*'s pirates and named all the villains involved, including Richardson's own workmen. It earned hearty support in leading London newspapers and periodicals, including the *Public Advertiser*, *Gray's Inn Journal*, and the *Gentleman's Magazine*.[1] The *Address* specifically denounced George Faulkner, the Dublin printer/bookseller with whom Richardson had contracted for the Irish rights to *Grandison* but whom the London author now charged with collaborating with the pirates.[2] Quickly, such London luminaries as David Garrick and Samuel Johnson rallied to the support of their friend Richardson.[3] Needless to say, the vociferous, united London front historically overshadowed Faulkner's futile attempts, both in letters to friends in London and in his *Dublin Journal*, to justify his role in the *Grandison* affair.[4]

Although it would be witless to propose that the majority of Irish reprints of London editions had been authorized by their copyright holders, recent studies have begun to put together bits of evidence that suggest that the Dublin–London publishing relationship was closer than originally

133

thought, and that collaboration between the two publishing centres was broader than previously allowed. Such a notion is also supported in at least two of three major pioneering studies of the Irish press published in the last half century. All three studies have gone a long way in setting the path for the definitive study alluded to at the outset, particularly by identifying and exploring appropriate resources. The first, a yet unpublished PhD thesis (Trinity College, Dublin, 1952), James W. Phillips's 'A Bibliographical Inquiry into Printing and Bookselling in Dublin from 1670 to 1800', compiled evidence from 18th-century imprints, contemporary correspondence, pamphlets, and newspapers to document many instances of publishing collaborations between Dublin and London from the 17th century through to the end of the 18th. The second is a more recent work, Richard Cargill Cole's *Irish Booksellers and English Writers 1740-1800* (1986). It examines auction catalogues of 203 18th-century Irish private libraries, thousands of extant copies of Dublin reprints of original London editions, and a corresponding number of newspaper advertisements in both the London and Dublin press in order to establish hard evidence for assessing the extent of the Irish reprint industry.[5]

The most recent work, Mary Pollard's Lyell Lectures at Oxford (1986-7) revised for publication as *Dublin's Trade in Books 1550-1800* (1989), also employs as its chief sources contemporary imprints and Dublin newspapers.[6] What is more, Pollard's book announces the discovery of the first contemporary Irish printer's records to come to light, those of Graisberry and Campbell, covering much of the last two decades of the century. Regrettably, however, because their discovery came too late, Pollard was unable to incorporate this evidence in the revised lectures.

None of these major works on the Irish press, however, pretends to offer a comprehensive, in-depth study of publishing relations between the two trade centres during the 18th century. Both Phillips and Cole have other fish to fry. Phillips's book-length thesis takes up all aspects of the Irish book trade – including printing, bookbinding, paper, ink, presses, and type – and gives over only one chapter (pp.186-205) to a consideration of Dublin–London publishing collaborations. Like Phillips, Cole's interests are also broader, as is evident in his spending three of his ten chapters on the work of Irish tradesmen who, after emigrating from their native country to America during the latter half of the century, continued to reprint the works of English authors in their new land. Pollard, although she has more to offer of positive value on the subject at hand, quite rightly regards our knowledge of Dublin–London publishing relations during the period as still elementary and looks upon her own lectures as 'a preliminary survey, a plotting out of some of the areas requiring more thorough investigation.'[7]

Perhaps national origins have some influence on the perspectives of the three works when commenting on the nature and extent of the Irish trade's intrusion on English copyright during the 18th century, but I do not think so. Each is a solid work of responsible scholarship that does not step beyond the evidence. By discovering materials long overlooked, both Phillips and Pollard attempt to counter the historical weight of the 18th-century London trade's loud protests of piracy, which, as Pollard says, 'have passed unchallenged into folk memory.'[8]

While all three scholars concede that the reprinting of English authors was the staple of the Irish trade, the collective impact of Cole's major statements, however unintentional, seems to prejudice the Irish trade. Employing extensive evidence of the reprint trade from Irish imprints, together with his discovery from newspaper advertisements that such reprints were consistently executed within a month or two of the appearance of the London editions, Cole concludes that 'More often than not their [i.e. the Irish] practice was to acquire the printed sheets surreptitiously and without paying the copyright holder or securing his permission.'[9] Although the conclusion might not be wide of the mark, Cole pays almost no attention to the many instances of collaboration between the Dublin and London trades discovered by Phillips, Pollard, and others, and so his treatment loses a little balance. The bare context he provides, implicitly at least, leaves the impression that Irish opportunism was the sole basis for the extensive Dublin trade in reprints of English editions.

Cole does not take sides in the issue; in fact, his first chapter attempts some explanation of the Irish practice by showing that the Copyright Acts of 1709 and 1739 did not cover reprints produced in Ireland for distribution in Ireland. Moreover, his book maintains that contemporary English writers enjoyed a positive advantage by reason of the Irish reprints: between 1740 and 1800, 'cheap reprints . . . augmented the audience for these writers not only in Ireland but in Britain and the United States of America.'[10] However, finding a secondary gain to compensate for the losses to English copyright holders does little to offset the received impression that the Dublin trade in English authors was entirely a product of Irish opportunism and enjoyed no collaboration from London booksellers. In effect, the inner workings of Dublin-London trade relations are almost completely ignored, and the dumb testimony of book imprints becomes the whole reality.

The kind of evidence of collaborative publication that Phillips and Pollard present (but Cole overlooks) has begun to build up in recent years, particularly in the case of George Faulkner, perhaps the most active and best known of contemporary Irish booksellers. Doubtless Faulkner overstates his case when, attempting to justify his publishing activities late in his career, he claimed that he had obtained all his texts 'in the fairest Manner from the different Authors and Proprietors in Great Britain and Ireland, at much Trouble and Expence, in his Journies to and fro'.'[11] Nonetheless, evidence is now in hand, if not to justify his claim, at least to give some basis for a modified version.

Faulkner's connections with the London book trade began very early, actually before he opened his Dublin shop. After serving his apprenticeship under the printer Thomas Hume in Dublin, he came to London in the early

1720s to work at the shop of William Bowyer the elder. Here he struck up a relationship with the younger Bowyer, who handled the printing of the classics for his father. Back in Dublin in 1724, he set up his own printing shop and carried on a correspondence and exchanged copyrights with the younger Bowyer, a relationship that lasted well after the mid-century.[12] From Dublin, he also corresponded with such other London booksellers as Robert Dodsley, Andrew Millar and Lockyer Davis, and he regularly visited London where he negotiated collaborations with Richardson, Dodsley, and James Rivington and where he often dined with the English authors he reprinted. His successful negotiations with Richardson for the Irish rights to *Clarissa* and *Sir Charles Grandison* in themselves support the case for active co-operation on the part of the London trade.

As pointed out some time ago, one of the most notable of Faulkner's London connections concerned his business and personal relationship with Robert Dodsley, mid-century London's eminent publisher of *belles lettres*.[13] From Dodsley's letter to Faulkner on 28 October 1757, it is clear that the London bookseller was not only one of Faulkner's London dining companions but, more important, a supplier of his own publications for Faulkner's reprints. In that letter, Dodsley says he is sending Faulkner a copy of his own poem *Melpomene*, inviting him to publish a Dublin edition, and, surprisingly, that he is delivering to Faulkner's nephew in London, Mr Smith, sheets for the fourth (revised) and fifth volumes of his hugely successful *A Collection of Poems by Several Hands*, long before their scheduled appearance from Tully's Head.[14]

Further testimony of Dodsley's collaboration with Faulkner emerges in letters from other Dodsley correspondents. On 13 March 1753, Robert Lowth wrote to remind Dodsley of his promise to send some copies of Louis Devisme's *Brief Account of the Vaudois* to Dublin for Faulkner's shop.[15] On 12 November of the same year, Benjamin Victor wrote to Dodsley, reminding him of the planned simultaneous publication by Faulkner of his *Widow of the Wood*.[16] As late as 1759, Faulkner's *Journal* (27 February-3 March) advertised Dodsley's shop as the only London house taking in subscriptions for *Miscellanies in Verse and Prose* by Samuel Derrick, Faulkner's friend.

Although unsubstantiated by similar first-hand evidence, Dodsley's collaboration with Faulkner may extend to as early as 1749. In April of that year, almost simultaneously from both their shops was issued Henry Brooke's *The Songs in Jack the Gyant Queller*. Two years later, on 28 May, Faulkner advertised for sale in his *Dublin Journal* a forthcoming edition of William Melmoth's translation *The Letters of Pliny the Consul*, a Dodsley copyright of 1746 for which the London bookseller would be issuing another edition the next month. Given what seem to be amiable relations between Dodsley and Faulkner during these years, the list of collaborations may include the following Dodsley copyrights that Faulkner reprinted during the period: William Melmoth's *Letters on Several Subjects. By the Late Sir*

Thomas Fitzosborne, 1749; *The Letters of Marcus Tullius Cicero to Several of His Friends: with Remarks by William Melmoth*, 1753; *The World. By Adam Fitz-Adam* (1755-6). Finally, on 12 March 1761, Faulkner and Dodsley's Tully's Head (Robert had now been succeeded by his brother James) simultaneously issued editions of Frances Sheridan's *Memoirs of Miss Sidney Bidulph*.

Unfortunately, extant evidence does not explain the terms of Dodsley's recompense, if any, for providing texts for Faulkner's Dublin reprints. It is not clear whether Dodsley was simply happy to have the additional exposure for his publications, whether he sold Faulkner copies at the usual trade discount and expected remuneration, or whether his working relationship with Faulkner was based, in whole or in part, upon the mutual exchange of copies of Irish and English works. It is possible, of course, that their agreements reflected some attempt on Dodsley's part to control the quantity of reprints or their distribution. In the end, probably Pollard has the correct answer when she says that 'Even without the reprinted texts the Irish market was of great importance to the English,' and consequently, like other London booksellers, Dodsley was simply cashing in on an extended market.[17] What is certain, however, is that at least some of the works Faulkner received from Dodsley were not acquired 'surreptitiously'. The London bookseller willingly and happily collaborated with the production of Irish reprints from texts of his own publication.

Now an unpublished Faulkner letter has come to light that shows at least one other Faulkner connection in the London trade, the influential publisher of the *Gentleman's Magazine*, Edward Cave (1691-1754). Although brief and clearly not referring to a joint publishing effort, this note from Faulkner to Cave does reveal Cave's having offered the Dublin printer a copy of a London imprint, and perhaps for a Dublin edition. Furthermore, Faulkner's acknowledgement of other correspondence with Cave, as well as his offering compliments to Cave's wife, suggests a cordial relationship extending beyond the piece's immediate business. This holograph note – as far as I know, the earliest piece of Faulkner correspondence extant – is here published for the first time:[18]

Sir,

I have been extreamly ill for three Weeks past, which prevented my answering your last Favour. as we do not lay by our News Papers, I cannot send those you writ for, but if you please I will send you the whole Volume published by the Dublin Society. Inclosed I send you a Pamphlet, but how it will answer I cannot say. You need not send me the Czar's Life. My Respects to Mrs. Cave.

I am, Sir,

Your Most Obedt

Dublin July   humble Servt

17. 1739.   George Faulkner[19]

Although Cave is not greeted by name in the salutation, he is most certainly its recipient, for the note appears in a sequence of some 40 letters addressed to Cave and listed as such in the *Catalogue of the Stowe Manuscripts in the British Museum* (2 vols, 1896). For the sceptical, the holograph itself affords additional evidence that Cave is the recipient. The note's concluding line carries Faulkner's compliment: 'My respects to Mrs. Cave.' Such closing gestures – typical among 18th-century letter-writers – are almost invariably addressed to the correspondent's wife.

Further support for such a conclusion emerges from the address found on the manuscript's verso. Although the entire right half of the address has been torn from the manuscript, enough remains to point to Cave. The remnant of the first line provides us with the addressee's first name: 'To Mr Edward . . .' The second line, before breaking off, adds the significant address: 'at the Post . . .', suggesting the Post Office as the note's destination. The pieces come together when one recalls that Edward Cave was an employee of the Post Office, at least from 1735 through 1742: that is, during the period when this note was penned.[20] Furthermore, when the note's contents are taken into account, it seems evident that the recipient was also associated with the publishing trade.

The unnamed works alluded to within the note also submit to tentative identification when associated with Cave. Cave's apparent request for recent issues of Faulkner's 'News Papers' – obviously the *Dublin Journal* – in his 'last Favour' can be explained in terms of one of Cave's current interests.[21] Each issue of the *Journal* carried a column entitled 'From the Dublin Society', a piece usually addressing the Society's mission of improving Ireland's agriculture and practical arts.[22] A series of these columns four months earlier, in March, had been concerned with the successful growing of flax for the production of linen. Although the connection is tenuous, the very next year Cave would be purchasing a spinning machine and setting up a mill on Turnmill Brook, near the river Fleet.[23] It seems reasonable to assume that Cave would have had a particular interest in what the *Journal* had to say about the making of linen. Similarly, the unnamed pamphlet Faulkner says he is enclosing might well have been the one Faulkner would be advertising in the *Journal* the very next week (24-28 July): *Some Thoughts on the Importance of Linnen Manufacture to Ireland. How to Lessen the Expense of It.* 'How it will answer' Cave's interests, Faulkner could not say, but it was close at hand for dispatch, and it responded to an inquiry laid out in Cave's previous letter.

More to the point of this paper, Cave's collaboration with Faulkner's publishing interests surfaces in the allusion to the 'Czar's Life'. It appears from Faulkner's statement that Cave had earlier offered to send Faulkner a copy of a work he had listed in the *Gentleman's Magazine*'s monthly register of books two months earlier, in May: the three-volume *History of the Life of Peter the Great, Emperor of Russia*, written by John Mottley and published in London by J. Read. In the circumstances, Cave must certainly have understood that, by sending Faulkner a copy of Mottley's work, he was potentially, at least, assisting the Dublin bookseller to produce another reprint of a London edition. However, apparently between the London appearance of Mottley's work two months earlier and the present Faulkner note, the Dublin printer had managed to secure the text from another London supplier, for not only does he here refuse Cave's offer but this very day he advertised in his *Dublin Journal* (14-17 July 1739) that Mottley's work was 'Now in the Press and will be speedily published by the Printer hereof.'

Obviously Faulkner had more than a few London 'agents' shuffling English imprints across the sea shortly after their London debut. That the publisher Read himself supplied Faulkner with a copy is impossible to say; no present evidence links Faulkner with the London bookseller. Nor is it clear what Cave himself stood to gain by the offer revealed, but perhaps it involved favours 'in kind'. Whatever the recompense, this case shows that another prominent figure in the London publishing scene was willing to supply a London edition, shortly after its publication, and apparently for a Faulkner reprint. Significantly, it was not Cave's own publication, and another London 'agent' had beaten him to it.

It is unlikely that Faulkner could have maintained such congenial relations with both London booksellers and their authors had his business practices rendered him *persona non grata*. What seems much more likely is that at least a portion of the London trade appreciated his Dublin reprints, or at least stood to gain in some way by the collaboration, and that they actually assisted in the production of his Dublin reprints.

The foregoing argument, drawing upon available evidence relevant to George Faulkner's relations with the London trade, attempts to distinguish him from the stereotype 'pirate' made so notorious by the 18th-century London trade's indictment of Irish publishing practices. Little has been said of other Irish publishers except to direct attention to those collaborations listed by Phillips and Pollard. These other instances seem fertile ground for similar stories whenever specific details of their interaction with the London trade are uncovered. On the other hand, it may be that the stereotype 'pirate' is justified in many other cases.

In the end, however, it seems reasonable to assume that the full story of the collaboration between Dublin and London booksellers will never be known. While there are libraries full of books whose imprints testify to the fact of the Irish reprint industry, there is no equivalent body of material extant that reveals the terms by which they came into existence. Comparably speaking, few — Irish or English — booksellers' records, correspondences, and publishing agreements have survived to document the extent of London's co-operation in the production of Irish reprints. Perhaps most significant, negotiations contracted orally are lost forever. A little evidence does survive, and more will certainly turn up, but inevitably the argument advanced here must rest with an appeal to the iceberg analogy.

References

1. 30 October; 13 October; xxiii (October), pp.465-7.
2. See T. C. Duncan Eaves and Ben D. Kimpel, *Samuel Richardson. A Biography* (Oxford: Clarendon Press, 1971), pp.379-83, where the story of Richardson's *Sir Charles Grandison* and the Irish booksellers is fully recounted.
3. *The Letters of David Garrick*, ed. David M. Little and George M. Kahrl (London: Oxford University Press, 1963), i, pp.201-2; 26 September 1753 in *The Letters of Samuel Johnson*, ed. Bruce Redford (Princeton: Princeton University Press, 1992), i, pp.74-6.
4. In his *Address to the Public* published in *Sir Charles Grandison* (vii, pp.424-42), Richardson claimed that Faulkner 'wrote letters to several persons of character in London, endeavouring to justify himself, without having that strict regard to veracity in them which becomes a man of business'. Among them was Samuel Johnson, who mentions Faulkner's letter in his letter to Richardson on 28 March 1754. See *Letters*, i, p.80; *Dublin Journal*, 3 November 1753.
5. London: Mansell; Atlantic Highlands, N.J.: Humanities Press, 1986. I am indebted to Andrew Carpenter, the first editor of the journal *Eighteenth-century Ireland*, for calling my attention to both Cole's and Phillips's studies and for providing help on this piece several years ago.
6. Oxford: Clarendon Press, 1989.
7. *Ibid.*, p.vii.
8. *Ibid.*, p.66.
9. *Ibid.*, p.x.
10. *Ibid.*, p.ix.
11. *Dublin Journal*, 2 June 1767.
12. Robert E. Ward, ed., *The Prince of Dublin Printers. The Letters of George Faulkner* (Lexington: University Press of Kentucky, 1972), pp.6, 41-2.
13. See the author's note, 'Faulkner and Dodsley: A Publishing Link' in *The Library*, 5th ser., 32 (1977), pp.52-5, and also his edition of *The Correspondence of Robert Dodsley 1733-1764* (Cambridge: Cambridge University Press, 1988), pp.47-8, 300-1, the latter hereafter referred to as *Correspondence*.
14. *Correspondence*, pp.300-1. See also pp.47-8.
15. *Correspondence*, p.153.
16. *Correspondence*, p.163.
17. Pollard, p.90.
18. The note is not found in Robert E. Ward, *op. cit.*
19. British Library, Stowe MS 748, f.170. The letter is printed here by kind permission of The British Library Board.
20. *The Journal of the House of Commons, 1732-1737*, p.476, records Cave's being summoned in 1735, as a supervisor of franks, to give testimony regarding the abuses of the franking privilege. See also *The Parliamentary History of England, 1066-1803*, ed. William Cobbett and J. Wright (London, 1806-1820), x, pp.842-8. The Establishment Books, in the London Post Office Archives, list Cave, in 1742, as a 'Sorter' with a salary of £50 per annum.
21. Faulkner published the *Dublin Journal* from 1728 until his death in 1775.
22. Faulkner was an active member of this society, the Dublin Society for Promoting Husbandry and Other Useful Arts. It had been founded in 1731 and would be granted a royal charter in 1750. See D. G. C. Allan, 'The Society of Arts and Government, 1754-1800', *Eighteenth-Century Studies*, 7 (1974), pp.438-9.
23. See 'Cave, Edward', *DNB*.

A 'List of the Stockholders in the Worshipful Company of Stationers', 1785

MICHAEL L. TURNER

Gough London 138, in the Bodleian Library, is a collection of pamphlets and ephemeral items largely relating to City Companies. A supplementary volume, *Gough London 138**, was used for similar material which came into the Library at a later date. It contains some 22 items from the last decades of the 18th century and the first decade of the 19th century. Alongside pieces relating to charitable societies and institutions are a few more relating to City Companies. Several of them clearly belonged to John Nichols (ST/3:1022), but the subject of this article carries no such indication.

The item in question, a single gathering of eight pages, begins on the first page with a drop-title — LIST | OF THE | STOCKHOLDERS | IN THE | Worshipful Company of STATIONERS. | [Swelled rule]. Immediately below this rule begins a list of names and addresses of 229 partners in the English Stock which concludes just beyond half-way down page eight. There are, in fact, 230 entries as Thomas Evans appears twice. There is no further comment, nor is the item dated. Perhaps the most unusual feature of the list, for those familiar with Stationers' Company documents, is that the order of the names is not hierarchical. The order bears no relationship to seniority in the Company nor to categories of shares in the English Stock. It appears to be random.

The only other printed lists specifically devoted to the Partners in the English Stock in the 18th century, of which I am aware, all date from the 1730s — 1 June 1735; 7 June 1737; and 4 December 1739. They were clearly produced early in the month of a distribution of dividends, and they are in strict hierarchical order — the Master, the Wardens, the Assistants, the Livery, and the Widows. Each is a broadside and they closely resemble the more familiar broadside Livery Lists. They possess a formality in their appearance, whereas the octavo *List* has a totally informal character.

The purpose of the present piece is to present this *List* and to comment on it.

Dating the list

As part of the work done on the Stationers' Company archives for the *London Booktrades Database*, maintained in Oxford, an attempt is being made to record the details of the ownership of shares in the English Stock and the dividends paid out. For the period 1695 to 1830 this is more or less completed. We have, therefore, a very useful tool on hand for working on the Partners of the English Stock during the period in which the *List* was produced.

A glance at the names on the *List* would indicate that it was produced in the last quarter of the century, but we can be much more specific.

In the annotations to the *List* I have given the inclusive dates for all the dividends received by each individual during their Partnership in the English Stock. These are expressed, as in the *Database*, by three digits representing the year and an 'M' for the Midsummer dividend and an 'X' for the Christmas dividend, e.g. '790M' or '810X'. The first date in the case of the men would be that following their election to their original share. By the date in question this would have invariably been for £40. For the women, it would be the first date following the death of their husband. The *List* must have been prepared before the latest 'starting date' of any of those on it. That date proves to be 785X (i.e. 22 December 1785) and is provided by entry no.133 – Samuel Hayes (ST/3:3821); and entry no.185 – William Caslon (ST/3:1543). No widows began their receipt of dividends on that date.

On checking the new £40 shareholders appearing on the Dividend List 785X (i.e. 22 December 1785) we find four names – Hayes and Caslon who, as we have just seen, appear on the *List*; and also Charles Treadgold (ST/3:4597) and John William Galabin (ST/3:4746) who do not appear. Presumably, the *List* was prepared between the elections of Hayes and Caslon on the one hand, and those of Treadgold and Galabin on the other.

It turns out that Hayes and Caslon were both elected at the earliest opportunity in the new Guild year, at the Court held on 5 July 1785. In 1785 the Midsummer Dividend had been paid on the last Court day (i.e. 23 June 1785) before the election of the new Master and Wardens on 2 July 1785. The election of Treadgold and Galabin followed that of Hayes and Caslon at the next regular monthly meeting of the Court on 2 August 1785. This provides a window for the preparation of our *List* between the two dates – 5 July and 2 August 1785.

We can approach the problem another way. It follows that if the last dividend date for anyone on the *List* happens to be 785M (i.e. 23 June 1785), then the *List* must have been prepared before they were known to be dead or had otherwise forfeited their share. Three entries meet the requirement. They are entry no.109 – William Strahan (ST/3:7992); entry no.225 – Charles Clavey (ST/3:3994); and entry no.177 – Elizabeth Emonson (ST/3:0995W). We know that Strahan died on 9 July 1785. We also know that the Court was made aware of both Charles Clavey's and Elizabeth Emonson's death on 2 August 1785, the very day that Treadgold and Galabin were elected to their £40 shares.

The *List* would appear to have been prepared and printed some time after the elections of Hayes and Caslon on 5 July 1785, but before the news of the deaths of Strahan, Clavey and Emonson, and the election of Treadgold and Galabin – possibly before 9 July 1785 or, at the latest, 2 August 1785. As Strahan's share would have passed to his widow there was no need to report his death to the Court for disposal of the share, but it seems unlikely that the officials of the Company would have remained ignorant of his death for any length of time. It would seem likely that the *List* was prepared early in July 1785.

A further confirmation of the 5 July date is afforded by those who had received dividends on 23 June 1785 but were not included on the *List*. Elizabeth Mount (ST/3:3167W) was such a case. Her death was reported to the Court on 5 July 1785.

The occasion

Another rather important Partner in the English Stock received his dividend on 23 June 1785, and does not appear on the *List*. John Wilkie (ST/3:4287), the Treasurer or Warehousekeeper, had died on 2 July 1785, the day that the Court was electing the new Master and Wardens for the ensuing year. As we have already seen, there was a meeting of the Court on Tuesday 5 July 1785 and it was then ordered that the election of a Treasurer or Warehousekeeper for the remainder of the year (i.e. until 1 March 1786) should take place on Friday 15 July 1785. The Court and the Partners duly met on that day and Robert Horsfield (ST/3:5147) was elected to succeed Wilkie as Treasurer of the English Stock.

Horsfield's name, without an address, appears last on our *List*. Whether or not this is significant I do not know. He was not sworn into office until a special Court held for that purpose on Tuesday 16 August 1785. It will be seen that the people at the end of the *List* are those living out of town, and we might suspect that Horsfield was one of those, because less than a year later—on 13 June 1786—he was reprimanded by the Master for absenting himself from sleeping in the House allowed him as Treasurer without permission and was told that he should forthwith give up his 'Lodging in the Country'. However, it may just be that Horsfield was regularly around at the Hall and no address was felt necessary. Marshall Sheepey (ST/3:4028), the Beadle, is also in this group—though the Hall is given as his address.

It would seem that the occasion for the preparation of the *List* was clearly to do with the events surrounding the election for a new Treasurer or Warehousekeeper after the death of Wilkie.

The order of the *List*

The order of the *List* is perhaps not so random as it at first appears. It is worth considering the *List* not as of people but as a series of addresses. It is fairly rough and ready and there are some peculiarities, but I believe that it basically represents a route, or possibly three routes, that might have been taken by anyone delivering notices to the Partners listed. Let us try and follow the journey—

The Eastern Circuit

After a quick and, as we will see below, rather unnecessary foray south into Blackfriars we would re-emerge on Ludgate Hill (1-5) and, possibly by way of Stationers' Alley, return to Catherine Caslon's (6) opposite the Hall. We then go out into Ave Maria Lane (7-11) and Warwick Lane (12), then east along Paternoster Row (13-24) taking in premises just off the main thoroughfare — Queen's Head Alley (17) and Ivy Lane (21). Then comes a turn around St Paul's Church Yard (25-29).

This might have been a short preliminary round after which we would return to the Hall, for at this point the journey makes something of a jump to the north-west and Snow Hill (30-31). Then begins a long journey east along Newgate Street and Cheapside (32-48) taking several excursions off the main line, particularly northwards — e.g. Staining Lane (36), Wood Street (37), King's Street (44) to the Guildhall (45-46), and Coleman Street (48). At the eastern end of Cheapside, we go south-east down Bucklersbury (49-50) into Walbrook (51), then back north to the Poultry (52).

The main thrust is still eastwards along Cornhill, but around the Bank (59) and the Royal Exchange (64) there have to be many excursions — to the north Finch Lane (56), Old Broad Street (58), Bartholomew Lane (60-61); to the south Exchange Alley (65), Abchurch Lane (66-68), Lombard Street (69-70), into Gracechurch Street (71-72), and across it into Fenchurch Street (74).

Heading back north to Leadenhall Street we continue the easterly progress (75-77), out on to Aldgate as far as the corner of Houndsditch (78).

William Walton on London Wall presents an awkward diversion, for at this point the journey really takes a southerly direction to the district around the Tower of London (80-89).

Then begins the journey back west heading along Little Tower Street (90) to Pudding Lane (91). At this point we have to make another diversion south to London Bridge and across into Southwark (93-94). Back northwards across the bridge in order to recommence our journey westwards along Cannon Street (95) and Watling Street (97-98) to Doctors Commons (99-100).

Finally, this eastern circuit may have been completed by returning to the Old Bailey (101) and Ludgate Hill (102-103). One wonders why the southerly diversion at the beginning of the *List* (1-5) was not included at this point.

The Western Circuit

It may have been that Isherwood (102) and Morgan (103) on Ludgate Hill were the beginning of a second journey westwards. However, we will commence with Henry Baldwin in Fleet Street (104). There are immediate diversions south into Dorset Street (105), and north along Shoe Lane to the New Street vicinity (106-111). Generally pushing westwards along Fleet

Street and the courts and lanes off it to the Temple (112-128), we arrive for the first time at the area around St Clements and whilst in the Strand go south down Essex Street (129).

Here is a further rather large jump westward to Pall Mall (130), followed by a northerly turn up St James's Street (131), on into New Bond Street (132) and out on to Oxford Street (133). Having taken this route, it is necessary to head south again into Mayfair to Hertford Street (134) returning north again to Oxford Street, via Park Street (135).

We go north of Oxford Street to Titchfield Street (136-137), then back in a south-easterly direction to Lisle Street (138) and eastwards to Drury Lane (139) and Lincoln's Inn Fields (140). The addresses causing a quick diversion north across High Holborn into Red Lion Square (141) and Lamb's Conduit Street (142-143) would seem to make more sense in the Northern Circuit to be described later.

After heading south via Chancery Lane (144-145), it is necessary to turn east again to Clare Market (146), which might have been dealt with earlier when going between Drury Lane and Lincoln's Inn Fields (139, 140). South-east again, crossing the Strand into the Temple to King's Bench Walk (147). Returning to the Temple Bar area a number of people can be dealt with on Fleet Street and the Strand around St Clements (148-153). These include, apparently, Thomas Evans (150), whom we visited on our way out (123).

The route now mysteriously heads west again down the Strand (154, 157) via Craven Street (155-156) to Charing Cross (158-159) and into Westminster (160). Then turning back to Charing Cross for Mews Gate (161) and going into Pall Mall for a second time (162). It would appear that this group is somewhat out of place and should have been taken in on our first trip westwards between William Sandby in Essex Street (129) and Paul Vaillant in Pall Mall (130).

At this point, I suggest we return to the Hall before starting a third circuit in a northerly direction.

The Northern Circuit (or meander)
We begin at Warwick Court, Holborn (163-164), and go north to Bedford Row (165-166), only to dart south again into the previous circuit for Wild Court (167-168). Again this could easily have been taken in earlier, as suggested above for Clare Market, between Drury Lane and Lincoln's Inn Fields (139, 140).

However, we now return north to Holborn (169-171) and beyond to Kirkby Street, Hatton Garden (172), then progress eastwards via Holborn Hill (173) through Smithfield (175) to Aldersgate Street (176). We will ignore the insertion of William Collins of Salisbury at this point, though there may have been some point of contact on our route. We must slightly turn back again to the north-west, to Clerkenwell (177) returning by St John's Square (178) to the Aldersgate Street area (179-182). Nichol's Square (179) being beyond Aldersgate Street to the east may have been better as the last of this group rather than the first, since — after the intrusion of another Collins — we must head north-east towards Finsbury for Chiswell Street (184-185). Finally comes a tour of the Islington area to the north (186-194).

This is the point at which any discernible pattern in our *List* of addresses ends. Other than that, the remaining names are Partners who lived in the more remote suburbs, the near country and the further provinces. John Miller was in New York and the Rev. William Tooke, apparently, in Russia.

If I am right about the ordering of the list as a guide to delivering notices to Partners in the English Stock, then it may have been that the *List* was prepared between 5 July 1785, after the election of a new Treasurer was ordered, and 9 July 1785 when William Strahan died, for there would undoubtedly have been a need to take out notices of the election on 15 July 1785. However, one does wonder why anyone went to the trouble of printing it if that was all.

The value of the *List*

This *List* supplements a number of other sources. The membership of the Stationers' Company throughout the 18th century is now pretty well established. Manuscript and printed lists of the Livery, of Bindings, Freedoms and Cloathings abound for given dates. The membership of the English Stock, together with the progression of share ownership, throughout the century is now determined with the exception of only one or two minor queries. All this information is recorded in the *London Booktrades Database*. Indeed, that is what made the fixing of a date to this *List* relatively simple.

But this *List*'s arrangement by perambulation is unusual and significant; it gives us a clear indication of who was topographically close to whom, information which can often be significant in disentangling the reasons for trade relationships. Moreover, any list which can be dated has some importance. With the usual caveats, it narrows down the months in which people might have died or otherwise been lost to the list makers. When a list contains addresses, then it has added significance. In his introduction to *The Earliest Directory of the Book Trade, by John Pendred (1785)* (London: The Bibliographical Society, supplement 14, 1955), p.53, Graham Pollard describes the (octavo) series of printed Livery Lists, which appear to be the first printed ones to contain addresses, as commencing on 1 July 1786 — just over a year after our *List*. This description appears to be made on the strength of a set at Stationers' Hall 'which lacks only the year 1794', but unfortunately this set is no longer to be found (R. Myers, *The Stationers' Company Archive*, p.41). Pollard's own set of these very rare lists did not begin until the issue dated 30 June 1792. Our *List* may be able to lay claim to being the first printed list of a group of its members produced by the Company which included addresses. Pendred, of course, also produced his listings in 1785 — another story!

The List

The consecutive roman numbering of the entries has been provided. The *italic* numbering represents the hierarchical order that the Partners would have had within the English Stock at the time the *List* was prepared. It is based on the 785M (i.e. 23 June 1785) dividend list amended to take into account the intervening election of the Master and Wardens, and such deaths and elections as had taken place.

The first line is a transcription of the entry as it appears on the *List*. On the *List* forms of address such as 'Mr.' and 'Mrs.' tend only to occur when a change is necessary, the subsequent entries being indented. The long-s has been dropped.

This is followed by any correction or expansion of the name as given in the *List* thought to be appropriate. In the case of widows the identity of the deceased husband is made clear. The widow's maiden name may also be given.

The number, of the form 'ST/3: . . .', is the identifying number in *The London Booktrades Database*. The final four digits are also the number for the first chronological appearance of the person in D. F. McKenzie's *Stationers' Company Apprentices 1701-1800* (Oxford: Oxford Bibliographical Society, new series, vol.19, 1978). By consulting McKenzie through that number information on apprenticeships, turn-overs, freedoms and cloathings can be readily obtained. *The London Booktrades Database* attempts to follow the person's career through the Company and provide further information. There are one or two persons in the *List* who have no entry in McKenzie. This fact is noted in the entry. Widows have a 'W' after their husband's number.

'Incl.Divs. =' records the first and last dividends received by the individual as a result of their membership of the English Stock. The three digits indicate the year; 'M' indicates the Midsummer dividend; and 'X' indicates the Christmas dividend. This is followed, in roman type, by the value of the final share held by the person. For members of the Company included in this *List* it can be assumed that they started with the lowest share of £40. The share value given in *italic* type represents the partner's holding at the time the *List* was prepared. Many in the *List* were affected by the additional shares that were instituted in the early years of the 19th century, so it cannot be assumed that they all followed the same sequence of shares during their careers. Full details of their progress through the English Stock, and all the dividends received, are given in *The London Booktrades Database*. For the widows the figure is that of the share they inherited from their husbands. As they were not eligible to progress any further it will obviously be the same in both occurrences. During the last decades of the 18th century and throughout the period which concerns these people, a member of the stock had to bequeath his share to his widow — it did not pass to her automatically.

Finally, an indication of the date of death of the person is given. This date should follow shortly after the date of the last dividend mentioned — unless the person had requested to give up their share, had re-married in the case of a widow, or had been declared bankrupt in which case they forfeited their share. Once bankrupts had satisfied the Commissioners, however, they were eligible to be re-elected into the Stock. Some entries will conceal such lapses. If there was no widow to inherit the share, the death would be reported to the Court, but rarely the actual date of the death, and the share was disposed of to another member of the Company. If there was a widow there was no need to report the death to the Court, so it would go unnoticed in the Court Minutes. The only indication would be that payment would be entered under the widow on the next distribution of a dividend. A widow could retain that share for the rest of her life, as most of them did, but if she re-married the share had to be returned to the Company and it was disposed of as though she had died. '*d.before*' may be the date a death was reported to the Court, the date of a grant of probate or administration of a will, or the date of the first dividend after the death of the person. Notes of pay-outs and re-marriages are given in the entry. Specific dates of death when known from other sources are given as '*d.*'.

[1, *229*]   Mrs.Tricket, Broad Way, Black Friars
        Sarah, widow of William Trickett[s].   ST/3:8297W   *Incl.Divs.* = 780X-809X
        (£40, *£40*)   *d.before* 3 Apr 1810
[2, *177*]   Mr.John Barker, Broad Way Black Friars
        ST/3:4941   *Incl.Divs.* = 779M-830X (£400, *£40*)   *d.* 25 Mar 1831
[3, *153*]   Samuel Brooke, No.7, Chatham Square
        ST/3:3728   *Incl.Divs.* = 776X-797X (£80, *£40*)   *d.* 20 Jan 1798
[4, *227*]   Mrs.Newbery, Ludgate Street
        Elizabeth [Bryant], widow of Francis Newbery.   ST/3:2799W   *Incl.Divs.* =
        780X-821M (£40, *£40*)   *d.before* 6 Nov 1821
[5, *23*]   Jenour, at Mr.Lawrence's Ludgate Street
        Eleanor, widow of Joshua Jenour.   ST/3:4532W   *Incl.Divs.* = 774X-802X
        (£320, *£320*)   *d.before* 1 Feb 1803
[6, *73*]   Caslon, opposite Stationers Hall
        Catherine, widow of Thomas Caslon.   ST/3:1769W   *Incl.Divs.* = 783M-786M
        (£160, *£160*)   *Re-married* to Thomas Prosser of Monmouth. Reported to the
        Court 5 Sep 1786
[7, *25*]   Mary Say, No.10, Ave-Maria Lane
        Widow of Charles Green Say.   ST/3:0792W   *Incl.Divs.* = 775X-787M
        (£320, *£320*)   *Re-married* to Edward Vint of Crayford at St.Mary, Ludgate on
        11 Nov 1787. Reported to the Court on 4 Dec 1787
[8, *33*]   Mr.Bedwell Law, No.13, Ave-Maria Lane
        ST/3:8508   *Incl.Divs.* = 759M-797X (£320, *£160*)   *d.* 25 May 1798
[9, *54*]   Thomas Pote, Eton, at Mr.Law's, Ave-Maria Lane
        ST/3:6442   *Incl.Divs.* = 763M-794X (£320, *£160*)   *d.* 28 Dec 1794
[10, *118*]   John Bird, No.5, Ave-Maria Lane
        ST/3:0842   *Incl.Divs.* = 772M-804M (£160, *£80*)   *d.* 12 Aug 1804
[11, *178*]   George Ferebee, at Mrs.Say's Ave-Maria Lane
        ST/3:3965   *Incl.Divs.* = 779M-788X (£40, *£40*)   *d.before* 9 Jan 1789   Though
        bound to Luke Hinde, Ferebee was turned over to, and freed by, Edward Say
        —Mary Say's father-in-law
[12, *182*]   Charles Heath, No.21, Warwick Lane
        ST/3:6169   *Incl.Divs.* = 779X-817X (£160, *£40*)   *d.before* 2 Feb 1818
[13, *30*]   Thomas Longman, Paternoster Row
        ST/3:5069   *Incl.Divs.* = 758M-796X (£320, *£160*)   *d.* 5 Feb 1797
[14, *19*]   Thomas Harrison, No.35, Paternoster Row
        ST/3:5985   *Incl.Divs.* = 756X-791M (£320, *£320*)   *d.* 4 Nov 1791   Harrison, in
        fact, requested to be paid out on 4 Aug 1791. This was granted
[15, *115*]   John Bew, No.28, Paternoster Row
        ST/3:0385   *Incl.Divs.* = 771X-792X (£80, *£80*)   *d.before* 7 Aug 1792   If this is
        true then the 792X dividend should clearly have been recorded as being paid
        to his widow, Jane
[16, *203*]   John Robinson, No.25, Paternoster Row
        ST/3:3873   *Incl.Divs.* = 784M-813M (£200, *£40*)   *d.* 2 Dec 1813
[17, *229*]   Mrs.Crowther, Queen's Head Alley, Paternoster Row
        Ann, widow of William Crowther. ST/3:7056W   *Incl.Divs.* = 781X-785X
        (£40, *£40*)   *Re-married.* Reported to the Court on 7 Feb 1786

[18, *136*] Mrs.Elizabeth Baldwin, at Mr.Baldwin's, Paternoster Row
Widow of Richard Baldwin. ST/3:0376W *Incl.Divs.* = 770M-809M (£80, *£80*)
d. 19 Aug 1809

[19, *156*] William Goldsmith, Esq; No.24, Paternoster Row
ST/3:1132 *Incl.Divs.* = 777M-795X (£80, *£40*) *d.* 4 Aug 1795

[20, *89*] Mr.H.S.Woodfall, No.22, Paternoster Row
Henry Sampson Woodfall ST/3:9078 *Incl.Divs.* = 768M-805X (£320, *£80*)
d. 12 Dec 1805 In fact H.S.W. was dead eight days before the 805X dividend
date, though his death was not reported to the Court until 4 Feb 1806. He also
appears to have been elected to a £400 share on 6 Aug 1805, though there is
no evidence that he accepted it

[21, *98*] John Boys, No.2, Ivy Lane
ST/3:2226 *Incl.Divs.* = 769X-802X (£160, *£80*) *d.* 21 Jan 1803

[22, *183*] James Buckland, jun. No. 57, Paternoster Row
ST/3:7956 *Incl.Divs.* = 780M-809M (£40, *£40*) *d.before* 19 Dec 1809 Buck-
land's entry in the 809X dividend list is crossed out and annotated 'Dead no
Widow' & 'paid to Geo Wilkie by G.G.'

[23, *125*] Henry Goldney, No.15, Paternoster Row
ST/3:6795 *Incl.Divs.* = 773M-806M (£400, *£80*) *d. c.*Sep 1806

[24, *18*] Stanley Crowder, No.12, Paternoster Row
ST/3:4021 *Incl.Divs.* = 756X-794X (£320, *£320*) *d.* 23 May 1795

[25, *224*] Mrs.Smith, at Mr.Lewis's, St.Paul's Church Yard
Mary, widow of Joseph Smith. ST/3:5060W *Incl.Divs.* = 777X-789X
(£40, *£40*) *Paid out* at her request 2 Mar 1790

[26, *10*] John Rivington, Esq; No.62, St.Paul's Church Yard
ST/3:6844 *Incl.Divs.* = 750M-791X (£320, *£320*) *d.* 16 Jan 1792

[27, *117*] Mr.Francis Rivington, No.62, St.Paul's Church Yard
ST/3:6885 *Incl.Divs.* = 772M-822M (£400, *£80*) *d.* 18 Oct 1822

[28, *212*] Charles Rivington, No.62, St.Paul's Church Yard
ST/3:6884 *Incl.Divs.* = 785M-830X (£400, *£40*) *d.* 26 May 1831

[29, *148*] James Simons, Canterbury, or at Mr.Johnson's St.Paul's Church Yard
ST/3:3421 *Incl.Divs.* = 770M-806X (£40, *£40*) *d.* Feb 1807

[30, *94*] Fenwick, Snow Hill
Henry Fenwick ST/3:5901 *Incl.Divs.* = 769M-822M (£160, *£80*) *d.* Nov
1822

[31, *41*] William Clarke, Snow Hill
ST/3:3993 *Incl.Divs.* = 757M-794X (£160, *£160*) *d.before* 3 Feb 1795

[32, *90*] Thomas Curtis, No.10, Newgate Street
ST/3:2937 *Incl.Divs.* = 768M-812X (£400, *£80*) *d.* 21 Apr 1813

[33, *2*] William Fenner, No.31, Newgate Street
ST/3:6481 *Incl.Divs.* = 758M-809M (£400, *£160*) *d.* 30 Oct 1809. Fenner had
been elected Upper Warden on 2 Jul 1785

[34, *68*] Thomas Bowles, No.49, Newgate Street
ST/3:0980 *Incl.Divs.* = 766M-787X (£160, *£160*) *d.* 28 May 1788

[35, *127*] Mathew Brown, Windmill Court
ST/3:1241 *Incl.Divs.* = 773X-817X (£200, *£80*) *d.* 10 Jan 1818

[36, *48*] Charles Rivington, Staining Lane
ST/3:6782 *Incl.Divs.* = 760M-790M (£160, *£160*) *d.* 22 Jun 1790

[37, *155*] Peter Wynne, Wood Street
ST/3:6258 *Incl.Divs.* = 778X-806M (£320, *£40*) *d.* 30 Jun 1806

[38, *129*] Thomas Vallance, No. 120, Cheapside
ST/3:0415 *Incl.Divs.* = 775M-822X (£400, *£80*) *d.* 28 Feb 1823

[39, *130*] Samuel Simmons, at Lincoln, or ditto
ST/3:8058 *Incl.Divs.* = 775M-819M (£200, *£80*) *d.* Sep 1819

[40, *135*] Mrs.Johnson, Wood Street, Cheapside
Mary, widow of Job Johnson. ST/3:4571W *Incl.Divs.* = 765X-791M
(£80, *£80*) *d.before* 22 Dec 1791

[41, *140*] Sarah Peck, at Mr.Wynn's, Wood Street, Cheapside
Widow of Ken[d]rick Peck. ST/3:9154W *Incl.Divs.* = 772X-802M (£80, *£80*)
d. 7 Dec 1802

[42, *29*]   John Boydell, Esq; Alderman, Cheapside
ST/3:1027   *Incl.Divs.* = 763M-804X (£320, *£160*)   *d.* 12 Dec 1804 J.B., in
fact, was dead eight days before the 804X was paid

[43, *187*]   Josiah Boydell, Esq; Cheapside
ST/3:1029   *Incl.Divs.* = 780X-816X (£320, *£40*)   *d.* 27 Mar 1817

[44, *85*]   Mr.William Chapman, No.36, King-Street, Cheapside
ST/3:1659   *Incl.Divs.* = 767M-800M (£320, *£80*)   *d.* 14 Aug 1800

[45, *50*]   John Gurr, Guildhall
ST/3:5014   *Incl.Divs.* = 762M-791X (£160, *£160*)   *d.before* 21 Jun 1792

[46, *97*]   Henry Parker, ditto
ST/3:6115   *Incl.Divs.* = 769M-809M (£400, *£80*)   *d.* 28 May 1809

[47, *123*]   Thomas Davidson, No.18, Size Lane
ST/3:2332   *Incl.Divs.* = 773M-821M (£200, *£80*)   *d.before* 22 Jun 1821

[48, *49*]   John Bailey, No.4, Packer's Court, Coleman Street
ST/3:0249   *Incl.Divs.* = 760X-787M (£160, *£160*)   *d.* 19 Jun 1787 J.B.
apparently died two days before the 787M dividend

[49, *179*]   James Wallis Street, No.2, Bucklersbury
ST/3:4141   *Incl.Divs.* = 779M-816X (£320, *£40*)   *d.* 10 Apr 1817

[50, *180*]   Mr.Richard Starkey, at Mr.Street's, Bucklersbury
ST/3:4140   *Incl.Divs.* = 779M-809X (£200, *£40*)   *d.* 22 Jan 1810

[51, *44*]   Thomas Hooke, No.8, Walbrook
ST/3:7720   *Incl.Divs.* = 759M-814X (£320, *£160*)   *d.before* 6 Jun 1815

[52, *101*]   Charles Dilly, No.22, Poultry
ST/3:2475   *Incl.Divs.* = 770M-806X (£400, *£80*)   *d.* 5 May 1807

[53, *75*]   Mrs.Moore, Grocers Alley, Poultry
Elizabeth, widow of John Moore. ST/3:9049W *Incl.Divs.* = 770X-787M
(£160, *£160*)   *d.* Jun 1787 possibly just before the dividend was paid

[54, *86*]   Mr.Richard Wells, No.11, Cornhill
Richard Welles. ST/3:8637 *Incl.Divs.* = 767M-802X (£320, *£80*)   *d.* 13 Mar
1803

[55, *223*]   Mrs.Pearch, at ditto
Ann, widow of George Pearch. ST/3:6315W *Incl.Divs.* = 775X-793X
(£40, *£40*)   *d.before* 4 Mar 1794

[56, *225*]   Davenhill, Finch Lane
Mary, widow of William Davenhill. ST/3:2891W *Incl.Divs.* = 779M-786X
(£40, *£40*)   *Paid-out* at her own request 3 Feb 1787

[57, *204*]   Mr.John Barnes Pearce, No.19, Cornhill
ST/3:5713   *Incl.Divs.* = 784M-788X (£40, *£40*)   *Bankrupt* reported to the
Court on 9 Jan 1789 and share disposed of

[58, *216*]   Mrs.Fielder, No.82, Old Broad Street
Elizabeth, widow of William Fielder. ST/3:2902W *Incl.Divs.* = 763M-820M
(£40, *£40*)   *d.before* 7 Nov 1820

[59, *167*]   Mr.Samuel Ethridge, Bullion Office, Bank
ST/3:0889   *Incl.Divs.* = 777X-804M (£160, *£40*)   *d.before* 3 May 1804

[60, *96*]   William Stephens, No.2, Bartholomew Lane
ST/3:9169   *Incl.Divs.* = 769M-816M (£400, *£80*)   *d.* 23 Oct 1816

[61, *120*]   Mathew Bloxam, Esq; No.34, Bartholomew Lane
Sir Mathew Bloxam. ST/3:1875   *Incl.Divs.* = 772X-822M (£400, *£80*)
d. 16 Oct 1822

[62, *92*]   Mr.Thomas Smith, No.13, Swithin's Alley, Cornhill
Sweeting's Alley. ST/3:7041   *Incl.Divs.* = 768M-792M (£160, *£80*)   *Bankrupt*
Share disposed of at Court on 6 Nov 1792

[63, *91*]   James Bate, No.7, Cornhill
ST/3:1874   *Incl.Divs.* = 768M-809M (£400, *£80*)   *d.* 5 Oct 1809

[64, *106*]   William Domville, No.95, under the Royal Exchange
Sir William Domville. ST/3:3065   *Incl.Divs.* = 770M-832X (£400, *£80*)
d. 8 Feb 1833

[65, *151*]   Thomas Smith, at a Sadler's, 'Change Alley
ST/3:4498   *Incl.Divs.* = 776M-829M (£400, *£40*)   *d.before* 22 Dec 1829

[66, *4*]   Thomas Wright, Esq; Alderman, No.30, Abchurch Lane, Lombard Street
             ST/3:8425 *Incl.Divs.* = 753M-797X (£320, *£320*) *d.* 8 Apr 1798
[67, *5*]   William Gill, Esq; Alderman, No.30, Abchurch Lane, Lombard Street
             ST/3:1158 *Incl.Divs.* = 755M-797X (£320, *£320*) *d.* 26 Mar 1798
[68, *207*] Joseph Gardner, at ditto
             Joseph Gardiner. ST/3:0555 *Incl.Divs.* = 784X-828X (£400, *£40*) *d.* 13 Apr
             1829
[69, *93*]   William Cooke, No.26, Nicholas Lane, Lombard Street
             ST/3:8521 *Incl.Divs.* = 869X-797X (£160, *£80*) *d.before* 6 Mar 1798
[70, *197*] Charles Edward Wilson, No.23, Lombard Street
             Charles Edward Wilsonn. ST/3:8929 *Incl.Divs.* = 783M-812M (£200, *£40*)
             Paid-out on 7 Jul 1812
[71, *84*]   Henry Clarke, No.72, Gracechurch Street
             ST/3:8057 *Incl.Divs.* = 767M-820X (£400, *£80*) *d.* 31 Dec 1820
[72, *100*] James Durnford, No.36, Gracechurch Street
             ST/3:3912 *Incl.Divs.* = 779M-785X (£80, *£100*) *d.* 16 Feb 1786
[73, *3*]   Thomas Greenhill, Esq; No.14, Gracechurch Street
             ST/3:8420 *Incl.Divs.* = 759M-797X (£320, *£160*) *d.* 16 Jan 1798. Greenhill
             had been elected Under Warden on 2 Jul 1785
[74, *74*]   Mrs.Mary Cocksedge, at Mr.Williams's, No.149, Fenchurch Street
             Widow of Thomas Cocksedge. ST/3:5863W *Incl.Divs.* = 772M-787M
             (£160, *£160*) *d.before* 3 Jul 1787
[75, *6*]   Mr.John Vowell, No.133, Leadenhall Street
             ST/3·8389 *Incl.Divs.* = 744M-800X (£320, *£320*) *d.* 26 Mar 1801
[76, *102*] John Vowell, jun. ditto
             ST/3:8390 *Incl.Divs.* = 770M-791M (£160, *£80*) *d.before* 28 Dec 1791
[77, *141*] Mrs.Stedman, No.24, Leadenhall Street
             Elizabeth, widow of Christopher Stedman. ST/3:0203W *Incl.Divs.* =
             774M-798M (£80, *£80*) *d.before* 3 Jul 1798
[78, *116*] Mr.Jonathan Moore, the Corner of Houndsditch, Aldgate
             ST/3:5552 *Incl.Divs.* = 772M-817X (£200, *£80*) *d.before* 3 Mar 1818
[79, *65*]   William Walton, London Wall
             ST/3:1850 *Incl.Divs.* = 761X-786X (£160, *£160*) *d.* 17 Feb 1787
[80, *13*]   John Mount, Esq; Tower Hill
             ST/3:5668 *Incl.Divs.* = 754M-786M (£320, *£320*) *d.before* 22 Dec 1786
[81, *79*]   Mrs.Sarah Page, Tower Hill
             Widow of Thomas Page. ST/3:6016W *Incl.Divs.* = 781M-805X (£160, *£160*)
             d.before 4 Feb 1806
[82, *20*]   Jane Page, Tower Hill
             Widow of Thomas Page. ST/3:6012W *Incl.Divs.* = 762M-792X (£320, *£320*)
             d.before 5 Feb.1793
[83, *159*] Mr.James Davidson, No.7, Postern Row
             ST/3:5656 *Incl.Divs.* = 777M-801M (£160, *£40*) *d.before* 30 Sep 1801
[84, *109*] John Davidson, No.7, Postern Row
             ST/3:2321 *Incl.Divs.* = 770X-798X (£160, *£80*) *d.before* 1 Sep 1798
[85, *53*]   John March, George Street, Tower Hill
             ST/3:5167 *Incl.Divs.* = 763M-797X (£320, *£160*) *d.* 15 Feb 1798
[86, *38*]   William Johnston, at Hampton Court, or Ordnance Office, Tower
             ST/3:5068 *Incl.Divs.* = 755X-804M (£160, *£160*) *d.before* 4 Dec 1804
[87, *132*] John Bullock, Battersea, or Ordnance Office, Tower
             ST/3:6642 *Incl.Divs.* = 774M-818M (£200, *£80*) *d.before* 7 Jul 1818
[88, *1*]   Robert Gyfford, No.35, Tower Street
             ST/3:2942 *Incl.Divs.* = 759M-805X (£400, *£320*) *d.* 12 May 1806. Gyfford
             had been elected Master on 2 Jul 1785
[89, *46*]   James Pritchard, Searchers Office, Custon House
             ST/3:2335 *Incl.Divs.* = 760M-806M (£160, *£160*) *d.before* 4 Nov 1806
[90, *164*] William Timson, No.6, Little Tower Street
             ST/3:4401 *Incl.Divs.* = 777X-818M (£200, *£40*) *d.* 23 Jun 1818
[91, *51*]   Bartholomew Penny, East Bourn, Sussex, or at Mr.Tims's, Pudding Lane
             ST/3:6288 *Incl.Divs.* = 763M-797X (£160, *£160*) *d.* 31 May 1798

[92, *64*]   John Burbank, Bridge House Yard
ST/3:6393 *Incl.Divs.* = 764X-792M (£160, *£160*) *d.* 7 Jun 1792. Apparently died 14 days before the 792M dividend

[93, *200*]   James Neatby, Brige-Foot, Southwark
ST/3:8655 *Incl.Divs.* = 783X-788X (£40, *£40*) *d.* 31 Dec 1788

[94, *163*]   Francis Green, Borough High Street
Francis Greene. ST/3:1747 *Incl.Divs.* = 777X-803M (£160, *£40*) *d.before* 20 Dec 1803

[95, *174*]   William Flower, No.47, Cannon Street
ST/3:2941 *Incl.Divs.* = 778X-805M (£160, *£40*) *d.* 13 Oct 1805. W.F. had been elected to a £200 share on 6 Aug 1805, his death was reported to the Court on 5 November and both shares were disposed of

[96, *26*]   Mrs.Flower, ditto
Martha, widow of George Flower. ST/3:8387W *Incl.Divs.* = 778M-804X (£320, *£320*) *d.before* 5 Feb 1805

[97, *60*]   Mr.Edward Gilberd, No.12, Watling Street
ST/3:3229 *Incl.Divs.* = 763M-806X (£160, *£160*) *d.before* 23 Jun 1807

[98, *186*]   Nathaniel Wilkinson, at Mr.Gilberd's, No.12, Watling Street
ST/3:3232 *Incl.Divs.* = 780X-824X (£200, *£40*) *d.before* 24 Oct 1823 for in spite of the change of dividends from Nathaniel to his wife Georgina not taking place until 825M, there is a clear note on his will at Stationers' Hall which gives the date of probate as 24 Oct 1823

[99, *168*]   John Crickitt, Esq; No.14, Doctors Commons
ST/3:2812 *Incl.Divs.* = 777X-811M (£320, *£40*) *d.* 30 Aug 1811

[100, *210*]   Mr.Thomas Moore, No.8, Wardrobe Place, Doctors Commons
ST/3:0983 *Incl.Divs.* = 784X-790M (£40, *£40*) *d.before* 23 Dec 1790

[101, *194*]   John Ryland, Old Bailey
ST/3:7089 *Incl.Divs.* = 782M-788X (£40, *£40*) *Bankrupt* reported to the Court on 3 Feb 1789 and the share was disposed of

[102, *122*]   Henry Isherwood, Ludgate Hill
ST/3:4391 *Incl.Divs.* = 773M-811X (£400, *£80*) *d.before* 4 Feb 1812

[103, *192*]   John Morgan, Ludgate Hill
ST/3:1872 *Incl.Divs.* = 781X-816X (£320, *£40*) *d.* 4 Mar 1817

[104, *59*]   Henry Baldwin, No.108, Fleet Street
ST/3:7198 *Incl.Divs.* = 763M-812X (£400, *£160*) *d.* 21 Feb 1813

[105, *133*]   William Woodfall, Dorset Street, Salisbury Court
ST/3:0390 *Incl.Divs.* = 776M-803M (£160, *£80*) *d.* 1 Aug 1803

[106, *112*]   John Walkden, No.5, Shoe Lane
ST/3:8423 *Incl.Divs.* = 771M-808M (£400, *£80*) *d.* 14 Jun 1808

[107, *208*]   William Wenman, No.144, Fleet Street
No record of a William, almost certainly Joseph Wenman. ST/3:4667 *Incl.Divs.* = 784X-789X (£40, *£40*) *d.* 3 Mar 1790

[108, *189*]   John Smith, King's Head Court, Shoe Lane
ST/3:7540 *Incl.Divs.* = 781M-799X (£80, *£40*) *d.before* 24 Jun 1800

[109, *9*]   William Strahan, Esq; New Street, Shoe Lane
ST/3:7992 *Incl.Divs.* = 749M-785M (£320, *£320*) *d.* 9 Jul 1785

[110, *170*]   Mr.Andrew Strahan, New Street, Shoe Lane
ST/3:8011 *Incl.Divs.* = 778X-831M (£400, *£40*) *d.* 25 Aug 1831

[111, *161*]   Edward Johnston, at ditto
ST/3:4595 *Incl.Divs.* = 777M-795X (£80, *£40*) *d.before* 7 Feb 1797 It would appear that on this day the Court made an exception in allowing Jane Johnson to inherit her husband's share

[112, *217*]   Mrs.Harrison, Red Lion Court, Fleet Street
Mary, widow of James Harrison. ST/3:7204W *Incl.Divs.* = 769M-796X (£40, *£40*) *d.before* 4 Apr 1797

[113, *37*]   Mr.John Hawys, No.6, Johnson's Court, Fleet Street
ST/3:7205 *Incl.Divs.* = 755X-785X (£160, *£160*) *d.* 27 Feb 1786

[114, *114*]   John Nichols, Red Lion Passage, Fleet Street
ST/3:1022 *Incl.Divs.* = 771X-826M (£400, *£80*) *d.* 26 Nov 1826

[115, *43*]   Harris Hart, No.12, Crane Court, Fleet Street
ST/3:3750   *Incl.Divs.* = 759M-786X (£160, *£160*)   *d.* 24 May 1787

[116, *7*]   Mathew Jenour, Fleet Street
ST/3:4534   *Incl.Divs.* = 743M-785X (£320, *£320*)   *d.before* 7 Feb 1786

[117, *99*]   Archibald Hamilton, Falcon Court, Fleet Street
ST/3:3536   *Incl.Divs.* = 770M-792M (£160, *£80*)   *d.* 6 Oct 1792

[118, *32*]   Robert Sayer, Esq; No.53, Fleet Street
ST/3:7235   *Incl.Divs.* = 759M-793X (£320, *£160*)   *d.before* 19 Jun 1794

[119, *17*]   Robert Gosling, Esq; No.21, Fleet Street
ST/3:3333   *Incl.Divs.* = 756M-793X (£320, *£320*)   *d.* 4 Jan 1794

[120, *172*]   Richard Waller, Esq; Foot's Cray, Kent, or Fleet Street
ST/3:8462   *Incl.Divs.* = 778X-808M (£200, *£40*)   *d.* 11 Jun 1808

[121, *173*]   Mr.Samuel Daniel Browne, Maidstone, Kent, or No.90, Fleet Street
Brown[e]. ST/3:1183   *Incl.Divs.* = 778X-832M (£200, *£40*)   *d.before* 1 May
1832.   Strangely, S.D.B.'s death was reported to the Court on 6 Jul 1830 and
his share was said to be disposed of.   His will is dated 29 Nov 1830 and
probate was granted on 1 May 1832.   Dividends are recorded until 832M

[122, *87*]   Charles Coles, Esq; No.21, Fleet Street
ST/3:5335   *Incl.Divs.* = 767X-817X (£400, *£80*)   *Bankrupt* reported to the
Court on 5 May 1818

[123, *209*]   Mr.Thomas Evans, ditto
ST/3:1878   *Incl.Divs.* = 784X-789X (£40, *£40*)   *d.* 23 Dec 1789

[124, *202*]   S.P.Pigott, Mitre Court, Fleet Street
Samuel Perchard Piggott. ST/3:2821   *Incl.Divs.* = 784M-816X (£200, *£40*)
d.before 26 Apr 1817

[125, *16*]   William Owen, No.11, Fleet Street
ST/3:5966   *Incl.Divs.* = 756M-793M (£320, *£320*)   *d.* 1 Dec 1793

[126, *42*]   George Booth, at Mr.Jones's, Temple Lane
ST/3:4628   *Incl.Divs.* = 759M-786M (£160, *£160*)   *d.* 7 Aug 1786

[127, *69*]   Richard Jones, Temple Lane
ST/3:4630   *Incl.Divs.* = 766X-791M (£160, *£160*)   *d.* 6 Sep 1791

[128, *131*]   John Furman, Middle Temple Lane
ST/3: 3120   *Incl.Divs.* = 775X-785X (£80, *£80*)   *d.* 9 Feb 1786

[129, *11*]   William Sandby, Esq; Essex Street, Strand
ST/3:5148   *Incl.Divs.* = 753M-799M (£320, *£320*)   *d.* 2 Nov 1799

[130, *8*]   Paul Valiant, Esq; Pall Mall
Vaillant. ST/3:0399   *Incl.Divs.* = 745M-801X (£320, *£320*)   *d.* 1 Feb 1802

[131, *83*]   Mr.Richard Ware, at Mr.Britchke's, St.James's Place, St.James's Street
ST/3:4001   *Incl.Divs.* = 767M-817M (£200, *£80*)   *d.before* 19 May 1817

[132, *201*]   George Michell, New Bond Street
ST/3:2211   *Incl.Divs.* = 784M-803X (£80, *£40*)   *d.before* 16 May 1804

[133, *213*]   Samuel Hayes, No.332, Oxford Street
ST/3:3821   *Incl.Divs.* = 785X-831M (£200, *£40*)   *d.before* 2 Aug 1831

[134, *128*]   Henry Holland, Harford Street, May Fair
Hertford Street. ST/3:1871   *Incl.Divs.* = 775M-806M (£200, *£80*)   *d.before*
26 Jun 1806

[135, *137*]   Mrs.Gardener, Park Street
Lucy, widow of Thomas Gardner.   ST/3:2599W   *Incl.Divs.* = 765M-788X
(£80, *£80*)   *d.before* 3 Mar 1789

[136, *57*]   Mr.Thomas Rider, Titchfield Street, Cavendish Square
Ryder. ST/3:0254   *Incl.Divs.* = 763M-803M (£160, *£160*)   *d.before* 23 Nov
1803

[137, *185*]   Thomas Ryder, jun. ditto
ST/3:0501   *Incl.Divs.* = 780M-810X (£80, *£40*)   *Paid-out* — ordered on 5 Feb
1811

[138, *215*]   Mrs.Plowman, No.6, Lisle Street, Leicester Fields
Margaret, widow of Henry Plowman. ST/3:8370W   *Incl.Divs.* = 744X-788M
(£40, *£40*)   *d.before* 3 Feb 1789

[139, *175*]   Joseph Cooper, No.134, Drury Lane
ST/3:6850   *Incl.Divs.* = 778X-799X (£160, £40)   *Bankrupt* reported to the
Court on 10 Jun 1800 and share disposed of

[140, *58*]   James Basire, Great Queen Street, Lincoln's Inn Fields
ST/3:7281   *Incl.Divs.* = 763M-802M (£160, £160)   *d.* 6 Sep 1802

[141, *119*]   Abraham Cutler, Drake Street, No.4, Red Lion Square
ST/3:2091   *Incl.Divs.* = 772X-796X (£160, £80)   *d.* 14 Feb 1797

[142, *126*]   Nathaniel Conant, Esq; No.19, Lamb's Conduit Street
Sir Nathaniel Conant.   ST/3:7201   *Incl.Divs.* = 773X-821X (£400, £80)
d.before 7 May 1822

[143, *158*]   Rev.John Henry Brown, at N.Conant's, Esq;
Browne.   Not identified in McKenzie's *Apprentices* ST/3:9302
Incl.Divs. = 777M-830M (£200, £40)   *d.before* 6 Sep 1830

[144, *190*]   Mr.John Warren, Corner of Cursitor Street, Chancery Lane
ST/3:2722   *Incl.Divs.* = 781M-792X (£40, £40)   *d.* 13 Jan 1793

[145, *142*]   Mrs.Edwards, Tooke's Court, Chancery Lane
Rebecca, widow of William Ewards.   ST/3:3119W   *Incl.Divs.* = 775X-800X
(£80, £80)   *d.before* 3 Feb 1801

[146, *77*]   Stichall, Stanhope Street, Clare Market
Mary, widow of Benjamin Stichall.   ST/3:2669W   *Incl.Divs.* = 779X-795M
(£160, £160)   *d.before* 1 Sep 1795

[147, *82*]   Sir Charles Corbett, at Mr.Bicknell's, No.10, One Pair of Stairs, King's Bench
Walk, Temple
ST/3:9026   *Incl.Divs.* = 763M-807X (£80, £80)   *d.* 8 May 1808

[148, *184*]   Francis Gosling, Esq; No.19, Fleet Street
ST/3:3329   *Incl.Divs.* = 780M-816X (£320, £40)   *d.before* 18 Mar 1817

[149, *71*]   Lady Gosling, No.19, Fleet Street
Elizabeth, widow of Sir Francis Gosling.   ST/3:3332W   *Incl.Divs.* =
769X-806M (£160, £160)   *d.before* 2 Sep 1806

[150, *209*]   Mr.Thomas Evans, No.21, Fleet Street
This would appear to be a second entry for Thomas Evans, *cf.* no.123

[151, *199*]   Edward Brooke, Bell Yard, Temple Bar
ST/3:7139   *Incl.Divs.* = 783X-828X (£400, £40)   *d.before* 6 Apr 1829

[152, *188*]   George Freer, Bell Yard, Temple Bar
ST/3:7970   *Incl.Divs.* = 781M-791X (£40, £40)   *d.before* 16 May 1792

[153, *111*]   H.L.Gardiner, No.207, opposite St.Clement's Church, Strand
Henry Lasher Gardiner.   ST/3:3143   *Incl.Divs.* = 770X-807X (£400, £80)
d. 29 Feb 1808

[154, *108*]   Thomas Cadell, No.144, Strand
ST/3:5461   *Incl.Divs.* = 770M-802X (£320, £80)   *d.* 27 Dec 1802

[155, *52*]   Robert Withy, No.24, Craven Street
ST/3:6889   *Incl.Divs.* = 763M-803M (£160, £160)   *d.* 19 Sep 1803

[156, *134*]   Mrs.Baylis, at Mr.Withy's, ditto
Sarah, widow of Stephen Baylis.   ST/3:4117W   *Incl.Divs.* = 764M-787X
(£80, £80)   *d.before* 6 May 1788

[157, *154*]   Mr.Thomas Smith, No.46, Strand
ST/3:3422   *Incl.Divs.* = 777M-829M (£400, £40)   *d.before* 22 Dec 1829

[158, *166*]   Samuel Hawksworth, Charing Cross
ST/3:9028   *Incl.Divs.* = 777X-828M (£400, £40)   *d.before* 19 Dec 1828

[159, *152*]   H.Woolsey Byfield, Charing Cross
Henry Woolsey Byfield.   ST/3:9024   *Incl.Divs.* = 776X-826X (£400, £40)
d. 6 Dec 1826

[160, *222*]   Mrs.Elizabeth Griffin, Westminster
Widow of William Griffin.   ST/3:7974W   *Incl.Divs.* = 775M-818X (£40, £40)
d.before 6 Apr 1819

[161, *193*]   Mr.Thomas Payne, Muse Gate, Castle Street
Mews Gate, Charing Cross.   ST/3:5992   *Incl.Divs.* = 781X-830X (£400, £40)
d. 15 Mar 1831

[162, *55*]   James Dodsley, Pall Mall
ST/3:2506   *Incl.Divs.* = 763M-796X (£320, £160)   *d.* 19 Feb 1797

[163, *105*] H.Simmons, the Corner of Warwick Court, Holborn
Humphrey Simmons.   ST/3:2823   *Incl.Divs.* = 770M-816X (£200, *£80*)
d.before 1 Apr 1817

[164, *144*] Mrs.Dymott, Warwick Court, Holborn
Mary, widow of Richard Dymott.   ST/3:7877W   *Incl.Divs.* = 778X-810X
(£80, *£80*)   *d.before* 5 Feb 1811

[165, *157*] Mr.Henry Hughs, No.41, Bedford Row
Hughes.   ST/3:4237   *Incl.Divs.* = 777M-810M (£320, *£40*)   *d.* 5 Sep 1810

[166, *22*] Mrs.Ann Hughs, ditto
Widow of John Hughes.   ST/3:4186W   *Incl.Divs.* = 771X-795M (£320, *£320*)
d. 1 Nov 1795

[167, *72*] Ann Hett, Wild Court, Wild Street
Widow of Richard Hett.   ST/3:1771W   *Incl.Divs.* = 766M-787X (£160, *£160*)
d.before 4 Mar 1788

[168, *28*] Hett, Wild Court, Wild Street
Ann, widow of Richard Hett.   ST/3:6776W   *Incl.Divs.* = 785M-798X (£320,
£320)   *d.before* 5 Feb 1799

[169, *104*] Mark Baskett, Esq; No.26, Bartlet's Buildings, Holborn
ST/3:0537   *Incl.Divs.* = 770M-785X (£80, *£80*)   *d.before* 22 Jun 1786

[170, *14*] Mr.Lockyer Davis, Middle Row, Holborn
Lockyer John Davis.   ST/3:2365   *Incl.Divs.* = 754M-790X (£320, *£320*)
d. 23 Apr 1791

[171, *162*] John Noorthouck, Barnard's Inn, Holborn
ST/3:5776   *Incl.Divs.* − 777M-816M (£200, *£40*)   *d.before* 17 Aug 1816

[172, *176*] Thomas Jones, Kirby Street, Hatton Garden
ST/3:4632   *Incl.Divs.* = 779M-793X (£80, *£40*)   *d.before* 4 Feb 1794

[173, *12*] Daniel Richards, Holborn Hill
ST/3:6719   *Incl.Divs.* = 754M-802M (£320, *£320*)   *d.* 8 Aug 1802

[174, *171*] Mr.William Collins, Salisbury
ST/3:7965   *Incl.Divs.* = 778X-810M (£200, *£40*)   *d.before* 8 Aug 1810

[175, *220*] Mrs.Meers, No.38, Smithfield
Marthanna, widow of William Meres.   ST/3:5409W   *Incl.Divs.* = 771M-809M
(£40, *£40*)   *d.before* 5 Sep 1809

[176, *226*] Isherwood, Aldersgate Street
Elizabeth, widow of James Isherwood.   ST/3:4396W   *Incl.Divs.* = 780X-806M
(£40, *£40*)   *d.before* 2 Dec 1806

[177, *78*] Emonson, Warren Court, Clerkenwell
Elizabeth, widow of James Emonson.   ST/3:0995W   *Incl.Divs.* = 780X-785M
(£160, *£160*)   *d.before* 2 Aug 1785

[178, *113*] Mr.Bye, at Mrs.Rivington's St.John's Square
Deodatus Bye.   ST/3:1577   *Incl.Divs.* = 771X-825X (£400, *£80*)   *d.* 12 Feb
1826

[179, *196*] Tho.Saunders, No.14, Nichol's Square, near Falcon Square
Thomas.   ST/3:7166   *Incl.Divs.* = 782X-818X (£200, *£40*)   *d.before* 3 Jun
1819

[180, *160*] Anthony Collambell, No.100, Aldersgate Bars
ST/3:1887   *Incl.Divs.* = 777M-818X (£200, *£40*)   *d.before* 8 Jun 1819

[181, *165*] John Ramsbottom, No.74, Aldersgate Street
ST/3:4399   *Incl.Divs.* = 777X-825X (£200, *£40*)   *d.before* 4 Dec 1826

[182, *169*] Richard Ramsbottom, ditto, Aldersgate Street
ST/3:4400   *Incl.Divs.* = 778M-812X (£200, *£40*)   *d.before* 2 Mar 1813

[183, *62*] Robert Collins
ST/3:3995   *Incl.Divs.* = 763X-785X (£160, *£160*)   *d.* 3 May 1786

[184, *76*] Mrs.Caslon, Chiswell Street
Elizabeth, widow of William Caslon.   ST/3:0512W   *Incl.Divs.* = 778X-795M
(£160, *£160*),   *d. c.*Oct 1795

[185, *214*] Mr.William Caslon, Chiswell Street
ST/3:1543   *Incl.Divs.* = 1785X-810M (£80, *£40*)   *Paid-out* −ordered after
dividend on 22 Jun 1810

[186, *181*]   Joseph Collyer, White Lion Row, Islington
ST/3:1940   *Incl.Divs.* = 779X-827X (£400, *£40*)   *d.* 24 Dec 1827
[187, *81*]   John Johnson, No.4, Clement's Buildings, Islington
ST/3:6157   *Incl.Divs.* = 771M-787M (£80, *£80*)   *d.before* 6 Nov 1787
[188, *139*]   Mrs.Spackman, High Street, Islington
Mary, widow of Isaac Spackman.   ST/3:0392W   *Incl.Divs.* = 771M-793M
(£80, *£80*)   *d.before* 12 Sep 1793
[189, *47*]   Mr.Field, Colebrooke Row, Islington
Thomas Field.   ST/3:7968   *Incl.Divs.* = 759M-794M (£320, *£160*)   *d.* 28 Aug
1794
[190, *61*]   John Curtis, at Mr.Curtis's, Islington
ST/3:2411   *Incl.Divs.* = 763X-800M (£160, *£160*)   *d.before* 2 Sep 1800
[191, *103*]   Joseph Ellis, near the Church, Islington
ST/3:7284   *Incl.Divs.* = 770M-793M (£160, *£80*)   *d.* 23 Aug 1793
[192, *198*]   John Bennett, Cross Street, Islington
ST/3:7231   *Incl.Divs.* = 783X-787X (£40, *£40*)   *d.before* 19 Jun 1788
[193, *107*]   Rev.Mr.Strahan, Islington
Rev.George Strahan.   ST/3:7991   *Incl.Divs.* = 770M-823X (£200, *£80*)
d.before 12 Jun 1824
[194, *150*]   Mr.Cumberledge, Upper Street, Islington
Stephen Austen Cumberlege.   ST/3:3972   *Incl.Divs.* = 776M-828M
(£400, *£40*) *d.* 29 Aug 1828
[195, *219*]   Mrs.Hazard
Kezia, widow of Joseph Hazard.   ST/3:2792   *Incl.Divs.* = 770X-794X
(£40, *£40*)   *d.before* 18 Jun 1795
[196, *56*]   Mr.James Fletcher, Oxford
ST/3:2920   *Incl.Divs.* = 763M-798M (£160, *£160*)   *d.before* 18 Jun 1798
[197, *211*]   Thomas Beecroft, Esq; near Norwich
ST/3:0646   *Incl.Divs.* = 784X-786X (£40, *£40*)   *d.* 21 Jun 1787
[198, *138*]   Mrs.Hinde, Tottenham High Cross
Mary, widow of Luke Hinde, who has not been identified in McKenzie's
Apprentices . . . .   ST/3:9307W   *Incl.Divs.* = 766X-807M (£80, *£80*)   *d.before*
2 Feb 1808
[199, *143*]   Goadby, Sherborn
Rachel, widow of Robert Goadby, who has not been identified in McKenzie's
Apprentices . . . .   ST/3:9305W   *Incl.Divs.* = 778X-789X (£80, *£80*)   *d.before*
13 Apr 1790
[200, *147*]   Warham, Greenwich
Caroline, widow of James Warham.   ST/3:8424W   *Incl.Divs.* − 784X-831M
(£80, *£80*)   *d.* 2 Aug 1831
[201, *146*]   Hasker, at Mr.Hammond's Charlotte Street, Rathbone Place
Ann, widow of Edward Hasker, who has not been identified in McKenzie's
Apprentices . . . .   ST/3:9308W   *Incl.Divs.* = 784X-811X (£80, *£80*)   *d.before*
5 May 1812
[202, *145*]   Towes, Vauxhall Walk
Mary, widow of George Towes.   ST/3:0608W   *Incl.Divs.* = 783M-797M
(£80, *£80*)   *d.* 7 Nov 1797
[203, *218*]   Mason
Frances, widow of William Mason.   ST/3:8421W   *Incl.Divs.* = 769M-807X
(£40, *£40*)   *d.before* 2 Feb 1808
[204, *21*]   Osborn, Dulwich Common
Mary, widow of Thomas Osborn.   ST/3:5950W   *Incl.Divs.* = 767X-786X
(£320, *£320*)   *d.before* 8 Feb 1787
[205, *24*]   Lady Hodges, Highgate
Jane Mary [Bullock], widow of Sir James Hodges.   ST/3:5821W   Incl.Divs. =
774X-787M (£320, *£320*)   *d.* 4 Aug 1787
[206, *27*]   Mrs.Harris, Bath
Amelia, widow of Charles Harris.   ST/3:6830W   *Incl.Divs.* = 781M-816M
(£320, *£320*)   *d.before* 19 Aug 1816

[207, *221*]   Raven,
                 Ann, widow of William Raven. ST/3:1079W   *Incl.Divs.* = 773X-786M
                 (£40, *£40*)   *d.before* 1 Aug 1786
[208, *70*]   Mrs.Knapton, Richmond
                 Elizabeth, widow of Paul Knapton.   ST/3:0800W   *Incl.Divs.* = 755X-796X
                 (£160, *£160*)   *d.before* 13 Jun 1797
[209, *31*]   James Leake, Esq; Knightsbridge
                 ST/3:4930   *Incl.Divs.* = 759M-791M (£320, *£160*)   *d.* 15 Aug 1791
[210, *34*]   John Ausitor, Esq; Southall Green
                 John Awsiter.   ST/3:0194   *Incl.Divs.* = 748M-786X (£160, *£160*)   *d.before*
                 20 Feb 1787
[211, *35*]   Samuel Buckley, Esq; Watford, Hertfordshire
                 ST/3:1318   *Incl.Divs.* = 748M-794M (£160, *£160*)   *d.before* 4 Nov 1794
[212, *80*]   Mr.Thomas Fletcher, Walthamstow
                 ST/3:2924   *Incl.Divs.* = 742X-792M (£80, *£80*)   *d.before* 4 Dec 1792
[213, *36*]   Thomas Simpson, Cumberland Row, Kennington Lane
                 ST/3:7432   *Incl.Divs.* = 754X-787M (£160, *£160*)   *d.* 18 Jul 1787
[214, *39*]   John Sharp, Redman's Row, Mile End
                 ST/3:7334   *Incl.Divs.* = 756M-785X (£160, *£160*)   *d.before* 22 Jun 1786
[215, *40*]   Marshal Sheepey, Stationers Hall
                 ST/3:4028   *Incl.Divs.* = 756M-786X (£160, *£160*)   *d.* 29 Jan 1787
[216, *45*]   Richard Wilson, Bath
                 Richard Wilsonn.   ST/3:1144   *Incl.Divs.* = 759M-785X (£160, *£160*)
                 d.before 22 Jun 1786
[217, *63*]   Robert Raikes, Gloucester
                 ST/3:6518   *Incl.Divs.* = 764X-810X (£400, *£160*)   *d.* 5 Apr 1811
[218, *66*]   John Townsend, Wandsworth
                 ST/3:0025   *Incl.Divs.* = 765X-804X (£320, *£160*)   *d.before* 19 Mar 1805
[219, *67*]   John Loveday, Walcot Place, Lambeth
                 ST/3:5085   *Incl.Divs.* = 765X-786M (£160, *£160*)   *d.before* 22 Dec 1786
[220, *195*]   Richard Snagg, No.4, Lambeth Marsh
                 ST/3:5913   *Incl.Divs.* = 782X-829M (£200, *£40*)   *d.before* 21 Jul 1829
[221, *88*]   Thomas Hunt, Ewell, Surrey
                 ST/3:4293   *Incl.Divs.* = 768M-785X (£80, *£80*)   *d.* 7 Jun 1785
[222, *95*]   Nathaniel Bray, Hertford
                 ST/3:8652   *Incl.Divs.* = 769M-799M (£160, *£80*)   *d.* 14 Sep 1799
[223, *124*]   John Payne, Hackney
                 ST/3:6196   *Incl.Divs.* = 769X-795M (£160, *£80*)   *d.before* 17 Dec 1795
[224, *110*]   Rev.Mr.Tooke, Russia
                 Rev.William Tooke.   ST/3:1025   *Incl.Divs.* = 771M-820M (£200, *£80*)
                 d.before 28 Nov 1820
[225, *121*]   Mr.Charles Cavey, at Froome, Somersetshire
                 Charles Clavey.   ST/3:3994   *Incl.Divs.* = 773M-785M (£80, *£80*)   *d.before*
                 2 Aug 1785
[226, *149*]   John Miller, New York
                 ST/3:7189   *Incl.Divs.* = 774M-812M (£40, *£40*)   *d.before* 4 Aug 1812
[227, *191*]   Daniel Isaac Eaton, Nightingale Hall, Deptford
                 ST/3:8632   *Incl.Divs.* = 781X-814M (£40, *£40*)   *d.* 22 Aug 1814
[228, *205*]   Richard Cruttwell, Bath
                 ST/3:1479   *Incl.Divs.* = 784M-798X (£80, *£40*)   *d.before* 20 Jun 1799
[229, *206*]   William Cruttwell, Sherborne
                 ST/3:4329   *Incl.Divs.* = 784X-804X (£160, *£40*)   *d.before* 15 Mar 1805
[230, *15*]   Robert Horsfield
                 ST/3:5147   *Incl.Divs.* = 755X-797X (£320, *£320*)   *d.* 4 Mar 1798. Horsfield
                 was elected Treasurer or Warehousekeeper of the English Stock on 15 Jul
                 1785

Alphabetical Index

HOLLAND, Henry	[134]	RIVINGTON, Francis	[27]
HOOKE, Thomas	[51]	RIVINGTON, John	[26]
HORSFIELD, Robert	[230]	ROBINSON, John	[16]
HUGHES, Ann	[166]	RYDER, Thomas	[136]
HUGHES, Henry	[165]	RYDER, Thomas	[137]
HUNT, Thomas	[221]	RYLAND, John	[101]
ISHERWOOD, Elizabeth	[176]	SANDBY, William	[129]
ISHERWOOD, Henry	[102]	SAUNDERS, Thomas	[179]
JENOUR, Eleanor	[5]	SAY, Mary	[7]
JENOUR, Mathew	[116]	SAYER, Robert	[118]
JOHNSON, John	[187]	SHARP, John	[214]
JOHNSON, Mary	[40]	SHEEPEY, Marshall	[215]
JOHNSTON, Edward	[111]	SIMMONS, Humphrey	[163]
JOHNSTON, William	[86]	SIMMONS, Samuel	[39]
JONES, Richard	[127]	SIMONS, James	[29]
JONES, Thomas	[172]	SIMPSON, Thomas	[213]
KNAPTON, Elizabeth	[208]	SMITH, John	[108]
LAW, Bedwell	[8]	SMITH, Mary	[25]
LEAKE, James	[209]	SMITH, Thomas	[62]
LONGMAN, Thomas	[13]	SMITH, Thomas	[65]
LOVEDAY, John	[219]	SMITH, Thomas	[157]
MARCH, John	[85]	SNAGG, Richard	[220]
MASON, Frances	[203]	SPACKMAN, Mary	[188]
MERES, Marthanna	[175]	STARKEY, Richard	[50]
MICHELL, George	[132]	STEDMAN, Elizabeth	[77]
MILLER, John	[226]	STEPHENS, William	[60]
MOORE, Elizabeth	[53]	STICHALL, Mary	[146]
MOORE, Jonathan	[78]	STRAHAN, Andrew	[110]
MOORE, Thomas	[100]	STRAHAN, Rev.George	[193]
MORGAN, John	[103]	STRAHAN, William	[109]
MOUNT, John	[80]	STREET, John Wallis	[49]
NEATBY, James	[93]	TIMSON, William	[90]
NEWBERY, Elizabeth	[4]	TOOKE, Rev.William	[224]
NICHOLS, John	[114]	TOWES, Mary	[202]
NOORTHOUCK, John	[171]	TOWNSEND, John	[218]
OSBORN, Mary	[204]	TRICKETT, Sarah	[1]
OWEN, William	[125]	VAILLANT, Paul	[130]
PAGE, Jane	[82]	VALLANCE, Thomas	[38]
PAGE, Sarah	[81]	VOWELL, John	[75]
PARKER, Henry	[46]	VOWELL, John	[76]
PAYNE, John	[223]	WALKDEN, John	[106]
PAYNE, Thomas	[161]	WALLER, Richard	[120]
PEARCE, John Barnes	[57]	WALTON, William	[79]
PEARCH, Ann	[55]	WARE, Richard	[131]
PECK, Sarah	[41]	WARHAM, Caroline	[200]
PENNY, Bartholomew	[91]	WARREN, John	[144]
PIGGOTT, Samuel Perchard	[124]	WELLES, Richard	[54]
PLOWMAN, Margaret	[138]	WENMAN, Joseph	[109]
POTE, Thomas	[9]	WILKINSON, Nathaniel	[98]
PRITCHARD, James	[89]	WILSONN, Charles Edward	[70]
RAIKES, Robert	[217]	WILSONN, Richard	[216]
RAMSBOTTOM, John	[181]	WITHEY, Robert	[155]
RAMSBOTTOM, Richard	[182]	WOODFALL, Henry Sampson	[20]
RAVEN, Ann	[207]	WOODFALL, William	[105]
RICHARDS, Daniel	[173]	WRIGHT, Thomas	[66]
RIVINGTON, Charles	[28]	WYNNE, Peter	[37]
RIVINGTON, Charles	[36]		

Note

The *London Booktrades Database* is a biographical database on members of the book trade in London from the beginning of printing until the year 1830. It grew out of work being done by the present author on the period 1800-30, and was pushed back to 1605 through the support of Prof. D. F. McKenzie, who suggested that it should be expanded to include the material in his three volumes of *Stationers' Company Apprentices*. Subsequently, with the assistance of the Leverhulme Trust, Dr Christine Ferdinand added a great deal more material, particularly in the period before 1700. So far, most of the entries are based on the membership of the Stationers' Company, but non-Stationers are gradually being entered into the database. In this article, where a parenthetical number follows the name of a person—e.g. William Strahan (ST/3:7992)—it is the number by which the individual can be identified in the database.

The changing role of the trade bookbinder, 1800-1900

ESTHER POTTER

THE HISTORY OF TRADE BOOKBINDING in the 19th century is the story of how the bookbinder adapted to changes in methods of publishing and the concept of edition binding. This paper is not about the binding of a single copy of a book to suit the taste (and the pocket) of the owner. Trade binding is done in bulk to the order of a bookseller or publisher. In the 18th century this did not imply the identical binding of large numbers of books. Individual orders could be quite small. Books were then published by booksellers or a consortium of booksellers who kept part of the edition to sell in their own shops and also sold copies, usually in quires, to other booksellers. The publisher/bookseller towards the end of the 18th century would frequently advertise his publications in two or three styles of binding at different prices. Similarly the booksellers who bought from him would have some copies bound to suit their own class of trade, and if they issued catalogues (which usually included both new and second-hand books) they might well include copies of a recently published book newly bound in several different styles at a range of prices. An edition might thus be split between many booksellers and several styles of binding and be shared among a number of binders.

At the lower end of the market there were, however, some categories of publication that reached the binders in larger quantities. There was an enormous output of pamphlets (political and religious controversy was conducted by vigorous pamphlet wars), sermons, newspapers, periodicals, books issued in parts (and a surprising number were), government publications and the like, all of which needed folding, stitching or stabbing, and often putting into wrappers. That part of an edition which was not given a binding by the bookseller would be given a temporary covering—paper wrappers early in the 18th century and paper-covered boards later—with a printed paper label for identification, and edges untrimmed so that the purchaser could have it bound to suit himself. Westley, who became one of the largest trade binders in the middle of the 19th century, was said to have in 1809 or 1810 about 12 men all on 'common boarding'.[1] Towards the end of the 18th century a more or less standardized style of binding was being developed for some classes of books—a tough unbleached canvas for school books, red roan for almanacks and directories, green roan for Sir Richard Phillips's guide books.

In general, however, 18th-century trade binding was an *ad hoc* business and carried on in small units. In 1794, 69 master bookbinders were recorded in London and 165 journeymen.[2] A typical business would then consist of a master with one or two journeymen and perhaps an apprentice. In the early years of the 19th century circumstances were changing fast. The output of books was rising rapidly to meet the needs of a growing population and expanding literacy. The number of master bookbinders rose dramatically from 69 in 1794 to 121 in 1808 and 151 in 1813.[3] The size of firms was growing with comparable rapidity. The 12 men that Westley had in 1810 on 'common boarding' probably did not represent his entire workforce. The printers were better able to cope with the demand because of the introduction of iron-framed presses, but the binders had no such mechanical aid. They achieved some increase in productivity by breaking down the process of binding into separate procedures which could be performed rapidly on a kind of production line.[4]

This period saw what Graham Pollard called 'the emergence of the publisher', the separation of publishing from bookselling and the rise, from the ranks of the larger booksellers, of publishers who sold only their own publications and concentrated on the publishing function.[5] More of the bookbinder's work then came from the publishers, who came to exercise increasing control over the binding, though the concept of a publisher's house style did not come until much later. In the first quarter of the 19th century it was still usual for reference books such as dictionaries and gazetteers to be bound in roan or sprinkled sheep, while history, poetry, novels and the like were issued in boards in the expectation that the purchaser would have his own binding put on them.[6]

The introduction in the 1820s of gift books and annuals, which achieved instant popularity and were published in editions of unprecedented size, had far-reaching consequences.[7] The publishers of literature and *belles lettres* awoke to the publicity value of an attractive and individual binding. It was no longer good enough to hand the sheets to the binder to provide one of the standard styles of the day. The binding was now as much part of the book as the text; each book or series had to have its own binding to distinguish it from competing publications. The earliest annuals appeared in glazed paper boards with matching slip-case like their German prototypes. As their popularity was seen to be well-established, bindings became more and more sumptuous. Silk was introduced in 1828 and some publishers issued presentation copies in gold-tooled morocco.

The development of embossed leather, first produced in England by the binder Frederick Remnant about 1825, provided a suitable binding for the top end of the gift book market. It also enabled elaborately decorated leather covers to be mass-produced. The leather is impressed with a design by hard pressure between an engraved die and a counter-die in an adaptation of the engineer's fly press. Once the die has been cut an almost unlimited number of covers can be produced quite quickly. The piece of leather, cut to size, had to be embossed before it was put on the book and any gold title or decoration had to be applied separately after the book was

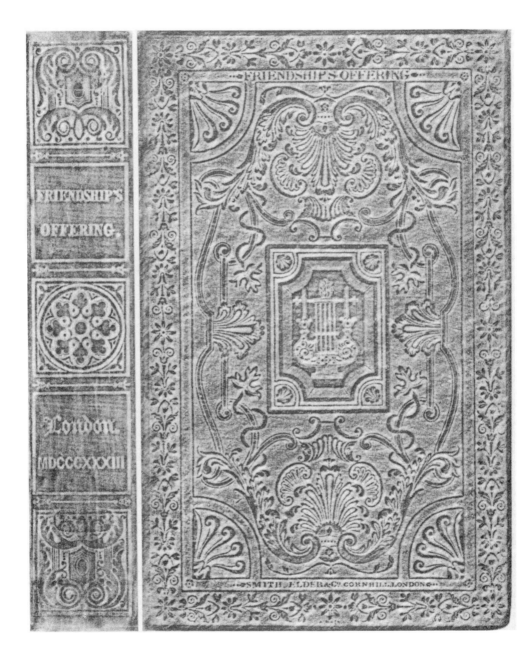

Fig.1. Rubbing of an embossed arabesque binding signed at the foot of the cover by the die-cutter, A. Bain: *Friendship's Offering* (London: Smith, Elder & Co., 1833). Reproduced by permission of the Cambridge Bibliographical Society.

covered. Cutting the dies was a highly skilled and therefore expensive process and so embossed leather was economic only for large editions. It was ideal for Bibles and prayer books for which there was a large and continuous demand, and for gift books and annuals since the same design could be used year after year for the same title as the date was not part of the die. It was much used for albums, pocket books, card cases and the like.

Embossed leather also provided the binder with a ready-made cover and removed from him the design function as well as the tooling. The bindings are well designed but there is little to tell us who designed them. A very few of them bear the names of publishers, Ackermann, and Smith, Elder and Scott, Webster and Geary, incorporated in the designs of the covers.[8] The other signatures recorded by Mrs Jamieson in her pioneer study of embossed bindings are nearly all of the embosser or the die-cutter.[9] When the name of a binder occurs — Remnant & Edmonds, Westley or De La Rue — it is most likely to be in his capacity as embosser since all three supplied embossed leather to the trade.[10] A name in minuscule letters is a good indication of a die-cutter or embosser.[11]

Obviously the publishers would exercise some supervision over the covers which bore their names, but for the majority of designs the key figure would appear to be the embosser. The technique for embossing book covers was devised by Jacob Edmonds, then Frederick Remnant's foreman and later his partner, and it is known that his first dies were cut for him by an engraver, James Barritt, who was working for a neighbouring silversmith. Barritt then took to embossing leather on his own account and selling it to bookbinders.[12] The obvious person to commission the design was the embosser, who evidently would have been a substantial businessman, since he had the capital to buy a huge fly-press and a basement with a strong floor in which to install it.

The bindings on the gift books and the bindings of embossed leather were special bindings on a limited range of expensive books, and although they have survived well because of their charm, they are not typical of trade bindings at that time. The most usual bindings in the 1820s and early 1830s were half calf or morocco with paper-covered boards for temporary covers and, for reference books, plain roan. Embossed leather may have been cheaper than hand-tooled leather, but it was still expensive, and there was a need for a cheaper decorative covering.

Book cloth was devised by the binder Archibald Leighton for the publisher William Pickering about 1825, originally as a neater alternative to paper for books in boards, but as the quality improved and it came to be embossed with a surface texture, it became a tolerably long-lasting covering in its own right. For some years book cloth was looking for a role. Pickering and other publishers used a plain calico with printed label in place of paper on boards. Cloth with an embossed pattern and printed label followed; paper-covered boards looked better on the shelf with a cloth spine and a dark green or black paper label printed in gold on a cloth binding transformed the label from a convenient identification to a decoration.[13] Costs could be cut by casing the book instead of lacing the cords into the boards but a prejudice against casing prevented its general adoption.

The idea of a uniform binding for an edition seems to have evolved slowly from the uniform binding of sets such as John Bell's *British Theatre*, which were of course in leather. Between 1829 and 1839 Robert Cadell issued four series of Sir Walter Scott's works, 98 volumes in all, in uniform red cloth. The logistics of blocking made it almost essential for all, or most, of an edition to have uniform blocking. It would have been expensive to keep changing the block – though not the colour of the cloth.

It was the introduction in 1832 of the iron-framed blocking press that made possible the production of case-bound gold- or blind-blocked books at a low enough price to open up a wide market for publishers' bindings. It also greatly enlarged the capacity of the binding trade for this work. Only a few of the largest binders could afford a fly-press for embossing leather, but one or two blocking presses were not beyond the means of a medium-sized binder. Publisher's cloth made slow progress for the first few years but from about 1840 it gathered speed and by the middle of the century a large part of the output of books was issued in case-bound blocked cloth publisher's binding.

Now the bookbinder was no longer just adding an optional embellishment to a book after publication. The binding was an essential part of the book and required close co-operation between publisher and binder. The binding had to be designed and planned before printing was completed, and a considerable number of copies had to be bound before the book could be published. This required from the binder a large, well-equipped and well-organized workshop. A substantial part of this trade was in the hands of a few long-established binding firms which had expanded to meet the needs of a growing book trade, and had taken a major part in the technical developments which made it possible. Remnant & Edmonds, Westleys & Company and Leighton, Son & Hodge, known collectively in the trade as 'the big three', were now operating in multi-storied factories and employing perhaps 200 or 300 workers. They were equipped to handle any type of binding from hand-tooled morocco to paper wrappers, but their principal output was in blocked cloth case bindings for the publishers. A little-known binding firm of comparable size was run by Lorinia Watkins and did all the binding for the British and Foreign Bible Society. James Burn, a former Bible Society binder, was by 1850 working mainly for the publishers.

It may not be a coincidence that these large publisher's binders all have a history starting in the 18th or very early 19th century. Archibald Leighton's father began business in London as a binder in 1764. James Burn's father, Thomas, was apprenticed to one of the top London binders, John McKinlay, in 1775 and set up on his own in 1781; Francis Westley, the son of a bookbinder, was apprenticed to his stepbrother George in 1792; Frederick Remnant's father was a master bookbinder in 1785 and Lorinia Watkins'

Fig.2. An example of blind and gold-blocking on cloth: *My Crochet Sampler* (London, 1844).

father, Thomas, was binding for the British and Foreign Bible Society in 1812. They all expanded, as trade grew, businesses that had started on a very small scale.

At that time a journeyman bookbinder, after serving a seven years' apprenticeship and perhaps working for his master as a journeyman for a few years longer, would need only a small capital to set up in business for himself. But by 1850 the proprietor of a large firm specializing in publisher's binding was no longer a craftsman working at the bench beside his journeymen; he was an entrepreneur, building and equipping factories, buying materials, employing labour.[14] The journeymen who could bind a book from start to finish, from folding the sheets to tooling the cover, were a dying breed. Folding and sewing were done by women who outnumbered the men in large businesses; forwarding and finishing were separate occupations; an increasing number of men were employed who had not served a regular apprenticeship, and those who had complained that blocking was often done by semi-skilled men. On the women's side outworkers were sometimes employed in folding, by Miss Watkins and William Clowes for example. In the second half of the century a few binders managed to establish themselves in the flourishing trade of binding Bibles and prayer books; some took over an existing business and developed it, as did Matthew Bell, and some, like Virtue Brothers & Company, Eyre & Spottiswoode and Blades, East & Blades, added a binding department to a long-established printing and publishing business.

In the middle of the century the number of binders was still growing but more slowly. The 151 of 1813 had grown to about 200 though not all of them would be engaged on publisher's binding. The expansion in capacity came mainly from the growth in size of the major firms. It is possible to identify which bookbinders worked for which publishers by the convenient habit which prevailed from the 1830s to the 1870s of sticking a little printed label inside the lower cover of the book (occasionally the upper cover) with the binder's name and address. The printed ticket was preceded by the binder's name and address stamped on a flyleaf. It is not nearly so common as the ticket but it is found in the 1820s in some books bound for major publishers and for the British and Foreign Bible Society. The Society's *Directions for binding the Society's Bibles and Testaments* issued to their binders on 10 February 1820 instructed each of them 'to affix his name and place of abode in the front cover of every book'.[15] Before that, from 1812 to 1820, the Society required their binders to include an identifying code letter in the block with the Society's name which was used on the upper board.

Not all binders used these little tickets, though all the largest firms did, and those who used them did not stick them in every copy (except the Bible Society's binders). It is evident that the Bible Society wanted, in the case of a complaint, to identify the binder responsible (in the early days they employed nearly 20). Why these tickets should otherwise be used, whether as an advertisement for the binder or for the convenience of the publisher, is one of the minor mysteries of 19th-century bookbinding. Nor do we know why some binders did not use them at all. Was it because the publisher objected? At least one publisher co-operated with his binder. The first volume (all I have seen) of *Memoirs of extraordinary popular delusions*, published by the Office of the National Illustrated Library in 1852, has for endpapers a list of the publisher's other works with a lithographed border in which is incorporated the name and address of the binder, Leighton, Son & Hodge of Shoe Lane, in the place where a ticket is normally found.[16]

Douglas Ball has used these tickets to trace the connections between publishers and binders. His conclusions are that a few publishers remained faithful to one binder.[17] Macmillan, who used James Burn exclusively, is a notable example, and after 1845 the Bible Society employed only Watkins. Many, not surprisingly, had one principal binder but gave some work to another, perhaps when their regular binder was too busy, or perhaps because a specialist type of binding was required. James Hayday, one of the principal fine binders, was known to do the extra morocco work for the Bible Society and many other publishers.

It was not usual for a binding order to be divided between two binders except for exceptionally large editions like some of the gift books. It involved duplicating the blocks. The normal way of dealing with a rush job was to work overtime. Periodicals were published at the end of the month and the binders were well accustomed to coping with the panic that invariably arose a couple of days before. The major binders had capacity for a large edition. Westleys were binding Macaulay's *History* in 1855 at the rate of 6,000 volumes a day, but Stanley's *In Darkest Africa*, 1890, was divided between Burn and Leighton, Son & Hodge who between them bound about 40,000 volumes in a fortnight.[18]

When the binding became an integral part of the book one might have expected the publisher to assume direct control over it and to exploit it to publicize his name, but this crept in only slowly. John Carter observed that the familiar device of the publisher's gilt-stamped name at the foot of the spine was not commonly found before 1840 on publisher's cloth.[19] Ackermann and Smith, Elder, however, had their names on the covers of two early embossed bindings, and Scott, Webster & Geary had their name at the foot of the embossed spine of one volume in their English Classic Library in 1836, just before the first example noted by Carter.[20]

By the 1850s publishers were using the endpapers to advertise their other publications, and before the end of the century are found decorative endpapers such as appear in the early Everymans, designed to co-ordinate with the title-page. When it came to the design of the cover the publishers seem to have left it largely to the binder and his tool-cutter. A contemporary account of the patrons of bookbinding listed 'Firstly the large publishers whose work is chiefly indebted for its ornament to the taste of the tool cutter and the working of the blocking press.'[21]

The earliest gold-blocked cloth bindings have simply the author and title within an elegant shield in gold on the spine — as in the Byron of 1832-3, the collected edition of Maria Edgeworth's works of 1832-3 and Crabbe's works of 1834 where, in addition, the cloth has in the centre of each board a lozenge design on a textured ground, both embossed in the piece before the case was made. This soon gave place to blocked designs on the boards. A common pattern was a decorative border or frame in blind round both boards with, in the centre of the upper cover, the title in gold, or a vignette illustrative of the subject-matter of the book and often reproducing one of its illustrations, or both title and vignette.

At first it was necessary to have a separate block cut for each book but soon it was possible to buy from the tool-cutters small ornamental blocks which could be arranged to form a design for the boards (perhaps a wide border with a lozenge motif in the centre). After the edition had been worked off the blocks could be taken apart and used in a different arrangement for other books.[22] The spine could be put together in a similar fashion. The binder would equip himself with a selection of these blocks, and he had a vast range to choose from. At least one tool-cutter, Morris and Co. of Ludgate Street, issued in about 1850 a catalogue illustrating well over 1,000 tools from their stock and 30 pages of designs for boards and spines that could be worked from them.[23] The central blocks, if they had a specific reference to the subject matter, may have been suggested by the publisher; the borders would be assembled by the binder. Uniformity in the binding of a series was not important. Three editions of the first series of *The Ladies' Knitting and Netting Book*, John Miland, 1837, 1839 and 1840, all in green cloth of varying shades, have the same title in gold in the centre of the upper board but different blind-blocked frames. The second and third series have the binder's ticket of E. Curtis (the first series was not signed) and have a gold vignette in addition to the title. One has purple cloth, the other brown, and the frames of all five are different.

The Great Exhibition of 1851 focused attention on design. Thereafter and until the end of the century a binding was increasingly likely to be designed as a whole and for a specific book. The identity of the designer is rarely known before 1851 but thereafter a certain number of bindings were signed by the designer, or can be attributed to him on other evidence. The most prolific designer was John Leighton who worked principally between 1845 and 1870 and whose bindings are regularly signed with his initials JL or sometimes LL (for his pseudonym Luke Limner).[24] John Leighton was a great-nephew of the Archibald Leighton who created book cloth and other members of the family were engaged in one or another sector of the printing and bookbinding trades. John was author, publisher and book illustrator. Bindings designed by him were shown at the Great Exhibition and among his regular clients were bookbinding members of his family, Josiah Westley and other binders. Another designer whose work featured prominently in the Great Exhibition was Owen Jones, who did much work for De La Rue, a major binder of stationery at that period, and who designed 400 tools for him at the time of the Exhibition.[25] Other regular designers were William Henry Rogers and Albert Henry Warren.[26] Some designers in other fields were occasionally called in when a special binding was wanted on some prestigious book. Some binding designs were prepared by Dante Gabriel Rossetti and William Morris.[27]

While we may know the names of the designers it is not always clear whether the commission came from the binder or the publisher. Much of John Leighton's work was done for the binders; Rossetti's was for the publishers. It seems likely that the freelance designers who produced only an occasional binding design were called in by the publisher. On the other hand a great deal of designing must have been done by the staff of the binder with a greater or lesser degree of direction from the publisher. James Burn had an active design department. In 1868 'a new man, Harvey Orrinsmith, trained as an artist, was engaged to look after the design of blocks and book covers'.[28] He long remained an important and influential member of the firm. It is clear from the memoir quoted above that, while publishers might hold strong views about the binding, and presumably had to approve the final design, James Burn's designers still had a decisive part to play. And even in the London bindery of the Oxford Press 'for some years the workers at Aldersgate Street were allowed a free hand in matters of design, despite occasional interference from York Powell, and contributed enormously to the prestige of the Press.'[29]

It would seem obvious, as Douglas Ball observed, that the publisher would keep the blocks for the bindings of his own publications, and yet there is a certain amount of evidence to the contrary.[30] When the Bible Society in 1828 ceased to employ one of the Wylie brothers, Christopher or Robert, they refused to buy from him the block he had had cut for stamping their name on the covers.[31] Again, the sale of the stock and equipment of Josiah Westley, bookbinder, who went bankrupt in 1852, included blocks for the *Illustrated London News* and also letterings for publications of Whittaker & Co., Tegg & Co., Bentley's Standard Novels and Sayer's *Modern Housewife*.[32] And, much later, James Burn lost thousands of brass letterings when a bomb fell on their Kirby Street factory in London in October 1940.[33]

One can see the influence of the publisher growing. Technological developments tempted binders and publishers into using novel techniques, mainly — one suspects — for their publicity value. Black ink was possible in the 1840s but was more popular in the 1860s and after. Coloured inks followed and led designers to produce covers more suited for illustrations than for bindings, until D. G. Rossetti and William Morris and the Arts and Crafts Movement restored some sense of style into bookbinding. Not all books were bound in cloth. There was an enormous output of popular literature issued in paper wrappers, stiffer than the old blue paper wrappers of the 18th century and printed with a suitable design. The binder can have had little to do with these except to attach them to the book. Then there were series of books, Yellow Books and the like, with stiff boards to be covered with printed paper again supplied by the publisher.

Why then, when the binding had become an important part of the book, did not the publishers do their own binding and have it entirely under their own control? Other large organizations with a regular need for binding had it done 'in-house'. King George III had established a bindery in Buckingham House about 1780; when the British Museum opened it was equipped with a bindery. The Bank of England bound its own account books; journeymen bookbinders were employed in several government departments, and in the last quarter of the century Mudie's Select Library had extensive binding workshops.

The answer seems to be that the publisher's demand for bookbinding was not regular. Publishing is a seasonal trade and the publishers would have had the problem of finding work during slack periods for skilled workers whom they could not afford to lose. It is said that when the Oxford University Press established its own bindery in London many titles were added to its list just to keep the bindery occupied. The Oxford Press took over an existing binding business in 1870 and built up a large bindery principally for binding its own books. By 1900 it was able to compete with the finest binders and won a *grand prix* at the Paris Exhibition of 1900.[34] Other publishers were slow to follow. When Longman bought the bookbinding business of Gates, Darnton & Co. in 1887 and announced their intention of binding all their own books in the future it 'created no small stir and comment in the trade', to quote *The Bookbinder*.[35]

One might have expected bookbinding to be combined with printing to avoid unnecessary transport of heavy and bulky paper, but when William Clowes set up in London as a printer in 1803 and not long afterwards added a binding department it was 'a thing almost unheard of at that time'.[36] That was in London. Some Scottish publishers had printing, binding and publishing together in one building in the first half of the 19th century, and it was inevitable that sooner or later integration would take place in London. It came in the last quarter of the century when many London-based industries were moving to sites outside London where costs were lower. Hazell, Watson and Viney, for example, who had been printing mainly periodicals in London, expanded into Aylesbury in 1868 where they printed and bound books for some of the major publishers.[37] J. M. Dent integrated the reverse way. Having built a binding plant in 1906 in Letchworth and finding themselves with space to spare they put in printing machines.

An important factor in this combining of printing with binding must have been the development of efficient machines for most of the binding processes. The blocking press had speeded up the decoration of bindings, but the only mechanical assistance available in the 1830s for the forwarding

Fig.3.   Some typical tickets used by London bookbinders. Books bound by John Bird contained, instead of a ticket, a printed advertisement on the front flyleaf. (With acknowledgement to Maurice Packer, *Bookbinders of Victorian London* (London: British Library, 1991).)

processes was the rolling press, and improved edge-trimming and board-cutting equipment. The paucity of machines was noted in the reports on the 1851 Exhibition. The need to mechanize folding, sewing, backing and case-making was indeed recognized and machines were invented, but they did not prove sufficiently reliable in operation to become generally established. In the last decades of the century an influx of machines from the USA transformed binding into a factory-based industry where the principal work of the operatives was in feeding books into the machines.[38]

Publisher's cloth binding then became to a large extent an adjunct of printing. Charles Batey of the Cambridge University Press wrote in 1954: 'Although many important binding plants continue to operate as separate units, especially in and around London, most large printers have now established their own binding departments which are themselves substantial businesses.'[39] But what these businesses were producing was not the exciting innovative bindings of the period following the Great Exhibition. The advent of the dust jacket marked the end of decorative publisher's bindings. By about 1910 the binding case was simplified to little more than the title and imprint on the spine. The publisher's statement of his individuality, and the work of the best designers, was transferred to the dust jacket provided by the printer.

The independent binders had to look to more specialized areas. The binding of books for libraries was a growing business and had been for some time. So was the production of presentation bindings. Two of Zaehnsdorf's advertisements at the end of the century are typical of many. 'School prizes and presentation books tastefully bound at moderate prices' and 'special attention to the binding of library books, binder to various medical and other societies; law binding a speciality.'[40]

A forward look into the 20th century shows that the independent binders were still needed by publishers who demanded stylish bindings. Burn was binding for Basil Blackwell, Chatto and Windus, and Faber among others in the early decades of the century.[41] Many Nonesuch Press books were bound by Leightons, now merged with Straker Brothers.[42] The binding of commercial publications offered considerable scope; the issue of trade catalogues and the like was a rapidly growing business. Burn's innovative talents turned to ring binders and their publicity in the 1920s and 1930s was dominated by 'Spirax' (a spiral wire binding), 'Wire-O', ring binders and more of the same kind.[43] The binders had shown they could adapt to a rapidly changing world.

References

1. British Library, Jaffray papers, 667.r.19, f.96.
2. *Finishers' Friendly Circular* (1845-51), pp.153, 151.
3. *The corrected list of prices as agreed by the booksellers and bookbinders of London and Westminster July 1* (1808); *The bookbinders' price-book . . . to commence January 1st 1813* (London, 1813).
4. For more on the structure and growth of the bookbinding trade see Ellic Howe & John Child, *The Society of London Bookbinders, 1780-1951* (London: Sylvan Press, 1952) and Esther Potter, 'The London bookbinding trade; from craft to industry', *The Library*, 6th ser., 15 (1993), 259-80.
5. Graham Pollard, 'The English market for printed books', fourth lecture, 'The emergence of the publisher', reprinted in *Publishing History*, 4 (1978), 7-48.
6. *The Bookbinder*, 1 (1888), p.49.
7. There is an account of these gift books and annuals in Anne Renier, *Friendship's Offering; an essay on the annuals and gift books of the 19th century* (London: Private Libraries Association, 1964).
8. *Forget me not*, R. Ackermann, 1825; *Friendship's Offering*, Smith, Elder & Co., 1831-45; W. Robertson, *The History of the discovery and conquest of America*, Scott, Webster & Geary, 1835.
9. Eleanore Jamieson, *English embossed bindings, 1825-1850* (Cambridge: Cambridge Bibliographical Society, 1972).
10. Books are sometimes found with the name of one of these three in the embossed cover and the binder's ticket of a different binder inside the lower cover, e.g. *The Boys Own Book* (Vizetelly, Bromston & Co., 1834) has the embossed signature 'De La Rue & Co.: London' on the cover but the binder's ticket of F. Westley. Remnant & Edmonds, when they were also the binder, used a ticket reading 'Bound and embossed by Remnant & Edmonds' (Jamieson, *op. cit.*, no.4).
11. e.g. A. Bain in *Friendship's Offering* (see fig.1); Barritt in *Proper Lessons* (Oxford, 1834) (Bodleian Library, Oxford, Carter g.11).

12. *The Bookseller*, 31 August 1863.
13. John Carter, 'Publishers' cloth 1820-1900', in *Aspects of book-collecting* (London: Constable, 1935), p.28.
14. George Dodd, *Days at the factories* (London, 1843) describes Westley's factory. Remnant & Edmonds' factory provided the material for Charles Tomlinson's article 'Bookbinding' in his *Cyclopaedia of useful arts and manufactures* (London & New York, 1854).
15. British & Foreign Bible Society, Minutes of Sub-Committee of Depository, vol.1.
16. Oliver & Boyd of Edinburgh printed their name as binder in a precisely similar fashion in 1858 on the end-leaf advertisements for their educational works. Copy in Bodleian, John Johnson Collection.
17. Douglas Ball, *Victorian publishers' bindings* (London: Library Association, 1985).
18. *British Bookmaker*, vol.4, no.38, pp.21-3.
19. John Carter, 'Notes on the early years of cloth binding', *Book Collector's Quarterly*, vi (April-June 1932).
20. Mrs Sherwood, *History of Henry Milner*, part 4 (London: Hatchard, 1837).
21. *Finishers' Friendly Circular*, 12 (May 1848), p.98.
22. John Hannett, *Bibliopegia*, 6th edn. (1865), pp.382-3.
23. There are copies in the St Bride Printing Library, London, and in the Bodleian, John Johnson Collection.
24. His work is reviewed in Douglas Ball, *op. cit.*, chapter 9.
25. *Official descriptive and illustrative catalogue*, vol.II, class xvii, nos.76, 543.
26. The work of these and other binding designers is summarized in Douglas Ball, *op. cit.*, chapter 10 and Appendix D.
27. Giles Barber, 'Rossetti, Ricketts and some English publishers' bindings of the Nineties', *The Library*, 5th ser., 25 (1970), 314-30.
28. Lionel Darley, *Bookbinding then and now* (London: Faber, 1959), p.50.
29. Peter Sutcliffe, *The Oxford University Press: an informal history* (Oxford: Clarendon Press, 1978), p.100.
30. Douglas Ball, *op. cit.*, pp.109-10.
31. British & Foreign Bible Society, Minutes of Depository and Printing Sub-Committee, no.2, 31 January 1928.
32. British Library, Jaffray papers, JAFF 162.
33. Darley, *op. cit.*, p.106.
34. The illustrated catalogue shows many fine leather bindings in the style of the period.
35. *The Bookbinder*, 1, 4 (October 1887), p.102.
36. W. B. Clowes, *Family business, 1803-1953* (London: Clowes and Sons, 1953), p.12.
37. H. J. Keefe, *A century in print. The story of Hazell's 1839-1939* (London: Hazell's, 1939), p.84.
38. See Darley, *op. cit.*, chapter 8.
39. Charles Batey, *The printing and making of books* (privately printed, 1954).
40. *The binding of a book* (Zaehnsdorf, [1890]); *A short history of bookbinding* (London, 1895).
41. Darley, *op. cit.*, p.72.
42. Adam Mills Rare Books, catalogue 20, no.169.
43. Darley, *op. cit.*, pp.100-1.

Magdalen College and the book trade:
the provision of books in Oxford, 1450-1550

CHRISTINE FERDINAND

JOHN FOXE, writing in the mid-16th century about good and mediocre bishops, favourably compared William Waynflete, Bishop of Winchester, with his predecessor Cardinal Beaufort; for Waynflete, 'thoughe he had lesse substaunce, yet hauyng a mynde more godly disposed, did found and erect the colledge of Mary Magdalene in Oxford. For the which foundation, as there haue bene, and bee yet many studentes bounde to yelde gratfull thankes unto God, so I must nedes confesse me selfe to be one, except I wilbe unkynd.'[1] The provision of books was generous at Magdalen in the 15th and 16th centuries, and possibly its library was inspirational of some of the scholarly gratitude Foxe describes.

When William Waynflete began planning his college in Oxford, one of his first concerns was to provide a fitting collection of books, one that would give the library a central position in the intellectual and cultural life of the College.[2] His campaign to promote and establish this new project included persuading his friends and their executors to furnish the library room he had in mind for Magdalen College. Indeed the first recorded intention to contribute – Sir Thomas Ingledew's donation of volumes 'of school matter and moral matter' described in an unsealed indenture of 1454 – came more than three years before the College actually received its charter.[3] For its first two decades the College occupied parts of the suppressed Hospital of St John the Baptist while funding was secured and plans drawn for more appropriate accommodation. The hospital buildings included a chapel, possibly furnished with an *armarium* or a wooden chest to secure valuable chapel books, but no particular room for storing books. The early fellowship no doubt kept books in their own rooms, while books intended for communal use may have been stored with the chapel books or in another chest.

By the time Waynflete came to design college buildings for his St John's Hospital site, he had already accumulated practical knowledge of construction programmes – at Eton, where he had worked with the architect and master mason William Orchard, and at King's College Cambridge.[4] That he himself was interested and unusually able to direct Orchard in the design and construction of a library, cloisters, chapel, muniments room, and great hall in Oxford is evident in his experience and in a surviving contract that shows that the building was to proceed according to the plan Orchard had submitted for the Bishop's approval. The Founder's interest in the architectural finish of his project even induced him to provide 16 statues for the College chapel. Construction of a precinct wall (particularly important for an institution outside the Oxford city walls) began in the 1460s; work on the new buildings began in the spring of 1474.[5] An indenture from mid-way through the project suggests a self-conscious attention to the architectural details of academic buildings, particularly the library, with instructions that 'each window to have two lights, as good as or better than the windows in the library of All Souls' Coll., [and William Orchard to] have for every window 13/4ᵈ'.[6] The ashlar buttresses and battlements for the building – the stone to come from the Headington quarry Orchard leased from the College – are described in another indenture.[7] The library room, on the first floor of the west range of the cloisters, just to the left of the ceremonial entrance to the College, was completed before 1480. In broad description the room probably had a floor covered with tiles similar to those still in the College's Muniment Tower and windows of much the same design as the present ones, and was furnished with the two-sided lecterns that were more or less standard library furniture of the period.[8] The books arrived the next year, in a sort of 800-volume fanfare to the Founder's state visit in 1481: 'Et duxit secum ad collegium suum et praemisit ante se diversos libros quam plurimos pro nova libraris: octingentos aut circiter praeter libros prius ibidem repertos datos et legatos ex diversis benefactoribus.'[9]

With more than 800 volumes, Magdalen's library was doubtless very well stocked for the time. To the description of the physical room can be added chains for the books that were to be stored on the lecterns there, shutters for the windows, candles for readers who worked there in the evenings, and possibly benches for them to sit upon. Respect for the value of the library collection is evident in College statutes outlining the behaviour of the readers and the care of books.[10] All this is documented in College records. And there is no question that Waynflete paid energetic attention to the library. He may have collected books for the library to a plan, perhaps following a model, as he had for the library windows – a plan that is no longer known and may never be recovered. He was among the first bishops in England to see the possibilities of the printing press, when he had indulgences printed rather than copied out by hand, and he may have enlisted the help of the book trade, as well as of other benefactors, to build the 15th-century library. The original arrangement of the collection is unclear too, although suggestions may be found in the stone figures representing four university faculties (theology, the arts, medicine, and law) mounted just outside the library windows, and in two relatively early lists of parts of the collection. Thomas James's numbered list suggests an arrangement of the manuscripts in the late 15th century, and it is possible there are clues in John Bale's earlier list, but there are no Magdalen Library catalogues to give definitive answers.[11]

The College's account books, *libri computi*, begin about the time the first phase of building was complete, and from the first include a heading for library expenditure, *custus librariae* and later *custus bibliothecae*. The accounts provide solid evidence for a pattern of growth and management that seems in many respects typical of late medieval English college libraries, starting with the first entry for 1481:

In primis pro legacione libri S^{ti} Thomae super phisicam xiiij^d. Et pro uno libro textuali naturalis philosophiae pro lectore naturalis philosophiae ix^s Et pro redempcione unius libri naturalis philosophiae expositi in cista de Nelle pro caucione per M Galffridum Recley vi^s viij^d. Et solutum pro v libris vocatis Alexanderis De anima xxxiij^s iiij^d. Et pro veccione unius libri qui vocatur Augustinus De civitatis dei a Waltam ad collegium vi^d.[12]

So one book was bound, a St Thomas for 14d, and a natural philosophy text was purchased for 9s. Another natural philosophy volume was redeemed for 6s 8d, evidence of the practice of leaving books for security on loans. In this case the loan may have been made by John Neele ('Nelle'), Bishop Waynflete's chaplain from 1460, the same John Neele, Fellow, who was later to give the College a substantial book collection.[13] Sixpence was spent on carriage for Augustine's *De civitate dei* from Waynflete's palace in Waltham to Oxford, and the largest sum, 33s 4d, was paid for five copies of a commentary on Aristotle's *De Anima* attributed to Alexander de Hales,[14] to make a total library expenditure of 50s 8d.

The bookbinder is unnamed, and it is unclear from whom the book purchase was made, yet these entries suggest that a natural relationship between the book trade and Magdalen College had already been established. The Aristotelian commentary was one of the first books to come from the press of Theodoric Rood, Oxford's first printer, in October 1481; certainly it is the first book to bear the printer's name; and it is the earliest Oxford edition of any original text.[15] The College must have bought its five copies hot off the press, perhaps directly from Rood himself, who was renting a tenement from the Hospital of St John below Oxford's East Gate — 35 or 36 High Street, just up the road from the College — from about 1478.[16] The College acquired another Oxford imprint from the same press, a luxury edition of John Lathbury's *Expositio ac moralisatio tertii capituli threnorum Jeremiae prophetae* printed by Theodoric Rood on vellum, dated 31 July 1482.[17] The book was probably a gift, possibly severally sponsored by members of the College, as is the vellum copy at All Souls.[18] The number of surviving copies and fragments discovered in later bindings suggests that it was printed in a fairly large edition. At any rate the College took care that it was well bound, paying 12d for binding in 1483.[19] The volume was probably chained, which should have helped its chances for survival, but the book (even in a fragmentary state) is no longer in the Magdalen collection.

Theodoric Rood's career in Oxford was brief, but not unusual in that.[20] Short-term printing was already a pattern on the Continent where many printers moved from town to town, setting up shop and then moving on within a few years.[21] Cambridge had no printer at all until John Siberch's arrival in about 1520, and even then he stayed only a few years.[22] As did

Oxford's second printer, Siberch's contemporary John Scolar, who was evidently in the printing business for about a year (1518-19).[23] Rood had emigrated from Cologne – a university town somewhat overcrowded with printers in the late 15th century – and seemed to bring with him the ability to size up the academic market. He was in business as a printer around 1478 when he anonymously printed Rufinus de Aquileia, *Expositio Sancti Hieronymi in Symbolum Apostolarum,*[24] and he seems also to have worked as a goldsmith.[25] By 1483 he had joined Thomas Hunt, University stationer, with whom he published John Anwykyll's humanist Latin grammar, further evidence of a link with Magdalen, since Anwykyll was at that time master of the College School.[26] Rood and Hunt appear together in the imprint of a Latin translation of Phalaris in 1485.[27] As printers, they would have had to compete with the better established continentals (particularly for the Latin trade) and they seem to have found a workable formula in their English-language books, but their business was not limited to printing. They bound books: examples of their bindings are in a number of Oxford college libraries.[28] And there is evidence of their activities as wholesale booksellers who retailed continental imports, something that was positively encouraged by the English government for a time.[29] In 1483 Hunt had books on a sale-or-return basis from Johannes de Aquisgrano and Peter Actors; and he is known to have traded with John of Westphalia.[30] Their names are last found in the imprint to John Mirk's *Liber Festivalis* of 1486.[31] Seventeen books in all can be associated with Theodoric Rood and the first Oxford press.[32] Despite his connections with the continental trade, some success with the academic community, and the diversification of his business, Rood disappears from Oxford in about 1486. It is uncertain whether he succumbed to the inhospitality of an English market that traditionally supported the continental book trade, or to the recurring outbreaks of plague that regularly drove the Oxford colleges to find temporary accommodation outside town.

Magdalen, in common with other Oxford colleges in the 15th century, followed the practice established earlier in religious communities of dividing the book collection into two parts, one to circulate amongst members, and the other to remain within the institution for reference. At Oxford a series of 'elections' was held at which the fellowship, often in order of seniority, could select from the college's circulating collection books relevant to their studies. The Magdalen 1480 Statutes ordered that

the Books regarding any Faculty whatsoever, which by a like bounty have been conferred on the said College, or acquired in any other manner (excepting those Books which may chance to be deposited, fastened, and chained in the common Library of the same College, by the will of the Donors, or the disposition of the President, or Vice-President, and Deans, and Bursars, for the common use of the Fellows and Scholars of the same,) be lent out to the Fellows of the same College who want them, for their special use, by way of new choice thereof to be every year made by election of the same Fellows.[33]

The wording here suggests that at Magdalen, as at the other Oxford colleges, the larger part of the collection circulated: for example Merton College Library, probably the best-documented of any in Oxford, has a 14th-century theological catalogue listing 250 manuscripts, of which only 31 were to remain in the library.[34] The trouble with the circulating collection was (and *is*) that the books disappeared. The system seemed to falter when the collection was large, the elections were held irregularly, rules against pawning borrowed books were not taken seriously, and the Fellows could borrow dozens of books at a time. Merton's Fellows developed a cavalier attitude: at an election of theological books in 1508 the 'mildest offender' was unable to produce five of his books, while another had lost all 28. Soon after this Merton abandoned book elections. Magdalen's collection at the same time was nearly as large, and its readers probably of similar disposition.

Outright book purchases were seldom made, so Magdalen's purchase of a commentary of Aristotle's *De Anima* reveals a somewhat unusual and purposeful attention to the reading needs of its members, service that extended beyond the usual provision of book chains and clasps, or bindings for gifts. The nature of the work suggests that it was purchased in multiple copies by Magdalen for circulation among Fellows studying natural philosophy in the Faculty of Arts. The College accounts show that four of the copies were bound the following year for 4s 8d.[35] Two of these copies — in later bindings, one with the woodcut borders on the section pages, the other without — are fortunately still in the collection, both of them showing signs of hard reading (the many doodles in one copy suggest that at least one reader did not find the material fully engaging). Neither bears any evidence of chaining in the 15th or the 16th century, although both were certainly chained in the library some time after 1610, when the College moved its books from lecterns to shelving, long after the election system had ceased.[36]

Records of early gifts to the library, which far outnumber outright purchases, give some sense of the character of the College library. In 1485 Thomas Rushall, BA, gave the College Antonius on Aristotle's *Metaphysics*, printed by John Lettou for William Wilcock in 1480. The volume was intended for the use of the bachelors and remains in the library, imperfect, but a rare survival.[37] In 1494 William Rydyall and Richard Lagharne gave the library 80 volumes: Rydyall, who was Chaplain in 1476, Fellow and Dean of Divinity in 1482, and Bursar in 1485, gave about 20 of the volumes; Lagharne, Principal of Inge Hall in 1455 and probably a Fellow of Magdalen, gave the others.[38] When Richard Lagharne's books were ready to be shipped from Salisbury, his nephew wrote to the President specifically to ask that they be chained.[39] 42 of those books were professionally chained and fastened with gilded hooks, possibly with some of Rydyall's books left for the circulating library. Three of these gift books can be identified in the present collection: a printed Lactantius, *Opera* (Venice,

1478), a manuscript collection of sermons called 'Filius matris' (15th century), and a manuscript copy of a standard text, Peter Lombard's *Sententiae* (14th century).[40] Lagharne records that he had purchased this last volume from Thomas Mason, former keeper of the Guildhall Library, London, for 13*s* 4*d* in 1468. The College paid 12*d* to a Fellow of the College, Robert Thay, for lettering the vellum labels that recorded the benefaction, which were mounted on the back board under horn, still present on two of these three survivors.

Another important gift began to arrive the following year: John Neele, a Fellow of the College and master of Holy Trinity College, Arundel, sent a chest of books from London, for which the College paid carriage at 2*s*. He died in 1498, and in 1505 the College received another 19 books. His gift is better recorded than most, for Neele left a list of the books he intended for Magdalen dated 'Henrici 7mo IIII°' (1488-9) on the flyleaf of another volume now in the College collection, Franciscus de Platea's *Tractatus restitutionum usurarum et excommunicationum* (Paris, 1476).[41] It is unclear whether Neele intended his books for the election or for the library: the few volumes still in the collection bear chain marks from the middle of the bottom of the front board—not the usual Magdalen style—which suggests that they had been chained before coming to Oxford, but probably then became part of Magdalen's circulating collection.

Meanwhile the College continued to make use of the professional book trade in various ways. Thomas Uffington the bookbinder was employed for six days in 1482; Lathbury was bound for 12*d* and the College Statutes for 16*d* in 1483-4.[42] A few of the books given by Lagharne and Rydyall evidently arrived in quires, and the College paid for them to be professionally bound; the chaining too, seems to have been the work of a professional, called here Thomas the Bookbinder. He was also paid to make up parchment rolls (the payment is 'pro conglutinacione rotuli') of the history of the Old Testament, and maps of the Holy Land and the world. The binder was doubtless still Thomas Uffington, who had been employed by the College earlier. Book chains constructed by the local binders were a regular expense until the late 18th century when the books were finally unchained. An illuminator named John Lylly painted the capital letters in the antiphon prepared by a College Fellow, John Wymark, after the Founder's death in 1486. Peter 'bokebynder', almost certainly the same Peter Actors who had been selling books to Thomas Hunt earlier, was a College guest at dinner in 1497. Actors was stationer to the King (from December 1485), bookseller, and bookbinder. Although he was based in London, he travelled on book business and had firm Oxford connections through his son Sebastian and son-in-law John Hewtee, both of them Oxford stationers.[43]

The late 15th century witnessed a general transition in academic life that affected library collections in particular ways. In Oxford the university curriculum was changing, in a move towards humanism and away from medieval schools. At Magdalen College and Magdalen College School – the free school established by Waynflete in the late 1470s – there was a remarkable concentration of literary humanists and grammarians who encouraged the trend from within: John Anwykyll was the school's first headmaster; John Stanbridge was usher and then master; Thomas Wolsey was headmaster briefly, and College Bursar.[44] Waynflete was instrumental in establishing the first free university lectures in England: his 1480 statutes required two Magdalen Fellows to lecture without charge to any members of their faculties who wished to attend.[45] College library accessions and *de*-accessions had to support a changing curriculum, then as now. At Magdalen the innovative momentum started by its founder continued for a time, and is reflected in the library's history, particularly in its purchases of printed books.

The introduction of the printing press into England in the 1470s (just when the College library was under construction) offered a new means of book production, and was of course an important part of the invigorating process. Waynflete was himself among the first to exploit its possibilities. Yet the transition from manuscript to print was not immediate and the boundaries between the two were often indistinct: early printed books often looked like the manuscripts from which they were copied; space was left in printed books for manuscript initials and handmade illustrations; readers often felt free to annotate the printed text; the manuscript book trade continued along with printed books, and indeed the circulation of books in manuscript continued for centuries. By the same measure, the book trade was more fluidly defined in the late 15th century. There were of course moves to organize the trade and protect various interests, but the Stationers' Company was not to receive its charter until the middle of the next century.[46] An Oxford student who needed a book might borrow a copy, buy a ready-made copy, or commission a copy from a professional scribe or an academic colleague if he had the money. He might copy it out himself. He could pay for a binding, or be happy to read the book in quires. Textbooks were sometimes made up from a scholar's lecture notes and the books usefully passed down from student to student.

This transitional state is reflected in the College accounts. At the same time as professional binders are employed to deal with new acquisitions, and purchases made from the established booksellers, there are entries for payments to different Magdalen Fellows and others not identified with the trade, for 'lettering' books, copying them in manuscript, or selling them to the College. The College rented accommodation to the book trade, dined with its members, and, in the 16th century, even welcomed members of at least one bookselling family into the fellowship. The relationship the College had with the trade through much of the 16th century was a very close one, founded in the seriousness with which it has usually viewed the provision of books for its members.

If 15th-century college libraries had acquisitions policies, they were determined for the most part by the inclinations of benefactors. The development of Magdalen's library was often guided by gifts during its first half-century, but occasional considered book purchases clearly played a part. The next century had an auspicious start, when a seven-volume set of Hugo of Vienna was bought for 46s 6d at the St Frideswide Fair in 1502,[47] but from then until the late 1530s there was little detectable energy in library acquisitions. The local book trade was still involved, mainly as suppliers of chains and bindings and the odd chapel book, and donated books continued to arrive (two-hundredweight in 1505), but the College's earlier momentum seems to have been lost. This might have had to do with Richard Mayew's absentee presidency after he was appointed Bishop of Hereford in 1504. Indeed there was a complaint that 'The servants of the Bishop of Hereford have done much harm in the College, as, for instance to the glass windows, and in emptying chamber-vessels upon the tiles over the library', which might represent the nadir of Magdalen College Library's history.[48] Unless that was the transformation of the library into a detention centre in 1520 when Roger Baynthrop was sentenced to write sentences on Aristotle there for posting a threatening letter on the President's privy door.[49]

There was a dramatic recovery by 1538-9. Extraordinary sums were paid to the Oxford bookseller Herman Evans for library books that year: there is one entry to him for £11 3s 8d, another for £12 2d. 'Raynarde bibliopolae Londoni', almost certainly Reyner Wolfe, sold the College books to the value of 29s. Entries in the libri computi suggest a healthy Oxford book trade that continued to supply most Magdalen library requirements, while the occasional, sometimes ambiguous, references to London indicate that the College maintained contact with the trade there, either directly or through the fellowship. Obviously Oxford booksellers had to establish their own networks with London and continental colleagues. Members of the College, including the Vice-President and Michael Drumme, took an active, if not clearly defined, role in procuring books. The works of Augustine (£3 6s 8d), the works of Actuarius (14d), and the works of George Valla (10s) were bought, and there are entries for shipments of books from London in the Library accounts.[50] This is not to mention books and stationery supplied for the Chapel. The relative strength of the Library budget at this time is all the more remarkable when viewed against the background of continuing domestic, political, and religious turbulence. It is tempting to see a relationship between books and the senior members of the College who looked after them: the politic Owen Oglethorpe was President from 1535 to 1552, and Michael Drumme was Reader in Greek and Dean of Arts in 1539 for example.

The College continued to spend a great deal at Herman Evans's shop, but a more important book-trade association began about the same time. The first entry in the accounts for Garbrand Harkes is not a very promising one, 17s for securing ('compingenti') various books in the same year that more than £23 went to Herman Evans.[51] That the relationship was taking an unusual turn is evident in 1539, when Garbrand Harkes and Magdalen's Henry Bull (then a Demy, but later the first Fellow Librarian) were brought to the attention of the authorities for participating in an orgy of meat-eating one Lent. Their fellow carnivores included most of the Oxford Protestant book trade. Herman Men, bookseller, 'confesses to having eaten this Lent with his family 20 legs of mutton, 5 rounds of beef, and 6 capons . . . Garbarande, bookbinder, Bull of Maudelyn College, Persephall Bertoune and his wife, Nicolas Hosier, Christopher, bookbinder, and Jenyns, bookbinder, have eaten flesh in his house or with him . . . He was examined before the mayor of Oxford, Aldermen Frere and Pye, and the principals of Pecwater's Inn and Edwarde Hall.'[52]

Four years later, in 1543, the College paid 34s to Garbrand Harkes for Theophylact and Eustathius in Greek.[53] The other library book purchase that year was of an Epiphanius from an unidentified Master Olivarius.[54] The Eustathius and Epiphanius are gone, but by coincidence there is in the library a copy of Theophylact in Greek on the Evangelists of about the same year (Rome, 1542), which Bloxham thought must be the book in question. However that volume came to the College as part of its purchase of John Jewel's library.[55] A more likely candidate is a volume containing Theophylact on the Evangelists (Cologne, 1536) and on the Epistles (Cologne, 1531). While not in Greek (and the entry in the accounts is ambiguous on that point), the two are bound in a 16th-century Oxford binding, which has the title inscribed on the back board in a contemporary hand. Thereafter Garbrand, from his shop in Bulkeley Hall, supplied the College fairly regularly with books for the chapel and occasionally for the library. His son Richard followed the same business, as did *his* son Ambrose.

Garbrand Harkes is Oxford's most famous Protestant bookseller, yet he demonstrated an ability not just to survive the vicissitudes of the Reformation, but to take advantage of them. He bought up stocks of books from monastic libraries under Edward; his cellar became a meeting place for Oxford Protestants during the Marian persecutions; and he is said to have rescued a cartload of Merton manuscripts – and doubtless many others – destined for an ignoble fate 'in tyme of the lamentable spoyle of the libraryes of Englande' as John Bale put it.[56] Garbrand and his son Richard stored them until times were more propitious – some of them were no doubt sold, and others may have eventually found their way back into academic libraries. John Bale, who was very concerned about the fate of books during these turbulent times, took care to include 13 manuscripts in Garbrand's hands, along with those in academic libraries, when he compiled his lists of extant English manuscripts. It is not improbable that John Foxe went to Garbrand Harkes for books, and perhaps some of the manuscripts from the Foxe library now in the College collection came from this source.[57] Certainly Foxe knew Garbrand, and mentions him in the letter he wrote to the President when he presented a copy of *Actes and Monumentes* to the

College. Indeed Foxe suggests with some diffidence that it was his bookseller Garbrand who persuaded him to give the book — written in English — to his old College ('huc me, nescio quo pacto, pertraxit, vincens pudorum et judicum meum, Garbrandi Bibliopolae, pellax oratio, sic ad persuadendum instructa').[58] At least one Magdalen manuscript, a copy of the *Chronicon Angliae*,[59] has annotations in Bale's hand and came to the College as part of the gift of John Foxe's books.

Garbrand Harkes was not himself a member of Magdalen College, but his sons and grandsons were.[60] Thomas Garbrand (b.1539) was a Magdalen chorister (1551), Demy (1553), and then supplicated for the BCL in 1568. He was as firm as his father in his religious beliefs, and just as ostentatious, going so far as to shave his head in a mock-tonsure on one occasion. He resigned his fellowship when his brother William (b.1549) was elected. Richard Garbrand (d.1602) joined his father in the book business. Another son John (1542-89) was the distinguished friend and editor of Bishop Jewel. Two grandsons were booksellers: John (1585-c.1618) in Oxford, after a fellowship at New College 1606-8, and Ambrose (b.1584) in London; two others, Tobias (b.1579) and Nicholas (b.1600), were Fellows of Magdalen in the 17th century.

This brief survey of the relationship between an Oxford college and the book trade begins with Waynflete and his concerns to build a creditable library, and includes the earliest members of Oxford's printed book trade. It concludes — about the time the Stationers' Company was incorporated — with Garbrand Harkes, his associations with John Foxe, Bishop Jewel, and others, and his extensive family of booksellers and Magdalenses, just before Laurence Humphrey was unanimously elected to the College presidency in 1561. Both the Garbrands and Humphrey were deeply persuaded by Protestantism, but Garbrand managed to save many books from destruction and Laurence Humphrey, who may have been happy to have the chapel statues smashed, was too much of a scholar to extend that policy to the Library. Their commitment to books and scholarship, as well as to a particular brand of religion, makes a fitting prelude to the history of Magdalen College and the book trade in succeeding centuries.

References

1. John Foxe, *The First Volume of the Ecclesiastical History contayning the Actes and Monumentes* (London: printed by John Daye, 1570), p.835, col.2; Magdalen's copy is the one Foxe presented to the College. STC 11223.
2. Virginia Davis, *William Waynflete: Bishop and Educationalist* (Woodbridge: The Boydell Press, 1993), and R. Chandler, *The Life of William Waynflete, Bishop of Winchester* (London: printed for White and Cochrane, 1811).
3. Magdalen College Archives (MCA), Misc. 436.
4. Davis, *William Waynflete*, 100-5. For William Orchard, see J. Harvey and A. Oswald, *English Medieval Architects: A Biographical Dictionary down to 1550*, 2nd edn. (Gloucester:

Alan Sutton, 1984), 199-200; E. A. Gee, 'Oxford Masons, 1370-1530', *Archaeological Journal*, 109 (1952), 54-131.

5. MCA CP/2/67/1, f.18v.

6. MCA Misc. 349.

7. *Ibid.*

8. Unfortunately Streeter is in error when he suggests that Magdalen inaugurated the very first 'stall' system of book storage (incorporated shelving and desks). This did not happen until early in the 17th century (Burnett Hillman Streeter, *The Chained Library: A Survey of Four Centuries in the Evolution of the English Library* (London: Macmillan, 1931), 1).

9. MCA Register A, EL/1, f.7v.

10. G. R. M. Ward, *The Statutes of Magdalen College Oxford Now First Translated and Published* (Oxford: printed for the author by Henry Alden; London: Jackson and Walford, 1840).

11. Thomas James, *Ecloga Oxonio-Cantabrigiensis* (London: impensis Geor. Bishop, & Io. Norton, 1600); John Bale, *Index Britanniae Scriptorum: John Bale's Index of British and Other Writers*, ed. Reginald Lane Poole and Mary Bateson; with an introduction by Caroline Brett and James Carley (Cambridge: D. S. Brewer, 1990). Bale's original notebook is in the Bodleian Library (MS. Selden supra 64 (S.C. 3452)). Missing lists include one that the College's first Fellow Librarian, Henry Bull, was paid 20s to compile in 1549-50 (MCA LCE/5, f.86v), and the list of books the College was required to submit to the Marian visitors in 1556.

12. MCA LCE/1, f.11v.

13. John M. Fletcher, 'A Fifteenth-Century Benefaction to Magdalen College Library', *Bodleian Library Record*, 9 (1974), 169-72. Another Magdalen book redemption is recorded in 1485, when 6s 8d was paid for redeeming from — Holem, Exeter College, a book of philosophy that had been pawned to him by Geoffrey Radcliffe 'nuper socio' (W. D. Macray, *A Register of the Members of St. Mary Magdalen College, Oxford, from the Foundation of the College* (London: Henry Frowde, 1894), i. 93). Malcolm Parkes records numerous other Oxford examples in his chapter on the provision of books in Oxford in the 14th and 15th centuries (M. B. Parkes, 'The Provision of Books', in J. I. Catto and T. A. R. Evans (eds.), *The History of the University of Oxford*, ii: *Late Medieval Oxford* (Oxford: Clarendon Press, 1992), 407-83).

14. The STC attributes the commentary to Alexander ab Alexandria (STC 314).

15. *Printing and Publishing at Oxford: The Growth of a Learned Press 1478-1978* (Oxford: Bodleian Library, 1978), no.4; Dennis E. Rhodes, *A Catalogue of Incunabula in all the Libraries of Oxford University outside the Bodleian* (Oxford: Clarendon Press, 1982), 55 [hereafter Rhodes].

16. An annual rent of 26s 8d is recorded for the years 1480-1 ('De domo in qua manet Dyryke Dowcheman') and 1481-2 (*A Cartulary of the Hospital of St. John the Baptist*, ed. H. E. Salter (Oxford: Oxford Historical Society, 1917), iii. 272, 276). A record for what seems to be the same accommodation 'infra portam orientalem ex parte boriali' shows that 'Ioh' Ducheman' was the tenant in 1478-9 (*ibid.*, 267, and i. 272).

17. STC 15297; Rhodes 1080; N. R. Ker, 'The Vellum Copies of the Oxford Editions (1482) of Lathbury on Lamentations', *Bodleian Library Record*, 2 (1947), 185-8.

18. Rhodes 1080(a).

19. LCE/1 (1483), f.75v (the accounts for this year are misbound over ff.34-9, 57-8, 66-77).

20. A résumé of Rood's career may be found in Harry Carter, *A History of the Oxford University Press* (Oxford: Clarendon Press, 1975), i. 1-16.

21. David Rogers, 'Printing in 1478: The Background to the First Press at Oxford', *Journal of the Printing Historical Society*, 13 (1978/9), 67-77.

22. David McKitterick, *A History of Cambridge University Press*, vol.1: *Printing and the Book Trade in Cambridge 1534-1698* (Cambridge: Cambridge University Press, 1992), 38-9; E. Gordon Duff, *A Century of the English Book Trade* (London: The Bibliographical Society, 1905), 147-8; STC iii. 154-5.

23. Scolar does turn up a few miles away in Abingdon about ten years later to print one more item (STC iii. 150).
24. STC 21443.
25. Carter, *History of the Oxford University Press*, i. 6.
26. STC 695-6; a revised (and definitive) list of early Magdalen College School headmasters and ushers may be found in Nicholas Orme, *Magdalen College and Its School: English Education 1480-1540* (Magdalen College Occasional Papers; Oxford: Magdalen College, forthcoming).
27. STC 19827; Rhodes 1393.
28. Examples of Rood and Hunt bindings may be found in most older Oxford college libraries (Strickland Gibson, *Early Oxford Bindings* (Oxford: The Bibliographical Society, 1903), pp.4, 5, 21, 46).
29. 1 Ric.3.c.ix, which encouraged the import of printed continental books.
30. F. Madan, 'Day-Book of John Dorne, Bookseller in Oxford, A.D.1520', in *Collectanea*, first series, ed. C. R. L. Fletcher (Oxford: Oxford Historical Society, 1885), 142-3; Rogers, 'Printing in 1478', 73; for a good overview and assessment of the import trade see R. J. Roberts, 'Importing Books for Oxford, 1500-1640', in *Books and Collectors 1200-1700*, ed. James P. Carley and Colin Tite (London: British Library, 1997).
31. STC 17958.
32. Listed by Harry Carter, *History of the Oxford University Press*, i. 10-11.
33. Ward (ed.), *Statutes of Magdalen College Oxford*, 110-11.
34. H. W. Garrod, 'Library Regulations of a Mediaeval College', *The Library*, 4th ser. 8 (1928), 312-35; F. M. Powicke, *The Medieval Books of Merton College* (Oxford: Clarendon Press, 1931), introduction; and G. H. Martin on the Merton College Library in G. H. Martin and J. R. L. Highfield, *The History of Merton College, Oxford* (Oxford: Oxford University Press, 1997).
35. MCA LCE/1 (1482-3), fo.3^v.
36. STC 314; Rhodes 55(c), 55(d).
37. STC 581; Rhodes 80.
38. Macray, *Register of the Members of St. Mary Magdalen College*, i. 40.
39. MCA MS 367, letter 29.
40. Lactantius: Rhodes 1069(a); sermons: Magd. MS. Lat. 81; Lombard: Magd. MS. Lat. 114.
41. The list is transcribed and discussed in Fletcher, 'A Fifteenth-Century Benefaction to Magdalen College Library'.
42. LCE/1 (1482), f.31v; (1483), f.75v.
43. Duff, *Century of the English Book Trade*, 1.
44. A revisionist description of the first decades of Magdalen College School, and of its influence through its grammarians is to be found in Nicholas Orme's *Magdalen College and Its School*. See also R. S. Stanier, *Magdalen School: A History of Magdalen College School* (Oxford: Blackwell, 1958).
45. J. M. Fletcher, 'Developments in the Faculty of Arts 1370-1520', in *History of the University of Oxford*, ii. 335.
46. Graham Pollard, 'The Company of Stationers before 1557', *The Library*, 4th ser. 18 (1937), 1-38 and 'The Early Constitution of the Stationers' Company', *The Library*, 4th ser. 18 (1937), 235-60.
47. MCA LCE/2, f.128v.
48. Macray, *Register*, i. 40.
49. Macray, *Register*, ii. 72.
50. MCA LCE/4 (1538-9), ff.132v-133r where payments to the Vice-President and Master Drumme 'pro diversis libris' are recorded; for Evans, see Duff, *Century of the English Book Trade*, 44; Wolf, *ibid.*, 171-2; the wills of Reyner Wolf and his wife Joan Wolf are abstracted in Henry R. Plomer, *Abstracts from the Wills of English Printers and Stationers, from 1492 to 1630* (London: The Bibliographical Society, 1903), 19-23.
51. MCA LCE/4, f.133r.

52. Examination of Herman Men 3 April 1539, 30 Hen. VIII (*Letters and Papers, Foreign and Domestic, Hen. VIII*, vol.xiv, pt.1, p.339).

53. MCA: LCE/4 (1543-4), fo.172v.

54. Olivarius evidently was not a member of Magdalen College, and is not recorded in A. B. Emden, *A biographical register of the University of Oxford, A.D. 1501 to 1540* (Oxford: Clarendon Press, 1974).

55. It is clearly marked on page one with Jewel's 'Bel ami' stamp, and bears the fore-edge title characteristic of books in his library. Garbrand Harkes's son John (who was a Fellow of New College) was a close friend of Jewel and edited his works.

56. John Bale, *Index Britanniae Scriptorum*, xi.

57. Magdalen MSS Lat. 36, 43, 53, 69, 70, 84, 170, 172, 180, 181, 199 and 200 were identified by Neil Ker as gifts of John Foxe's son Samuel Foxe (Demy 1574, Fellow 1577-90), identification that Thomas Freeman is presently investigating (N. R. Ker, *Medieval Manuscripts in British Libraries*, vol.iii (Oxford: Clarendon Press, 1983), 644-5).

58. The letter is tipped into the volume at Magd. Arch.B.I.4.13. The first two editions were evidently gifts to the College; nevertheless £6 13s 4d was paid to Foxe for each, an arrangement possibly suggested by Garbrand as a tactful way of assisting the author. I am very grateful to Thomas Freeman for his timely assistance on matters relating to John Foxe and his library.

59. Magd. MS Lat. 36.

60. For a summary account of the Garbrand family, see *DNB*.

The library of Sir Edward Sherburne (1616-1702)

T. A. BIRRELL

BODLEIAN LIBRARY MS Rawlinson Q.b.3 is described as follows in the *Summary Catalogue* (S.C. 16031):

In English on paper: written in about A.D.1681. 16½ × 10½in. 53 leaves.

A catalogue of a library of 2000 or 3000 volumes, arranged alphabetically by the first letter of the heading. The type of pressmark is 'E.15', 'V.48'. The owner lent books to Flamsteed in 1681-84 and records his purchases at several sales.

There are in fact about 2,000 *titles*; the first leaf of the letter 'A' is missing; the leaf containing the letter 'Y' has been very obviously torn out; and the most recent book in the catalogue is dated 1684. But what is very striking to the eye of a non-palaeographer is that the catalogue has an alphabetical thumb-index. This immediately reminded me of a similar feature in another library catalogue, British Library MS Sloane 857; this is a catalogue dated 1670, of about 1,000 titles, of the library of Sir Edward Sherburne. A comparison of the two manuscripts makes it quite clear that MS Rawlinson Q.b.3 is a later and considerably expanded version of Sherburne's library catalogue. Both the catalogue, and the *curriculum vitae*, of Sherburne are remarkable examples of 'the two cultures', the easy combination of the arts and the new science, in Restoration England.[1]

Sherburne's family history is an illustration of social mobility, up-down-and-up, in four generations. His great-grandfather was a Lancashire squire from Haighton near Preston—a strongly recusant enclave—who sold the family estates; his grandfather came south and was in charge of the stables at Corpus Christi College, Oxford; his father became secretary of the East India Company and later Chief Clerk of the Ordnance at the Tower. On the death of his father in 1641, Edward Sherburne succeeded to the job at the age of 25.

Sherburne had received a ten-year classical education at the London school of Thomas Farnaby, and later private tuition from Charles Aleyn, Farnaby's usher and a minor poet and translator. Sherburne went on to find a place in the world of the Caroline poets, Pope's 'mob of gentlemen who wrote with ease': Thomas Stanley, Thomas Randolph, Tom May, James Shirley, Robert Herrick and Richard Lovelace. But he presumably acquired his scientific knowledge from private study: he speaks of having lost, at the outbreak of the Civil Wars, a library of 2,000 books, which must have included his father's books as well as his own.

In 1642 Sherburne was removed by the Parliament from his post in the Tower. He served the King as captain and commissary general of artillery at Edgehill and the siege of Oxford. In 1646 he retired to lodgings in the Middle Temple with his friend Thomas Stanley; in 1651 he became agent to the young George Savile (later Marquis of Halifax) at Rufford and, after the abortive Royalist rising in 1655, retired to the continent and travelled in France, Italy, Germany, the Netherlands, 'and some parts of Hungary'. He returned to England shortly before the Restoration and eventually got his old job back. At the Glorious Revolution he was once more outed from his office and lived on in lodgings in Holborn, ill and poor, till his death in 1702 at the age of 86.[2]

His literary publications include two translations from Seneca, published in 1648, the *Answer to Lucilius; why Good Men suffer misfortune*, and the *Medea* (in verse); and *Poems and Translations, Amorous, Lusory, Moral and Divine* (1651). In a sense all three publications were political acts: the first was dedicated to Charles I, a very obvious consolation for *his* misfortunes; the plot of the second is a not too fanciful analogy of a society chopped into pieces in the futile hope of an improved revivification; and the third, chiefly translations from the Italian *concettisti* Marino and Preti, the French *libertin* St Amant, and the Polish neo-Latinist Sarbiewski, were evocations of the lost international baroque culture of the days of Charles I.

After the Restoration the Ordnance Office ledgers show Sherburne at his daily routine for nearly thirty years: ordering tarred rope, checking the quality of gunpowder, sending snaphanses for repair, and putting on displays of pontoon bridges over the lake in St James's Park for the edification of Charles II. And besides this, he was Clerk of the Works for the building of Greenwich Observatory, during which he became, surprisingly, a friend and confidant of that very paranoid astronomer John Flamsteed (1646-1719), who frequently borrowed books from his library (and dutifully returned them). The atmosphere in the office was congenial: the mathematician Sir Jonas Moore (1617-79) was Surveyor General of the Ordnance; the old warhorse and almanack-maker Sir George Wharton (1617-81) was Paymaster; and there were olympian but stimulating visits from Lord Berkeley of Stratton (d.1678), Master of the Ordnance, and from Lord Brouncker (1620-84), first President of the Royal Society. There were often festive departmental dinners to which other scientists or *virtuosi*, such as Robert Hooke, John Collins, Richard Towneley and John Aubrey, might be invited.[3]

It was within this congenial environment that Sherburne put down his marker as a member of the scientific community: in 1675 he published his translation of Book I of *The Sphere* of Manilius. In its own day, it would have been called a 'pompous' folio, in no pejorative sense: one has to see it, in a large-paper edition, to believe it. Perhaps the best idea of its tone, as well as of its contents, is conveyed by the advertisement in the *Term Catalogues*:

The Sphere of Marcus Manilius made an English Poem, with Annotations: and an Appendix containing the Original and Progress of Astronomy; a Catalogue of the Writings of the most eminent Astronomers, Antient and Modern; The several Mundane Systems; A Cosmographical, Astronomical Synopsis; A description of the Nature, Light, Place, Magnitude, Distances, and other Adjuncts, of the Fixed Stars and Planets; Of Comets and other fiery Meteors, their original Causes and History. In Folio. Price, bound, £1. 10s.

It was Sherburne's grand scientific statement, in which he displayed himself both as a 'modern' scientist and as an historian of science. The text of Manilius ploughs its way majestically through a thicket of textual criticism and commentary. But it is in the 'Catalogue of the most eminent Astronomers, Antient and Modern' that Sherburne displays the depth of his reading and the width of his circle of scientific friends.

Some such brief biographical sketch is a necessary preliminary to the consideration of Sherburne's library catalogue and its contents. The first striking feature of the catalogue is the demonstration of its owner's organizational methods. To quote the Bodleian description once more, it is 'arranged alphabetically by the first letter of the heading [in most cases the surname of the author if known]. The type of pressmark is "E.15", "V.48".' In fact, the pressmarks relate to the format of the books — more strictly, the height of the spine — and the catalogue is a combined accessions register and finding register. Sherburne's system is the simplest, and least time-wasting, method of managing a private library — provided of course that you have plenty of space.

He began with a press of seven shelves lettered A to G: A = folio; B = folio; C = folio and quarto; D = quarto; E = octavo; F = octavo *et infra*; G = duodecimo. The shelving began at the bottom with A, running upwards to G. On a rough calculation each press was about 10 to 12 feet long. As each book was acquired, it was put on the shelves according to *size*, and without any consideration whatever for *subject*. Each book had two diamond-shaped labels, at the top and bottom of the spine; the lower label had the alphabetical shelfmark and the upper label had the number on the shelf.[4] When the first press began to fill up, a second press was constructed with another seven shelves H-O (I and J counting as one letter), with the same arrangements for size. The third press must have run from P-W (with U and V as one letter). The pressmark X certainly exists, chiefly for quartos; and the most recently acquired duodecimos were put in at E, where there seemed to be some space left over. Only one book has the pressmark P, Minsheu's *Dictionary* 1611 (P11), so presumably that shelf was used for other things, perhaps manuscripts and files. A few very recent acquisitions have indeed no pressmark at all, and they occur at the end of each alphabetical list: it is by the dates of publication of these books that it can be calculated that the cut-off date of the catalogue is about 1684.

To get a clearer impression, let us take a random sample: the first 20 quartos on shelf M of the second press, which was constructed about 1667.

M.1   Alfragani, Elementa Astronomica Arabica. Lat. per Jacobum Golium. Amst. 1669.
This was the *editio princeps*. Golius gives first the Latin text, then notes, then the Arabic text.

M.2   Meursii, Jo., Miscellanea Laconia. Amst. 1661.
Classical antiquities: on the history of Sparta.

M.3   Bibliotheca Bodleiana per Tho. James. Oxon 1620.
Sherburne also had two copies of Hyde's 1674 catalogue.

M.4   Waseri, Gasp., De antiquis Mensuris Hebr. Heidelb. 1610.
Weights and measures in the Bible (Sherburne was fascinated by Biblical *realia*) together with other forms of ancient weights and measures.

M.5   Heydon, Sir Christopher, Defence of Astrologie, Cambr. 1603.
A large book, full of misprints.[5] Like other scientists of his day, Sherburne certainly believed in the astrological influence of birth dates and times.

M.6   Lachmundi, Frederici, ὀρυκτογραφια Hildesheim, &c., Hildesheim 1659.
Printed for the author. Palaeontology: a book on fossils in and around Hildesheim.

M.7   Hygini & Polybii, de Castris Rom. per H. R. Schelium, Amst. 1660.
Military, ancient. Edited by Hermann Rabod.

M.8   Leipstorpii, Danielis, Specimina Philosophiae Cartesianae cum eiusden Copernico Redivivo. L.B. 1658.
A defence of Descartes's mathematics and of the Copernican system.

M.9   Reusneri, Eliae, Thesaurus Bellicus, Francf. 1609.
Military. Classical and biblical authorities quoted on the nature and laws of war. 530pp.

M.10   Hervarti, Jo. Frederico, de Magnete &c. Monachii 1626.
On the history and cult of the loadstone. Hard to classify: as much cultural anthropology as history of science.

M.11   (a) Scylacis Cariendens., Periplus. per Isaacum Vossium &c. Amst. 1639 (b) una cum Galilaei Discorsi Mathemat.
(a) Ancient geography, though the text is not in fact by Scylax.
(b) The 'system' breaks down here, for the book is not cross-referenced under Galilei. It was in fact the *editio princeps* of Galilei's *Discorsi*, smuggled out of Italy and published by the Elzeviers at Leiden in 1638.[6]

M.12   Maimonides. Mosis, de Jure Pauperis et Peregrini apud Judaeos, Hebr. Lat. per Humfridum Prideaux. Oxon 1679.
Word for word parallel translation for the beginner in the study of Hebrew.

M.13   Goesii, Wilelmi, Rei Agrariae Authores Legesque variae cum notis Nicol. Rigaltii. Amst. 1674.
Classical antiquity. Classical texts on agriculture plus a commentary on the chrestomathy.

M.14   (a) Chaloneri, Thomae, Poemata. Lond. 1579. (b) una cum Ubbonis Emmii, Guilelm. Ludov. Com. Nassov. Groning 1621.
Once again the system breaks down. (a) Neo-Latin verse. The book includes Chaloner's *De republica Anglorum instauranda*: 'a major philosophical and political work, one of the longest Latin poems to appear in sixteenth century England . . . a landmark in English humanism that has been almost completely ignored by literary historians and by students of the period.'[7]
(b) Military biography. Willem Lodowÿk Count of Nassau (1560-1620) campaigned with Sir Edward Norris in the Low Countries, and became Stadtholder of Friesland, Groningen and Drenthe.

M.15   Bangii, Thomae, Caelum Orientis. Hafniae 1652.
Hebrew philology; esoterica.

M.16   Street, Tho., Astronomia Carolina. Lond. 1661.
       Astronomy and mathematics. Street (or Streete) lived on Tower Hill: for his biography
       see Taylor (n.3). A modern mathematical practitioner who greatly influenced
       Flamsteed.
M.17   Bonarelli, Guidubaldo, Philli de Sciro favola Pastorale. [Ferrara] 1607.
       Pastoral drama. Sherburne was contemplating a new English translation of this, and
       asked Anthony Wood to borrow for him a copy of the 1655 translation in the
       Bodleian. This of course Wood was unable to do, but he obligingly sent transcripts of
       specimen portions.
M.18   Ἴκων ἄκλαστος, being an Answer to Jconoclastes against Jcon Basiliche.
       [London] 1651.
       By Joseph Jane. Though the lemma is in fact 'εἰκων', Sherburne has catalogued it
       under I/J because it is a point by point refutation of Milton's 'Jconoclastes'.
M.19   Brerely, Jo., Protestants Apollogie for the Roman Church. [St Omer] 1608.
       Roman Catholic apologetics. Virtually unreadable: 750 pages on each of which a small
       portion of text is completely surrounded by notes.
M.20   Alberti, Leandro, Descrittione d'Italia. [n.p., n.d.: Bologna or Venice 1550-88].
       Historical geography. An extremely thorough 600 page account, with maps.

This brief random sample shows how the juxtaposition of Sherburne's
manifold but active interests—Mathematics, Astronomy, Astrology,
Bibliography, Classical antiquity, Palaeontology, Militaria, Philosophy,
Philology, Geography, Neo-Latin and Pastoral poetry, Politics and Theology
—is mirrored in the haphazard juxtaposition of his books on their shelves.
The preponderance of books printed in the Netherlands (seven) is not
wholly fortuitous: Dutch scholarly books were relatively cheap and
accessible. But there are other books in the library with very out-of-the-way
imprints.

The catalogue also contains some miscellaneous notes. Besides recording
loans of books to Flamsteed, Sherburne also lent very extensively to a Mr
Newman (whom I have not been able to identify), a book to Dr Thomas
Gale FRS (1635-1702), then High Master of St Paul's, and a couple of
books to the notorious Hadrian Beverland.[8] The Bodleian description says
that the catalogue 'records his purchases at several sales.' To be sure,
Sherburne notes considerable numbers of books from the auction sales of
John Lloyd (3 December 1682), Sir Jonas Moore (3 November 1684), and
Nicolas Heinsius (Leiden 1682), but it is not altogether clear that these are
notes of actual purchases: it is more likely that he was using auction
catalogues for bibliographical reference. His notes of books from Sir Jonas
Moore's sale catalogue are very different from the books he actually bought.
In fact, he was a selective buyer at auction and did not attend the sales, but
placed his bids with the auctioneer: occasionally his name appears scratched
in *over* the title, which was the auctioneer's way of reminding himself of the
name of a bidder outside the room. Of the 20 marked auction sale
catalogues (1680-95) known to me, I have only been able to trace Sherburne
at five sales.[9]

   At the Bysshe sale (15 November 1680),[10] where he is referred to as
'Capt. Sherburne', he bought two books of Isaac Vossius; two books of

William Schickard on the Hebrew and Persian kings; Scaliger's *Poemata* (Leiden 1615); Meursius's *Arboretum Sacrum* (Leiden 1642); two books on Roman history by Leo Allatius, the Vatican Librarian; a book on chronology by J. Lalamantius ([Geneva] 1571); and two books by the prolific Italian Paganino Gaudenzio (Pisa 1644 and 1646) of whom more later. At the Ralph Button sale (7 November 1681) he bought a single, expensive, lot: Strabo's *Geographia* (folio, Paris 1620) for £1 15s 2d. At Sir Jonas Moore's sale (3 November 1684), where he is referred to as 'Sir Edward Sherburne' — 17th-century auctioneers were very punctilious about titles — he bought four lots: two mathematical books; Naudé's *Considerations Politiques* (n.p. 1667) for 2s 6d; and Habington's *Castara* (London 1639) for a shilling. At the Henry Coventry Sale (9 May 1687) he bought four lots, Italian and Spanish. And finally, at the Thomas Jacomb sale (31 October 1687), he bought five lots, including Lavater's *De Spectris* (Geneva 1530) for a shilling, and two books of Hieronymus Magius (Basle 1502 and 1563) for £1 7s 6d together — he must have had a very special sympathy for Girolamo Maggi (1523-72), press-corrector, lawyer, classicist, poet, and military engineer, who defended Cyprus against the Turks and was subsequently captured and strangled.

A number of Sherburne's books have been found in institutional libraries. In a fascinating article, 'Acidalius on Manilius' (*Classical Quarterly*, 41 (1991)), M. D. Reeve has traced a considerable amount of Sherburne's material on Manilius. The Belgian scholar Caspar Gevartius died at Antwerp in 1666 and Sherburne bought a box of his books and papers on Manilius.[11] In 1697 Sherburne presented some, but not all, of his Manilius material to the Bodleian.[12] Reeve has traced eight of these items, and two more in Cambridge University Library from the collection of John Moore (1646-1714), Bishop of Ely, the well-known collector.[13] Reeve has also established the significance of Sherburne's cryptic *ex libris*, 'FSLA' to be found on the title-pages of his books, even when there is no signature. The initials stand for '*Felix Servator Lympidarum Aquarum*': Edward means 'happy guardian' (felix servator) and Sherburne means 'bright stream' (lympidarum aquarum).

   With the help of this information Alison Walker, of Collections and Preservation at the British Library, has already been able to trace 16 printed books with the 'FSLA' *ex libris*, formerly belonging to Sir Hans Sloane (1660-1753), the details of which she has very kindly made available to me. Three of these are of special interest. On a copy of Andreas Arnold, *Denarius S. Petri*, Altdorf 1679 (Arnold's university thesis), Sherburne has written 'ex dono authoris doctissimi, mihique amicus'. Andreas Arnold (1656-94) was in England from 22 May 1681 till about November 1682. In his extremely thorough book *Christoph & Andreas Arnold and England* (Nÿmegen 1981, Nuremberg 1982), Frans Blom was unable to establish any connection between Arnold and Sherburne. On a copy of G. B. Hodierna,

MEDICAEORVM
EPHEMERIDES
NVNQVAM HACTENVS APVD MORTALES EDITÆ

Cum fuis Introductionibus

IN TRES PARTES DISTINCTIS.

A V C T O R E

DON IO. BAPTISTA
HODIERNA.

Romæ: 1658. a P.Su: Car. de Thomasys
Theatino.

Fig.1. G. B. Hodierna, *Medicaeorum Ephemerides*, [Palermo] 1656, with Sir Edward Sherburne's inscription on the title-page (British Library, 531.l.12.(3)). Reproduced by permission of The British Library Board.

Medicaeorum Ephemerides, [Palermo] 1656, Sherburne has written 'Romae 1658: a Patri Car. de Thomasiis Theatino.' (fig.1). Carlo Tomasi was a voluminous Theatine theologian who had just arrived in Rome from Palermo.[14] Hodierna was a distinguished astronomer from Palermo, who published all his books there, so presumably Tomasi was able to get the book from Palermo for Sherburne. The date 1658 establishes the period of Sherburne's stay in Rome. On F. Verbiest, *Astronomia*, Dilingen 1687, Sloane has put his date and price code, which Alison Walker has kindly 'cracked' for me: '1697 2s 6d'.[15] So Sherburne, in straitened circumstances — financial as well as spatial — in lodgings in Holborn, was disposing of some of his books before his death: 1697 was also the date of his gift of Manilius material to Bodley.

In the course of a recent hasty search in Bodley I have found three more Sherburne books:[16]

(a) Tobias Wagner, Chancellor of the University of Tübingen, *Breviarium totius orbis terrarum geographicum*, Ulm 1663. Sherburne's signature has been heavily deleted, but the ownership is established by the *ex libris* 'FSLA': the pressmark is 8° E.8.Linc., but this does not necessarily mean that it was part of the library of Thomas Barlow (1603-91), Bishop of Lincoln.

(b) J. Bisselius, *Argonauticon Americanorum*, Munich 1647, at 8° H.108. Linc., with Sherburne's original labels on the spine.

(c) Rawl. 8° 270, Sherburne's own interleaved copy, with notes and additions, of his translation of Seneca's *Troades* (1679), later in the possession of Thomas Rawlinson (1681-1725). Sherburne turned to Seneca's most anguished drama during the period of the Popish Plot, as he had done during the tribulations of the Civil Wars.

Unlike an institutional librarian, who has to think in terms of subject categories in order to satisfy a variety of readers, the private bookbuyer has only to think of himself and his particular needs — and for Sherburne, books *were* 'needs'. Both as a War Office administrator, and as a poet, his concerns were 'professional'. Or, to look at it another way, his whole mind-set was 'scientific' — his approach to 'the arts' was in terms of *realia* and cultural anthropology. It was of course an attitude which he shared with the *savants* of his day, perhaps even more in France and Holland than in England — one could, for instance, compile from Sherburne's library a succinct bibliography of Gassendi and his circle. Sherburne's library not only represents a combination of the sciences and the arts, but also a combination of the ancients and the moderns.

Bibliography and library science
The strength, and the efficiency, of Sherburne's library in this field, stands out immediately.

1. *Catalogues and accounts of institutional libraries.* Sherburne has material for Augsburg, Frankfurt a/d Oder, Leiden, Nuremberg, Oxford (1620 and 1674 catalogues), Padua, Venice and Wolfenbüttel. There was not much else available.

2. *National bibliographies.* France: Du Verdier (1585), Du Chesne (1618), Sorel (1664), and, most notably, *Bibliotheca Gallica Universalis* (1646-54) by L. Jacob, the founder of French national bibliography.[17] Belgium: Valerius Andreae (1643); Denmark: Bartholinus (1660); England: Bale (1557) and Pits (1614, two copies), virtually all there was before Wood's *Athenae*; Germany: Hertzius (1679); Ireland: Ware (1639); Spain: Schottus (1608). Sherburne would obviously have liked something for Italy, but the Italians have never been any good at producing national bibliographies.

3. *Subject catalogues.* Theology: Labbé (1653, 1664), Spizelius (1668); drama: Allatius (1660); orientalia: Leon Pinelo (1629), Hottinger (1658, 1664); medicine: *Miscellanea Curiosa Medico-Physica* (Rostock 1671-6).[18]

4. *General Reference.* Gesner (1583); Draud (1625); à Beughem (1680, 1681); Moreri, *Grand Dictionnaire* (1678), the precursor of Bayle; and, to illustrate the point concerning ancients and moderns, G. M. Koenig, *Bibliotheca Vetus et Nova* (1678).

5. *Auction Catalogues.* Besides those already mentioned: *Bibliotheca Cordesiana* (1643) compiled by Naudé – the library of Jean Descordes was bought *en bloc* by Mazarin and formed the nucleus of the Mazarine till it was dispersed after the Fronde, so it could also be considered as the catalogue of a Paris institutional library; Adrian Pauw (1654) of Heemstede, the Dutch anglophile; H. Vander Hem (1674 – not in Archer Taylor), the Amsterdam jurist – Sherburne specially styles him 'Dominus', which suggests that he knew him personally.

6. *Library Science.* Library theory: Clemens (1635); Jacob (1644); Lomeier (1669), but not Naudé. Cataloguing: Placcius (1674) for anonyma. Typography: Malinkrot (1641).

With this kind of bibliographical support for a library of 2,000 titles, it is clear that Sherburne was not a dilettante *collectionneur*.

Science and military science
The basis of Sherburne's scientific collection is mathematics. Mathematics leads to cosmology, astronomy, physics, optics and horology – and also leads to military science, for navigation and gunnery. His mathematical books include the ancient and the modern: nine editions of Euclid and several editions of the Arabic mathematicians. For the moderns he has Copernicus,

Galileo, Kepler, Brahe, Vieta, Clavius, Mersenne, Briggs; and also the humbler modern mathematical practitioners: Michael Dary, John Collins, Thomas Streete and Richard Towneley.

Sherburne has remarkably little on chemistry. The only book that stands out is the *Opera Omnia Chemica* (1649) of the 15th-century alchemist, George Ripley. This is rather alarming, particularly in view of the fact that the building of the Greenwich Observatory was financed by the sale of 'old and decayed gunpowder.'[19]

Military science is similarly a mixture of the ancients and the moderns. There are the basic texts on ancient warfare: Aelian, Frontinus, Hero Mechanicus, Polybius and Vegetius; and also the commentators on ancient warfare: Brancaccio on Caesar (1585); Schefferus on ancient naval warfare (1654); and Witsen's *Scheepsbouw en Bestier* (1671). There are also theoretical books: Ruscelli's *Praecetti* (1583) and Medoça's *Theorica y Practica de Guerra* (1596). Besides more or less 'intermediate' books, like C. Lucar's translation of Tartaglia on artillery (1588) and Basta's *Maestro di Campo* (1606), there are more recent works: Ufano's *Artilleria* (1621), from whence Norton's *Art of the Great Artillery* (1624) is derived — Sherburne does not bother with Norton; Freitag's *Fortification von Regular Vestungen* (1642), from whence Hexham's *Principles of the Art Military* (1642) is partly derived — Sherburne does not bother with Hexham; Gentilini's *Il perfetto Bombardiero* (1626); and Furtenbach's *Halinitro-Pyrobolia, Beschreibung einer newen Büchsenmeisterey* (1627). There is also a group of really state-of-the-art books for gunners: Noizet's *Grand Art de l'Artillerie* (1651), translated from Casimir Simienowicz; Chevillard's *L'oeil du Canon* (1657) and Thomas Streete's *Genuine Use of the Gun* (1674).

Sherburne may have been a desk-bound brass hat, but he was still fighting the battle of Edgehill, as a gunner, 40 years on.

Astrology, demonology and witchcraft

A belief in judicial astrology was not inconsistent with post-Restoration science, and Sherburne's office colleague, Sir George Wharton, supplemented his regular income with the publication of almanacks. Sherburne's only incunable is Joannes Eschuid (or Eastwood) *Summa Astrologiae Iudicalis* (1489), and he also had Heydon's modern defence. On demonology and witchcraft, Sherburne was much more sceptical: he had the dialogue of Michael Psellus, *De Operatione Daemonum* (1615), Delrio (1608) who believed in the punishment of witches, and Gödelmann (1676) who did not. Most significantly, he had the two English books which finally debunked the witch-craze: John Wagstaffe's *Witchcraft Debated* (1671) and John Webster's *Display of Supposed Witchcraft* (1677). 'How can the obscure and tipsy Oxford scholar John Wagstaffe or the crotchety Yorkshire surgeon–parson John Webster compete with the names of Sir Thomas Browne and Richard Baxter and the Cambridge Platonists Ralph Cudworth, Henry More and

Joseph Glanville?' asks Trevor-Roper rhetorically.[20] For Sherburne they certainly did.

Biblical criticism

As has already been said, Sherburne's biblical interest is in *realia*, not in devotional commentary. He has Bochart's *Geographia Sacra* (1651) and *De Animalibus Sacrae Scripturae* (1663); Eusebius's *Onomasticon* (1659); and three books on Old Testament polity: Bertramus, *De Politia Judaica* (1651); Cunaeus, *De Republica Hebraeorum* (1666); and Schickard, *Jus Regum Hebraeorum* (1674). He obviously tried to teach himself Hebrew, by means of an English translation of Buxtorf's *Hebrew Grammar* (1655) and Prideaux's text of Maimonides (1679). Sherburne's attitude to the Bible is critical and scientific: Richard Simon (1638-1712), the father of modern biblical criticism, is just a little too late for the catalogue, but Sherburne would certainly have been sympathetic to Simon's approach.

Languages

Sherburne's interest in oriental languages extended beyond Hebrew. He has the Arabic grammars of Erpenius (1636, 1638), Martelotti (1620), Metoscita (1624) and Dominicus Germanus (1636, 1639 – published at Rome by Propaganda Fide), as well as Scaliger's Arabic proverbs (1623). He would obviously have liked to read the Arabic scientists in the original, but whether he ever mastered Hebrew or Arabic is another matter.

With Latin, Greek, French, Italian and Spanish he is evidently quite at home, and he also has books in German and Dutch. For dictionaries he has Scapula (1652); Pollux (1502 *ed. princeps*, and 1608); one of the many 'eight-language' dictionaries (1631); and, remarkably, Du Cange (3 vols, 1678). For Italian, Florio (1611) and Torriano (1640); for Spanish Minsheu (1623) and Franciosini (1640) – *Tacito Español* (1614) and Nuñez y Guzman, *Refranes o Proverbios Españoles* (12° Paris 1659)[21] were probably used as reading texts.

Literature ancient and modern

1. *Latin and Greek*. As a pupil of Farnaby, Sherburne has all the major classical, and post-classical, texts. Furthermore, his library is rich in Neo-Latin poetry, not only Sarbevius and the major Dutch Neo-Latinists, but a 32-volume set of the *Deliciae Poetarum*.

2. *French and Italian*. Certain aspects of French and Italian literature concerned Sherburne professionally, as a translator. He has a mixture of French pastoral poetry, Mairet's *Sylvanire* (1631); *libertin* poetry, de Viau (1631), Mathurin (1642) and Dehénault (1670); and novels, Nervèze (1602). For Italian the principal concern is, as expected, with the *concettisti*, not only Marini's *L'Adone* (1623) and Preti (1656, the best edition), but a late example like Fulvio Testi (1658). Sherburne also has the Italian pastoralists, Tasso's *Aminta* (Italian and French,

1598), and Malvezzi's *I Delirii della Solitudine* (1634). Other French and Italian writers can be considered later as part of Sherburne's light reading. The general impression is that he knew exactly what he wanted, and a considerable number of his editions are not to be found in English academic libraries today.

Literary criticism

Most striking is the amount of what, in the 17th century, passed for literary criticism. Sherburne has the standard works: the *Poetica* (1536) of Daniello, the commentator on Dante; Castelvetro's *Poetica* (1576); Paluzzi's *Della Poetica* (1586); the editions of Longinus by Langbaine (1636) and Tanaquil Faber (1663); Boileau (1675) and Rapin (seven titles); Heinsius on classical tragedy (1643); J. C. Boulenger on comedy (1603) and Hédelin on theatrical production (1669 – there was an English translation in 1684); and Huet on translation (1664). There is the pious defence of classical tragedy by the Italian Jesuit Galuzzi (1621, 1633), and the warning on the moral dangers of reading poetry by the Jansenistic Oratorian Bernard Lamy (1668). For English criticism there is Puttenham (1589) and Rymer (1678).

Archaeology, numismatics and emblems

Like so many classicists, Sherburne had a wide interest in classical and post-classical antiquities — *altertumswissenschaft* was something that you did not get at school. Pride of place in the library (A1) was given to *Roma Sotteranea* (1632) by Antonio Bosio, 'the Columbus of the catacombs', and other early acquisitions were Cluverius *Italia Antiqua* (1624) and *Sicilia Antiqua* (1619). There was Panvinio (1648) for epigraphy, and the catalogue (1678) of the cabinet of remains from the Roman encampment at Nÿmegen collected by Joannes Smetius. For numismatics there was Erizzo (1578), Antoine Le Pois (1579), Gorlaeus (1608), Occo (1626), Menestrier's *Médailles* (1642), Sequin (1666), Vincencio de Lastanosa on Spanish medals (1645) and Patini on medals ancient and modern (1672).

Numismatics leads naturally to the study of emblems. Sherburne has Ruscelli (1566 – *ed. princeps*), Alciati (1599), Otho van Veen (1612), Estienne's *L'art de faire les Devises* (1646) and Menestrier's *L'art des Emblèmes* (1662).

Geography and travel

Once again one can discern the phenomenon of ancient and modern. Besides a Strabo (1620) and a range of books on the geography of the ancient world, Sherburne has Ferrarius's *Lexicon Geographicum* (1670) and a complete set of the handy national guidebooks issued by Elzevier between the late 1620s and early 1640s. Coryate, Purchas, and Lassels's *Voyage of Italy* (1670) are the only English travel guides; Jouvin, *Le Voyageur de l'Europe* (1672, 6 vols) is the most up to date.[22] But Sherburne's interest is not confined to Europe: he has travel books on the Near and Far East, on Africa, and on the Americas – as befits the son of a secretary to the East India Company.

Political theory

In contrast to his friend Thomas Stanley, Sherburne had little interest in philosophical speculation in general, but his books on political theory suggest a more intelligent outlook than that of a romantic and traditional royalist. For a start, he had Naudé's *Bibliographia Politica* (1673); then Osorius, *De Regis Institutione* (1588) for the traditional view; and for the moderns Machiavelli ('1550', i.e. 1610-45); *La République* (1583) of Bodin the *légiste*; and a handy volume of Grotius's political aphorisms edited by Gruter (1652). Most significant of all is the absence of Hobbes's *Leviathan*, but the presence of a considerable number of books *against* Hobbes – almost a bibliography for J. Bowle, *Hobbes and his Critics* (London, 1951).

Religion

Sherburne's religious position is something of a puzzle. His Lancashire family background was Catholic, he certainly considered himself a Catholic, and Anthony Wood turned to him for information on the biographies of Catholics. But as the holder of an office of profit under the Crown he had to take the Oaths of Supremacy and Allegiance. In theory, he should have taken the Oaths when he succeeded to his father's job in 1641; he definitely took the Oaths in 1673, after the Test Act. The wording of the Oath of Allegiance was officially disapproved of by the Catholic church authorities, though there were a number of English priests who argued that it could be taken. But the Oath of Supremacy was quite impossible for a practising Catholic. Charles Dodd describes Sherburne as a Catholic who 'managed his religion with so much caution as not to come under prosecution'.[23] Sherburne's library affords some hints as to his religious position.

He had two copies of the Rheims–Douay translation of the Bible (3 vols, 1625); a Roman *Pontificale* (1645), *Rituale* (1652), *Processionale* (1666) and *Breviarium* (1673); Harpsfield's *Historia Anglicana Ecclesiastica* (1622), the decrees of the Council of Trent (1653), and Labbé's *Concilia* (1672) – all solidly orthodox material. For apologetics he had *Catholics No Idolaters* (1672) by Thomas Godden, *Roman Catholic Doctrines No Novelties* (1663) by Serenus Cressy, and *A Rational Account of the Doctrine of Roman Catholics* (1673) by Abraham Woodhead – the very titles are revealing: the emphasis is all on rationality. As for ecumenism, he has Grotius's edition of Cassander's *Via ad Pacem Ecclesiasticam* (1642) which makes Cassander even more ecumenical than he really was. But what stands out is Sherburne's considerable collection of the works of the group Thomas White, Kenelm Digby, Henry Holden and John Sergeant – all dogmatic 'minimalists', who sought to reduce Roman Catholic belief to what they considered to be its bare essentials, and as independent of Rome as possible. Even more extreme is the *Irish Remonstrance* (1662) of Peter Walsh, the Irish

Franciscan pensioner of the Duke of Ormonde, which advocated a Gallican–Erastian church polity.

The evidence of his library (including the Biblical section), suggests that Sherburne was a well-informed but independent-minded and somewhat sceptical Catholic of the Erasmian type — his 11 volumes of Erasmus included theological as well as humanist works. Wood's picture of Sherburne after the Glorious Revolution, 'spending his time altogether in Books and Prayer', is probably not far wrong — as soon as he was dismissed from office he could be *pratiquant* as well as *croyant*.

Light reading

Most of Sherburne's literary reading was related to his professional interests as a translator, so that light reading (i.e. reading to pass the time) forms a very restricted category.[24] The most noticeable fact is that there are only two books in English which qualify: William Painter's *Palace of Pleasure* (1567), translations of novels by a former Clerk of the Ordnance in the Tower, and Mary Carleton's *Memoirs* (1673), a piece of feminine 'rogue' literature. All the rest is continental — ancient, medieval, and modern: Apuleius, Petronius and Heliodorus (three editions); Boccaccio; and for the moderns, Barclay's *Euphormio* (1674) and Garzoni's *Piazza Universale* (1638), recommended by both Florio and Torriano, and rammed with life.[25] Bartholinus's *De Usu Flagrorum in Re Medica et Venerea* (1670) is probably not in the library for its purely scientific interest, and one's suspicions are confirmed by the presence of Aloisia Siga, *Satyra Sotadica* (c.1660) by Nicolas Chorier, a pornographic classic which was being peddled around in 1676 by an Amsterdam bookseller in London.[26]

A final consideration is Sherburne's method and policy in building up his library. At an educated guess, Sherburne must have used Robert Scott as his principal library agent; Scott was active in buying books from the continent, was Sir Jonas Moore's publisher, and frequented scientific circles.[27] But a comparison of Sherburne's library with Scott's printed catalogues shows that Sherburne was not dependent on selections from the booksellers: his acquisitions policy was far more purposeful, clearly directed, and specialized. His extraordinarily efficient bibliographical apparatus, already described, was his guide to acquisitions: he discovered exactly what he needed, and went for it.

Policy is determined by resources: Sherburne's resources were not unlimited. In his heyday, he had his civil service salary and perks, including free lodging in the Tower; a personal pension of £100 p.a. from Charles II; and some capital — he made enquiries of Anthony Wood concerning the possible purchase of an Oxford college annuity. He spent a lot of money on his library but every penny had to count. In the first place, books in English are only about 15% of the total, and he rarely bought translations if the original was available — the originals were probably cheaper anyway.

Secondly, there is very little that cannot be accounted for as answering to his specific needs. The only books that stand out as being quite superfluous are the ten titles of Paganini Gaudenzio, a negligible Italian scholar-scribbler and papal pensioner—perhaps he knew the man personally. To be sure, Sherburne subscribed to ten of John Ogilby's folio productions of the Book Beautiful, but Ogilby was a business partner of the father of his friend, Thomas Stanley.[28] By contrast, what is really striking is Sherburne's willingness to commit himself to what must have been an extraordinary capital outlay on sets of books that he really wanted: 10 volumes folio of the works of Cardanus, 12 volumes folio of Baronius, 18 volumes folio of Labbé's *Concilia*, and 22 volumes folio of the *Byzantinae Historiae Corpus*. Sherburne's library was not a hobby, it was an essential part of his working life—and he devoted to its formation all his intellectual and financial resources. But then, of course, he was a bachelor.

References

1. In an article on Flamsteed's library (*Notes and Records of the Royal Society*, vol.28 (June 1973)), E. G. Forbes, who had been led to MS Rawl. Q.b.3 by the *Summary Catalogue* index s.v. Flamsteed, conjectured that the catalogue may have been that of Dr Edward Bernard. I am most grateful to Dr J. M. Blom for having provided me with a xerox of this article.

2. This summary account is arbitrarily condensed from the extremely thorough introduction by F. J. van Beeck SJ to *The Poems and Translations of Sir Edward Sherburne* (Assen: Van Gorcum, 1961). Van Beeck must be consulted for a full and proper account of Sherburne's life and friendships. Unfortunately I did not realize the identity of Sherburne's library catalogue in Bodley till after van Beeck's book had gone to press.

3. See index to H. W. Robinson and W. Adams (eds.) *The Diary of Robert Hooke* (London: Taylor & Francis, 1935). All but Towneley are in *DNB*: for Towneley see E. G. R. Taylor, *The Mathematical Practitioners of Tudor and Stuart England* (Cambridge: Cambridge University Press, 1970), p.248.

4. The labels are still visible on Bodley 8° H.108.Linc., Bisselius, *Argonauticon*, Munich 1647.

5. For publication details see D. J. McKitterick, *History of the Cambridge University Press*, vol.I (Cambridge: Cambridge University Press, 1992), pp.240-1.

6. A. Willems, *Les Elzevier* (Brussels, 1880), pp.116-17.

7. J. W. Binns, *Intellectual Culture in Elizabethan and Jacobean England* (Leeds: Francis Cairns, 1990), p.26.

8. Wood *Fasti* s.v. 1672, and *Nieuw Nederlandsch Biografisch Woordenboek*, ed. P. C. Molhuysen and P. J. Blok (Leiden: A. W. Sijthoff, 1911-37), 7: 197. In his MS apologia, bound up with Bodley 8° H.247(4) BS, Beverland names some of his friends: Lord Pembroke, Lord Carbery, Lord Spencer, Dr Aldrich (of Christ Church, Oxford) and 'Sir Edward Scherborn'. (Philip Herbert (1653-83) fifth Earl of Pembroke, was a homicidal maniac, and John Vaughan (1640-1713) third Earl of Carbery was, according to Pepys, 'one of the lewdest fellows of the age, worse than Sir Charles Sedley'.)

9. Owing to pressure of time, I have not been able to re-examine the Anglesey catalogue (25 October 1686) at Lambeth.

10. Not 15 November 1679, as in A. N. L. Munby and L. Coral, *British Book Sale Catalogues 1676-1800* (London: Mansell, 1977), p.3.

11. For references to Gevartius see A. Gerlo and H. Vervliet, *Bibliographie de l'Humanisme des Anciens Pays-Bas* (Brussels: Presses Universitaires de Bruxelles, 1972), pp.339-40.

12. Auct. O.5.19, Sherburne's copy of the Venice edition of Manilius, c.1498-1500, formerly owned by Isaac Vossius, was bought for Bodley in 1841.

13. He also draws attention to the notebook (Cambridge University Library MS Kk. 5.38) of Abednego Seller (1646-1705) the nonjuror, which includes evidence that Sherburne lent his Gevartius material to Seller, who was living at the time (1692-6) at Red Lion Square, Holborn, and thus a neighbour.

14. A. F. Vezzosi, *I scrittori de' Cherici Regolari detti Teatini* (Rome: Propaganda Fide, 1780, 2 vols), 2: 349 *seq*.

15. See M. A. E. Nickson, 'Sloane's codes; the solution to a mystery'. *Factotum* 7 (December 1979), 13-18.

16. I am most grateful to Mr William Hodges, Superintendent of Duke Humfrey, for permitting me to order up a large number of books per day, in the summer holiday period, when staff resources were under even more than usual pressure.

17. See L. N. Malclès in *Mélanges . . . Frantz Calot* (Paris: Librairie D'Argences, 1960).

18. See F. J. Cole, *History of Comparative Anatomy* (London: Macmillan, 1944), pp.341-69.

19. Cambridge University Library, MS RGO 1/35/81.

20. 'The European Witch-Craze' in *Religion, the Reformation and Social Change* (London: Secker & Warburg, 1984), p.168.

21. There is a copy of this edition in the British Library, 12305.aaa.24. I am most grateful to Giles Mandelbrote for identifying this edition and its translator, César Oudin.

22. For a very full study of the significance of Lassels's remarkable book, see E. Chaney, *The Grand Tour and the Great Rebellion* (Geneva: Slatkine, 1985).

23. Charles Dodd (*vere* Hugh Tootell, a Catholic secular priest), *Church History of England . . . chiefly with regard to Catholicks* (Brussels [*vere* Wolverhampton] 1742), 3: 453.

24. See T. A. Birrell, 'Reading as Pastime: the place of light literature in some gentlemen's libraries of the 17th century' in Robin Myers and Michael Harris (eds.), *Property of a Gentleman* (Winchester: St Paul's Bibliographies, 1991).

25. For Garzoni see J. L. Lievsay, *The Englishman's Italian Books 1550-1700* (Philadelphia: University of Pennsylvania Press, 1969).

26. See David Foxon, *Libertine Literature in England 1660-1745* (New York: University Books, 1965).

27. Leona Rostenberg's study of Scott in her *Literary, Political, Scientific, Religious and Legal Publishing, Printing and Bookselling in England 1551-1700* (New York: Burt Franklin, 1965), pp.281-313, is helpful but must be used with caution.

28. See K. S. van Eerde, *John Ogilby* (Folkestone: Dawson, 1976), p.137. Sherburne was one of the 'overseers' of Ogilby's will.

Richard Lapthorne and the London
retail book trade, 1683-1697

MICHAEL TREADWELL

WHEN, IN THE AUTUMN OF 1993, Colin Tite came to the third and last of his Panizzi Lectures on *The Manuscript Library of Sir Robert Cotton*, he chose to begin it with the most vivid surviving description of that library as it had existed in the autumn of 1692:

scituated adjoyning to the house of Com*m*ons at Westm*inster* of a great highth & part of that old Fabrick but very narrow as I remember not full 6 foot in breadth & not above 26 in length ye books placed on each side of a tollerable highth so that a man of an indifferent stature may reach ye highest[.] Over ye books are ye Roman Emperors I meane their heads in brass statues, w*h*ich serve for standards in ye Catalogue to direct to finde any perticular book Viz. under such an Emperor^s head, such an Number . . . some relicts I took notice of besides ye books. . . . I had in my hand ye sword of Hugo Lupus Earle of Chester y^t came in with ye Conquest.

Since this was the lecture in which Tite was to advance his theories both of the origin of Cotton's imperial classification system and of the actual physical layout of the library, such testimony was a godsend and Tite showed his gratitude by omitting an intervening sentence in which his witness confessed that he 'had not time to look into the books'. The man who thus escaped the obloquy of having fondled the sword of Hugo Lupus while the unique manuscript of Beowulf lay all undiscovered before him Tite identified simply as 'Richard Lapthorne', the source being 'one of his regular newsletters from London to John [*recte* Richard] Coffin of Portledge, Devon, for whom he acted as agent'.[1]

This is reasonably accurate as far as it goes, but naturally it went no further than the Cottonian library, thus relegating Richard Lapthorne, not for the first time, to the footnotes of the history of the book.[2] He deserves much better, and my explicit aim in this paper is to introduce Lapthorne to the mainstream of book trade history. Moreover, I hope, through a brief account of his career and activities, to suggest that Lapthorne is not only our best witness to the appearance of the Cottonian library in the 1690s, but one of the very best sources we have for the day-to-day functioning of the book trade, from book auction records to views on binding conservation, in a period which was as crucial for the trade as it was for the nation.

Richard Lapthorne first appears in the modern scholarly record in 1876 when Henry Thomas Riley published brief extracts from more than 140 of his letters to Coffin in the *Fifth Report of the Royal Commission on Historical Manuscripts*.[3] Included was the account of the Cottonian library quoted above, but in general reports of fire, assault, and sudden death vastly outweighed news of books. Nor did this balance alter significantly when, 50 years later, two members of the Coffin family published a far more extensive selection from 400 of Lapthorne's letters as *The Portledge Papers being extracts from the letters of Richard Lapthorne, Gent, of Hatton Garden London, to Richard Coffin Esq. of Portledge, Bideford, Devon from December 10th 1687-August 7th 1697.*[4] The editors began by confessing to the omission of the 'one or two of the earliest letters [that] survive . . . on account of their lack of interest', but went on to claim that 'all the letters of the 1687-1697 period have been included', that correspondence being 'given in full except for a few unimportant passages'.[5] Nothing could be further from the truth, and a careful examination of the originals, on deposit in the Devon Record Office in Exeter, reveals that the published version omits not only several complete letters, but also literally hundreds of shorter passages, many of them of the greatest interest and importance to the historian of the book trade.[6] Clearly it was the printed word which was 'unimportant', for of the more than 350 books, pamphlets, or broadsheets which Lapthorne refers to or reports purchasing in the course of the correspondence, fewer than half appear in the printed selection.

Moreover, although the recipient of the letters, Richard Coffin (1622-98), was easily identifiable as the leading 17th-century member of a family which by 1928 had been lords of the manor of Portledge for roughly eight centuries, the editors were forced to confess that of Richard Lapthorne 'nothing is known . . . other than what can be gleaned from the letters themselves'. In their abridged form these revealed apparent Devon origins, a home address in Hatton Garden, London, a wife who was sister to a Master in Chancery, and, in 1688, two small sons, one of whom subsequently went on to Eton and then to Pembroke College, Oxford.[7] However, the complete correspondence, together with a little biographical research, reveals considerably more about Richard Lapthorne and his various activities.

To begin with, he certainly came from Devon, for he writes to Coffin of Devon as 'our cuntry' (7 March 1691) and of other Devon men as 'our cuntryman' (30 April 1692), and news from Portledge in July 1694 that one of Coffin's daughters was to marry Charles Kelland of Painsford in Ashprington parish evoked the reply that Lapthorne was 'better acquainted wth his father [John Kelland (c.1635-92)] being schoolfellows' (28 July 1694).[8] Ashprington is near Totnes in South Devon and presumably Lapthorne grew up nearby. Certainly he was not from the north, for when he was planning a trip into Devon, in the late summer of 1694, it was because he had 'some few houses at Plymouth' and he expressed the hope of calling on Coffin at Portledge since 'I never was yet in yt part of the Cuntry' (21 July 1694).[9]

Unhappily there were so many Lapthornes in parishes in the Plymouth-Dartmouth-Totnes region in the 17th century that it has not been possible to trace Richard Lapthorne's parentage.[10] The earliest record I have found in which he can be positively identified is his marriage licence allegation, dated 21 October 1675, in which he describes himself as a bachelor of about 38, and as a gentleman of Lyons Inn, one of the ancient Inns of Chancery, most of whose records have unfortunately disappeared.[11] The woman whom Lapthorne married in 1675 came from a much better-known family. She was Macrina Keck, daughter of Thomas Keck, Bencher of the Middle Temple, who had died in 1671 leaving her £400. Her mother, Hannah (*née* Sommer), was almost certainly the 'one dangerously ill in my house . . . yt is now on a recovery tho very aged', mentioned by Lapthorne on 9 January 1691, and who died there three years later and 'is this night to bee caryed . . . to ye Temple Church to bee layd by her husband' (27 January 1694). No fewer than five of Macrina's brothers followed their father to the Middle Temple, the most distinguished being the eldest, Samuel, a Master in Chancery from 1689, who is referred to in passing by Lapthorne, by office though not by name, in a letter of 24 February 1694.[12]

Far and away the wealthiest and most powerful of the Keck family, however, was Macrina's uncle, Sir Anthony Keck (1630-95), a distinguished barrister in the Court of Chancery who served briefly as second commissioner of the Great Seal under William and Mary.[13] That appointment was from 5 March 1689 and almost brought Lapthorne's series of letters to an end. As he wrote to Coffin in early August 1689, he was 'at present put on some publique Imployment' by 'the lords Commissioners of the great Seale' and was therefore seeking to 'recomend another to serve you in my roome' (3 August 1689). We can only guess at Coffin's response to this attempted resignation for there are gaps in the surviving correspondence during three of the four months which follow. Those letters that do survive, however, show no sign of any change in Lapthorne's role, and Sir Anthony's early resignation in May 1690 restored the status quo.[14] But this is to anticipate.

The 'roome' in which Lapthorne served Coffin was that of his London agent, writing a weekly letter of news and gossip, purchasing periwigs, a cane, a saddle, and endless batches of seeds for the Portledge family, or forwarding money to a young Coffin at Oxford. But what set Lapthorne apart from the conventional agent and made him ideal for Richard Coffin's purposes, was his knowledge of and passion for books. Many other agents could have collected as much gossip, and most would have collected better information on the price of hops and collected it faster. Few if any others, however, would have been willing to sit through a book auction lasting seven weeks to exercise commissions, or to visit 20 shops in pursuit of an elusive book – unless, of course, that was how they spent their time in any case.

And in this context it is significant to notice that when Lapthorne was intending to resign his charge in 1689 the person he recommended as his replacement was John Bagford, not known for his skills as a correspondent, but certainly the most celebrated book runner in late Stuart London.[15] And in recommending him to Coffin, Lapthorne says nothing whatsoever about Bagford's other skills, sticking entirely to the essential facts that 'his Genius has run much in collecting books & of late yeares has bin assisting to Auctions, & hath bin Imployed by Mr. Powle, Mr of ye Rolls & Speaker of parliamt to collect books for him'.[16] These, Lapthorne knew, were the qualifications Coffin was looking for, and the particular skills for which he was prepared to pay, though, as Lapthorne modestly put it, '[Bagford] is a man yt will expect no great matters from you. wt you allow mee, I know will content him' (3 August 1689).[17]

Indeed some surviving evidence suggests that Lapthorne was not so much a traditional agent with a particular passion for books, as a freelance dealer in books and manuscripts willing to perform other tasks for a client-friend. First, during the period of his correspondence with Richard Coffin he was apparently the principal consignor in one of the largest London auction sales of the time, a sale to which I will return in a moment. Second, among the Rawlinson manuscripts in the Bodleian Library are two with the inscription 'liber Petri le Neve, 1691', one 'formerly Mr Lapthrons and bought of him' and the other 'bought of Mr Lapthorne'.[18] And third, from the period immediately following the end of the Coffin correspondence there exist two private letters in which Lapthorne offers carefully selected collections to well-known potential buyers. The first of these letters, dated 27 August 1698, is addressed to Thomas Tanner at All Souls and reports the sending of a package of books before going on, apparently in response to a query, to offer a 'choyce Collexion conteyning as I take it about 250 volumes' of Lapthorne's 'Old English bookes', the collection to be sold 'intire'.[19] The second letter, dated 18 June 1701, is to Under-Secretary of State John Ellis making him a present of two pamphlets, offering him for purchase a collection of 'upwards of 600 . . . State Pamphletts' and asking Ellis, should he himself not be interested, if he 'would recomend them to one to whom you think they may bee acceptable'.[20]

Certainly books seem to have been at the root of Lapthorne's relationship with Coffin. His first two surviving letters to Coffin, of 20 and 27 June 1683, already provide us with several clues to the nature of his activities, for while they contain some political news and the usual reports of storm and sudden death, their main preoccupation is with books.[21] The first in particular ends with a detailed bill for more than six pounds (the shillings and pence have been lost) for the purchase of a dozen separate works, new and old, and the gilding of three of these and two others, together with a note of a previous bill of more than £27, presumably at least partly for books. The second also concludes with a bill (badly mutilated), this time totalling only £2 4s 3d, for two new purchases and some more gilding, but this time specifying an unexplained 3d 'for the bookbindr' and 2s for '[Ba?]temans man for his pains in [torn] em up wch took up much tym' (27 June 1683).

1683 is thus the earliest date we have for any book-dealing by Lap-thorne on Richard Coffin's behalf, but it is also the date of the earliest record I have found of his book-dealing in any other context. In December of that year he appears as the purchaser of 80 lots in the London auction of the libraries of the Rev. Dr John Lloyd and Sir Thomas Raymond.[22] He may of course have participated in earlier auctions, some 40 of which had taken place in England since the initial Seaman sale of 1676. However, none of the surviving marked catalogues for book sales prior to December 1683 names Lapthorne as a buyer, and the fact that his name appears throughout the Lloyd-Raymond catalogue as 'Clapthorne' also suggests that he may then have been a relative newcomer to the salerooms.[23] It may even be that it was the new fashion for selling books at auction which gave rise to Lapthorne's book dealing, or at the very least to his dealing for Coffin, whose other correspondence reveals that he had previously bought new books directly from the publishing bookseller, but who may well have preferred a gentleman rather than a player for the more delicate business of the auction.[24]

Auctions, in fact, form the major preoccupation of the book-related portion of the main body of the Lapthorne–Coffin correspondence, over its first four years from its opening in December 1687 to the climax of the sale of 9 November 1691 at which Lapthorne bought more books for Coffin than he records for all previous auction sales combined.[25] Thereafter, it is as if both men had shot their bolt, and although books and their pursuit remain major preoccupations throughout the final six years of the correspondence, auctions are rarely mentioned and there is no surviving record of Lap-thorne's having purchased a single lot at auction after 1691, either for Coffin or for anyone else.

Earlier, things were very different. Lapthorne's second surviving letter of 27 June 1683 already speaks of a work 'haveing bin sold at a great value an [torn] auction' and much of the first letter of the main series (10 December 1687) is taken up with a description of his purchases on Coffin's account at the sale of the Bibliotheca Jacombiana, between 31 October and about 11 November 1687. In that same letter, moreover, Lapthorne is also commenting on the progress of the Burleigh sale, then nearing completion, while at the same time defending himself against a charge that he has been remiss or even devious in not sending two catalogues for an unspecified sale in sufficient time for Coffin to profit by them.[26] The eight lots purchased for Coffin at the Jacomb sale were not finally sent until 14 January 1688, the delay presumably being partly due to the care with which they were first examined, Lapthorne having given

a man orders to take speciall care in the collating of them & hee informs mee they are perfect, saving Boxhornius and hee sayth there wants nothing only yt ye leafes yt are foaled [sic] down there is some things double printed [21 January 1688].

Over the five-month period from early November 1687 to late March 1688, Lapthorne's letters reveal that he attended at least four different auctions at which he bought a manuscript and three dozen lots of printed books for Coffin, as well as other lots, possibly for other clients.[27] By far the largest of these sales was that of the bookseller Robert Scott, the progress of which over seven weeks can be followed in some detail in Lapthorne's letters and at which he bought almost two dozen lots for Coffin. However, even the Scott sale takes second place in its importance for the Portledge Library to a later sale at which Lapthorne bought an unprecedented 60 lots for Coffin, a sale which his letters reveal to have been, at least in part, Lapthorne's own.

This was the sale of 9 November 1691 of the *Bibliotheca Selectissima librorum omnigenorum* collected, in the words of its preamble, 'by a Bookish Gentleman, who constantly attended and frequently advised with men of the greatest Judgment in the Affairs of Learning'. On the title-page of Hans Sloane's copy of the sale catalogue a 17th-century hand has written 'D. Lapthorne', which led Munby and Coral to suggest D. Lapthorne as the consignor, though with a query, and which may now lead us to guess that some at least of Lapthorne's contemporaries referred to him as 'Dick'.[28]

The first reference to the sale seems to be in Lapthorne's letter of 17 October 1691 in which he hopes the 'Catalogue sent by Torrington Carrier this day sevenight' has been received. It had not been, but after lengthy explanations of precisely how it had been sent and how it was packed (31 October), it finally turned up and by 7 November, two days before the sale was to begin, Coffin's commissions had been received. By the following Saturday Lapthorne was able to report that, up to that point at least, 'The most part of yor bookes are bought', though he was forced to apologize that he had so little news to offer, being 'so taken up about this Auction at present yt I can have litle conversation a broad' (14 November 1691). On Tuesday 17th November, having 'compared ye Auction booke wth yor instructions', Lapthorne was able to send a preliminary list, with prices, of the 14 lots bought for Coffin down to the end of the miscellaneous folios, and on the following Saturday, 21 November, added 12 more from the Libri Miscellanei of smaller sizes. He warned of possible errors, but was sure that the final account would be correct, 'There being two writers'. By that date they had 'gon over ye 2d page of ye Medici 4°: & proceed to ye remaynder Monday night'. On Saturday 28 November Coffin was assured that his 'direccons for English bookes' would also be observed. Sale of these was to begin on Monday 30 November with the Divinity folios, and by Tuesday they had reached the octavos. By Saturday 5 December, after four full weeks of sale, Lapthorne was admitting to being 'tyred out wth attending every night at the Auction by reason of our ending at unseasonable hours'.[29] However, the end was also in sight, possibly the following Wednesday when 'wee sell ye Comon law' and hope 'god willing to conclude ye Sale'.

By Saturday 12 December 1691, it was all over though 'wee are in such a hurry in making bills & delivering of books' that Coffin's patience was asked in the matter of his own account. After further delays, and still more corrections, this account was finally sent on 22 December, accompanied by Christmas best wishes. But making the books match even the corrected list proved no easy matter and it was not until Saturday 23 January that the box containing the books themselves was finally delivered to Morris, the Exeter carrier, though still without one book, particularly valued by Coffin, that had disappeared 'by knavery & not by accedent' (30 January 1692), as Lapthorne thought.[30]

Had it all been worth it? Lapthorne's summary of the experience was succinct, but inconclusive. 'As to our Auction ye books were 22 days a selling some went off very cheape & some at good rates but considering the great charges in preparing & selling it prooved a hard market' (2 January 1692). Whether he ever participated in another such sale the letters do not reveal, but that he did not immediately abandon the possibility is evident from a curious anecdote which Lapthorne recounted to Coffin three years later on 3 March 1694:

Thursday night between six & seaven of ye clock (I having by the favour of ye Treasurer of Lyons Inn ye use of some old chambers there gratis to put some books in) when I came to unlock ye dore & a youth being wth mee wth some things I had bought, I could not open ye dore forasmuch as ye Latch was depressed & kept down; so yt I was faine to have ye dore broken open by a Smith. but when I came in I met wth a youngster yt was gotton in how I canot tell & kept mee out what his design was God knows. hee was a young clerk to one of ye House.

This unique glimpse of Richard Lapthorne returning to his private book-store, a young porter or bookseller's apprentice following behind with his day's catch, seems to have caught Coffin's attention much as it catches ours. Presumably he asked by return what Lapthorne was up to filling old chambers with books, and what he intended to do with them, for on 17 March 1694 Lapthorne replied: 'I have a small collection of bookes, but whether I shall expose them to sale by Auction I ha[ve not yet?] . . .' and the end of the sentence is obscured by a tear. Perhaps he did expose them, but perhaps he had already begun to concentrate on putting together the sort of specialist collections he was later to offer to Tanner and Ellis, precisely the kind for which the modern antiquarian bookseller issues a special catalogue.

While it is possible, therefore, that Lapthorne participated in no further auctions as a seller after 1691, what is more surprising is that his 1691 sale is also the last at which he seems to have bought books for Coffin. In August 1692, having failed to find the recommended edition of DuFresne's *Glossary* in any London shop, he was still reassuring Coffin that 'ye next winter wee are to have Auctions for severall collections of Generall books & then I make no doubt but you may have yt Edition at a cheaper rate' (18 August 1692). However, there is no evidence, in the letters at least, that he attended any of those auctions, and when he finally bought a DuFresne for Coffin it seems to have been from 'Mr Smyth' (22 October 1692), almost certainly Samuel Smith of the Prince's Arms, St Paul's Churchyard.[31] There are still occasional references to catalogues sent, but they seem generally to be the *Catalogues of Books* which we now know as the *Term Catalogues*. Lapthorne may, of course, have continued to attend the sales either on his own behalf or for other clients, but if so he does not mention it to Coffin, whose apparent decline in interest we may perhaps put down to increasing years or the rising land tax, as the war with France pressed harder and harder on the country gentry.

Auction sales were not, of course, the only, or even necessarily the cheapest way to obtain old or scarce books, as Lapthorne himself was quick to point out to Coffin in explaining why he had not executed a commission to buy Vossius's *De . . . Idololatriae* at Robert Scott's auction:

As for yt of Vosius de Adolitrea &c. It was sold for neer 40s. and I remembered I had seen the booke a litle before at Mr. Batemans a booke sellere in Holborne ye 2 vol. bound in one & his man sayd cost his master a guyny in quieres; but sayd hee my master would now take 27s. for it so yt when I saw it goe at such an excessive rate at the Auction I went imediately to Mr. Bateman and bought yt at ye price of 27s. [11 March 1688].[32]

'Mr. Bateman' was presumably Stephen Bateman (*c.*1642-98), one of the greatest antiquarian booksellers of the day, but Lapthorne knew all the leading members of the antiquarian trade.[33]

I was with Mr Litlebury yisterday & hee hath sold his Buchartas in fol & also Weavers Monumts—but Mr Scot hath one not so good as Mr Litleburys & Mr Bateman another but will not take under 30s for either [20 June 1683].

What stand out in Lapthorne's correspondence, however, are not the routine bookhunting expeditions, but his accounts of the lengths to which he would go to fulfil a commission — and the detail he provides of his efforts. Higden's *Polychronicon*, for instance, was evidently on Coffin's list of *desiderata* and Lapthorne does not even wait to see it before reporting that 'Mr. Millington lately told mee hee had a policronicon and would use me kinde for it. I intend to see it' (21 January 1688). Evidently either the copy or the price was not right, for six months later he is still looking in vain. 'I was also yisterday wth Mr. Litlebury ye most likliest man for Higdons policron: but hee hath none. I shall continew my Inquest . . .' (28 July 1688). Three weeks later Lapthorne was still pressing Littlebury who, like the occasional bookseller since, was reduced to promising that 'ye first hee meets with hee will give mee notice of it' (19 August 1688). But the very next week Lapthorne's luck changed:

Going this weeke to buy some old books for my selfe of one yt had lately bought some. I found amongst them Higdon's policronicon, ye Bookeseller, tho an old & cuning Artist, it fell out was ignorant of ye Author. I bought ye booke for 8s. and I suppose may have twenty shillings of a bookseller for my bargaine. I think its perfect which is very rare. It hath an old deformed dress but I think you had best let it goe so because of its Antiquity & not new binde it [25 August 1688].

In his conservationist approach to a 'deformed' original binding Lapthorne seems far ahead of his time,[34] but unfortunately he was less skilled than the professional he had retained to collate Coffin's books at the end of major auctions, for subsequent correspondence makes it clear that Lapthorne's copy was not perfect at all. Perhaps the bookseller was less ignorant or more cunning than Lapthorne had given him credit for.

The problem of the perfecting of the *Polychronicon* was then to hang on for well over a year — though in justice to Lapthorne we should observe that communications with the south-west were somewhat impeded by William's invasion that November, and the smooth functioning of the London book trade by its aftermath. It is not, therefore, until 2 November 1689 that we find Lapthorne reassuring Coffin that 'as to ye transcribing of ye policronicon if you write in your next what is wanting I make no doubt but to have it transcribed ether out of yt at ye Auction or from another'. Unfortunately that at the auction, the Maitland sale of 28 October-*c*.20 December 1689, was itself incomplete, being 'filled up wth manuscript & indeed its very rare to meet wth one perfect'. Moreover, Lapthorne had determined that it was of a different edition, having 'compared your leafe wch is much longer & a litle broader'. And to top it all, when he had raised the subject of transcription 'they asked unreasonable . . . above 20*s* for doing it at ye Auction house', though he still hoped that 'possibly some acquaintance or one yt I may oblidge may buy [it] Then I may borrow it for some time & get one to transcribe it at a cheape rate' (16 November 1689). The Maitland copy of the *Polychronicon* came up for sale sometime in the week of 9-13 December, but by then Lapthorne had a better solution still, having

found at a Booksellers an old imperfect Policron English & I gave your paper to his man an honest fellow who told by compar. hee found all yt was missing in yors in yt & yt ye paper leafe agreed wth yt I have since spoken wth his master & I think I may have it at 6*s* price wch I would advise you to take [15 December 1689].

Presumably Coffin followed this advice though, as so often happens, the disappearance of all letters between 20 December 1689 and 8 March 1690 means that we will never know.

The chronicle of Lapthorne's long search for the perfect — or at least perfected — *Polychronicon* tells us a great deal about the avenues open to the resourceful book-hunter in late 17th-century London, but a much shorter search tells us even more about the reference materials available to the contemporary antiquarian bookseller. This search involved the *Phonurgia nova* of Athanasius Kircher, the Jesuit polymath whose works Coffin particularly coveted and of which he eventually formed an impressive collection. On 24 September 1692, obviously in response to Coffin's request for a copy, Lapthorne replied that as for . . . Kirchers phonourgia nova its very scarce here. I made great inquiry after it & perceived ye Booksellers were strangers to it, yn I went to Mr. Litlebury who is our standard for knowing Authors & hee knew nothing of such a booke, hee lookt into ye Oxford Catalogue & could not finde it, but going to an Ingenious man yt hath taken paines to keepe an alphibiticall Register of most books & prices yt have been sold in our London Auctions, And in one Voets Auction found this booke printed beyond sea 1673 fol. wth figures, price 9s. 6d, Its a scarce booke, & you may now use your own measures about buying it.[35]

Coffin's library was eventually to contain a copy of the *Phonurgia nova*, though whether obtained through Lapthorne's agency or not is never revealed.[36] But the search is, in any case, more revealing than the eventual find, for while we might learn from other sources of Littlebury's pre-eminence in the contemporary antiquarian trade, or deduce the importance as a reference tool of Thomas Hyde's magnificent 1674 folio catalogue of the Bodleian Library's collections, nothing but Lapthorne's passing reference could have told us of the existence in late 17th-century London of a manuscript Book Auction Records, which, like the Cottonian library itself, was open to inspection by those with the right credentials and with a serious interest in its contents.

New books naturally posed different problems for the would-be purchaser than did old ones, and the first essential skill was the ability to tell the two apart. Thus Lapthorne was forced to explain to Coffin, who had received the 1672 first edition of Ashmole's *Institution of the most noble Order of the Garter* instead of the 1693 'reprint' he had expected, that

they tell mee there is but one edition, but its true Mr Dring buying ye stock of ye remaynder in quiers printed a new tytle & put to ye old books & made as if there were a new edition, but there was nothing added saving a list of ye Kts created since ye printing of ye booke wch shalbe transcribed for you . . . [18 August 1694].

Coffin's source of information on new publications was sometimes Lapthorne himself, sometimes the *London Gazette*, of which Lapthorne sent him each week's two issues under cover of his own weekly letter, and sometimes the *Term Catalogues*. These were published four times a year, in February, May, June and November, for the Hilary, Easter, Trinity and Michaelmas law terms, according to their modern editor, though in fact they appeared irregularly.[37] To Coffin they were indispensable, as Lapthorne clearly understood when he wrote 'I presume you have collected them for many yeares & intend to binde them & therefore its necessary you should have ye set intire' (27 February 1692). The occasion for this comment was his promising to track down the number for Michaelmas 1690 which had somehow been missed, and which neither Lapthorne nor 'my friend', the bookseller Christopher Wilkinson, was then able to procure. He had no more success five months later, though 'I went my selfe to pauls church yard & from Bookseller to Bookseller making inquiry' (18 August 1692), nor three weeks later still, this time 'at Stationers Hall . . . where they were printed . . . & Mr Tooke ye Clark of the Hall told mee . . . yt they are now wanted by many'.[38] Moreover, it was not only private customers who wanted the missing catalogue, for Lapthorne had also tried 'Mr Chiswell who is making up of severall setts & wants yt Terme as well as yor selfe' (6 September 1692). Whether Coffin ever got his missing *Term Catalogue* the correspondence again does not say, though we know that Lapthorne was still searching as late as 27 May 1693.

Happily, however, Lapthorne's failures almost always tell us more than his successes. Thus the item in Lapthorne's bill to Coffin of 27 May 1693 for 'Du Pines Bibliotheca. . . 0 13 0' tells us nothing beyond the fact that Coffin apparently acquired at that time the first two volumes of Louis Ellies Dupin's *New History of Ecclesiastical Writers*, advertised in the *Term Catalogue* for Hilary Term 1693 at '13s. in sheets'. Prices were, however, often omitted in the *Term Catalogues*, as, for example, in the Easter 1692 advertisement for 'the Third Part, in two Volumes' of Rushworth's *Historical Collections*, and it is then only from Lapthorne that we learn 'yt ye Generall price . . . is 45s & ye lowest is 42s & yt is but at one place to witt Mr Daniell Browns at Temple bar, where I often buy books' (11 June 1692). Most revealing of all, however, are Lapthorne's reports on delayed or aborted publications, like that which he refers to as 'Dr Lightfoots 3d vol.', advertised in Trinity Term 1693 to supplement his *Works* (2 vols, 1684) but 'throwne . . . aside' by 'ye undertakers . . . for yt it seems the manuscript thereof conteyn[s] much of his other works wch they perceived not wn they printed ye proposalls' (13 February 1697).

Often it was Lapthorne himself who was the direct source of information on new books and there can be no more striking example than his report of how

Coming through St. paul's Churchyard Mr. Ketleby called to mee & gave mee notice of these books lately come fourth (viz) Bishop Overalls Convocation &c. 4° price 0.6.0. & Dr Burnetts 2d part of the Theory of ye earth fo: price 0-8 0 & ye life of Cardinall pole in Latine oct price 0 2 0 I leave it to you whether any of them are for your use [12 April 1690].[39]

Here Lapthorne leaves the final choice to Coffin, but there were times when he felt sure enough of his client's tastes to take a risk, though a carefully calculated one in the case of the 1693 edition of Bede's *Opera* 'sent without order . . . wch was newly come out & I thought fit for your purpose but I bought it wth this caution yt if you returned it hee is to take it againe at ye price'. The price, as the accompanying bill shows, was seven shillings, 'hee' being 'Mr Wilkinson . . . yt bought my Ld Anglessies Library' (17 December 1692). Sometimes, however, Lapthorne would take the full risk, though generally on a relatively inexpensive book of antiquarian interest like *The English Historical Library,* 'an octavo being a Bibliotheke written by Nicholson ye price 3s wch I make no doubt wilbe welcome unto you' (12 December 1696).

It was a miscalculation on Lapthorne's part on a considerably more expensive work to which we owe a good deal of information about one of the very few new continental works discussed in the correspondence. This was the *Museum Regium seu Catalogus* (Hafniae [Copenhagen], 1696), a heavily illustrated folio which Lapthorne refers to as 'the King of Denmark's Musaeum'. Coffin had inquired about it and Lapthorne quickly determined

yt a few of them about 20 are brought over & Smith & Walford nor Swall wch are ye great dealers in yt sort of learning had none of them, but Mr Bennett at the Halfe Moone had one, . . . its a thin fol. wth many fine Scluptures [*sic*] [6 February 1697].

Two weeks later Lapthorne had been back again to see Bennett, 'who only hath these books & as I take it sayth hath but 3 more left', and confessed to Coffin that although the bookseller 'would not abate mee one penny of 25*s*' he knew Bennett 'hopes to make more of ye rest so yt I have bought one for you' (20 February 1697). Unfortunately this letter crossed with one of Coffin's declining the purchase which left the too precipitate Lapthorne to confess of his initiative that 'I ye rather hastened it because I was apt to think they would bee all bought up' (27 February 1697). Lapthorne was fortunately able to dispose of the unwanted copy, but the sequel provides a scarcely credible picture of the rationalizations of the inveterate collector prostrate before the twin idols of rank and rarity:

My Lord Keeper hath yt for his Library wch I first bought . . . Now because hee is a great Judge of learning & bookes & there being but 2 left of these bookes (20 only brought over) I thought yt wn you should heare yt his Lpp had yors yt you might wish for one wn it could bee had & therefore have this day bought another at ye same price & put it into ye box so yt now there is but one left & I suppose who ever buys it will pay sawce for it, I hope it wilbe an ornamt to yor Library [17 April 1697].

It duly appears in Lapthorne's bill of 24 April 1697 at the original price of £1 5*s* 0*d*; one wonders how many Bennett actually had in his warehouse.

It was not, however, that Lapthorne would buy—or recommend the purchase of—just anything, even where Coffin had first expressed an interest. Thus Joshua Barnes's *History of . . . Edward IIId* proved, on enquiry, to be 'a work of litle merritt & ye booke but of a smale Bulk for such a price' (11 August 1688), and Samuel Clarke's very popular *Annotations on the Bible* merely 'usefull for the lower & meaner order of people & not so much for the learned' (6 July 1695). Lapthorne's most outspoken opposition, however, was reserved for Nathaniel Crouch's potted histories, which he permitted himself to denounce even after Coffin had ordered them, writing bluntly that

I am apt to think you are mistaken in yor choyce of Crouches bookes for they are generally but trifles & not much regarded by the skilfull in learning being collections jumbled togeather and exposed to make a present penny, & fit only for the purchase of ordinary people but however unless you contradict your order they shalbe sent [27 March 1697].

They were, and half a dozen of them appear in Lapthorne's bill of 24 April 1697 at 1s 4d each, Lapthorne having had them bound 'in calves leather' rather than the sheep he obviously felt was their proper dress, that being the only thing left for him to do to try to fit them for a gentleman's library.

The revealing anecdotes — like Stillingfleet's very popular *Christ's Sufferings* having been 'ingrossed by Martlock [the bookseller Henry Mortlock] — & hee puts his own price on it' (26 June 1697), or the fact that Thomas Guidott's *De Thermis* was not in fact available from its supposed publisher Samuel Smith who was 'very angry wth ye Doctor to print it in his name [i.e. with his imprint] & not to send him any books' (20 August 1692) — are far more numerous than there is space for here.[40] I hope, however, that I have included enough to make at least a *prima facie* case in support of my initial claim that Richard Lapthorne, in particular in his correspondence with Richard Coffin, is one of the richest sources of information we have on the operation of the retail book trade in London in the final years of the 17th century.

The correspondence ends, with rumours of the coming peace, on 7 August 1697 in a letter which is almost certainly not the last, merely the last surviving, of the series. A more personal climax comes, however, in the immediately preceding letter in which Lapthorne describes how 'On Thursday last [29 July] I caried my [torn] son about 16 yeares old aboard ye Shipp calle[d] [torn] lying at anchor below Graves End bound for Chi[na] [torn] had a mynd to goe god bless him' (31 July 1697). This was Peter (b.1681), the second of Lapthorne's three surviving children, and for the father who had written to Coffin three years earlier that after that summer's trip 'its not probable I may ever see Devonshire againe' (21 July 1694), it must have been a bleak parting. In the event, however, Lapthorne himself was to live for another 26 years, with at least two of his three children surviving him.[41]

After his letter to John Ellis of 18 June 1701, mentioned above, by which time he was already into his sixties, Lapthorne seems to have left few traces. In June 1714 he was a party to the marriage contract between his youngest child, Hannah, whose birth had been announced to Coffin on 14 July 1688, and John Pocklington of Hatton Garden, apothecary, Hannah's portion being £850.[42] Lapthorne's address when writing to Ellis in 1701 had been Kirby Street, Hatton Garden, but by 1714 he was living in Ormond Street, and it was from Ormond Street that Macrina Lapthorne, his wife of almost 50 years, was carried for burial to St Andrew Holborn on 19 April 1723, to be followed three months later, on 26 July, by Lapthorne himself. Both died intestate, administration of their goods being granted on the same day, to their eldest child, the Reverend Anthony Lapthorne (b.1678).[43] Just over a year later Anthony also died, apparently unmarried, administration of his goods in turn being granted, on 2 April 1725, to his brother Peter, safely returned from China.[44] It was thus presumably Peter Lapthorne who was responsible for the sale 'of Uncommon and Valuable Books . . . Being the entire Collection of Richard Lapthorne, Esq', which was sold at Joseph Pote's shop at Charing Cross beginning at 9 a.m. on Wednesday 22 March 1727, almost four years after his death. It was a relatively small sale of just over 1,300 lots which may well have included Anthony Lapthorne's books along with his father's, and which had certainly been conventionally augmented by the trade, there being no fewer than 30 works dating from 1726 or 1727 alone. Nevertheless the sale attracted the attention of Sir Hans Sloane, who perhaps remembered the name, and who purchased 19 lots at a combined price of £6 13s 0d. They were a mixed bag ranging from the 'History of Barbary with the Adventures of Sir Anth. Shirley' of 1609 to the 'Constitutions of the Free Masons' of 1723, but they filled gaps in Sloane's swelling collections and thus passed in time to form the foundations of the British Library.[45] That would surely have pleased Richard Lapthorne who, but for the chance survival of 400 of his letters in a remote country house, would, like so many of the books which filled his life, have passed into obscurity.

References

1. Colin G. C. Tite, *The Manuscript Library of Sir Robert Cotton* (London: The British Library, 1994), pp.79-80. I quote *literatim* from Tite, who gives as his source '*The Portledge Papers*, ed. by R. J. Kerr and I. C. Duncan (London, Jonathan Cape, 1928), pp.149-50', while adding that 'The words, "yᵉ books placed on each side . . . may reach yᵉ highest", are written in the margin of the original letter'. This fact is nowhere mentioned in the 1928 edition which also expands all contractions and brings down all superior letters, so that Tite's source must in fact be the original and not the 1928 printed edition, though his 'Viz.' should be '(viz)' and his 'Number', 'number'.
2. The author of the original *DNB* article on Sir Henry Powle cites Lapthorne's letters as extracted in '*Hist.MSS.Comm.* 5th Rep. p.379' as evidence that John Bagford helped Powle in the formation of his extensive library, and Galbraith M. Crump cites *The Portledge Papers* for the report of 'Richard Lapthorne, a young student' [sic], concerning 'the stir caused by "a lampoon relating to the late thanksgiving"' in his introduction to *Poems on Affairs of State. Vol.4: 1685-1688* (New Haven: Yale University Press, 1968), p.xxxviii, to mention only two such earlier references.
3. 'The manuscripts of John Richard Pine Coffin, Esq., at Portledge, North Devon. (Second report)' in *Fifth Report* . . . (London: HMSO, 1876), pp.378-86. Riley had initially noted the existence of the letters, though without quoting from them, in his original report on the Pine Coffin manuscripts, *Fourth Report of the Royal Commission on Historical Manuscripts* (London: HMSO, 1874), p.375.
4. Edited by Russell J. Kerr and Ida Coffin Duncan (London: Jonathan Cape, 1928). Sir Russell James Kerr (1863-1952), who seems to have been the original transcriber of the letters in the 1890s, had married Miriam, eldest daughter of John Richard Pine-Coffin in 1888; Ida Coffin Duncan I have been unable to trace, but her name makes it almost certain that she too was a family member.
5. *The Portledge Papers*, p.11. In fact three letters survive and are omitted from the earlier period, those of 20 and 27 June 1683, and 21 May 1685, while a further eight are omitted from 1687-97, those of 13 January and 16 October 1688, 29 March and 5 April 1690, 1 December 1691, 2 December 1693, and 6 January and 6 October 1694. Moreover, all Lapthorne's surviving bills, whether forming part of a letter or submitted separately, are systematically omitted.

6. The letters, which form part of a larger Portledge deposit, are contained in four large bound volumes, Z19/40/3-6, labelled as letter books A (20 June 1683-17 January 1691), B (20 January 1691-9 December 1693), C (16 December 1693-13 June 1696), and D (20 June 1696-7 August 1697). With a few insignificant exceptions the letters have been tipped on to the right-hand page of each opening, while the left-hand facing page contains a generally accurate, handwritten, 19th-century transcription. In what follows I quote from the original letters (though all superior letters have been brought down), which are cited by date. I am most grateful to the staff of the Devon Record Office for their kindness to me throughout the time I was at work on the letters.

7. *The Portledge Papers*, pp.11-12.

8. For Charles Kelland, who married Bridget Coffin on 23 August 1694, and for his father John, both of whom sat for Totnes in the 1680s, see Basil D. Henning, ed., *The Commons 1660-1690* (London: History of Parliament Trust, 1983), ii, 669-70.

9. The Charity Commissioners' *Report of the Commissioners concerning charities; containing that part which relates to the county of Devon*, vol.I (Exeter: T. Besley jun., 1826), p.279, in an account of William Hill's Gift in the parish of St Andrew, Plymouth, mentions a lease for three lives on a messuage on Southside Quay, Plymouth, 'granted in 1681, by Richard Lapthorne to Johanna Dyer'. I am most grateful to Ian Maxted for bringing this reference to my attention.

10. The normal difficulties of such research have been increased by the loss in the 1942 blitz of all the testamentary and other records of the Archdeaconry of Totnes which covers the entire south-west part of the county.

11. Lapthorne's marriage allegation is in the Vicar General's series, at 21 October 1675, his marriage being recorded the same day at St Mary Magdalen, Old Fish Street.

12. The Keck family is too vast to document thoroughly here, but Thomas and Samuel can be traced in J. Bruce Williamson, *The Middle Temple Bench Book*, 2nd edition (London: The Masters of the Bench, 1937), and the other sons in H. A. C. Sturgess, *Register of Admissions to the Middle Temple*, 3 vols (London: Butterworth, 1949). Thomas was buried in the Temple Church on 6 November 1671, and his will, proved 13 December 1671, is in the PRO, PROB 11/337/145. See The Rev. H. G. Woods, ed., *Register of Burials at the Temple Church 1628-1853* (London: Henry Sotheran, 1905), which also records the burial of 'Hanah Keck' on 27 January 1694.

13. For Sir Anthony Keck see *DNB*.

14. Keck resigned in sympathy over the dismissal of Sir John Maynard and Lapthorne reported to Coffin that although Keck had been offered Maynard's place as first commissioner 'hee desired to bee excused', adding cryptically 'a great act of selfe denyall in him, but his relations will suffer by it' (8 June 1690).

15. The term is applied to Bagford by T. A. Birrell whose 'Anthony Wood, John Bagford and Thomas Hearne as bibliographers' in Robin Myers and Michael Harris, eds., *Pioneers in Bibliography* (Winchester: St Paul's Bibliographies, 1988), pp.25-39, is the best account of Bagford's book-hunting activities, though Birrell himself cites Milton McC. Gatch, 'John Bagford, Bookseller and Antiquary', *British Library Journal*, 12 (1986), 150-71, as a fuller general summary.

16. See note 2 above, and the 'Note on the Powle collection', one of the most important legal collections of the period, in J. H. Baker, *English legal manuscripts*, vol.II, *Catalogue of the manuscript year books, readings, and law reports in Lincoln's Inn, the Bodleian Library and Gray's Inn* (Zug and London: Inter Documentation Company, 1978), pp.134-8. I am most grateful to Giles Mandelbrote for calling my attention to this account of the Powle collection.

17. Further evidence that Lapthorne was a paid agent rather than simply an obliging friend is an item for £2 in the bill of 20 June 1683 'allowed mee for my paines'.

18. Respectively MS Rawlinson C. 44 'A booke of reasons for precedency both of doctors of the lawe and maisters of the chancery before serieants of the lawe 1615': W. D. Macray, ed., *Catalogi codicum manuscriptorum Bibliothecae Bodleianae partis quintae fasciculus*

secundus (Oxford: Clarendon Press, 1878), col.13; and MS Rawlinson D. 1142 'Of the coronation of the emperor Charles the fifth' (17th century): *ibid., fasciculus quartus* (Oxford: Clarendon Press, 1898), col.313.

19. Bodleian Library, MS. Tanner 22, f.91. The card index summary gives the number of volumes as '500', but the letter clearly reads '250'. Tanner may eventually have seen a listing of the collection since British Library Add. MS 6261, ff.101-5, contain his notes on 'Mr Lapthorn's Catalogue Jun.2.99', notes almost exclusively concerned with English books of the 16th century.

20. British Library Add. MS 28,887, ff.143-4.

21. References in the letter of 20 June to 'my last bill' and to the sum of £10 received '13 March by Bill' reveal that the correspondence was already of some months' duration, and the fact that both letters are badly damaged suggests that they have survived merely because they were *less* badly damaged than those which surrounded them.

22. All the sale catalogues in what follows may be found, listed chronologically, in A. N. L. Munby and Lenore Coral, *British Book Sale Catalogues 1676-1800* (London: Mansell, 1977). For convenience I cite them by date, in the present case, for example, as Munby and Coral, 3 December 1683, the particular copy containing the names of buyers, including 'Mr Clapthorne', being British Library 11906.e.40. I am most grateful to Professor T. A. Birrell for having identified this annotated copy.

23. The six catalogues for which buyers' names survive in at least one copy are Munby and Coral, 19 April 1680, 4 July and 7 November 1681, 15 May and 30 November 1682, and 16 November 1683.

24. Devon Record Office, Z19/40/8b, folder 6, contains a letter to Coffin of 9 May 1682 from the London bookseller Moses Pitt promising to send 'the Bookes you desire', three of which, all published with Pitt's imprint, are included in a bill at the end of the letter.

25. Munby and Coral, 9 November 1691. No annotated copy of the catalogue is known to survive, but Lapthorne's purchases for Coffin can be traced in the correspondence and are summarized in a bill which probably dates from 22 December 1691 when Lapthorne wrote 'I have inclosed sent you your account of ye bookes bought', but which is now tipped in with his letter of 30 January 1692.

26. Munby and Coral, 31 October 1687 (Jacomb) and 21 November 1687 (William Cecil, Lord Burleigh). The second catalogue had been sent 'because the first miscarried', and both may, in fact, have been for the Burleigh sale since it had begun on 21 November; and in his letter of 10 December Lapthorne may be consoling Coffin for earlier lost opportunities when he writes that 'Yor Letter comes time enough for the manuscripts', which formed the last section of the catalogue and which were to begin selling the following Monday, 12 December. See the *London Gazette*, 8 December 1687.

27. Besides the Jacomb and Burleigh sales these were Munby and Coral, 1 February 1688 (Massauve), and 13 February 1688 (Scott). The correspondence contains no direct evidence of Lapthorne's acting for other clients, but during the Scott sale he wrote to Coffin 'I finde in ye margin of my catologue Num:772 & 773 Euseb: Nuremburg—but I know not well whether for you, pray if not let mee know in yor next' (11 March 1688). They were not bought for Coffin and so were presumably not his commissions, and the fact that Lapthorne might be expected to remember which were his own *desiderata* makes it possible that these were commissions from another client.

28. Munby and Coral, 9 November 1691, Sloane's copy being British Library S.C. 1033.(1). I am most grateful to Giles Mandelbrote for calling my attention to Sloane's ownership of this copy, and also to the fact that Robert Hooke's copy of Nicolo Antonio Stelliola's *Il Telescopio over Ispecillo Celeste* (Naples, 1627), British Library 529.h.33, bears the inscription in Hooke's hand, 'R Hooke pr 5d. Lapthorn Auct. Nov.27 1691'. The book does indeed appear as lot 79 of the 'Libri Gallici, Italici, &c. in Quarto' on p.71 of the catalogue of the 9 November sale, which Hooke too clearly regarded as Lapthorne's.

29. The catalogue announces the daily starting time as 4 p.m., an unusually late hour, but of the four advertisements I have noted in the *London Gazette* three, those of 15 October and

9 and 12 November, give a 2 p.m. start, though the fourth, that of 26 November, does give 4 p.m.

30. This was lot 61 of the Libri Theologici on p.2 of the catalogue, 'Andr. Piscarae Castaldi Sacr.Rom.Eccles.Rituum accurata Tractatio *Neap.*1625' which had sold for 6*s* 4*d.* Although Lapthorne's letter of 17 October 1691, quoted above, reported a catalogue 'sent by Torrington Carrier', he generally used Morris of Exeter, who left from the Saracen's Head, Friday Street, every Saturday and whose business is described in Dorian Gerhold, *Road transport before the railways. Russell's London flying waggons* (Cambridge: Cambridge University Press, 1993), pp.6-16.

31. The edition Lapthorne examined in Smith's shop according to his letter of 22 October 1692 was '2 vol. fo: . . . both Greek printed at Lyons 1688 . . . ye lowest price 55*s.*' His bill of 17 December 1692 for the copy actually bought gives simply 'DuFregns Glossary . . . 2-14-0', a shilling below Smith's price, and the copy listed for sale a century later as lot 20 in the *Catalogue of the Portledge Library* (Exeter: S. Woolmer, 1801), p.3, was 'Du Fresne Gloss. ad Script. . . . Graecitatis, 2 vol. in 1, . . . *Lug.*1688', now priced at only £1 5*s* 0*d.*

32. Munby and Coral, 13 February 1688, p.10, lot 443 of the Libri Theologici Folio is 'Gerh.Joh. Vossius de Origine & Progressu Idololatriae (Charta Magna) [Large Paper] Amst. 1668' which the annotated copy of the catalogue, British Library 821.i.13(1) shows as selling for '1-18-6'. The 1801 sale catalogue of the Portledge library (see note 31, above) lists two copies of this edition (p.26, lots 951 and 952) under its main title '*de Theologia Gentili*' [*et Physiologia Christiana, sive de Origine ac Progressu Idololatriae* . . .]. 951 is the standard issue '2 vol.', now selling at 7*s* 6*d*, but Lapthorne's bargain must be 952, '*large paper and fine*' like the Scott copy, and '2 *vol. in* 1' like the Bateman copy, though now valued at only 18*s.*

33. Presumably, since Stephen was the much longer established in Holborn. However, Christopher Bateman, Stephen's son-in-law and one-time apprentice (freed 1684), also eventually established himself at Holborn, and on 17 October 1689 Hooke recorded in his diary 'Calld at both Batemans'. See R. T. Gunther, ed., *Early science in Oxford*, vol.x (Oxford: for the author, 1935), p.157.

34. Lapthorne may, perhaps, have merely been relaying professional advice, for a year later he reports that 'I was overruled agt ye new binding of Zwinglius for yt ye taking off of ye covers would have defaced ye books so they are only guilt' (6 August 1689).

35. The sale catalogue of the library of 'Gisbert Voetius' is Munby and Coral, 25 November 1678, and the annotated copy in the British Library (C.120.c.2) confirms that the *Phonurgia Nova*, lot 250 of the 'Libri Historici, Philosophici, Mathematici, &c. in Folio' (p.47), sold for '0-9-6'.

36. The 1801 sale catalogue of the Portledge library contains a separately labelled section of 'KIRCHER'S WORKS', lots 362-74 among the 'Libri Miscellanei . . . Folio', the *Phonurgia Nova* being lot 368, priced at 10*s* 6*d.*

37. See, for example, Lapthorne's report in his letter of 19 December 1696 that 'Michas Terms Catalogue of books [is] not yet come out.'

38. John Garrett was Clerk of the Stationers' Company at this date, but Benjamin Tooke Sr., as Warehouseman of the English Stock, was also prominent in Company affairs, though it has not previously been suggested that he had responsibility for the *Term Catalogues*, generally regarded as a private, rather than a Company undertaking. Nor are the *Term Catalogues* known to have been printed at the Hall itself, which had no printing facilities, though they may perhaps have been printed in the printing houses of Robert Roberts or Robert Everingham, both of which were located in Stationers' Court, right beside the Hall.

39. The three are Wing O607, B5954, and B1641, the first two printed for Kettilby himself, and the third for his near neighbour James Adamson of the Angel and Crown, St Paul's Church yard.

40. I hope eventually to publish a fully annotated and indexed edition of the entire bibliographical portion of the Lapthorne correspondence.

41. Both Lapthorne's sons survived him and his daughter may have done so. After her marriage to John Pocklington in 1714 she bore six children (including one set of twins) whose baptisms are recorded at St Andrew Holborn between 12 May 1715 and 20 December 1719 [*sic!*], after which I have found no further trace of the family.
42. Library of the Inner Temple, Barrington MS 60, ff.68-76.
43. PRO, PROB 6/100/7, granted 24 January 1724. Joseph Foster, *Alumni Oxonienses . . . 1500-1714* (Oxford: Parker, 1891-2), calls Anthony the rector of Sherborne St John, Hants, in 1702, but his residence at the time of his death is given as Waltham Abbey, Essex.
44. PRO, PROB 6/101/55.
45. Munby and Coral, 22 March 1727, the copy with Sloane's list of purchases tipped in being British Library S.C. 550.(12). The titles are quoted from Sloane's list, the 'History of Barbary' presumably being STC 4300, C., Ro. *A true historicall discourse of Muley Hamets rising to the three kingdomes. The adventures of sir A. Sherley, and other[s] in those countries*, 1609.

Note

Robin Myers's abiding research interest having always been the great antiquaries and bibliophiles, from Ducarel to Blades, Richard Lapthorne struck me from the moment I first stumbled upon him as very much her sort of person. Accordingly, I present him to her here as a small token of my gratitude for more than a decade of the most generous friendship and hospitality, and in the hope that she will agree with me that he really is worthy of her acquaintance. And given Robin's genius for bringing her myriad friends together she will, I know, be pleased to hear me acknowledge that this paper could never have been written without the unfailing help and kindness of three more of her friends, Jill and Ian Maxted in Exeter, and Giles Mandelbrote at the British Library.

The antiquarian satirized:
John Clubbe and the Antiquities of Wheatfield[1]

ALISON SHELL

WITS AND ANTIQUARIANS were each other's enemies throughout most of the 18th century, a warfare which has been of only tangential interest to bibliographers. But John Clubbe's extraordinary pamphlet *The history and antiquities of the ancient villa of Wheatfield* (1758), which sends up Philip Morant's *History and antiquities of the most ancient town and borough of Colchester* (1748) and antiquarianism in general, testifies that wits could make inventive use of a book's physical make-up to satirize the antiquarian malaise of bookishness. The history of the transmission of the two texts, insofar as it can be traced, is further testimony to a near-total incompatibility of ideals between satirist and victim. Satire at this period was a kind of ethical engagement with folly, and so had the property of radiating outwards from the text into many forms of personal behaviour.

The points at issue were not just factual, or disagreements on methodology; on either side they were critiques of the misapplication of meaning, since the antiquarian and the wit had very different ideas of how to pursue truth. The articulation of this difference can be seen as part of the long-running battle between Ancients and Moderns: as Stuart Piggott has put it, 'It is obvious that antiquarian pursuits should be regarded as trifling by the historians of the old school, devoted to the grand manner and the presentation of the great and good of the past as moral exemplars.'[2] It was from this type of historian that wits derived both their normative assumptions and their prejudices. Whereas antiquarians derived knowledge from the inductive accumulation of individual facts, wits conceived it as having more to do with the application of moral imperatives; to antiquarians etymological speculation was legitimate, but wits saw it as destabilizing meaning. Though wits frequently accused antiquarians of turning irrelevancy into an art form, this conceals a fear that the free play of speculation might prove only too influential. This ideological clash informs the bibliographical satire of *Wheatfield*, where every feature down to the typography invites the reader to address the antiquarian's interpretative rashness. In *Colchester*, archaeological inscriptions are minutely transcribed and ponderously explicated; in *Wheatfield* text is shattered, its gaps irresponsibly filled in and the whole adorned with ludicrous woodcuts.

John Clubbe

If Clubbe was a wit, Morant was certainly a thorough-going antiquarian. His *History and antiquities of Colchester* was published in 1748: the first in-depth treatment of Colchester to be compiled, and published to be bound with Nathanael Salmon's *History and antiquities of Essex* (1740).[3] Morant's preferred method of compilation made few concessions to literary style, with its long transcriptions of documents and the kind of factual density which pleased other scholars more than the common reader. Even an antiquarian contemporary wrote of him, 'Our author is not a very lively writer.'[4] Then, ten years after *Colchester* had been published, *Wheatfield* appeared anonymously.

Who was the man taking such pains to subvert Morant's book? With an anonymous publication, giving the name of a village helps to identify the author. Wheatfield—or, more commonly, Whatfield—was a real Suffolk parish just outside Ipswich, and Clubbe was rector of it from 1735 up to the year of his death, 1773. He does not seem to have had especial antiquarian interests himself, and the few surviving anecdotes about him tend to give the impression of a genial and successful humorist. His portrait (fig.1) was painted by Gainsborough, a fellow East Anglian resident; and in a letter dating from the same year that *Wheatfield* was published, Gainsborough reported of the experience, 'I'm sure I could not paint his picture for laughing . . .'.[5]

Wheatfield was the most successful piece Clubbe ever wrote, but it was followed by another humorous pamphlet, *Physiognomy* (1763), with a frontispiece engraved by Hogarth.[6] Other pamphlets are to do with his calling as an Anglican clergyman: a sermon preached in 1751 before the Incorporated Society for the Relief of Widows and Orphans of Clergymen, and his *Letter of free advice to a young clergyman* of 1765. Another suggests he was a hunting parson: *The farmer's queries and resolutions concerning the game* [1770?].[7] It is very much the *curriculum vitae* of an occasional writer, when Clubbe's writings were reprinted by the Ipswich bookseller John Shave, they were deservedly given the title *Miscellaneous tracts*. But in terms of a writer's life, miscellaneity is sometimes not as accidental as it appears. So much of Clubbe's writing was issued by Ipswich publishers that one gains the impression of an author who intended his writing primarily to have a *local* utility: an extension of his pulpit on the one hand, and of his role as a local dignitary on the other. The ideal is for publication not to be sought, but to arise naturally from popular demand. This is a gentlemanly version of self-promotion, too pastoral to be called *sprezzatura*, but with the same determination not to be mistaken for a professional.

But, as will be described below, Clubbe had good contacts in London through his local literary acquaintances and would have been able to choose between London and Ipswich as a place of publication. In this context, the fact of a London publisher—Mary Cooper—for *Wheatfield* is suggestive. Research for this article in the copious Morant archives has yielded no

Fig.1.   Portrait of John Clubbe by Thomas Gainsborough, oil on canvas, 29½ × 24½ in. (private collection, USA, courtesy of Historical Portraits Ltd.)

evidence of how Clubbe's dislike of Morant's book reached such a pitch; indeed, they leave one with the suspicion that all references to the dispute have been deliberately excised.[8] But given the proximity of Ipswich and Colchester, it may well have had elements of a local feud. The book would, for this reason, have found a large and attentive local audience; naturally, when it was published, it was advertised in the *Ipswich Journal*.[9] It is, of course, possible that Ipswich booksellers refused to print the book; yet at the same time, provincial publication would have lessened the impact of the satire. The imprint of Clubbe's *Letter of free advice* suggests that difference between London and the provinces should not be exaggerated, as far as distribution networks went;[10] but Morant's book had been a London production, and from London, Clubbe's pamphlet had a relevance to myopic antiquarians of all counties. Though it may have been inspired by a local squabble, it would, from Ipswich, have appeared like nothing more. In effect, London publication of the pamphlet was a recognition that the community of wits had to be based in the metropolis.

But this could exist side by side with a local culture of wit based on the community of manuscript circulation. There are a number of jokes which depend on knowledge of Whatfield, strongly suggesting that the piece began life as a *jeu d'esprit* for local consumption. Soon after it was printed, *Wheatfield* was put into hudibrastic verse: possibly by William Myers, vicar of Walton in Suffolk. As it survives in manuscript, it is given a dedicatory epistle where the writer expresses his desire to make his rhymed version a best-seller.[11] It is heavy with irony – possibly simple, possibly inspired by envy of Clubbe's metropolitan success, but at all events dissociating itself from the mercantile world of print.

> You say, this Version will not sell,
> (That's more, learn'd Sir, than you can tell).
> Did e'er the World see such sad Stuff,
> Dull Sense, low stile, hobling & rough?
> Why, Sir, it rhimes, & that's enough.
> Pray, don't you see, how yt. the Town,
> For Cantos five will give a Crown?
> If't does but rhime, it will go down.
> Besides, this is a Subject new;
> All Novel Things will sell, tis true. (ll.243-52)[12]

It was not only Clubbe's admirers who joined in. *Wheatfield* was republished in 1761, three years after its original appearance, in Robert and James Dodsley's anthology *Fugitive pieces*.[13] The title is disingenuous, since the very fact of the pieces being collected and printed accords them a permanency; and since *Colchester* had not been a commercial success, the frequent reappearances of Clubbe's piece must have been exceptionally provoking to Morant. He seems likely to have been the author of a manuscript poem in 136 quatrains: 'Laus Britanniae. or The Panegyric. An Epistle, written upon Mr. Dodsley's Republication of the Antiquities of

Wheatfield, To the Author by Morantia. With explanatory Notes, by Historicus. . . . 1762.'[14] Its irony, even heavier than that of the versified *Wheatfield*, pivots around the assertion that publishing success is a reliable index of worth.

> When proud Colonia [i.e. Colchester], Sir, espy'd
> Your Title fix'd on Dodsley's Post;
> She sigh'd, she groan'd, & falt'ring said,
> Ah! me, now all my Honour's lost . . . (stanza 74)

But ultimately, the existence of *Laus Britanniae* is more important than anything it actually says. Not confident enough in the validity of his research, Morant must also have wished to be seen worsting Clubbe in the rhetorical battle of wits.

Antiquarians versus wits

Morant's initial preface to *Colchester* includes an apology for the book's format. 'By the advice of Friends I have chosen to print it in Folio, as the most commodious form; and tho' it is but thin, it contains full as much as might easily have been run out into a bulky Quarto' (π2a). It is an unusual point to stress, and Clubbe's text begins by mocking it, supplying Morant's text in quotation marks: 'By the Advice of Friends I have chosen to print it "in" *Quarto*, "as the most commodious Form; and though it be but thin, it contains as much as might have been run out into a more bulky *Octavo*;" [because one fourth of a Sheet contains two eighths, and one Fold of the paper more would have made the Bulk just double]' (p.x).

Perhaps Clubbe knew how exquisitely annoying this particular shaft would be. Morant's correspondence with the publisher Charles Davis and his printer William Bowyer survives, and reveals that the size of the book was the single most tendentious issue between them. Morant's original dream of having it in quarto was discarded in favour of a folio format, partly to make it uniform with Salmon's *Essex* — another work printed by Bowyer — but partly too to make it more economical to print; Clubbe's sneer was commonsensical, but not correct. However, Morant objected greatly to the text being set in two columns to decrease the book's cost still further. Suspecting that Bowyer was being deliberately obstructive in failing to listen to his repeated objections, he asked his own bookseller Henry Whitridge to commission another printer to set up a specimen sheet with the text in long lines. This soon got back to Bowyer, and Whitridge reported how he 'complains of ill Usage in this Affair as he had indeavoured to serve you in the prosecut[io]n of the Work and told me that I had shut him out of the Job, . . . though he had got you four subscribers with great difficulty.'[15]

Financial considerations eventually prevailed with a book that, as Morant was repeatedly told, was unprofitable to print at all; and the book's two-column format shows who won. Charles Davis pulled out shortly afterwards, and Bowyer saw the project through to publication; indeed,

Morant's comment was a reflection on Bowyer which might well be construed as ungrateful. But it is the toilsome history of the negotiations with printer and publisher that lies behind the apology, rather than any real exiguity of text. *Colchester* is not an especially thin book by most standards, and Clubbe's dapper quarto points to the incongruousness of Morant's comment.

Another implication is latent in Clubbe's mockery: bulkiness and wit can never co-exist.[16] The point is brought home further in the preface to *Wheatfield*, where the author gently complains, 'I have spent the major part of a long life in this Study, and I have inverted, as it were, the very Form of my Body in your Service; which was once plumpish, and inclining to fat upwards, but by my Sedentariness is now fallen downwards, to the no small Increase of my Legs . . .' (pp.vii-viii). This contrasts unfavourably with the healthy georgic picture which Clubbe paints of himself at the end of the main text: 'The Parson has begot himself Children, made himself Gardens and Orchards, and planted Trees in them of all Kinds. He hath made himself Pools of Water . . . and he has had possession of great Cattle above all that were in Wheatfield before him' (pp.30-1).

Commentators in the succeeding centuries have been grateful for Morant's bulk, and somewhat puzzled by Clubbe; *Wheatfield* has, for instance, been called a 'rather pointless joke'.[17] Even to a sympathetic 20th-century reader, *Wheatfield* in its printed form invites two questions: why should it have taken so long to appear? — and why should Clubbe have taken so much trouble over it? The first may not be as puzzling as it seems. If — as already suggested — the piece was first circulated in manuscript, it may well not have taken the whole ten years between 1748 and 1758 to brew. The length of time taken may be negative evidence that Morant and his friends did not know about it till print-publication; certainly, there seems to be no evidence of any attempt to suppress it beforehand. Unfortunately, the Morant papers preserved in the Essex Record Offices are barren of reference to the dispute, and the only comment on the book which I have found could be either a short-term or long-term reflection: in response to what must have been an incendiary letter of June 1758 from Morant, A. C. Ducarel wrote that *Wheatfield* was 'a work wch has done [Clubbe] no Honor'.[18] But the relationship of *Colchester* to *Wheatfield* is like that of Richardson's *Pamela* to Fielding's *Joseph Andrews*; the specific satirical inspiration is made obvious at the beginning, but the finished artefact has an integrity that goes beyond it.

This leads one on to the second question, why Clubbe took so much trouble over the joke. This can only be answered by emphasizing the seriousness of a number of the points that Clubbe is making, which in turn demands a brief consideration of 18th-century mentalities. Antiquarians had long been an object of ridicule; and within the early 18th century, they violated the gentlemanly assumption that a man of sense studied nothing to excess.[19] The *Memoirs* of Martinus Scriblerus, dreamt up between 1714 and

1727 by a coterie of wits including Pope, Swift and Dr Arbuthnot, was perhaps the most influential contemporary incarnation of the stereotype. His birth presaged by his mother's dream of an overflowing inkhorn, Scriblerus has a turn for fluent miscellaneous nonsense which, in his antiquarian modes, shades into Stygian pedantry. The wits' particular target was the polymath Dr John Woodward, whose interests embraced everything from palaeontology to classical antiquities. Admiration among the learned for his prize acquisition, a Roman shield depicting the victories of Scipio Africanus, was matched only by learned opprobrium what it was discovered to be a Renaissance imitation.[20]

By the middle of the 18th century, antiquarian studies encompassed both miscellaneity and a considerable degree of specialization; wits could assume a public which was familiar with the parameters of many sorts of antiquarian writing, and well able to detect when these were being subverted. County and town histories were appearing in increasing numbers from a growing band of gentlemen or clergymen with antiquarian interests, anxious to find some especial virtue in the county or parish where they happened to live. Their fitness for the task varied widely, and they are often most useful nowadays where they describe rather than interpret. But their education was overwhelmingly classically-based; the paths taken by university learning encouraged the assumption that worthwhile knowledge was philologically oriented; and the 18th-century passion for aetiology had the effect of making speculative etymologists out of most antiquarians. As with commentaries on physical remains, the quality of the interpretation was bound to vary; some genuine discoveries were made, and some red herrings created a diversion.

But it sometimes seems as if the antiquarians' critics are not in favour of any speculation, good or bad. James Davis's *Origines Divisianae.*[21] *Or the antiquities of the Devizes* (1754) is made up of a series of letters, not so much giving an antiquarian account of the town as offering a solemn warning against those who already have.

They who are but moderately acquainted with the study of the early English antiquities must soon have been convinc'd, that they are engag'd in a dry and uncomfortable task, and oblig'd to plunge thro' many difficulties and puzzle through a variety of perplexities: The originals of Facts lying confus'd, and involv'd; and are to be found out only, like Rattle-Snakes, by their Tails. . . . Would the writers upon these subjects permit modesty and reason now and then to step into their minds, they would restrain their loose imaginations . . . Their readers too would be freed from perusing long and lifeless books, made up chiefly of fanciful suppositions instead of well-grounded facts . . . (pp.2-3).

Like *Wheatfield, Origines Divisianae* combines well-grounded fact with parody and satirical abuse. Though this is generically surprising to the 20th-century academic, it demonstrates the greater academic seriousness of satire two centuries ago. Chief among Davis's complaints is the antiquarian proclivity for speculative etymologies: 'These . . . have furnished out great attempts for wonderful discoveries, the words having been tortur'd and wove into a delicate contexture of flimsy probabilities' (p.5). In a later letter he describes 'Roots of Hebraic, Celtic, Saxon, all finely powder'd but not search'd' as an essential ingredient in the making of a 'compleat modern Antiquarian' (p.71). Embedded in a humorous recipe, the joke acts more as a homoeopathic prescription. The *History of Wheatfield*, too, begins with a cheerful burlesque of all tenuous philological excursuses.

WHEATFIELD was called by the Romans VILLA FRUMENTARIA, and sometimes, hyperbolically, SICILIA BRITANNICA, for the Excellency and Plenty of Wheat growing therein. The Saxons called it ['Whatefield' in Saxon type] [whate] signifying Wheat, and [feld] Field; which the Moderns, for want of Skill in the Saxon Tongue, mistaking its Etymology, now corruptly call WHATFIELD. There are not wanting learned Men, I confess, who adhere to the vulgar Reading; and in support of it suppose, that the Saxons, out of Surprize and Amazement at the Fertility of the Place, cried out, *What Feld!* and from that Moment, according to the capricious and licentious Nomination of Men and Things of those Times, called it WHATFELD. (p.16)[22]

The capricious and licentious nomination of contemporary antiquarians is, of course, the real target. It was a common fear, further brought out by one particular hudibrastic expansion of *Wheatfield*; Clubbe hints in the preface that 'The particular Motives that induced me, at this Time, to publish the following Work, were really no other, than to establish the World in their present belief of Antiquities, which I greatly suspect some ill-designing Men, both at Home, and Abroad, are now endeavoring to subvert' (pp.viii-ix), but the versifier makes this into an explicit reference to the antiquarian abuse of aetiology.

> The motives which do me induce,
> To write now for the publick use,
> Is really (If you'll me believe) . . .
> That you, & all Mankind, should credit give.
> To what we Antiquaries write,
> And your attention to excite
> To the Belief of all such Things
> as we trace back to their first Springs. (ll.130-2, 134-8)

Antiquarian interpretations of inscriptions come in for a similar douche of scorn. At the end of *Colchester*, Morant spends some time proving why an inscription previously thought to date a house in Colchester to 1090 has been misread; in his quest for accuracy, he even includes a plate 'taken from the Date itself with wet paper' (Book III, p.29). Had the date of 1090 been correct, it would have proved that the house was one of the oldest still standing, and that Arabic numerals were in use in 11th-century Britain. Though here Morant is sceptical enough to have pleased even Clubbe, his refutation gives evidence of his brother-antiquarians filling the *lacunae* of an incomplete text with nothing more substantial than hope.

Clubbe took the hint; and his other authorial persona, a hopeful antiquarian, has various adventures. First he is delighted to find what he thinks to be a Roman inscription in Clubbe's rectory. 'In a Cornice of exquisite Workmanship, there is a large Roman C, and some imperfect Figures of the Date U.C, but the Ignorance of some modern Inhabitant has defaced it, either by prefixing the initial Letter of his own Christian Name, or by giving a ridiculous Tail to another Roman C, (inscribed perhaps C.C. *Claudius Caesar*) . . . whom, upon searching the Parish Register, I take to have been the simple Rector, one George Carter' (pp.17-18). Then he finds an inscription in a farmhouse cut by one John Warter; he decides the inscription is Saxon, and 'by frequently repeating WARTER JOHN, I discovered the Sound of VORTIGERN[23] . . . I concluded the Author, through Ignorance, or Punning, or Ænigmatic Ingenuity, which are much alike in their Operations, has inveloped and perplexed the Thing' (p.27). A point of wide applicability is being made.[24] This is not just satire on a particular bad habit of the learned; it derides the very condition of bookishness.

Clubbe's text takes typographical hints from Morant's: type is filed to reproduce the broken text of an ancient inscription (p.18) and black-letter and Anglo-Saxon types are used to dignify his extraordinary etymologies.[25] The preoccupation with true and false meaning returns in this physical condemnation of misreading, though — sadly — reprints show considerable dilution of these and other bibliographical jokes.[26] If Pope described a little learning as a dangerous thing, the real fear in *Wheatfield* is of too much learning, and of certainties illegitimately drawn from the poor remains of ancient texts and the semantic instability of sound. Clubbe is accusing the etymologists almost of a regression to Renaissance theories of correspondence, doomed attempts to make trifling coincidences yield up real meaning. The boundaries have shifted from when it was enough to ridicule the antiquarian's penchant for accumulating mounds of fact; Clubbe is identifying an opposite fault, that of theorizing from insufficient evidence. Despite wits' sharp criticism of scientists in the early days of the Royal Society, they themselves made demands recognizably similar to those of the new scientific methodology.

It is not entirely clear what the wits would have approved as a legitimate scholarly method of dealing with the etymological problems of English. Certainly all critics and scholars were standard targets for humorists; their interest in textual problems was read as a morbid preoccupation with trifles, and the charge of small-mindedness rendered more piquant by the contrast between author and commentator. Swift identified true critics by 'their talent of swarming about the noblest writers, to which they are carried merely by instinct, as a rat to the best cheese, or a wasp to the fairest fruit.'[27] But the pusillanimity of critics was not felt to impugn the greatness of the texts they inhabited; about antiquarians, though, there still existed a genuine feeling that their preoccupations were with worthless material.

Antiquarians were associated with the Gothic: not because they were interested in nothing else, but because Gothic remains played a large part in British history. In the mid-18th century, a continued prejudice against Gothic co-existed with the general revival of interest in it. *Wheatfield* is testimony to the symbiotic relationship of the two trends, but its sympathy is firmly that of Pope's fifty years earlier. Pope and most of his generation conflated the two ideas of vandalism and the sleep of learning when using the term: in 'A Gothic Library! of Greece and Rome / Well purg'd . . .' (*Dunciad*, I, ll.145-6) or in the *Essay on Criticism*:

> With Tyranny, then Superstition join'd,
> As that the body, this enslav'd the mind;
> Much was believ'd, but little understood,
> And to be dull was constru'd to be good;
> A second deluge learning thus o'er-run,
> And the Monks finished what the Goths begun. (ll.687-92)[28]

It was also a time when there were many competing ideologies of British-ness to choose from; yet an admirer of Pope, such as Clubbe, might still have found Roman-influenced ideals of English virtue compelling, and disliked the various mutations of Gothic for that reason. Stuart Piggott has commented that 'the remains of the remote British province of the Empire long continued to share something of the esteem attributed to classical studies. . . . It had a foot in both camps, the prestige of the Ancients combined with the techniques of the Moderns.'[29] Antiquarians themselves could be pro-Roman to a fault: in the preface to his study of Roman Britain, *Itinerarium Septentrionale* (1726), Alexander Gordon expressed the hope that through the Society of Antiquaries 'Antiquity and Learning may flourish in the Island, to the total Extirpation of Gothicism, Ignorance, and a bad Taste' (f.C1a). But where the anti-antiquarian prejudice was strongest, this could – paradoxically – have engendered an exactly opposite feeling: that the classical tradition was a less appropriate subject than Gothic for antiquarian study.[30] A town history, of course, would always have needed to deal with both Roman and Gothic remains where both existed; but Colchester was one of the premier towns of Roman Britain, and could well have had particular symbolic importance for a British Augustan. Morant's book might have aroused Clubbe's hostility precisely because he felt that Roman subject-matter was being obscured by gothic spider-webs.

Bibliographical satire

To the 18th century, the idea of Gothic included intimations of the rough-hewn as well as the medieval. *Wheatfield*'s most conspicuous feature is its two extraordinary Gothic headpieces (fig.2), but they are not the only way that Clubbe exploits the physical medium of the book to enhance his satire. In this respect, *The history of Wheatfield* stands alongside much better-known 18th-century imaginative satires: Pope's *Dunciad Variorum*, and Sterne's *Tristram Shandy*.[31] Some features of this are more immediately striking than others. Metatextual features are pressed into satirical service: there are fulsome prefatory comments and verses, signed A. B., B. C., C. D., D. E., E. F., and F. G.,[32] an equally obsequious dedication to an unnamed lord, ending with the hope that 'Your Lordship may live to be Yourself a most venerable Piece of Antiquity' (p.v), and a preface to the reader, which explains how 'we durst not hazard our Works into the World, . . . but are obliged previously to point out the Beauties, &c. lest they should not strike the Reader so forcibly as, perhaps, they have us, the Authors or Editors' (p.[vii]). Within satires on antiquarianism, there is a long tradition of criticizing metatextual features: for example, Johann Burkhard Mencken's *De charlataneria eruditorum* (1st editions 1715, Leipzig & Amsterdam) complained of the academic misuse of dedications, prefatory letters, eulogistic verses and 'sonorous and arresting book titles'.[33]

Fig.2.

Clubbe's conscientious criticism of the metatext did not end with *Wheatfield*. In 'Scattered thoughts on title-pages, dedications, prefaces and postscripts', published in the *Miscellaneous tracts*, he even subjects the title of his own book to a devastating quick analysis: 'Miscellaneous Tracts, short Narratives, succinct Views, &c. are Taking Title-pages, because they promise the reader not to detain him long upon any one subject' (p.90). He suspects the motives of author, printer and bookseller in colluding to defraud the customer of true moral nourishment: 'Some Title-pages dress well, to insinuate themselves into our company, but with a view only to pick our pockets' (p.89). And, though criticism of fulsome dedications is so widely diffused as to be a commonplace, Clubbe gives it a distinctive moral twist, identifying their role in betraying innocence. 'In my younger days I was very fond of reading Dedications; . . . for the sake of those catalogues of virtues, with which such performances generally abound. . . . With this kind of knowledge of men I set out, furnish'd as I thought with as many toasts for

as many glasses as wou'd become me to drink: when the company told me
to my great confusion, that I had toasted four of the worst men in the
kingdom' (pp.91, 93).[34] There is nothing neutral about any element of a
book's physical and textual presentation: everything has been contaminated
by flattery and mercantile greed, and must be cleansed by satire.

Wheatfield's headpieces were almost certainly specially made for the
book. Before the main text is one featuring two little blank roundels, like
those on pedigrees: juxtaposed with shields, but also suggesting the shape
of a pair of spectacles and joined by a neat nose-piece. On the right is a
shield bearing the motto 'Antiquum obtineo' [I possess the antique]. To the
left, another bears Greek characters arranged in a triangle, and spelling out
Archimedes' exclamation of discovery, 'εύρηκα'.[35] A second headpiece,
discussed in more detail later, features a snake with its tail in its mouth, the
symbol of eternity.[36]

Who designed these ornaments? At present, this is not a question that
can be definitely answered. But, as this article will go on to remark,
Clubbe's satirical imagination was stimulated by architecture; and though
these ornaments are not especially architectural, the two disciplines of
architecture and book-design could both, at this period, take allusions latent
within the repertoire of conventional ornamentation and use them to make
specific points. Even if this were not the case, Clubbe as author would be
the most obvious person to have designed them. But the question of
influence is, perhaps, more interesting. Hogarth was a figure who impinged
upon literary East Anglia. Joshua Kirby's *Dr Brook Taylor's method of
perspective made easy* was first published in Ipswich in 1754,[37] and the book
is dedicated to Hogarth, who designed the frontispiece showing the
absurdities of lack of perspective. This does for visual language what satires
on speculative etymology do for verbal, making what is essentially a moral
point: lack of perspective, or true sense, results in a series of interconnec-
tions frightening because of their manifest absurdity.[38]

Kirby was a friend of Clubbe's as well, and it was through him that
Physiognomy was dedicated to Hogarth.[39] Ronald Paulson speculates that
the frontispiece was offered by Hogarth as a reciprocal gesture, and if this
is so, Kirby also seems to have acted as intermediary here. The frontispiece
shows a weighing-machine designed to calculate human *gravitas*, tried on
men ranging from the ponderous to the feather-headed; according to
Hogarth's first biographer John Nichols, Clubbe thought the figure called
'Good sence' in the centre was a portrait of himself, and that it must have
been drawn by Kirby since Hogarth had never met him. One hopes that
Clubbe finally managed to meet his literary mentor on a trip to London, but
since Hogarth died in 1764 there would have been little time for the
relationship to develop.

The text of *Physiognomy* has been recognized as having Hogarthian
traits. Clubbe's preface praises the moral efficacy of Hogarthian satire: 'For
such cautionary Exhibitions correct, without the Harshness of Reproof, and

are felt and remembered, when rigid Dogmatizings are rejected and forgotten.' More generally, the sheer *literariness* of the *Wheatfield* conceit, and its interpenetration of the verbal and the visual, shows an awareness of the possibilities of the medium that is also very Hogarthian. In this context, Clubbe's other headpiece is worth pausing upon. Hogarth had published his *Analysis of beauty* in 1753, and a woodcut ornament on its title-page gives emblematic form to his famous exposition of the serpentine line of beauty, a snake displayed against a pyramid. Transmuted to a pyramidal shell, this became part of Hogarth's crest.[40] The *Analysis* explains how the Greeks sought out perfect proportion and dedicated it to Venus in a triangular glass (pp.15-16). But the pyramid is also symbolic of eternity; like the snake, it can symbolize both the triumphs of art and the triumph of death.

Turning again to *Wheatfield*, the headpiece above the preface combines different attributes of Time: the hourglass, the scythe and a snake with its tail in its mouth, signifying eternity. The deliberate rusticity of the rendering aids the intended message: this is the iconography of the tombstone.[41] Prefatory puffs refer to the snake. The one signed C. D. remarks how 'your Stile, like the Emblem of your Subject, *serpit humi,* [crawls on the ground] as well as the best of your Contemporaries' (p.xi), and E. F. breaks into epigram:

> Old Time, with your Scythe, and your Snake, and your Glass,
> Have a Care of yourself, there's *a Snake in the Grass*!
> A Snake, like the Serpent in MOSES'S Hand,
> That will eat up your Snake at the Word of Command. (p.xii)

Two snakes are being polemically opposed. First is the antiquarians' snake of eternity — and there may be a gibe here at William Stukeley's notorious claim that the megalithic stones of Avebury were arranged in that shape.[42] The second snake is a snake in the grass, ambushing antiquarian Time by means of an anonymous parody; yet it is compared to Moses's snake, and consumes falsehood. In view of Clubbe's admiration of Hogarth, this strongly suggests an allusion to Hogarth's snake, and to a Hogarthian moral aesthetic.[43] The *Analysis of beauty* comments that 'there is scarce an Egyptian, Greek, or Roman deity, but hath a twisted serpent, . . . or some symbol winding in this manner to accompany it. . . . it is as remarkable, that the deities of barbarous and gothic nations never had, nor have to this day, any of these elegant forms belonging to them' (pp.xviii-xix).

The two writers shared a scepticism about patination, thought by satirists to be the main reason why ancient objects were highly prized by antiquarians. Pope's 'Epistle to Mr Addison, occasion'd by his dialogues on medals' is typical in the sequence of points it makes:

> With sharpened sight pale Antiquaries pore,
> Th'inscription value, but the rust adore;
> This is the blue varnish, that the green endears,
> The sacred rust of twice ten hundred years! (ll.35-8)

Hogarth's 'Time smoking a picture' was designed three years after the publication of *Wheatfield* in 1761.[44] Illustrating a commonly used metaphor for the depredations of age, it gives iconographical shape to an intuition first expressed in the *Analysis of beauty*, that Time is not a beautifier but a destroyer. 'Smoke' is used in the double sense of darkening and tricking, a deliberate ambiguity that Hogarth returned to in a later engraving, subtitled 'The Bathos, or Manner of Sinking, in Sublime Paintings, inscribed to the Dealers in Dark Pictures'.[45] The dispelling of smoke—or, to quote *Wheatfield*'s title-page epigraph,[46] *Ex fumo dare lucem*—is a central metaphor to both satirists.

Smoke and rust both create patination, enhancing the archaeological object or obscuring it. In *Wheatfield*, Clubbe comments that he distrusts the substitution of iron for brass implements in cookery, because it may lead to a prejudice against old coins. Apologists for iron lay 'the greatest Stress upon the Unwholesomeness of the Rust and Verdegrease Suffusions, which make these Coins so very valuable. I should be glad to find these Apprehensions of mine groundless; but the same indirect Attack (invisible indeed to common Eyes) . . . has been made upon Protestantism by Father Hardovin, and upon Christianity itself by Dr. Middleton' (p.ix).[47] Naturally, Clubbe is not implying that Christianity is only valuable for its verdigris. The comment is double-edged: his irony is directed against all who confuse accretion with the real thing, as well as those who find it a cause for alarm. Clubbe locates himself at the golden mean: half-way between the popish Hardouin and the godless Middleton, half-way between the philistines and the anti-scrapers. Again, one is struck by the relentlessness by which the passage of a joke is constantly short-circuited to moral absolutes.

The analogues with Hogarth's *œuvre* do not end there, since Hogarth too had burlesqued antiquarianism in the past. The *Peregrination*, written by Hogarth's friend Ebenezer Forrest, records their journey round Kent with a group of other friends in 1732, and alludes frivolously to the genre of the antiquarian journey which gave rise to books like Stukeley's *Itinerarium Curiosum*.[48] During the trip, Hogarth and Samuel Scott had drawn monuments, and Forrest had transcribed a number of inscriptions. As with *Origines Divisianae*, there is some ambivalence in their intention; clearly some contribution to antiquarian knowledge was intended, but the playfulness of the narrative creates an ironic distance between real antiquarians and Hogarth's cronies. Like *Wheatfield*, it was versified.

Though it now only exists in one copy, other copies may have been made—with or without imitations of Hogarth's illustrations—or Clubbe could simply have heard about it. In either case, reference to an unpublished work enhances the coterie quality of the jokes in *Wheatfield*, and further points up the distinction between the media of manuscript and print that Clubbe makes play with elsewhere. One joke, in particular, makes the identification almost certain. There is a hint at speculative etymology in the *Peregrination*, where Forrest exclaims of the Isle of Grain that it must certainly have acquired the name because of its fruitfulness. The fore-shadowing of Wheatfield seems too neat to be coincidental. It would be going far past the evidence to suggest that Hogarth had any direct hand in the decorative or conceptual schema of *Wheatfield*, but he must certainly have been among the inspirations.

Convention, ornament and meaning
Through the genre and practice of peregrination, antiquarian works and guidebooks overlapped in several ways. Inevitably, once a journey was described other travellers followed in the footsteps of the author; antiquarian works not written as peregrinations could also be used as guides by the traveller; and cheap guidebooks tended to derive their information from authoritative antiquarian works. Towards the end, *The history and antiquities of Wheatfield* is satirizing a sub-genre of the guidebook, printed vade-mecums to the garden buildings of estates such as Stowe. These were a very specific kind of traveller's progress, interpreting the iconographical meaning of the individual structures, and of the relations between them and the site. Stowe is also a well-known example of how architectural language could be used for satirical purposes: next to the handsome and well-appointed Temple of Ancient Virtue, the Temple of Modern Virtue is a ruin. The Gatton 'Town Hall', a classical structure built to house a simple urn, makes a similar point; its satire depends on the viewer making the connection between the use of urns for voting and the political status of Gatton, a tiny village and a notorious rotten borough at the time the 'Town Hall' was built.[49]

Clubbe refers to the conventions of the guidebook in every respect except one; by not identifying the buildings he describes, he makes them sound more antique and more interesting than they are. 'In a shady and obscure Part' of the Rectory garden, a Gothic arch built with black flints supports 'an Angel, in a full-bottom'd Wig' presenting the arms of Wheatfield, 'a Shield, *Pearl*, a Fesse, *Sable*, between three Garbes,[50] *Or*' (p.19). This is likely to be a poker-faced description of a feature on one of the parish buildings near the rectory: perhaps the parish reading-room, since demolished, which was built of flint against the tithe-barn and would have been a possible place to display the Whatfield arms.[51] It is a very local joke, and again points to the piece being intended first for a local audience.

Throughout *Wheatfield*, and perhaps for reasons already touched upon, Clubbe shows himself particularly impatient with Morant's going out of his way to identify remains in Colchester as Roman. There may be something of retaliation in Clubbe's description of an antique structure belonging to the rectory, a Grecian temple surrounded by 'Oak, Yew, and Box trees, planted there with a View to repair, or refit the Deity within' (p.18). He blandly explains away its modern appearance: 'This Temple is made of Wood and Plaister, and therefore cannot be supposed to be the identical

Temple first erected here . . . but, like the Royal Sovereign [a ship] has been built and rebuilt till scarce a plank is left of the original Structure' (p.19).

It is not clear whether there actually was a temple at the time when Clubbe was writing. But given that the point of *Wheatfield* is to describe existing objects in a grandiose manner, it would be surprising if it were pure invention; ironically, Clubbe's satirical description may prove to yield real evidence for 20th-century architectural historians. A temple was erected by John Plumpin, the rector who succeeded Clubbe, and stands to this day with a tablet commemorating Clubbe, but the two structures are not the same: the present one is brick and flint, rather than wood and plaster. Nevertheless, Plumpin's building may be a re-erection of a ruinous former structure which Clubbe himself had commissioned. As already commented, Clubbe remodelled the Rectory garden to incorporate a number of canals, and the temple is placed on a mound at the head of a small embankment which seems to be part of the waterworks. Another alternative is that the building was indeed imagined, but that Plumpin, having read *Wheatfield*, erected it as an appropriate tribute to Clubbe.[52] Whatever the precise chronology, the relationship of book and garden underscores the literariness of Clubbe's landscape; a trip round it, or round the village, becomes a mini-peregrination like the formal progression of reading.

Visually, too, there is a similarity between the traditional ornaments of book and building: one way of illustrating how very close the relationship between architecture and the book could be. As with architecture, ornament within a book is regulated in two ways: by being subservient to a utilitarian design, and by adherence to a limited aesthetic vocabulary superficially very unlike the representative freedom of pure art. Architects too could play with the similarities. Lane Cottage at Ravenstonedale in Cumbria has an assemblage of Gothic elements built into it, and the resemblance to a plate of architectural details is made explicit by a signature mimicking that on an engraving: 'T. Hewitson del. W. Hodgson sculp.'[53]

Conservatism and conservation

The incorporation of fragments into both buildings and books could also be utilized for polemical purposes. John Clubbe was not the only member of his family to indulge in building activities. His son, the clergyman and poet William Clubbe, erected a polemical pyramid in his vicarage garden at Brandeston to protest at the radical alterations that had been carried out to Letheringham church in the 1780s, during which the chancel was demolished and many funeral monuments cleared away. Built of fragments salvaged from the ruins, and carrying four inscriptions, it complained:

FUIMUS.
Indignant Reader!
These Monumental Remains
Are Not
(As Thou Mayest Suppose)
The Ruins Of Time,
But
Were Destroyed In An Irruption Of The Goths
So Late In The Christian Era
As The Year 1789.
CREDITE POSTERI !!! [54]

William Clubbe's use of the word 'Goths' to condemn those who destroy Gothic architecture accentuates – probably deliberately – the ambivalence in usage which the satirists had helped establish, and which continued as late as 1789. He was not alone in erecting a folly to condemn folly. Around 1769, the antiquarian Bryan Faussett erected a pavilion to display a selection of objects rescued from the depredations of the ignorant, including such items as the stone cover of an ossuary, the rest of which had been shattered by the ploughshare and the clumsy hands of the ploughman. Each item had an inscription that devoted as much space to condemning philistinism as to explaining historical background; the pavilion was a convenient means of displaying antiquarian finds, but it also served as a reproach to the careless.[55]

Small engravings of fragments appeared as head- and tailpieces within a whole range of 18th-century books on classical remains, utilizing the aesthetic convention of bricolage to perform a service that was at once ornamental and illustrative. Sometimes, especially with books on Pompeii and Herculaneum, this was related to a degree of urgency about the publication itself. Where conservational techniques were seen to be inadequate or positively dangerous, it was necessary to record and diffuse information about the remains before they disappeared altogether; in such cases the illustrated fragments allude to a lost wholeness, but also to a crisis that may result in even those fragments vanishing.[56] Like the buildings described above, they illustrate a reproach. A generation earlier than William Clubbe, Stukeley had gone one further; a satirical woodcut ornament in *Abury* (1743) caricatured the farmer who destroyed megaliths to obtain building-stone.[57]

Books are usually meant to be published, whether in print form or not, and buildings are meant to be seen; and so, where either enshrines a polemical message, they represent two different media for the diffusion of opinion. Of the two, buildings would have had a more local impact, but one that would probably have extended further down the social scale once the criticism was explained; a vicarage was a social centre, and to illiterate or semi-literate villagers, a conspicuous building in a vicarage garden would have been more obviously intriguing than a book. Because of this, the similarity between the satirical statements of Stukeley and William Clubbe should not be overstressed; the very fact of criticisms residing in a book does much to limit their implied audience. By definition modern-day vandals were thought illiterate, since reading would have taught them to respect antiquity; and Stukeley — in theory at least — was safe from retaliation when he caricatured them. Garden buildings such as those erected by William Clubbe and Faussett were a different matter. Even on private property, they were more striking than books and could serve more effectively as a perpetual reproach: one local landmark lamenting the loss of another.

Philistine alterations were not an especial characteristic of the late 18th century, so much as a more educated consciousness of the Gothic. The climate was changing, and antiquarians benefited. The Suffolk antiquarian John Ives, though parodied under the name 'Curiosus' in 1771, was able to write only the next year: '. . . amidst the every kind of literary improvement that has been made, especially in these two centuries, the study of Topographical Antiquities has not been the least; . . . Their authors are no more represented as men of uncultivated minds, fit only to pore over musty records, or grovel amongst ruined walls, and their accounts are no longer considered as the dull effusions of pedantry, or the verbose disquisitions of folly.'[58]

This, however, was the orthodoxy of a later generation than John Clubbe's. In the reprint of *Wheatfield* in *Miscellaneous tracts*, Clubbe's spoof continues.[59] 'A Letter to the Author, and his Answer on the late Discovery of a piece of Antiquity' describes how workmen employed in a church discovered in a cavity of one of the stone pillars 'two small *paterae* of wood that exactly fitted each other, and had been closely cemented together, and covered over with what is strongly suspected to have been cloth', containing what appeared to be the muscular parts of the human heart, with a few linen rags. 'It was covered over, with what? by the illeterate[60] might be taken for either hair or wool; but when examined by adepts was found to be neither . . . some conjectured they might be the finer vessels of the human body, others imagined them the fibres of plants, &c.' (sig.F*2b). He proposes that it is a relic of Richard the Lionheart, brought back by Crusaders. This hairy heart stands as a bizarre emblem of antiquarians' relic-hunting, and their fondness for dignifying revolting objects with an illustrious and fanciful pedigree. Its visual success is yet another tribute to Hogarthian emblematic, but the conception of it combines dismissiveness with fear. Clubbe's attitude to church restoration is very unlike his son's.

Buildings and books can both embody visual jokes, and in the artefacts described above, this is turned to serious effect. In its seemingly lavish frivolity, its artfully exaggerated employment of visual convention and its placement within a real landscape, *Wheatfield* could be termed a bibliographical folly; but as with some architectural follies, the term is only half-accurate. John Clubbe's humorous book conceals surreal fears about the instability of meaning and truth against the forces of poor scholarship;

William Clubbe's humorous pyramid wards off the opposed nightmare, the cataclysmic depredations of those who know nothing. Satirists tend to be conservative, and so by comparing them in different generations one can get a sense of how conservatism changes; but this particular comparison of father and son illustrates something rather different, the late 18th-century transition from conservatism to conservationalism in the way that antiquarian study was regarded. Both men use and subvert the conventions of ornament and inscription, one for a book and the other for a building; but in a curious, almost oedipal reversal, the father attacks antiquarians and the son philistines.

It is only fair, though, that the last word should go to the maligned Morant. Antiquaries had one unassailable argument on their side, how it was by the process of scholarship that reputation was made and immortality secured. In satirical terms, it translated thus: Clubbe might mock antiquaries now, but his works would be ancient in time; and then, without the antiquarian species, his works would all be vain. The present author was very pleased to discover the following lines in *Laus Britanniae*, where Morant addresses Clubbe.

> Be not dismay'd; — I do foresee,
> Like yours, a Genius will arise;
> When your learn'd works are perish'd all,
> Will your great Name immortalize . . .
> Take comfort then, & easy be,
> For by Experience we learn.
> Your Works in Time will antient be,
> This truth we have from Thomas Hearne. (st.123, 125)

References

1. Of all the works that make up Robin Myers's varied *œuvre*, I have found her studies of antiquarians to be the most engaging; but even if some of her subjects might not have seen Clubbe's joke, I think she will. I am also pleased to be able to thank David Allen, Hugh Belsey (of Gainsborough's House), John Blatchly, Robert Elwall and Paul W. Nash (of the British Architectural Library), John Feather, Richard Goulden (of ESTC), Arnold Hunt, Giles Mandelbrote, David Stoker, Anne Templeton, Ruth Wallis, John Walwyn-Jones, Joy Wellings.

2. *Ancient Britons and the antiquarian imagination* (London: Thames & Hudson, 1989), pp.23, 150-2 (quotation p.23). A typical riposte to this prejudice comes in John Horsley's preface to *Britannia Romana* (1732), where he begs leave to 'remove a common objection' and gives a justification for inductive reasoning. 'A minute inquiry into particular circumstances of time and place, separately considered, may be looked upon as a matter of no great moment; and yet what is all chronology and geography but a collection of these, digested into a regular body? . . . Why then should it be thought a trivial matter to trace them out from antient monuments, when they contribute so much to the light and pleasure of history?' (p.ii). Horsley's defensiveness is particularly interesting in that Roman Britain was commonly seen as the most acceptable face of antiquarian study: see above.

3. Morant himself was soon to supersede Salmon by his *History and antiquities of the county of Essex* (published in 3 parts, 1763-6, and in 2 vols in 1768).

4. Essex R.O., Chelmsford (D/DU 546/2): antiquary's notebook of Sir Alfred Savill, including abstracts from Scott family MSS (the above quotation comes from Scott's letters, March 1764-January 1765).
5. 13 March 1758. Printed in *The letters of Thomas Gainsborough*, ed. Mary Woodall (Ipswich: Cupid Press, 2nd edn., 1963), p.63. In *Thomas Gainsborough in his twenties: a memorandum based on contemporary sources* (Colchester: the author, 3rd edn. 1993), pp.16-17, John Bensusan-Butt suggests that the letter was addressed not to Robert Edgar, as Woodall and previous scholars have thought, but to William Mayhew of Whatfield Hall.
6. An apparently unique copy of an octavo reprint of *Physiognomy* [London, 1765?] is held by Chicago University Library (shelfmark BF 840.C64).
7. Not in ESTC; the Beinecke copy is described in Tony Copsey & Henry Hallam, *Book distribution and printing in Suffolk* (Ipswich: Ipswich Book Company, 1994), no.486. This list of Clubbe's publications combines the ESTC listings with those in Copsey & Hallam.
8. I have discovered no letters written by Clubbe himself, and would be grateful for further information.
9. Issues of 24 June and 1 July 1758.
10. 'Ipswich: Printed by E. Craighton and W. Jackson, for J. Shave, at the Stationer's-Arms, in the Butter-Market; and sold by T. Longman, in Pater-noster Row, and C. Bathurst, in Fleet-Street, London; and by all other booksellers in town and country. 1765.' (Copsey & Hallam 483). *Pace* John Feather, *A history of British publishing* (London: Croom Helm, 1988), p.97, who remarks that the provincial trade 'provided a distribution system rather than becoming a rival producer'.
11. 'The History & Antiquities of the Antient Villa of Wheatfield', BL Add.MS 19,202 (ex David Elisha Davy; hereafter, 'Davy MS'), ff.121-52a (provenance details on f.152a). The attribution is Davy's, and, as well as the preface, there are a number of other additions to Clubbe's text in the footnotes. It seems never to have been printed.
12. Cf. ll.195-200, mentioning its additions as a device to make the reader pay twice over, and ll.265-8, 282-6, mocking *Colchester* for being unprofitable. The hudibrastic poem can perhaps be dated between 1765 and 1768 (the year *Colchester* was reprinted) if the following lines are to be taken literally:

    > On Rubrick Posts, when they shall spy
    > High pasted up in Ken of Eye,
    > Fam'd Wheatfield's Story turn'd to Verse,
    > Each Booby strait will ope his Purse . . .
    > Pray, what Impressions has it run?
    > This is the fourth 't has undergone;
    > While that of forty eight stands still at one. (l.273ff.)

    This is assuming that the writer knew about the Dublin edition (see next footnote), since *Miscellaneous tracts* is usually dated to around 1770.
13. *Fugitive pieces* was reprinted in 1765 and 1771, with a Dublin edition in 1762; *Wheatfield* was first identified as Clubbe's in *Miscellaneous tracts* (see above).
14. Davy MS, ff.153-61a. Davy attributes this poem to Myers too because he saw two copies in Myers's hand, one a rough sketch and the other neat, with the notes only present in the former. Myers may have copied both pieces while having written neither, or he may have written the versification of *Wheatfield* and made two copies of Morant's piece, one rough and one tidy. Davy's implication that Myers wrote both for and against Clubbe, though unlikely, is also not to be excluded; and so, another possibility is that he is indeed 'Morantia' (though the soubriquet seems far more likely to be a thin authorial disguise for Morant, and this is what has been assumed above). Myers may also have been 'Historicus', the author of the footnotes. See also *The East Anglian*, n.s. 4 (1891-2), p.224 (query from W. E. Layton).
15. See the letters in Essex R.O., Colchester (to Henry Whitridge, 1739-49, acc.no. C286, no.158); and Chelmsford (to William Bowyer and Charles Davis, 1746-52, D/DQS 33 & 34). Morant's habit is to draft his reply on the letter itself.

16. See also the beginning of Chapter 1, where Clubbe imitates Morant's precise notification of the town's latitude and longitude, and p.16, where he pokes fun at Morant's thinking it necessary to give the post-times.

17. E. J. Rudsdale, 'Morant's *Colchester*, 1798-1948', *Essex Review*, 58 (1949), pp.90-5 (quotation p.92).

18. BL Add.MS 37,219, f.106, 24 June 1758.

19. There is a general discussion of anti-antiquarian satire in Beverly Sprague Allen, *Tides in English taste (1619-1800)*, 2 vols (Cambridge, Mass.: Harvard University Press, 1937), vol.ii, ch.xv. See also Piggott, *Ancient Britons*, pp.14-18.

20. See Charles Kerby-Miller (ed.), *Memoirs of the extraordinary life, works, and discoveries of Martinus Scriblerus* (New Haven: Yale University Press, 1950); Joseph M. Levine, *Dr. Woodward's shield: history, science, and satire in Augustan England* (Berkeley: University of California Press, 1977), esp. ch.13.

21. The pun on 'Devizes' and 'division' suggested by the Latin title is probably intentional.

22. Cf. Morant's comments on the derivations of 'Colchester' and 'Maldon' (*Colchester*, pp.11, 15). Clubbe may also be alluding to dismissive summaries in guidebooks: John Kirby's *The Suffolk traveller* (1735) remarks that 'WHATTISFIELD, WOTFIELD OR WHEATFIELD [is] at present of no great remark, but for its excellent Seed Wheat' (p.132).

23. Morant discusses Vortigern (*Colchester*, Book I, ch.iv).

24. Cf. Davies, *Origines Divisianae*, pp.58-9.

25. Morant uses Anglo-Saxon type for Saxon names (e.g. Book I, pp.11, 15, 39).

26. One can speculate that the first edition might also have been published from London because of the technical demands which the satire imposed on the printer, though Dodsley's London reprints were constrained by the format of an anthology and are not much more impressive than William Jackson's in Ipswich.

27. Angus Ross & David Woolley (eds.), *Jonathan Swift. A Tale of a Tub and other works* (Oxford: Oxford University Press, 1986), p.49.

28. All Pope quotations are taken from Herbert Davis, ed., *Pope, poetical works* (Oxford: Oxford University Press, 1978).

29. *Ancient Britons*, p.27.

30. Writing to Morant about his descriptions of Roman government in *Colchester*, Bowyer commented 'But the Antiquarians will not regard this Branch of learning, because it looks too classical. They are more critical about things that are more Gothic or more monastical.' (Essex R.O. Chelmsford (D/DQS 34), p.41, letter dated 3 May 1748.)

31. Clubbe's *Physiognomy* is based on an idea from *The Dunciad*. I am grateful to the British Architectural Library for allowing reproductions from their copy of *Wheatfield*.

32. Mistakenly printed E. G. in the 1758 edition.

33. *The charlatanry of the learned*, trans. Francis E. Litz, ed. H. L. Mencken (New York & London: Alfred A. Knopf, 1937), pp.66-7, 72, 75.

34. Cf. the criticism of dedications in the preface of the versified *Wheatfield*, ll.310-77.

35. I am grateful to Giles Mandelbrote for pointing this out.

36. The more conventional woodcut ornaments in *Wheatfield* have not been located in the (incomplete) files of printers' ornaments held by the ESTC project. (I am grateful to Richard Goulden of ESTC for help on this point.) A brief checking of other Mary Cooper imprints has, however, located the headpiece of Apollo (f.A2a) in *Odes on several subjects* (London: printed for Robert Dodsley, sold by Mary Cooper, 1745), f.A3a (with a border and a visible crack on the left-hand side, both cut away by the time *Wheatfield* was printed); the ornament on f.D4a of *Wheatfield* also occurs at f.E3b. The Apollo headpiece recurs in Clubbe's *Physiognomy* (1753), f.A3a, so may have been specially requested by him on either occasion.

37. Ronald Paulson, ed., *Hogarth's graphic works*, 3rd edn. (London: Print Room, 1989), no.232. It was engraved by Luke Sullivan, who is also said to have engraved the frontispiece to Clubbe's *Physiognomy*; and Hogarth heralds the book in *Analysis*, p.109. Clubbe and

Gainsborough are among the subscribers to the *Method of perspective*; and, more unexpectedly, Kirby subscribed to *Colchester*.

38. Six years later Hogarth was to design the frontispiece for Kirby's *Perspective of architecture*: Paulson no.235 (engr. William Woollett).

39. Paulson no.242; John Nichols and George Steevens. *The genuine works of William Hogarth, illustrated with biographical anecdotes*, 3 vols (London, 1808-17), vol.i, pp.379-81.

40. This too was first presented as a puzzle: Hogarth describes how 'in the year 1745, [I] published a frontispiece to my engraved works, in which I drew a serpentine line lying on a painter's pallet, with these words under it, THE LINE OF BEAUTY. The bait soon took; and no Egyptian hierogliphic ever amused me more than it did for a time . . .' (*Analysis*, p.x). It appears again in the 'Tailpiece' (see below).

41. Cf. *Wheatfield* on 'Grave Rails': 'these are ill proportioned, and needlessly inform us of their Use, by confused Representations of Hour-Glasses, Scythes, Skulls and Skeletons' (p.26).

42. Stukeley and Morant were friends: see Stuart Piggott, *William Stukeley, an eighteenth-century antiquary*, 2nd edn. (London: Thames & Hudson, 1985), p.147.

43. Hogarth's own feelings on the moral efficacy of the line of beauty were more ambivalent: see Paulson no.231, who quotes *Paradise Lost*, IX, 516-18:
> So vary'd he, and of his tortuous train
> Curl'd many a wanton wreath, in sight of Eve,
> To lure her eye . . .

44. Paulson no.208, mentioning the allusion to Addison's essay on Time in a picture gallery (*Spectator*, no.83, 5 June 1711).

45. Paulson no.216. This was Hogarth's last engraving; its actual title, 'Tailpiece', again reminds us of the referential usefulness of bibliographical conventions. See also Paulson's discussion in *Breaking and remaking: aesthetic practice in England, 1700-1820* (New Brunswick: Rutgers University Press, 1989), pp.213-14.

46. Horace, *Ars Poetica*, l.143. In context it mocks grandiose beginnings to a work: 'non fumum ex fulgore, sed ex fumo dare lucem . . .'. It is probably also to be seen as a riposte to Morant's own epigraph: 'Labore et Patientiâ. What Profit hath a Man of all his Labour which he taketh under the Sun?' (Eccles. ch.i, v.2). Morant's later Horatian epigraph in *Laus Britanniae* is a riposte to Clubbe's (*Dignus laudari, Hae Nugae in seria ducent*) and the versified *Wheatfield* continues Clubbe's metaphor with a disarming quotation from Persius (*Dare pondus idonea fumo*). Conceivably, too, *Ex fumo dare lucem* could refer to a poem of William Stukeley's which praises pipe smoke for clearing the brain, also given this epigraph (Beinecke Library, Yale: Osborn MS c 371, ff.12-15a).

47. The references are to the Catholic theologian Jean Hardouin (1646-1729) and Conyers Middleton (1683-1750), who engaged in a controversy with Daniel Waterland on the historical accuracy of the Bible. Both men combined antiquarian interests with theological.

48. See Ronald Paulson, *Hogarth*, vol.i (Cambridge: Lutterworth, 1992), pp.319-27. The manuscript has been edited by Charles Mitchell (Oxford: Clarendon Press, 1952); the verse version was first published in the 1782 edition of John Nichols, ed., *Biographical anecdotes of William Hogarth*.

49. Gwyn Headley & Wim Meulenkamp, *Follies* (London: Jonathan Cape, 1990), p.116. The first two lines of the explanatory inscription at Gatton are translatable as: 'When the lots have been drawn, the urn remains. Let the well-being of the people be the supreme law.'

50. i.e. sheaves of corn.

51. The portion of the road now running along by the tithe-barn was traditionally called 'The Grotto' (information from Joy Wellings). The tithe-barn still stands.

52. The earliest description of it is in John Blatchly, ed., *A journal of excursions through the county of Suffolk, 1823-1844. David Elisha Davy* (Boydell Press/Suffolk Records Society: Woodbridge, 1982), pp.85-6. There are oak, yew and box trees in the surrounding garden.

53. Headley & Meulenkamp, *Follies*, p.381.

54. This, with the other inscriptions, is transcribed in Richard Gough, *Sepulchral monuments in Great Britain*, pt.ii, vol.i (1796), p.cccxxiii. See also John Blatchly, 'The lost and mutilated memorials of the Bovile and Wingfield families at Letheringham', *Proceedings of the Suffolk Institute of Archaeology*, xxxiii, pt.2 (1974), pp.168-94; a drawing of the monument by Isaac Johnson is reproduced as pl.xvii in the volume.

55. R. F. Jessup, 'The Faussett Pavilion', *Archaeologia Cantiana*, 66 (1953), pp.1-14, transcribes the inscriptions and suggests that the building may have been inspired by the display of Roman tombstones in the walls of The Hermitage, Higham. See also Stephen Bann, *The inventions of history* (Manchester: Manchester University Press, 1990), pp.111-15 (inscription reproduced p.112), and *Under the sign: John Bargrave as collector, traveler and witness* (Ann Arbor: Michigan University Press, 1994), pp.101-3.

56. I discuss this point in 'Publishing Pompeii: a study in cultural censorships', *Biblion*, 4:2 (1996), pp.17-34.

57. Piggott, *Stukeley*, pp.62, 94, pl.14.

58. Preface to Henry Swinden, *The history and antiquities of the ancient burgh of Great Yarmouth* (Norwich, 1772), f.π3a-b. See also Norman Scarfe, 'John Ives, F.R.S. & F.S.A., Suffolk herald extraordinary', *Proceedings of the Suffolk Institute of Archaeology*, vol.xxxiii (1976), pp.299-309; John Blatchly, 'John Ives parodied as *Curiosus* in 1771', *Proceedings of the Suffolk Institute of Archaeology*, vol.xxxvi, pt.1 (1985), pp.38-9. Piggott, *Ancient Britons*, ch.5, gives a more pessimistic view of antiquarian scholarship at this date, based on the state of prehistoric archaeology rather than Gothic.

59. The volume collates 8°: π1 (=N8?) A-E^8 F^4 F*^{8} Ff$^2 \approx ^4$ G-L^8 M^{4}N^8(-N8) O^4. The 'Letter' and 'Answer' run from F*1 to Ff2, suggesting it was an afterthought.

60. *Sic* (probably a joke).

Gentlemen, pirates, and really respectable booksellers: some Charleston customers for Lackington, Allen & Co.

JAMES RAVEN

ONE OF THE GREATEST honours to be avoided in the 18th-century book trade was appointment as London Bookseller to the Charleston Library Society. It was true that few colonial orders were as valuable as those received from the planters and slave traders of South Carolina. Nor were there many customers who could match their credit-worthiness. Less inviting, however, was the Charlestonian expectation of service. Transactions between London booksellers and provincial clients were problematic enough, but orders from the Charleston Library Society were frequently propelled by unrealistic hopes of overcoming the delays and uncertainties of transatlantic book traffic.

Despite formidable obstacles of cost, risk and time, the transatlantic book trade greatly expanded after about 1740. This was partly a result of the limited and unbalanced development of colonial printing, but partly also a consequence of the strength of the cultural and economic bonds of empire. In addition to early supply constraints and direct political prohibitions, American publishing was frustrated by the tenacity and adaptability of British mercantile and monopolistic trade practices. North American newspaper advertising and colonial booksellers' catalogues were used to retail London wares in a manner similar to provincial English practice (where local book printing was also handicapped by the dominance of the London trade system). For wealthy individual customers and institutions like the Charleston Library Society direct correspondence with London agents and booksellers continued well into the 19th century. Yet little was easy about such trade, however rich and famous the customers, and however expansive overseas literary commerce appeared to be.

In South Carolina, demand for new and expensive literature was sustained by the ostentatious wealth of the Charleston élite. All were eager for their flourishing port to be accepted as a great city of the Empire. The Library Society, founded by 17 young merchants and men-about-town in 1748, aspired to imitate the shelves of European learned societies. Under the title 'Et Artes trans Mare Currunt', the printed rules of the Library declared that

The advantages arising to mankind from learning are so evident, that all civilized societies, both ancient and modern, have ever given the greatest encouragement to the promotion of it, and ever held it in the highest veneration and esteem. . . Let any person of common consideration and humanity, take a serious view of the Indianinhabitants of this extensive continent, and it will be impossible for him to reflect without very mortifying sentiments, how little human nature uncultivated differs from the brute; on the other hand with what exalted pleasure will he contemplate the splendid figure which Great-Britain, the admiration and envy of the world, at present makes when compared with its rude and savage state in the days of Julius Caesar.[1]

In pursuit of these ideals the Library Society achieved a swift accumulation of both members and volumes. The 1770 Catalogue listed 184 folios, 115 quartos, 555 octavos and smaller volumes, and an additional 135 classical titles. By 1819 the Library commanded 280 members, 13,000 volumes, a capital in funded debt of $10,000 and a yearly income of $3,000.[2]

Only in its supply of booksellers was the success story dimmed. Appointments included some of the most distinguished and successful London traders of the age, but they rarely served long. The gentlemen members elected and then sacked their Booksellers with equal gravity and regularity. William Strahan, James Rivington, Thomas Durham, David Wilson, James Dodsley, James Fletcher, William Nicoll and John Stockdale were successively elected and dismissed as Bookseller to the Society. Charles Dilly simply ducked and refused appointment. Elections were solemnly recorded each January at an 'anniversary' general meeting of all members. Names of respectable booksellers were recommended by members with knowledge of the London book trade, many from their own contacts made when in London. Majestic letters were then sent across the Atlantic informing a usually unprepared bookseller of his appointment (and sometimes reappointment). Letters detailed not only the Society's orders, but also binding, labelling, shipping and packing requirements. Failure to understand a commission or to prevent a slow sea-passage usually brought a termination of business — and quite possibly some relief in London.[3]

Faced by orders containing conflicting or incomplete information, cancellations of previous requests already packed and shipped, and invitations to use careful judgment to order additional new works of good taste and importance, the Bookseller was often in an impossible position. The request to Strahan to purchase 'any pamphlets or papers of Character useful or entertaining' was, several booksellers later, qualified in the form: 'no Subject is excluded, which is either usefull or entertaining, at all times avoiding polemical Divinity in every shape, unless, particularly Ordered'.[4] Such issues were, of course, no new source of dispute in long-distance book ordering. The Library Company of Philadelphia (founded 1731), and bibliophiles like James Logan of the same city, employed book agents to avoid enslavement to a bookseller's ignorance or deceit.[5] The Charleston Library's Secretary was always ready to convey the belief of members that the Bookseller was lazy, exercising bad judgment or unloading unsaleable books. James Fletcher narrowly escaped dismissal in the January 1768 vote, after which he was informed that members 'were highly Offended at your remissness in Several Particulars (especially in sending out the Classics unlettered contrary to the full and clear Instructions given you by their late

Secretary)'. When the next year's anniversary meeting did indeed sack Fletcher, the Secretary warned William Nicoll, the new supplier: 'the late Bookseller not attending to the spirit of the above General Instructions, supplied the Society not only with all the unsaleable hawk of his Shop, but with many books about the size of Plays & Pamphlets & which being Sewed in Boards too were often doubly unfit to have places in our Library'.[6] Nicoll tried his best, before the long disruption (and cessation of book ordering) caused by the War of Independence. In 1785, however, within a year of trade resumption, he was told that 'if you wish to continue in your present Connection with the Society, it will be necessary to be more attentive to Directions'. In the next letter Nicoll was summarily dismissed because of 'the backwardness you seem to shew in serving'.[7] After brief reliance on the exiled Charleston bookseller (and former Library Society committee member) Robert Wells, in 1787, the Society turned to and then away from the pro-American John Stockdale for the year 1791-2.[8] His dismissal for incompetence — against which Stockdale sent an aggrieved protest — was followed by a new policy of employing a firm of general merchants, Bird, Savage and Bird, to collect orders from the supplier booksellers. For ten years the firm served the Society well, until, in the early months of 1801, it encountered business difficulties and declined trade.[9]

Reverting, therefore, to direct correspondence with a bookshop, the Charleston Library Society elected Lackington, Allen & Company its Bookseller in September 1801. The appointment lasted eight years — well above the average term — but ended, predictably, in acrimony and confusion. Lackington, Allen was successor to the extraordinary enterprise of James Lackington, who had first set up shop in London in 1774. Lackington's lively early career, notorious in his own day and much remarked upon since, has overshadowed the later years of Lackington, Allen, even though the firm survived until fire gutted its then Piccadilly premises in 1841.[10] The empire was built from remaindered books sold at discount, from large and rapid turnover, and originally from the controversial refusal of credit. In 1793 Lackington sold a quarter of his business to his former apprentice Robert Allen, before opening his 'Temple of the Muses' a year later, in a block of houses converted to a great shop and warehouse in Finsbury Square. Lackington finally retired in 1798, disposing of the remaining three-quarter shares to his cousin and also one-time apprentice, George Lackington.

The bookshop was now in its prime, commemorated in a well-known print (fig.1). In 1801, the year in which the Library Society first addressed the firm, the ten-year old Charles Knight was taken by his bookseller father to this great mecca of literature:

We enter the vast area, whose dimensions are to be measured by the assertion that a coach and six might be driven round it. In the centre is an enormous circular counter, within which stand the dispensers of knowledge, ready to wait upon the country clergyman in his wig and shovel-hat; upon the fine ladies in feathers and trains; or upon the bookseller's collector, with his dirty bag. . . We ascend a broad

Fig.1.

staircase, which leads to 'The Lounging Rooms,' and to the first of a series of circular galleries, lighted from the lantern of the dome, which also lights the ground floor. Hundreds, even thousands, of volumes are displayed on the shelves running round their walls. As we mount higher and higher, we find commoner books in shabbier bindings; but there is still the same order preserved, each book being numbered according to a printed catalogue. This is larger than that of any other bookseller's, and it comes out yearly.[11]

Most of these annual catalogues survive for the years 1787-1820 and chronicle the expanding business.[12] Copies of the 1787 catalogue could be bought at six other bookshops in London and Westminster, but also at Vowell's in Cambridge and Palmer's and Merrick's in Oxford.[13] By 1792 the catalogue claimed four London outlets and bookseller-agents at Cambridge, Oxford, Sherborne, Bath, Coventry, Bury, Plymouth, Norwich, Bristol, Newcastle and Edinburgh. The firm gained increasing respect, not least because of its width of stock. In 1801 the business was still growing with 800,000 volumes in 21,868 entries in an annual catalogue now 516 pages long.

It is nonetheless remarkable that in preference to more conventional booksellers, the Charleston Library Society should have approached the firm of Lackington, Allen early in the new century. James Lackington, who lived on until 1814, remained the subject of public discussion and the target of hostile satirical prints. Sketches mocked the firm's cheapness and ostentation. In 1795 Peter Pindar (John Wolcot) had been moved to produce an *Ode to the Hero of Finsbury Square*. Lackington's notorious autobiographical *Memoirs* went through many editions—one of which rests in the collection of the Library Society—and in 1804 the 'cobbler-turned-tycoon' published his extraordinary *Confessions*.[14] Both accounts presented a very different character from the booksellers of repute and distinction selected by the Society in their first decades.

The choice can be explained in several ways. First, the Library Society had moderated many—although, as we shall see, far from all—of its exacting demands. The stentorian tone of the Society's early letters weakened. The enforced use of Robert Wells, when relocated to London, and the subsequent *débâcle* with Stockdale had proved a turning-point. Reports by Wells—a former Society committee member—and by the Carolinaphile Bird, Savage and Bird, offered a sympathetic appreciation of the difficulties faced by London suppliers. At the same time, the London book trade now included businesses capable of dealing more efficiently with the book-search demands of overseas literary societies and libraries. Lackington, Allen presented itself as such a firm, and the breadth of its stock, together with the thoroughness of its cataloguing, must have impressed the Society. Moreover, booksellers elected by the Library Society were always required to collect books from other wholesalers, and very often from antiquarian dealers to complete orders. This, as Bird, Savage and Bird explained, had become very difficult and time-consuming for a single bookseller like Stockdale. Lackington, Allen's emporium was a different matter.

The redirection of the Library Society's London orders was also accompanied by changes in the type of literature requested. As the Society's President admitted to Bird, Savage and Bird in 1793, 'the bulk of the Catalogue [the Society's requirements] inumerates Books of much lighter reading than our last, but in a Society such as ours, we are obliged to consult all tastes and to have many books of mere amusement as well as books of instruction and science'.[15] But if 'Et Artes trans Mare Currunt' was forgotten, the amnesia was widespread. In 1801, the Secretary of the New York Society Library declared that 'the Taste of several of the Members of the Library is so much turned to the reading of novels that it will be absolutely necessary to have a supply of this kind of Books'.[16] The change suited Lackington, Allen's shelves and connections very well.

So it was that 'The Cheapest Bookstore in the World' came to serve the Charleston Library Society, and for the next eight years we are able to follow in some detail the course of the relationship through a surviving letterbook recording out-going and in-coming letters, orders, and accounts. Correspondence opened on 7 September 1801 with a letter from Charles Cotesworth Pinckney, Federalist vice-Presidential candidate in 1800 and soon to be the party's Presidential candidate in 1804 and 1808.[17] As President of the Charleston Library Society, Pinckney wrote to Finsbury Square enclosing a bill of transfer for £230 and explaining that because the Society had been 'informed of your Attention and Punctuality in the supply of your Customers, & of the reasonable rates at which you dispose of your Books, they have determin'd to purchase of you while they shall be satisfied with your mode of dealing such Books as they shall want'. As usual, there were many instructions and conditions. Pinckney asked to 'have such Books carefully packed up in strong cases and shipped to us in one of the first American Vessels bound for this port, apprizing us of the shipment by two or three other opportunities that we may make insurance here'. Finally, emphasizing the concern about slippage in literary tastes, he trusted that

you will adapt your selection to suit as well those who are fond of serious & erudite subjects as those who have to amuse themselves with light & trivial reading . . . and to apprize us of every new publication of considerable merit or importance which may appear in the various branches of literature — All books sent us must be bound and letterd — you will be able to learn at the Caroline Coffee House in Birchin Lane Cornhill what vessalls are ready to sail for this port; & you will be careful to forward our Books to this port & to no other.[18]

Lackington, Allen's reply to the Librarian and Treasurer, John Davidson, sent in February 1802, savoured the prospects ahead:

We flatter ourselves that the execution of this Order will meet the approbation of the Society as we have been very diligent in collecting the several Articles, many of which being out of print & scarce could only be procured with difficulty — The

Omissions are principally Novels & such as we trust are least anxiously wished; many of these however are now reprinting & will be sent with your next Order—The binding we think will be found both neat & durable — To our prices we have annexed those generally charged by the trade & from the comparison anticipate your favorable opinion. . . We have inclosed our New Catalogue, which with the Reviews will be found an adequate guide to the further selections.[19]

The reversion to ordering from a bookseller, however, reintroduced old tensions. In his first response, Davidson noted that the two cases of books arrived some ten days before the letter of explanation from Lackington, Allen, which then arrived 'by the way of New York'.[20] He reminded the firm of 'the propriety of accompanying every Shipment with a few lines by the same Vessell'. The booksellers also claimed difficulties. In September 1802 Lackington, Allen wrote in explanation of their quest for the ordered volumes of *Philosophical Transactions* — 'We have searched every Library in London & have also sent to Oxford and Cambridge without being able to meet with a Copy made up by the Abridgement. We have therefore ventured on sending an entire set, the finest we are confident that ever was seen: the price is £120 which is very reasonable, considering the scarcity & value of the Article—we have every reason to hope that the difference in charge will be amply compensated by the utility of the work & its ornament to your Library'.[21] Whatever the truth of this argument, it must also have seemed like a familiar bookseller's ploy.

More telling was the emphasis that the credit-only Lackington, Allen gave to punctuality of payment and that the Library Society gave to the turn-round time of the transaction. Both concerns depended on book collection and packing times, the information available in London about departing ships, and the transatlantic conditions of weather and foreign hostilities. The swiftest passage from London to Charleston was about 32 days, but much more common was a sailing such as that of the ship *Montezuma* which left Gravesend 8 March 1802 and arrived at Charleston 64 days later.[22] Many Charleston members were ship-owners themselves or were related to the sea captains. The letter from the Library Society was usually written only a day or two before its carrier sailed. Davidson seems to have expected Lackington, Allen to have matching knowledge of when the ships sailed from London and also to be able to complete an order within the three weeks or so to enable the books to go back on the ship which carried the order. In July 1804 Davidson wrote that 'On the return of Capt[n] M[c]Neill to this Port the Society was much disappointed in not receiving a part at least of the Order transmitted by him'.[23] In the same month, Lackington, Allen are writing defensively that 'the return of Capt[n] M[c]Neill was so sudden that tho' the Order was put in hand immediately we were not in time for him: ever since which the books have lain pack'd waiting a vessel for Charleston direct'.[24]

Successive letters issued minor warnings about the firm's conduct, but, nearly four years after Lackington, Allen's appointment, broader hostilities brought the first real crisis. On 2 June 1805 the Library Society's large winter consignment was 42 days out from Gravesend and virtually within sight of Charleston when its journey was arrested. As the *Charleston Gazette* reported five days later:

It is with sincere regret we inform our readers that on Wednesday evening last, the regular trading ship Two Friends, capt M'Neil, from London, was captured when within a few miles of our bar, by the French privateer which has been cruising in the offing since Saturday last.

The privateer *Emerance* from Guadaloupe sailed under French letters of marque during the second year of renewed war between Britain and France. She carried seven guns and a total crew of 97. According to the Charleston newspapers the *Two Friends* was seized because she had no certificate from the American consul declaring her or her cargo to be American property. Neil McNeil, the cook and two boys were detained aboard, but the gentlemen passengers and the remainder of the crew were allowed to take the pilot boat to Charleston. On landing they reported the intention of the privateers to sail the *Two Friends* to Guadaloupe or Cuba.[25]

It was a catastrophe. The *Charleston Courier* of 7 June estimated that the full cargo was worth between £80,000 and £100,000, and observed that its plunder

has produced a sensation in this city of a stronger kind than any that has been felt for several years. . . The cargo of the Two Friends was composed of a considerable part of the Spring and Summer supply of Goods for this State – none other being expected till the Fall. . .

As a further report exclaimed, 'by the daring and piratical proceeding of a small picaroon, is our port completely blockaded, and our citizens wantonly robbed of their property!'[26]

The literary loss was especially severe. It included 13 trunks of books from Lackington, Allen containing the Library Society's books (worth a little over £170), but also a special order to supply a library and some scientific instruments to the South Carolina College at Columbia. The College order charged to Judge William Johnson was valued at over £970.[27] In addition, were 2,000 letters in the ship's bag 'all of which were detained by the Frenchman'.[28] The newspapers, with knowing political bias, proclaimed disgrace:

What must the nations of the world think of a country whose commerce extends all over the globe, insulted in all its ports by paltry privateers. . . It is said by some that America could not in many years build a navy able to cope with that of England – True; but it might build enough to make the country respected, in its harbours, to repress those paltry aggressions, which are disgraceful to us in proportion to their smallness.[29]

Moreover, although redress was unexpectedly at hand, the assistance was not American. First, the *Emerance*, together with two of her prize vessels, were captured by a British frigate early in July.[30] Then the British brigantine *Hunter* recaptured the *Two Friends* off Barracoa, and escorted her to Jamaica, with McNeil restored to command.[31] The *Two Friends* arrived at Kingston on 9 July, news reaching Charleston three weeks later. Documents certifying the ship and cargo as American property were then immediately sent to Jamaica. There the Admiralty Court had ordered the *Two Friends* and her cargo to be sold, to ascertain their value before salvage compensation was paid to the British recaptor. As part of this it was publicly reported that

Captain McNeil, having been deprived of all his papers, it became requisite, in order to get at the invoices, to open the greater part of the letters. This was to the navy agents a very disagreeable duty, but absolutely indispensable; and you may assure the parties that every scrupulous delicacy was observed, that was possible in such a case — not a single letter of them was read: the invoices were taken out of such as contained any, and the letters were instantly sealed again. One letter only is retained, that being written on the back of an invoice, could not be separated from it. The invoice appears to be from *Lackington* to judge Johnson, of articles for the South Carolina College.[32]

McNeil bought back the *Two Friends* in the Jamaica sale, and the ship and the books for the Library Society and the College finally arrived at Charleston under British naval convoy on 13 October.[33] By this time, the capture of the *Two Friends* had become a political *cause célèbre* up and down the East Coast. Many had been ready to question the exact ownership of the *Two Friends* and to explain the pained outrage as Federalist trouble-making. If Charlestonians had risked their cargoes on what were in reality British-owned ships, then they had to take the consequences. This was certainly the argument carried in the New York *Farmer's Register* and reprinted in the *Baltimore Evening Post*, denouncing the 'virulence' of the *Charleston Courier*, asserting that the *Two Friends* was London-owned, and concluding that 'sailing under the American flag is a mere cover to save risks'. The Federalists, led by the President of the Library Society, were accused of seeking vengeance against Jefferson (Pinckney had commanded only 14 electoral votes in 1804).[34] All this was refuted during the summer in the Charleston newspapers, notably by William Boyd, merchant of Charleston, and William Muir, the former part-owners of the ship who confirmed their American citizenship (at least since 1793) and the sale of the ship to Captain McNeil in 1799.[35]

Lackington, Allen were therefore unlikely to have remained ignorant for long about the fate of the *Two Friends*,[36] but it was only with the new winter order, conveyed by the redoubtable Captain McNeil himself in late December 1805, that the Library Society informed its booksellers of the events of the summer. The immediate concern was clear. As Davidson explained it, the Society's consignment 'was retaken & carried into Jamaica where it was exposed to public Sale & bought in . . . [by Captain McNeil] for the Society, as will appear from a certified copy of his Acc^t.' To reclaim the costs of buying back the books, the Library Society demanded full compensation from the £150 of their order that was insured from the underwriters engaged by Lackington, Allen. The South Carolina College pursued a similar claim for £950.[37]

The episode reaffirmed the importance of insurance. During the 18th century the effective charge on transatlantic insurance was lowered by between 10% and 15% with coverage increasing to within 1% or 2% of the loss. From the 1720s, rates on most crossings fell to a peace-time levy of 2%. This was a consequence of changes to business organization, economies of scale in inventorying, and later, the development of credit institutions. An apparent decline in piracy also contributed to more attractive terms.[38] With the decline in risks, crew sizes were also reduced, further cutting carriage costs. The insurance taken out on packages sent by the London bookseller, John Murray, to his customer Robert Miller in Williamsburg in the 1770s averaged just over 2% on each shipment. In the same decade the insurance bill for the much larger book cargoes sent by Thomas Longman to Henry Knox, bookseller of Boston, also claimed 2% of total charges.[39]

Nevertheless, insurance rates remained unpredictable and the outbreak of hostilities brought sudden hikes in charges. During the war years, 1757-8, the books sent to the New York Society Library by its bookseller, John Ward, were covered by an insurance which amounted to 16% of the total invoice.[40] During the American war British insurance rose again by 23%. For one of the small orders sent in 1772 Murray was forced to charge Miller 4% for the insurance, but in mid-1774 the London bookseller William Nicoll was only able to insure the order for the Charleston Library Society at 11.5%, much to the dismay of the committee.[41] Insurance rates were also volatile during the 1790s. Bird, Savage and Bird arranged an acceptable insurance costing 2% of the total charge to the Library Society in 1796, but a year earlier the charge had been 5%. The returns on claimed insurance also varied greatly, but it was rare for the bookseller or customer to recoup all losses. Judging by the complaints of others, Jeremy Condy, bookseller of Salem, was relatively fortunate in 1762 to recover £97 10s from his insurance on £100 of books carried in the *Lucretia* by Captain Green 'who was taken'.[42]

In Pinckney's opening letter of 1801, the Charleston Library Society excused Lackington, Allen from the task of securing insurers, but Davidson quickly reversed this and demanded the inclusion of insurance from the next order onwards.[43] Much in line with all the early Lackington, Allen invoices, the combined charge for insurance and duty paid on the confiscated cargo of 1805 was 3%. This, however, was taken out for £150 only of the total consignment value of £170 15s 11d. After the *débâcle* Davidson instructed Lackington, Allen in December 1805 'that in future Insurance may be made in full so as to cover the premium & all charges'.[44]

More aggravating than the uninsured portion, however, was the time that it took to settle with the underwriters. In June 1806, six months after the Library Society's instructions reached London, Lackington, Allen reported that the underwriters had not yet paid out but that at least 'we are now in expectation of the produce of the Sale being remitted from Jamaica'.[45] The 13 trunks of books for the Library Society and South Carolina College were sold for a little over £1,058 Jamaican; but from this the brokers, Tunno, deducted one third of the remittance, or just over £354 Jamaican to cover 'landing charges, public sale expences, Brokers, Agents & Registers Commissions, Salvage – 12½ p'Cent to Recaptors, Proctors Accounts, Premium on Bills 10 p'Cent'.[46] The total returned was £703 12s 10d Jamaican or £502 12s sterling. A year later, payment had still not been received from the underwriters, who, according to Lackington, Allen 'made many objections principally as to the sale & re-purchase at Jamaica which we have had to combat – these we believe are now done away with & the delay is occasion'd by their refusal to allow the heavy commissions & charges which the agents have put on them'.[47]

The settlement was finally made in August 1807, but by 14 November, when a new order was sent, the Library Society remained ignorant of its details.[48] These were not pleasing. 'We regret to find', wrote Lackington, Allen, 'that a loss tho small will fall on your Acc.' arising partly from the Policy not covering the whole amount of Invoice & partly from a refusal on the part of the Underwriters to admit the enormous charges on acc.' of Sale in Jamaica, as well as home expences. We have had great difficulty in bringing the matter to an issue; & after advising with our sollicitor, we thought it more to your interest to refer the affair to an arbitrator than adopt legal measures'.[49] The total claim against the insurers was for the £1,100 of the full loss of £1,149 5s 5d for the combined Library Society and South Carolina College books, excepting the total of £502 12s returned from the Jamaican sales. This last was reduced (and the insurance claim therefore increased) by a total claim against charges in London of £45 13s 10d, which included a proportion of the charge of sending pilot boats to Havana and Jamaica in search of the *Two Friends* and with documents to prove the neutrality of the cargo (£8 12s 4d), small brokers' and postage charges (£11 18s 10d), and Tunno's 5% commission (£25 2s 8d). It was this last commission that the underwriters would not accept.

Resentments hardened when another familiar grievance surfaced. Engraved and coloured plates were highly esteemed by the Library Society members, and many expensively illustrated botanical, natural history, topographical and travel volumes were the pride of the collection. On board the seized *Two Friends* was a keenly awaited copy of Thomas Holcroft's *Travels*.[50] When the consignment eventually reached Charleston, Davidson wrote to confirm that all 'arrived in good Order, but I must inform you that the Plates which should have accompanied Holcroft's Travels were omitted to be sent'.[51] In response Lackington, Allen argued that 'the volume of

Plates to Holcroft was assuredly packed, & we imagine, if you have not yet found it, that it must have been taken out & not replaced, either by the Captors or Recaptors'. The riposte did not go down well. Now some two years since the Holcroft was originally ordered, Davidson insisted that 'some mistake must have taken place with regard to the Plates for Holcroft, as the Packages had never been opened 'till deliver'd here when I took out the contents with my own hands'.[52] In April 1807 the London booksellers surrendered: 'As to the plates of Holcroft we cannot account for them being missing: we will however endeavour to procure another set'.[53]

In Charleston incompetence and obstinacy now seemed to accompany interminable delays for the latest publications from London. Library Society frustration turned to real anger, however, when not only its books and journals but also acknowledgements of payments and orders failed to arrive. Between August 1807 and March 1809 the Librarian heard nothing from Lackington, Allen, and therefore had no advance notice of whether any of the Society's books were carried by the vessels that did arrive at Charleston — or by those that were reported as lost or captured.

It might be argued that the Library Society was once again assuming that it could ignore worldly realities. Britain and France were still at war, and American vessels were especially disrupted by the Berlin Decree and the retaliatory Orders-in-Council of 1806. Within months, one attack too many led to the American Nonimportation Act against Britain and then the deeply unpopular Embargo Act of December 1807, suspending all commerce with the rest of the world. Although Pinckney, the Federalist candidate (and the Library Society's President), lost the American Presidential election of 1808, he benefited greatly from an anti-Jeffersonian resurgence. It contributed to the replacement of the 'dambargo' by a Nonintercourse Act in March 1809, but this still prohibited trade with Britain and France. There was, perhaps, a certain helplessness about the last closing courtesy from Lackington, Allen assuring Davidson 'that no change of circumstances affecting the amity of our countries (which would be deeply lamented here) will affect our situation with you'.[54]

By November 1808 patience in Charleston had worn thin. Davidson wrote to Finsbury Square:

It is now fully Twelve Months since I wrote you by the Ship Caledonia, Henderson, inclosing an Order for Books & the 1st of Exchange for £220 — Soon afterwards I forwarded a duplicate with the 2d of Exchange. — The Society feels much hurt & disappointed in neither having received the books, nor even an acknowledgement of the receipt of the Bills. — The Montezuma arrived here lately from London & another vessel is said to be daily expected, an opportunity of which it is hoped you have not neglected to avail yourselves. A new Order has been in readiness for some time but will not be forwarded till the receipt of the former.[55]

In the following March Lackington, Allen wrote to express surprise that their earlier receipt had not yet reached Charleston, and to insist that the books had been collected and packed although 'the only vessel our broker has apprised us of for Charleston direct . . . suddenly changed her destination, in consequence we imagine of the uncertain state of American Affairs. Since that time no vessel has sailed either from London or Liverpool for your port'.[56] By then, however, the new President of the Library Society, Henry William DeSaussure, had written to John Hopton, a leading London Carolina merchant and member of the Society,[57] noting that 'considerable sums of money' had been sent to Lackington, Allen for some years. The firm 'have had an Order for Books for nearly a Year & a half, which they have not complied with' and, since November 1807, 'a Bill of Exchange for £220 on Mess[rs] Harrison, the payment of which they have never acknowledged, tho' we have learnt collaterally that the Money has been paid them — Having behaved thus improperly, the Society have resolved to change their Correspondent.'[58] Hopton was asked to reclaim the outstanding balance from Lackington, Allen and

to retain the same in your hands until the commercial intercourse between Great Britain & America, now unhappily interrupted, shall be restored; & upon that event to cause a shipment to be made by some eminent bookseller on whom reliance can be placed. . . We should be glad to establish a regular correspondence with some really respectable & exact Bookseller whom you could recommend to us & beg that you would make such recommendation.

DeSaussure had no objection to Lackington, Allen completing the last order but he was clear that it would be their last: 'We know that this is a bad course in the unsettled state of affairs between the two countries, but it is better than bringing a suit for the recovery of it'.[59]

Two months later, in May 1809, the Library Society contacted a domestic supplier. Until then, the Society had appeared resolute in depending directly on London booksellers, even though New York, Boston, and Philadelphia wholesalers were now the main and often cheaper suppliers of London-imported books to American customers, and increasingly of American publications and reprints.[60] Davidson wrote to William W. Woodward of Philadelphia who was importing books from London as well as dealing in American imprints.[61] Davidson ordered $302 worth of books. In response, Woodward commended his new shipment of books from London — testimony to the poor enforcement of the Nonintercourse Act — offering to search through this for any books that he was unable to supply to date, but warning that 'if any should have been imported they will be extravagantly dear'.[62] The Librarian was horrified by the new charges, replying that 'as the Books from London come so high you will please to stop sending any more of that description'.[63]

From London meanwhile, John Hopton replied first to his Charleston brother-in-law, Nathaniel Russell, and then directly to the President and Vice-President of the Library Society, recommending that its affairs be entrusted to the general commercial firm of Goldingham.[64]

In future their Order for books & remittances to pay for them be sent to him, so that ho may take care to have them shipped in due time, d° the Custom House business, pay the duty, make the Insurance & forward the Invoice & Bill of Lading — All this part of the mercantile business is quite foreign to a Bookseller: from this cause arose the disappointment which the Society have just now experienced — to them, his trifling commission of £8 or £10 pr Ann: can't be any object, & in return for which their business will be faithfully & punctually executed.[65]

Of Goldingham, Hopton assured them, 'disappointment won't again occur — the books will be sent by the very first conveyance, but when, is not fixed; the amount of the first cost will exceed your balance about £100 which he will advance, besides the duty, freight &c — hence the whole will go on equal terms & prevent any more, already too long, delay'.[66]

After eight troubled years of service, a bookseller was for the second time rejected for a general mercantile firm. Hopton further reported on a visit he made to Lackington, Allen: 'I hinted that Interest should be allow'd on the Balance they held, to which they object, in my opinion without reason.' The firm had also 'protested their innocence' about the ship that had been sailing for Charleston a month before — an ignorance 'which I can readily believe as they are mere booksellers'.[67] In the same month, Lackington, Allen managed to send another letter defending their conduct and insisting that although they would now obey Hopton's instructions to deliver the books for shipment to Goldingham, 'it cannot expedite the business since it is a ship only that is wanting & that we shall ourselves make every search for, since we trust it must be evident to every person that the delay is as detrimental to our interest as to your convenience.'[68] In late August the firm reported that Goldingham had duly shipped their books to the Library Society and that they 'therefore anxiously solicit a return of your good opinion which from this unpleasant affair we shall undertake unusual care to preserve'.[69] It was not to be. Lackington, Allen's correspondence with the Library Society ceased, ending also this rare chronicle of long-distance ordering.

Despite the abrupt if familiar end to the trade, Lackington, Allen & Co. profited from service as the Society's *de facto* monopoly supplier at a period of relative decline in the general transatlantic book trade. Although credit services and supply and marketing expertise improved during the second half of the 18th century, imperfect information and transport and transaction costs had always threatened to make transatlantic trade unviable — and certainly did so once the handicapped domestic printing industry reached an effective stage of development at the turn of the 19th century. Many London booksellers had their fingers burned by the American trade. Creditors were greatly disadvantaged by distance, and pricing arrangements by the London trade offered little incentive to enlarge transatlantic commerce.[70] The evidence from John Murray's surviving correspondence and business records, for example, is that his relatively small colonial trade was hardly worth it.[71] English client-booksellers were notorious for holding long credit and being unresponsive to demands, yet not only did American booksellers and customers hold credit at 3,000 miles' distance but their attempts to pay were often unsuccessful and in some cases less than serious.[72] Similarly, many colonial booksellers and general merchants dealing in books found the import trade to be unpredictable and difficult. Both smaller traders and individual customers were also disadvantaged by economies of scale, and were more likely to count the cost of transport. This was particularly so given the constant risk of loss and the volatility of insurance rates.

The progress of Lackington, Allen's Charleston business exemplified the bifurcation of the American market between a continuing supply of high-quality books to élite customers or isolated communities, and, as American publishing and wholesale and retail networks advanced, the diminution of broad and cheap book supply to colonial booksellers. Other major American libraries, notably the Library Company of Philadelphia, also persisted with direct London suppliers. Its committee, like that of the New York Society Library, conducted its affairs through long-established agents.[73] In much the same way, the Charleston Library Society resolved to continue to elect a London Bookseller and ignore the possibility of ordering books through a Philadelphia or New York wholesaler. When, in June 1809, Hopton wrote to the President and the Vice President of the Library Society, he suggested that 'if you continue resolved to change your correspondent, I recommend to your attention Mess[rs] F. C. & J. Rivington, who as well as their Father & Grandfather, were Booksellers on the same site, St Pauls Church Yard, for about a Century, & are undoubtedly as respectable as any in that trade'. He added that the Rivington's prices were slightly higher than those of some booksellers, but that they supplied high-quality goods.[74] The irony, of course, was that their great-uncle, until declared incompetent, had previously served as one of the elected respectable Booksellers of the Library Society. How long the Rivingtons stayed the course this time is not known.

References

1. *The Rules and By-Laws of the Charlestown Library Society: Together with the Act of the General Assembly of South-Carolina for Incorporating the Society, Confirmed by his Majesty* (Charlestown, 1762), pp.iii-iv. I am greatly indebted to the Librarian, Miss Catherine Sadler, and the staff of the Charleston Library Society for assistance in the preparation of this paper. Library Society materials are reproduced here with their generous permission.
2. J. L. E. W. Shecut, *Shecut's Medical and Philosophical Essays: Containing: 1st Topographical, Historical and Other Sketches of the City of Charleston* (Charleston, 1819), p.41.
3. Booksellers' appointments: William Strahan to 1756; James Rivington 1756-9; Durham and Wilson 1760-4; Robert Dodsley 1764 (but already deceased); James Dodsley 1765-6; James Fletcher 1766-9; William Nicoll 1769-74, 1783-5; Charles Dilly 1786 (who declined); Robert Wells 1787-9; John Stockdale 1791; Bird, Savage and Bird 1792-1801; Lackington, Allen & Co. 1801-9. Of these, Rivington (serving until his bankruptcy in 1759) was apparently a controversial choice, but he is unfairly assessed by Strahan (his CLS predecessor) in the well-known Strahan–Hall correspondence. The early history is discussed in James Raven,

London Booksellers and American Customers: The Transatlantic Booktrade and the Correspondence of the Charleston Library Society, 1758-1812 (forthcoming, 1998).

4. Charleston Library Society Letterbook, 1758-1812, Robert Brisbane (CLS) to James Rivington, 10 Aug. 1758, William Mason (CLS) to James Fletcher, 27 May 1767 [letters 1 and 17; hereafter letters numbered as in Raven, *London Booksellers and American Customers*].

5. Edwin Wolf 2nd, *The Library of James Logan of Philadelphia 1674-1751* (Philadelphia: Library Company of Philadelphia, 1974); and in particular, Logan to John Whiston, 27 July 1748, copy, Hist. Soc. Pennsylvania, Logan Papers, Letterbook 1748-50, f.5.

6. Jno. Colcock (CLS) to Nicoll, 9 Mar. 1769 [letter 21]. Fletcher was informed of his dismissal in a letter sent the same day [letter 20].

7. John McCall (CLS) to Nicoll, 6 Aug. 1785 [letter 37]; McCall to Nicoll, 14 Jan. 1786 [letter 39].

8. Stockdale's American contacts are discussed in Eric Stockdale, 'John Stockdale of Piccadilly: Publisher to John Adams and Thomas Jefferson', in Robin Myers and Michael Harris, eds., *Author/Publisher Relations during the Eighteenth and Nineteenth Centuries* (Oxford: Oxford Polytechnic Press, 1983), pp.63-87.

9. Stockdale to CLS, 14 Sept. 1792 [letter 53]. Henry M. and Robert Bird and Benjamin Savage (the latter the son of John Savage, merchant of Charleston and later London exile). A leading firm in Anglo-Carolinan trade, the partners finally failed after the Peace of Amiens, March 1802, stopped payments in Feb. 1803 and were declared bankrupt five months later — see George C. Rogers Jr, *Evolution of a Federalist: William Loughton Smith of Charleston (1758-1812)* (Columbia SC: University of South Carolina Press, 1962), pp.99, 203, 273-5, 355.

10. Charles Knight, *Shadows of the Old Booksellers* (London: Bell and Daldry, 1865), pp.282-99; George Paston [pseud.], *Little Memoirs of the Eighteenth Century* (London and New York: Grant Richards and E. P. Dutton, 1901), pp.205-34; Richard G. Landon, 'Small Profits do Great Things: James Lackington and Eighteenth-Century Bookselling', *Studies in Eighteenth-Century Culture*, 5 (1976), pp.387-9; and others listed in James Raven, 'Selling One's Life: James Lackington, Eighteenth-Century Booksellers and the Design of Autobiography', in O. M. Brack Jr, ed., *Writers, Books and Trade: An Eighteenth-Century English Miscellany for William B. Todd* (New York: AMS Press, 1994), pp.1-23 (notes 33-5). In 1827 the firm moved to 4 Pall Mall East; it variously changed partners and was finally Harding, Triphook and Lepard.

11. Knight, *Shadows of the Old Booksellers*, p.283.

12. The British Library and Cambridge University Library hold annual catalogues, 1787-9, 1792-4, 1796-1811, 1814, and 1817-20.

13. *Second Part of Lackington's Catalogue for 1787: Consisting of About Thirty Thousand Volumes*, p.1.

14. Landon, 'Small Profits do Great Things', p.387; James Lackington, *Memoirs of the Forty-Five First Years of the Life of James Lackington* (London, 1791), dedicated to 'sordid and malevolent booksellers'; and *The Confessions of J. Lackington, Late Bookseller, at the Temple of the Muses, In a Series of Letters to a Friend* (London, 1804).

15. C. C. Pinckney to Bird, Savage and Bird, 17 Apr. 1793 [letter 57].

16. NYSL archives, Keep papers, J[ohn] Forbes, draft of a letter for the Purchasing Committee, to Revd John M. Mason, Glasgow, 1 Oct. 1801. I am indebted to Sharon Brown, NYSL, for her assistance in locating this.

17. The new parties developed largely from conflicts over Alexander Hamilton's financial and political aspirations. The anti-Hamiltonians or Republicans, now led by Jefferson, were opposed by the Federalists, favouring greater industrialization. Both parties soon drew upon complex geographical and sectional support. The southern Pinckneys balanced the more natural Federalism of the north (which by 1800 had lost its vitality). For a general account see Maldwyn A. Jones, *The Limits of Liberty: American History 1607-1980* (Oxford: Oxford University Press, 1983), pp.81-105.

18. C. C. Pinckney to Lackington, Allen [hereafter LA] 7 Sept. 1801 [letter 84].
19. LA to John Davidson, 15 Feb. 1802 [letter 86].
20. Davidson to LA, 12 June 1802 [letter 87].
21. LA to Davidson, 26 Sept. 1802 [letter 88]. Their concern is repeated, 20 Nov. [letter 89]. The 1811 *Catalogue of the Charleston Library Society*, p.134, lists 'Philosophical Transactions at Large', 91 vols, 4to.
22. *Charleston Gazette and Daily Advertiser* [hereafter *CG*] 24 Apr. and 22 May, 1802.
23. Return reported, after passage of 49 days, *CG*, 25 June 1804; Davidson to LA, 16 July 1804 [letter 97].
24. Given the recorded passage of 49 days to Charleston, McNeil must have left London 7 May 1804. He had left Charleston for London 30 Jan. An above-average passage of 65 days would have seen McNeil in London in the first week of April, giving a London docking period of 3-4 weeks. LA to Davidson, 20 July 1804 [letter 98].
25. *CG* and *Charleston Courier* [hereafter *CC*], 7 June 1805.
26. *Poulson's American Daily Advertiser*, 18 June 1805.
27. William Johnson (1771-1834), Judge of the SC Court of Common Pleas 1798-1804, Associate Justice of the US Supreme Court from 1804, and an early trustee of the college (later University of South Carolina), established by State Act in 1801 with a capital of $50,000 and an annual grant of $6,000. See Daniel Walker Hollis, *University of South Carolina*, 2 vols (Columbia SC: University of South Carolina Press, 1951-6), 1: 22-6. I am indebted to Robert Leath for clarification here.
28. *CC*, 7 June 1805.
29. *CC*, 7 June 1805.
30. Report from Savannah, *CG*, 15 July 1805.
31. Report dated 20 July from Charleston, in *Poulson's*, 2 Aug. 1805.
32. Report from Kingston dated 18 July, in a report from Charleston, dated 1 Aug., reprinted in *Poulson's*, 16 Aug. 1805; and Extract of a Letter from Kingston (Jamaica) received at Charleston 13 July 1805, in *The Political and Commercial Register*, 15 Aug. 1805.
33. *CG*, 30 July and 14 Oct. 1805.
34. See above, note 17.
35. *CC*, 31 July; *CC*, 1 Aug. and *CG*, 2 Aug. 1805.
36. The firm had not been informed by 6 July 1805 when writing to express the hope that the winter order had arrived 'in safety & we rely on its having given satisfaction'.
37. Davidson to LA, 24 Dec. 1805 [letter 103]; account enclosed with LA to Davidson, 5 Aug. 1807 [letter 107].
38. Gary M. Walton and James F. Shepherd, *The Economic Rise of Early America* (Cambridge: Cambridge University Press, 1979), pp.89-90.
39. Murray Archives, Albemarle Street, John Murray I Letterbooks 3 (Feb. 1771-Apr. 1773), 4 (Apr. 1773-Nov. 1774) [various entries] and Day Book, f.384 (July 1773); Massachusetts Historical Society, Henry Knox Papers 1719-1825, 56 vols, vol.48 [invoices from Thomas Longman].
40. NYSL Archives, First Minute Book 1754-72, f.29, 27 Mar. 1758 (order arrives) invoice copy (27 Sept. 1757) f.30.
41. Colcock to Nicoll, 10 Aug. 1774 [letter 31].
42. American Antiquarian Society, Condy Account Book, 1758-70, f.57, 29 Oct. 1762.
43. Davidson to LA, 12 June 1802 [letter 87].
44. Davidson to LA, 24 Dec. 1805 [letter 103].
45. LA to Davidson, 20 June 1806 [letter 104].
46. Tunno and Loughnan were regularly used by the Library Society as brokers for bills of exchange. John Tunno, a loyalist, had moved from Charleston to London. The firm were merchants of 3 New Court, Swithin's Lane, London, listed in *The Post Office Annual Directory* (1802) and *Holden's Triennial Directory* 4th edn. (1808), 2 vols. In Charleston, Eleazer Elizer, *A Directory for 1803* (Charleston, 1803), p.58, lists four Tunnos, including merchants Tunno and Price.

47. LA to Davidson, 20 Apr. 1807 [letter 106].
48. LA to Davidson, 5 Aug. 1807 [letter 107]; Davidson to LA, 14 Nov. 1807 [letter 108].
49. LA to Davidson, 5 Aug. 1807 [letter 107].
50. The exact title was not specified but it was probably Holcroft's recent *Travels from Hamburg through Westphalia, Holland, and the Netherlands to Paris*, 2 vols (London, 1804), rather than his earlier *Travels through Germany*, 2 vols (1796-7).
51. Davidson to LA, 24 Dec. 1805 [letter 103].
52. Davidson to LA, 12 Jan. 1807 [letter 105].
53. LA to Davidson, 20 Apr. 1807 [letter 106].
54. LA to Davidson, 5 Aug. 1807 [letter 107].
55. Ship *Caledonian* [*sic*], Henderson, cleared Customs House Charleston, bound for Liverpool, *CG*, 14 Nov. 1807; *Montezuma*, Smith, arrived from London after a passage of 45 days, and 'by this we received our regular files of London papers up to 31st July', 29 Sept., *CG*, 30 Sept. 1808; Davidson to LA, 26 Nov. 1808 [letter 109].
56. LA to Davidson, 1 Mar. 1809 [letter 110].
57. H. W. DeSaussure (1763-1839), Director of the Mint in Washington in 1794, returned to Charleston 1795, elected to the Chancery Bench in 1808, and served as President of the Library Society, 1807-12. John Hopton (1748-1831) partnered Robert William Powell in one of the largest importing / slave importing firms. In *Holden's Directory* of 1808 he is listed as merchant, 1 Angel Court, Throgmorton St., London.
58. The term 'Bookseller' is dropped.
59. DeSaussure to John Hopton, 31 Mar. 1809 [letter 111].
60. Two letters were received from Sarah Butler of Philadelphia in August and October 1792, but there was no continuation of orders.
61. William Wallace Woodward, printer, bookseller and stationer of Chestnut St. (1796-1801) and South Second St. (1802-20), Philadelphia. See H. Glenn Brown and Maude D. Brown, *A Directory of the Book-Arts and Book Trade in Philadelphia to 1820 Including Printers and Engravers* (New York: New York Public Library, 1950).
62. Woodward to Davidson, 24 May 1809.
63. Davidson to Woodward, 20 June 1809.
64. Nathaniel Russell (1738-1820), born Rhode Island, arrived in Charleston in 1765 as a commercial agent. He married the daughter of William Hopton (a frequent attender at Library Society meetings from at least 1759). Nathaniel Goldingham, merchant of 59 Old Broad St., as listed in *Kent's Directory* of 1808 and 1813 (but not in *Kent's Directory* of 1801 or the *Post Office Directory* of 1802).
65. Hopton to Russell, 10 June 1809 [letter 112].
66. Hopton to W. H. DeSaussure and Thos. Roper, 24 June 1809 [letter 114].
67. Hopton to Russell, 10 June 1809 [letter 112].
68. LA to Davidson, 9 June 1809 [letter 113].
69. LA to Davidson, 30 August 1809 [letter 115].
70. Stephen Botein, 'The Anglo-American Book Trade before 1776: Personnel and Strategies', in W. L. Joyce, *et al.*, eds., *Printing and Society in Early America* (Worcester: American Antiquarian Society, 1983), pp.48-82.
71. Of various examples, JML DB, f.409 (27 Nov. 1773); AL, f.170 (6 June 1774, 7 July 1774, 16 Feb. 1775), and invoice copy, DB, ff.295-6.
72. Examples are given in James Raven, 'The Importation of Books in the Eighteenth Century', in Hugh Amory and David Hall, eds., *The History of the Book in America*, vol.1 (Cambridge: Cambridge University Press, 1997).
73. Library Company of Philadelphia, Minute books, 2 (1768-85), 3 (1785-94), 4 (1794-1816), 5 (1816-32) copies of correspondence with Joseph Woods and William Dillwyn, 1783-1812 (and with Samuel Woods from 1812 to at least 1824).
74. Hopton to DeSaussure and Roper, 24 June 1809 [letter 114].

Francis Fry, a maker of chocolate and Bibles

DAVID J. HALL

IN 1869 THE COLLECTOR Robert Curzon was buying Bibles from the Bristol Quaker Francis Fry. Curzon described him as 'a maker of Chocolate and Bibles, which he makes up from imperfect copies'.[1] De Ricci's description gives us more detail.

Another collector of English Bibles was Francis Fry (1803-1886) of Bristol, a partner in the well-known firm of cocoa and chocolate manufacturers, who spent all his leisure hours in comparing copies of the early editions of the Scriptures in English and establishing the variations between the editions and issues. His publications are still the leading authorities on the subject. His unrivalled collection was purchased in 1890, for £6000, by the British and Foreign Bible Society and has been fully described in the catalogue published by that institution. A few of his duplicates have come on the market in various small sales.[2]

I shall attempt here to describe in turn the man, the collector and the bibliographer. Fry was a prominent member of one of the notable Quaker commercial dynasties that began in the 18th century. His grandfather Joseph, a medical practitioner, was involved in the manufacture of chocolate, porcelain, chemicals and soap and in printing and typefounding in Bristol and London. He was a partner in the Bristol printing and typefounding firm of Fry and Pine which moved to London in 1770, becoming J. Fry & Co. and then Edmund Fry and Son (Edmund was Joseph's son). The firm issued specimen books of type and was in 1786 'letter-founders to the Prince of Wales'. It passed out of family hands in 1828 but it is not fanciful to suppose that Francis was influenced by this background and in particular his grandfather's work in printing several Bibles of typographical interest.[3] Francis's father, Joseph Storrs Fry, was another of Joseph's sons. He took on the chocolate manufacturing, in partnership with his mother, then with another Quaker and finally with his three sons Joseph, Francis and Richard. Joseph Storrs Fry wrote an essay on the means of employing the poor for which he was awarded a silver medal by the Board of Agriculture, and as well as several other works *A Concise History of Tithes* (1819), reprinted at least six times. His wife Anne published three improving works, his daughter Henrietta Joan eight works and his son Richard a temperance tract. Francis's wife Matilda had two volumes of verse privately printed in Bristol.[4] With this literate background Francis Fry's own publications seem inevitable.

Francis was born at Westbury-on-Trym on 28 October 1803. He entered a school in a local village run by a Quaker and then trained for business at

Croydon in Surrey. From the age of 20 he was involved in the family business in Bristol and moved from the city to nearby Cotham in 1839. Cotham Tower in the grounds of his house appeared on his bookplate. Fry served as a special constable in the Bristol riots of 1831 when the warehouse containing the firm's stock of cocoa was burnt. His public service extended to membership of the Managing Committee of the Bristol Philosophical Society and of the subscription library. He was acquainted with local scientists and enjoyed collecting minerals, fossils and later shells. He turned down an invitation to serve on the Bristol City Council for lack of time. His business interests extended beyond the chocolate firm. He was a director of railway companies in the south-west of England and a closely involved director of the Bristol Water Works from its inception for 40 years. One of his publications proposed the setting up of a national parcel post system by the railway companies before the Post Office took up the idea. In later middle age he was able to spend less time on business and his deep interest in Bibles began in the middle of the century. It was then too that he undertook a major piece of service for the Society of Friends. Fry's Quakerism is usually evident from the language if not the dating of his letters and he certainly kept for some time to the traditional Quaker dress when it was becoming less commonly encountered. He was a founder of the first temperance society in Bristol and supported both the Anti-Slavery society and the British and Foreign Bible Society.

In 1850 Fry had joined with two other Quakers in one of a series of deputations sent by the Society of Friends to the monarchs of Europe in the anti-slavery cause. This mission took him to Northern Italy for three months. Later he travelled extensively in pursuit of his bibliographical interests both at home and on the continent. In 1860 he spent three months in Germany visiting centres of early printing. He published a brief account of the original cross bar of Gutenberg's press seen at Mainz. In Munich he discovered books printed at Worms by Peter Schoeffer which led him to the view that Schoeffer had printed the first Tyndale New Testament in Worms in 1526. No doubt he found opportunities to buy some of his older books illustrating the early history of printing on this and other journeys.

Fry died on 12 November 1886. An appendix to the *Memoir* prints some of the letters of condolence received by his family. George Bullen of the British Museum wrote:

A deal of knowledge has died with him, especially in the particular branch of research to which he chiefly devoted himself—the bibliography of our English Bible. Only one man that I ever knew at all approached him in that branch of knowledge, namely, the late Henry Stevens, who had a great admiration for your husband.

Edward Arber wrote similarly to Fry's son Theodore:

He was one of the pillars of English bibliography. Our losses in that department of late have been enormous. Francis Fry, Henry Bradshaw, Henry Stevens and Cornelius Walford all died within a short time, and I never expect to meet with their equals. I have many pleasant memories of your father, and I respected him with all my heart. He has rendered noble service in the bibliography of our printed English Scriptures, for which I hope his name will be held through many years in affectionate memory. (*Memoir*, pp.61, 62).

Though Fry appears to have been fairly single-minded as a collector he owned more books than just Bibles and owned more than just books. His home, though simply furnished, contained Greek and Etruscan vases. An important china collection centred on items from the Bristol factory. Apart from the Bibles and the accompanying material illustrative of early printing and for reference he had some medieval manuscripts, a complete set of Dibdin's works and a serious collection of Quaker books. The latter was particularly strong in books of the 17th and 18th centuries and at one point he seems to have aimed for comprehensiveness. Some of these books were probably inherited; some will have had family connections. The Library of the Society of Friends has a large-paper copy of the *Memoir of . . . Priscilla Gurney* (1834) edited by Fry's aunt Sarah Allen and given by her to Francis and Matilda. Joseph Smith acknowledged the help of Francis Fry in lending him many books when he was compiling his *Descriptive Catalogue of Friends' Books*.

The Bible collection, with its great strength in the editions of the English Bible, was Fry's most important. He collected thoroughly and extensively, aided no doubt by a fairly deep pocket. He sold or exchanged numerous duplicates too and occasionally acted as a broker between buyer and seller when he was not himself interested in acquiring the book. His selling may have been to supplement his buying funds as well as to clear duplicates (though these still accumulated); it was almost certainly trading up on the quality of the copies he retained. More controversially it also encompassed fragments of imperfect Bibles. However much the sheer scale of his activities made others believe that he was a dealer, all that was a by-product of his collecting. Certainly as a collector he was always interested in the value and rarity of his books and his annotations often include that information. In 1871 he wrote a memorandum about the value of the Bible collection, meaning quite clearly its monetary value as well as importance. Did he contemplate selling the collection at that point? Part of the memorandum was printed later and sheds light on both his preoccupations and methods:

In reference to my collection of Bibles, this must never be forgotten, viz: — the condition, and that they are Standards. Every book is collated throughout, unless so stated, good and in fine order, or in some cases well repaired. Most are picked copies, all bad and worn leaves taken out, and good ones put in before binding, several copies of some cut up to make a fine copy, always of the same edition. I have been *positive* to use the same edition always, and could have perfected copies with leaves of other editions that would read, and would never have been known, but I have not done so. I have bought many duplicates of most of the commoner editions, and more than one, where I could, of rare ones, and this has enabled me to compare and prove what is the true edition, for I have found so many Bibles and Testaments made up of different editions. I have cut these mixed books up, and therefore my Bibles and Testaments are *standard copies*, and the value that a copy might be sold at in a common way is no criterion of what such a copy of an edition as my copy is, should be valued at. My books are beyond dispute so much more valuable for condition and *correctness*. For what use is it to pretend to have an edition and not to *know* that you have it? There is no *perfect* and *correct* copy of four editions of Cranmer's (Bible) known but *mine*. No April, or July 1540, no May or December 1541. *I am sure of it.* My Cranmer's are worth more than I put them at. They are perfectly unique as a correct set; even Mr. Lenox has not made his up; he has not the two last leaves, December, and has mixed leaves. I have, by much labour, comparing copies, discovered various editions which no one else has noticed and this adds much to their value

1871.⁵

(Signed) FRANCIS FRY.

Fry has been rightly criticized for the harm he did by the perfecting of copies by replacing leaves with others from what he thought were the same printings and by inserting facsimiles, particularly of title-pages. These practices have often made the tasks of later bibliographers more difficult, occasionally even impossible. Nevertheless by the prevailing standards of his own time, as the extended quotation above shows, he was really quite a purist and entirely open about his methods. Many of his contemporaries did similar things and had other regrettable traits such as indulging in wholesale rebinding or the washing out of early annotations or provenance information. The London binder Lewis's work for Beriah Botfield is a good example.⁶ Making up nominally perfect copies was nothing unusual; the serious criticism of Fry is that he mixed leaves from different printings through ignorance. Even then he may have done less harm than others — how reliable were the three 1535 Coverdale Bibles that were being made up in the trade from the many imperfect copies in the Pickering stock in 1857? These had missing leaves provided in facsimile by Harris, one of the top craftsmen in the field.⁷ Fry too used Harris as did Sir Thomas Phillipps and Fry's rival Bible collector, the American James Lenox. Given the imperfections of well-used 16th-century bibles and other printed books there was constant demand for the work of skilled facsimilists.

Fry's acquisition of books from dealers has still to be investigated. Unless he felt it too expensive or too competitive he would surely have bought from the remainder of Lea Wilson's collection or a Henry Stevens trade sale. His contact with other collectors include some of the great names. Lord Lindsay wrote that in forming his collection of Bibles he 'owed most to two men outside the trade, Francis Fry and James Dix.'⁸ Fry wrote first to Sir Thomas Phillipps in June 1861. He said then that he had 'perhaps nearly 400 editions' of Bibles and Testaments. Fry surmised that Phillipps had purchased two imperfect Welsh New Testaments of 1567 and hoped to obtain any surplus parts of them on any terms 'sale or exchange'.

He continued 'I buy a great many copies of the same edition & I sell & exchange with the chief if not all the Bible Collectors in the Kingdom and thus we help each other.'[9] Other contacts were with less well-known people but to the same ends. In 1872 Fry wrote to a Mrs Acton Tindal on terms of personal friendship about her Tyndale Pentateuch. He offered to acquire it if she decided not to keep it, as his present copy had 15 facsimile leaves, or alternatively to supply her with spare leaves to perfect her copy.[10] Fry's first surviving letter to Henry Bradshaw (5 September 1879) offered him the first Dublin-printed Bible. Here Fry acted simply as intermediary. Bradshaw was pleased to obtain the book for 50 shillings and in his manuscript note on the letter says 'I am afraid if it had been in much worse plight and had been marked at twenty pounds I should not have refused the offer.' Fry said that this was only the second copy he had encountered, though Bradshaw ended up with three copies in his collection of Irish books.[11] Other correspondents included James Lenox, Henry Stevens, Henry Bohn, Henry Huth and numerous ecclesiastics. Fry, like the Bodleian and the British Museum, turned down a spurious Tyndale manuscript from George Offor's library. James Lenox bought it from Henry Stevens. Offor had been another source of Bible leaves to Lord Lindsay.[12] Among the libraries Fry visited were those of the Earls of Pembroke, Leicester and Ashburnham, Earl Spencer and the Royal Library at Windsor (*Memoir*, p.34).

Fry was a perfectly human collector. His first letter to the Secretary of the British and Foreign Bible Society, requesting a copy of the Society's library catalogue, demonstrates this:

Allow me to say that I am a Collector of the early editions of the Bible & should particularly value a presentation copy if the Committee will do me the honour to give me one. It is not to save 5/- but for the interest of a presentation copy & I think it may be in my power to contribute some facsimiles of rare leaves or something to help your imperfections.

Later in 1857 he wrote again offering facsimiles to fill some of the gaps he had noted from his study of the catalogue:

Some of my bibles are like yours minus what I wish they hd. Would your committee let me have 4 or 6 leaves out of your 2nd Cranmer by Petyt & R[edman] 1540 if I give you complete value for other books. I would benefit some of your early bibles much but I should like a little for a bible or two which you can help me with. No doubt I should give you 2 or 3 times the value of anything I should ask of you.[13]

Fry sold Bibles, psalters and prayer books to the Bodleian. These included Barker's octavo of 1631 (the 'wicked' Bible) for £40 in 1858, the Great Bible of 1539 for £100 in 1864, and a 1541 edition of Cranmer's Bible for £82 10s in 1869. The Coverdale Bible of 1535, listed by Macray in his *Annals* as exhibited in 1890, had a facsimile title-page provided by Fry.[14] The British Museum also acquired works from him. The Museum had been striving to build up its Bible collection, buying in competition with Lea Wilson, James Lenox and the Duke of Sussex. The best of Lea Wilson's collection was bought for Lenox by Henry Stevens later, but the Museum bought from the Duke of Sussex's sale. Fry was considered a major supplier of antiquarian material, including foreign Bibles, to the Museum. In 1866 he sold the first edition of the Bible in Polish (Cracow, 1561) for £60; later sales included two early German Bibles and a Polish New Testament.[15]

So far only hints of the contents of Fry's Bible collection have been given, often by mentioning its duplicates. Another clue could have been found in the 28 volumes he lent to the 1877 Caxton exhibition – mostly English and including his own publication of the Tyndale New Testament facsimile, but there were also a Venetian Bible of 1487 and a German Bible of 1534. His contribution was overshadowed by those of Earl Spencer and Henry J. Atkinson, the latter lending more than 400 of the 717 Bibles.[16] Much more information can of course be found in the records of the dispersal of the Fry books. The core of the English Bible collection was acquired after his death by the British and Foreign Bible Society. It was valued by George Bullen of the British Museum and his letter to Fry's son Theodore was reprinted as part of the Society's printed appeal for the acquisition of the collection:

BRITISH MUSEUM,
LONDON W.C.,
19th February, 1889.

DEAR MR. FRY,

I have at length concluded the examination and valuation of your late Father's Valuable Collection of Printed Bibles, chiefly English.

So important a Collection was, I have no hesitation in saying, never before brought together by a private individual, and for English Bibles, I know of none anywhere existing that can compare with it, whether in public or private Libraries. The copies are for the most part fine and perfect, and some even unique. To me it seems that it would be a pitiful thing indeed, and a serious loss to Biblical literature, that such a Collection should be dispersed to the four corners of the world instead of being reserved for scholars, as a whole to aid them in their researches. I should, therefore, strongly advise that efforts should be made to secure it as a kind of National treasure for Bible-loving England. Were it not that the British Museum is already rich in this direction, I should recommend its purchase by the Trustees; but there are other Institutions, notably, the British and Foreign Bible Society, in whose Library such a Collection might properly find a place.

After a careful examination of the works with a view to set a pecuniary value upon the same, and after comparing notes with Mr. Witson, my Assistant, I have arrived at a conclusion that they are worth altogether £8,837.

The English, Welsh and Irish being worth -   -   -   -   £7,589

And the Foreign   -   -   -   -   -   -   -   £1,248

I remain, Dear Mr. FRY,
Yours very truly,
(Signed) GEO. BULLEN.

The basic appeal reads:

BIBLE HOUSE,
146, QUEEN VICTORIA STREET, E.C.,
7th March, 1889.

The collection of Bibles made by the late Mr. F. FRY has now been carefully examined and valued by Mr. BULLEN, of the British Museum, whose authority on such a subject will be universally recognised.

We enclose a copy of his letter and valuation. Nothing that we can say can add weight to his testimony to the extraordinary value and importance of the collection, and we appeal with confidence to the generous friends of the Bible Society, to avail themselves of the opportunity thus presented, of obtaining for these splendid and unique Volumes their only fitting permanent resting-place in this Country, in the Library of this House.

(Signed) J. G. BARCLAY, *Treasurer.*
"   J. B. BRAITHWAITE, *Chairman*
of the Editorial Sub-Committee.
"   WILLIAM WRIGHT, *Editorial*
Superintendent and Librarian.

Papers in the Society's archives show the gradual progress of the appeal. There is a preliminary printed list of contributors with 68 names, headed by Theodore Fry, owner of the collection, giving £1,500, A. Peckover £500 and J. G. Barclay £250. Names added in manuscript to that list included Talbot B. Reed who offered three guineas, the Right Hon. W. H. Smith £25, Francis J. Fry £100 and the Syndics of the Cambridge Press and the Delegates of the Oxford Press with 50 guineas each. By the time that the list was sent out with the 7 March letter it had 141 names. The odd gift of £3 7s from each of seven individuals is explained in a later document: 'the collection, taken as a whole, costs about £3 7s per copy.' Among those approached and apparently not responding were the Dukes of Bedford and Westminster, Lord Justice Sir Edward Fry and the Goldsmiths' Company. The total sum needed had not been secured by early May of 1889 and Theodore Fry had received another offer for the whole collection. However a formal offer to purchase was made by the Society on 30 May and Theodore Fry wrote accepting it on the same day. It was to buy the English Bibles together with Irish, Welsh, Gaelic, Anglo-Saxon and Rheims versions for £4,500 (the nominal price being £6,000 before Fry's contribution) on 1 July 1889. 1,220 volumes were handed over, together with Fry's record of the collection in a specially printed ledger. A substantial range of English Bibles was excluded from the purchase and gradually came on the market later.[17] The original edition of Darlow and Moule's catalogue identifies the Fry copies in volume I, though this is dropped in the revision by Herbert.[18] The range and depth of the collection is clear from the original catalogue and the later sale catalogues. It would be impractical to attempt a summary of the core of the collection here but some approximate indication of what was dispersed later may be of interest.

Four later auction sales contained substantial elements of Fry's collections. Only one, the first, at Sotheby's on 15 January 1890 was devoted wholly to Fry books, described as 'the foreign and remaining English portions of the collection of Versions of the Scripture in various languages, of an eminent collector, deceased.' The first 132 of 458 lots were in foreign languages and included six incunabula, 74 16th-century and 25 17th-century Bibles. The remaining lots were mostly English Bibles, New Testaments and editions of the psalter with the main strength in the 16th and 17th centuries. It is possible that lots unsold from this sale appeared in one of the later ones.

A Puttick and Simpson sale on 4 December 1905 included a selection of books from the library of Francis Fry. These appear to have been lots 1-138. The Bibles included six incunabula (1475-93) and the first Bibles in Welsh and Swedish. The first Polish Bible had the title and several leaves in facsimile. There were 11 other continental 16th-century Bibles. There were also five medieval manuscripts, three of them Bibles (two from the 13th century) and 25 continental incunabula. A Puttick sale on 23 January 1918 included early English Bibles collected by Francis Fry. The 57 lots included 24 of Fry's own publications, a parcel of facsimile and genuine leaves from rare Bibles, some Quaker books and a volume described as Queen Elizabeth's copy of Cranmer's version 1560-1 with her signature authenticated by Fry. The lot numbers of the Fry material in this sale are given by Seymour de Ricci (see note 2).

In a Sotheby sale of 30 March-1 April 1931 there were 67 lots from the estate of Francis James Fry. These included two Flemish books of hours, three incunabula, three incunable papal indulgences, one of them block-printed, a run of English Bibles and New Testaments, and numerous copies of Fry's own works in various editions. The 1541 Great Bible had a facsimile title-page by Harris. All these presumably came from books retained by the family. These four sales were not quite the end of the dispersals. In the mid-1950s there was a collection of 68 titles in 42 volumes still owned by one descendant, mostly 17th-century English versions but including a 1524 New Testament.[19] Some foreign Bibles were sold to Blackwell's by a family source in the 1970s. The homes of the Fry family must almost have been awash with Bibles.[20] In addition there were Fry's own works: the most interesting of the English Bibles and New Testaments in the Pratley sale at Sotheby's on 13-15 January 1988 was a vellum copy of Fry's Tyndale facsimile, inscribed by him to both his daughter and granddaughter and bound by Tuckett in an elaborate Grolieresque style.

In turning to give some account more specifically of Fry as bibliographer there is inevitable overlap with his collecting activities. We have already seen something of his negative achievement in the perfecting of copies. He complained on occasion about the activities of others. Prayer Book collectors were blamed for mutilating Herbert 154, a 1578 Bible, by removing the rare version of the Prayer Book (Fry observes this in a note inserted in the Bible Society's copy). Criticism of Fry's practices began to appear not long after his death. W. E. Smith wrote in his 'Study of the Great 'She' Bible (1613 or 1611)':

May I slip in here a strong protest against Mr Fry's habit of tampering with Bibles, altering sheets, and inserting skilfully imitated facsimile title-pages?

In some cases, perhaps always, he inserts a paper with indication of what he has done, but it would be far more interesting to have a book left in its original state, and the facsimile titles hold out a great temptation to unscrupulous owners or booksellers to suppress his record, and turn a *facsimile* into a *forgery*. Mr Fry's proceeding could be understood on the part of anyone who was a mere collector; but from a patient and laborious investigator like Mr Fry, better things might have been expected.[21]

A. W. Pollard followed in 1911, writing about the 1611 Authorized Version:

Further investigation is rendered almost hopeless by the fact that collectors like Lea Wilson and Francis Fry (the latter of whom bought and sold an extraordinary number of copies), and many such more easily forgivable booksellers, have transferred sheets from one copy to another to bring them into accord with their own mistaken ideas of perfection, and the evidence has thus been hopelessly confused.[22]

This outspoken opinion is followed by criticism of Fry for muddling edition and issue in his terminology. Nevertheless Pollard recognizes the value of some of Fry's work, noting that he was correct in establishing the sequence of the editions of the Authorized Version, unlike F. H. A. Scrivener in his *The Authorised Edition of the English Bible* (1884).

More recently Dr B. J. McMullin's article 'Towards a bibliography of the Oxford and Cambridge Bible presses in the Seventeenth and Eighteenth Centuries', having first established that some other 19th-century works and the revision of Darlow and Moule are flawed, gives 'the impact of Francis Fry' as the first of various problems that need to be resolved before he can make progress. McMullin, echoing Pollard, states that 'seldom can the bibliographical waters have been so muddied as they have been by Francis Fry'. McMullin is clear that Fry must have been wrong in establishing many of his standard editions because:

the nature of bible printing (certainly in the seventeenth century) was such that it may be difficult to even establish what constitutes an edition, let alone establish that two copies are from the same one. In fact the King's Printer's practice of continuously reprinting individual sheets, and the consequent difficulty – if not impossibility – of defining 'edition', is perhaps the major hurdle to be surmounted by any future reviser of DMH.

He goes on to point out that Fry's criteria had been taken over uncritically by Darlow and Moule.[23]

Both the Bibles that had passed through Fry's hands and his own bibliographical writings must therefore be treated with caution. Despite Smith and Pollard they were accepted with enthusiasm for many years. De Ricci in 1930 said that Fry's publications 'are still the leading authorities on the subject'. In an account of the Scheide Library, a Fry provenance was accepted 'as a sufficient guarantee' of the perfection of a first edition of the Authorized Version. The copy had been given by Fry to his son Francis James Fry and carried a typical note 'This is a fine clean perfect copy. I have examined every leaf and certify that it is all the true first issue therefore a standard copy.' Others were not so sure. J. F. Mozley, writing on Coverdale, referred to Fry on mixed copies without perhaps realizing that Fry had done some of the mixing:

How then can we be sure what a standard (unmixed) copy is, or in other words what leaves belong to what edition? Fry devised elaborate tests, by which he claimed – at enormous labour to himself – to have solved the problem, and his conclusions have been accepted by bibliographers, and cataloguers, though some complain that it is difficult to check his results, because he so seldom tells us what copy he is using.

This is echoed in the note to Herbert 46, the first Great Bible of 1539:

By examining every leaf of a great number of copies, and tabulating his results, Fry attempted to ascertain what leaves properly belonged to each edition, and to make a list of the 'reprinted' leaves. Though his conclusions may not always appear convincing, and it is impossible now to test their accuracy, his work remains a monument of painstaking research, and the tests which he laid down are generally applied to copies of these editions.

H. M. Adams in his 'Table for identifying the edition of imperfect copies of the Book of Common Prayer, 1600-1640' used Fry's methods: 'The method is of course that used by Fry in his collations of the Great Bible and the 1611 Bibles except that here only one leaf, the second, in each quire is noted.'[24]

Henry Bradshaw valued Fry as a bibliographical correspondent as well as a source of Bibles. Referring to his 'indefatigable friends, Mr Francis Fry and Mr Henry Stevens' he adds that: 'I have said that, thanks to Mr Fry's labours, the sequence of the early editions of Tindale's version of the New Testament, issued during his lifetime, stands out clear.' In the same paper Bradshaw corrects Fry on the publisher/printer of the 1534-5 Antwerp Tyndale; he also says of Fry's *Bibliographical description of the Tyndale New Testament*:

It is simply a storehouse of facts upon the subject; and it is here that we have for the first time a clear statement of Tindale's work upon the New Testament, unclouded by the confusion caused by the want of knowledge from which previous writers suffered.

A letter from Bradshaw to Fry about the blocks used in the New Testaments of the 1530s says: 'You must forgive me for writing all this to you. There are so few who take any interest in my particular view of these things that I am bound to *pour out* when I once begin a letter on the subject.'[25]

Fry was responsible for a number of publications. Only two of them do not concern the Bible in some way, his 1852 *Remarks on Parcel Traffic* (Bristol) and the 1860 *Catalogue of Books in the Library belonging to the Monthly Meeting in Bristol* (Bristol, i.e. the library of the local administrative unit of the Society of Friends). Three publications are reprints from *Notes and Queries* and *The Journal of Sacred Literature*. Eight were listed in Appendix E to the *Memoir*, seven with prices and with Sotheran's address given as a source. It will come as no surprise to the reader that with his bibliographical works Fry catered to contemporary taste for special and de luxe copies, even producing one leaf-book. There were large-paper copies, old-paper copies and in some cases copies on vellum. Fry's facsimile of *The First New Testament printed in the English Language* (Bristol, 1862) was printed in an edition of 177 copies; 155 of these were standard octavo copies, 26 were quarto on old paper or vellum and could be obtained on special application with the woodcuts and initials illuminated. The introduction was issued separately cloth-bound with one of the facsimile leaves illuminated, thus acting as a prospectus, and in an abbreviated form also. The most lavish of his publications was *A description of the Great Bible, 1539, and the Six Editions of Cranmer's Bible* (1865) published at £5, or £20 on vellum. It contained a leaf from each of the editions described, 14 in all. Lord Lindsay wrote to acknowledge the gift of a copy:

a volume which is a *chef d'oeuvre* in its kind — a miracle of labour, the result of love. I have read the introduction with great interest, and nothing can be more clear and satisfactory than the data for verification supplied by the plates, as well as the other illustration matter. Your idea of adding original leaves of the different Bibles will facilitate comparison in a manner that nothing else could equal. I cordially congratulate you on having achieved a work which must always hold a place of high honour in the library of bibliography (*Memoir*, pp.51-2).

In this work Fry discounts Lea Wilson's work on early printings of the Authorized Version because he did not take account of his sophistication of his own copies! Later works by Fry were *The Bible by Coverdale, 1535* (1867), *Three New Testaments of William Tyndale compared with each other and with the first edition of Thomas Matthew* (Bristol, 1875), which appeared in 1878 with Sotheran's imprint as *A Bibliographical Description of Tyndale's New Testaments and of the two editions of the Bishops' Version*, and four small facsimile editions.

It will be evident to the reader that this account of Fry has no claim to be comprehensive. This is as much due to the limited amount of work undertaken in preparing it as to the limits of space suggested by the editors. More could be made of his life outside the world of books, a much more thorough account could be given of the Bibles and other books he owned, and further investigation of the processes of acquisition of the collection should prove fruitful. The reader is left to judge how far any of these themes deserve further study.

References

1. A. N. L. Munby, *Connoisseurs and medieval miniatures 1750-1850* (Oxford: Oxford University Press, 1972), p.104.
2. Seymour de Ricci, *English collectors of books and manuscripts (1530-1930) and their marks of ownership* (London: Holland Press, repr. 1960), pp.140-1.
3. This account and most of what follows about the family and Francis Fry the man is derived from Theodore Fry, *A brief memoir of Francis Fry, F.S.A., of Bristol* (London: Barclay & Fry, 1887; not published).
4. These and other printed writings of members of the family are detailed in Joseph Smith, *A descriptive catalogue of Friends' books* (Joseph Smith, 1867, 2 vols).
5. From the Fry papers in the Bible Society's archives in Cambridge University Library. I am grateful to the Reverend A. F. Jesson, Bible Society's Librarian, for permission to quote from this and for his kindly interest in my work on Fry.
6. See for example the instances in *Highly important incunabula, Bibles, early Greek printing and colour-plate books from Beriah Botfield's library* (Christie's sale on 30 March 1994).
7. Nicolas Barker, *Bibliotheca Lindesiana* (London: Bernard Quaritch for the Roxburghe Club, 1978), pp.156-7. For a more detailed account of one of the Harrises see Barry Gaines, 'A forgotten artist: John Harris and the Rylands copy of Caxton's edition of Malory', *Bulletin of the John Rylands Library*, 52 (1969), 115-28. Another dynasty of facsimilists was the Tuppers: see Robin Myers, 'An account of G. I. F. Tupper', in *Transactions of the Cambridge Bibliographical Society*, 7 (1978), 113-34. A. N. L. Munby gives an account of Sir Thomas Phillipps using a facsimilist much cheaper than Harris in his *Phillipps Studies*, no.iv, *The formation of the Phillipps library from 1841 to 1872* (Cambridge: Cambridge University Press, 1956), pp.139-41.
8. Barker, p.198. This is perhaps a reason for Quaritch's dislike of Fry. Dix was another Bristol Quaker.
9. Munby, pp.96-7.
10. Cambridge University Library MS Add. 8202 (an album of letters of book collectors collected by A. N. L. Munby). Quotation from this and other material in the Library is by kind permission of the Syndics of Cambridge University Library.
11. Cambridge University Library MS Add. 2592.537. The Bible is item 666 in *A catalogue of the Bradshaw collection of Irish books in the University Library Cambridge*, 3 vols (Cambridge: Cambridge University Library, 1916).
12. Henry Stevens, *Recollections of James Lenox and the formation of his library*, revised and elucidated by Victor Hugo Paltsits (New York: New York Public Library, 1951), p.53. Barker, p.159.
13. Bible Society archives, file Misc. Edit. Corresp. 1851-60B, letters of 16 February and 25 June 1857.
14. Sir Edmund Craster, *History of the Bodleian Library 1845-1945* (Oxford: Clarendon Press, 1952), p.72. William Dunn Macray, *Annals of the Bodleian Library Oxford*, 2nd edn. (Oxford: Clarendon Press, 1890), pp.383, 465. The 'wicked' Bible is part of a classic saga of perfecting. Henry Stevens sold an imperfect copy to the British Museum. The Museum bought the missing leaves from the Reverend Mr Jennings, who sold the remains of his copy to Francis Fry. Fry used it to make up another perfect copy which he then sold to the Bodleian. This information is in Stevens, pp.28-9.

15. P. R. Harris, 'The development of the collections of the Department of Printed Books, 1846-1875', *British Library Journal*, 10 (1984), 114-46 (pp.123-6).
16. Henry Stevens, *The Bibles in the Caxton Exhibition MDCCCLXXVII* (London: Henry Stevens, 1878). I am grateful to Robin Myers for the loan of this book.
17. Bible Society's archives, box of papers about the Fry collection.
18. T. H. Darlow and H. F. Moule, *Historical catalogue of printed editions of the English Bible 1525-1961*, revised and expanded from the edition of 1903 by A. S. Herbert (London: British and Foreign Bible Society, 1968).
19. Private information from the late Mrs M. I. Burkitt.
20. Blackwell's catalogue A1065 (1976) contained two Bibles given by him to his daughter. In 1979 they had another given by Francis to Francis James Fry. Bloomsbury Book Auctions on 2 September 1993 had a Bible presented to a grandson. (I am grateful to Mr Giles Mandelbrote for that reference.) A group of medieval manuscripts from the Fry family library was sold at Bloomsbury Book Auctions on 10 October 1996.
21. *The Library*, 2 (1890), 96-102 (p.97).
22. A. W. Pollard, *Records of the English Bible: the documents relating to the translation and publication of the Bible in English, 1525-1611* (Oxford: Oxford University Press, 1911), pp.70, 72.
23. *Bibliographical Society of Australia and New Zealand Bulletin*, 14 (1990), 51-73. Dr McMullin kindly provided an offprint of this article. His article 'The Bible and continuous reprinting in the early seventeenth century', *The Library*, 6th ser. 5 (1983), 256-63 also has references to Fry.
24. De Ricci, p.141. Julian P. Boyd, *The Scheide Library*, ([n.p.], [n.pub.], 1947), p.105. J. F. Mozley, *Coverdale and his Bibles* (London: Lutterworth Press, 1953), p.220. H. M. Adams, 'Tables for identifying the edition of imperfect copies of the Book of Common Prayer, 1600-1640', *Transactions of the Cambridge Bibliographical Society*, 1 (1949), 61-3.
25. 'Godfried van der Haghen (G. H.), the publisher of Tindale's own last edition of the New Testament in 1534-35' in *Collected papers of Henry Bradshaw, late University Librarian* (Cambridge: Cambridge University Press, 1889), pp.354-70. The quotation from Bradshaw to Fry is from Bradshaw's draft letter in Cambridge University Library MS Add. 2592.678.

Art and craft:
bookbindings in the National Library of Wales

EILUNED REES

'SPLENDOUR IN THE BINDING of books is a taste which dates back from remote times' – the opening sentence of the section on 'Bookbinding' in the *Reports by the Juries* on the Great Exhibition of 1851.[1] The craft of bookbinding evolved as the codex-book replaced the roll-book in early Christian times and essentially has changed but little: a bookbinder's primary concern continues to be the attaching of covers to a written or printed text in order to protect the pages and preserve their sequence. Good craftsmanship is closely bound with respect for the materials used and in its wake comes awareness of their artistic potential. Art and craft merge in bookbinding, with art reflecting regional culture and artistic fashion and with craft developing according to the availability of materials and state of technology.

The National Library of Wales was not founded until 1909, but even so the history of bookbinding in England and Wales can be comprehensively illustrated from the collections, with enough examples from European countries to place it in context. Serendipity accounts for the presence of most of the bindings. They came with the great collections donated to the Library[2] or as purchases chosen primarily for their textual significance or association value. Only during the last three decades have bindings been purchased in their own right to form a Fine Bindings Collection. Rare, fragile or interesting bindings found amongst the general book-stock are often transferred to this Collection; comparable bindings in Special Collections are recorded as such but are left *in situ*.

Medieval bindings are housed in the Department of Manuscripts and Records. The foundation collection of the National Library was that of Sir John Williams, who purchased the bulk of the richest repository of early Welsh manuscripts, the Peniarth Library, which in turn had incorporated the Hengwrt Library dating back to the 16th century.[3] Inevitably many manuscripts have been rebound over the centuries, but those which have escaped the misplaced zeal of past owners are of immense value as specimens of medieval craftsmanship, especially, ironically, if their condition is less than perfect. The techniques of the medieval binders can be studied in books such as Peniarth 381D, a manuscript of Bede's *Historia Ecclesiastica*. There are but fragments left of the leather which once covered the thick oak boards. Clearly visible are the two double thongs of whittawed leather on to which the book was sewn in neat kettle stitches and the pegs

279

which anchored the thongs to the covers. A pin on the lower cover and remains of a strap fastened by brass nails on the upper cover are evidence of a typical strap and pin fastening.

Appreciation for technical expertise is the reaction most likely to be evoked by medieval bindings of this nature. In contrast, there are medieval bindings whose artistic merit reflects the ritual role of certain ecclesiastical manuscripts. *Llyfr Llandaf* or *Liber Landavensis* contains St Matthew's Gospel, documents relating to the diocese of Llandaff and lives of saints, including St Teilo, patron saint of Llandaff Cathedral. The exquisite gilt-bronze figure of Christ which adorns the 12th-century lower oak board has been described by Neil Stratford as 'a unique survival of major English bronze-casting of the third quarter of the 13th century, probably *c.* 1250-75.'[4] Wales can boast of few extant medieval liturgical treasures and for that reason the binding will be described in greater detail than most (fig.1).

The lower board seems to be part of the original binding. Cut into it is a sunken panel, with a chamfered edge, which shows evidence of having been covered in metal and of having had the original central feature of the panel enclosed in a mandorla, probably another Christ in Majesty. The latter was replaced by the surviving figure, attached to the remains of thin silver plate. Nail holes, some still with their brass nails, indicate that the sunken panel, its frame and the outer edges of the board were all once covered with silver plate. The gilded figure of Christ is seated on a rainbow, blessing a book on his left knee, his feet resting on what was probably a smaller rainbow. The form of the longer rainbow suggests that there was a framing mandorla.

Daniel Huws surmises that the volume was first bound in the 12th century and has undergone two medieval rebindings, with the substitution of the figure accompanying the second rebinding. The book was again rebound in 1696 and in 1892. The Reformation rendered the medieval liturgical and administrative uses of the book obsolete; instead, *Liber Landavensis* attracted the attention of antiquaries. Theophilus Field, Bishop of Llandaff, lent the volume to John Selden, who did not return it. It fell into the hands of one of Selden's executors, John Vaughan of Trawsgoed, and subsequently reappeared in the collection of Robert Davies of Gwysaney, who had married Vaughan's granddaughter. It remained part of the Gwysaney library until 1959, when it was sold to the National Library of Wales, where it had been on deposit since 1942.

Proof that Robert Davies commissioned the 1696 rebinding lies in an inscription in the sunken panel of the upper board: 'Librum hunc temporis injurias passum novantiquo tegmine muniri curavit / R. D. / A° 1696.' In 1892, the book was rebound in the British Museum in a manner which would cause consternation in these more enlightened days. The book was cut into single leaves, which were overcast to form quires on five raised bands and glued to a leather back; some words in the inner margins can no

Fig.1. The 13th-century figure of Christ on the lower board of *Liber Landavensis*. Reproduced by kind permission of the National Library of Wales.

longer be read. At least the figure of Christ was unscathed, a figure whose beauty transcends all trends in fashion.

The style of binding exemplified by Peniarth 381D was somewhat austere, even in instances when the leather was decorated with blind-tooled stamps; the bindings associated with church ritual were often lavishly embellished with precious metals and gems. Neither style was suited for books designed for private use in affluent households, the handsomely illuminated missals, popular histories and romances which, like modern coffee-table tomes, were designed to impress as well as to be read. From the 13th century onwards, the art of book-covering was enriched by the use of silk and velvet. The crimson velvet covers of Peniarth 481D, with their five brass bosses and corner-pieces, would have appeared sumptuous in the 15th century, but they have suffered the fate of most textile covers: the pile of the velvet has worn thin and the joints have cracked; some of the bosses have disappeared. The volume comprises three manuscript works on parchment, which are listed in a bastard secretary hand on a vellum label covered in horn, placed in a brass rectangular frame and nailed to the top of the lower cover: 'Catonis versis î Inglishe & the stories of Alexander & of ye iii king^s of Colon î latinge writyn on p'chmêt & illûned.' Indistinctly stamped four times on the covers are the initials MC. The spine is padded with waste from a 13th-century manuscript. The binding is most likely of English origin and previous owners have been tentatively identified by Daniel Huws. On the flyleaf is an English quatrain in an Elizabethan hand signed 'Jhon Cutts', probably Sir John Cutts of Childerly, Cambridgeshire (d.1615). The 'Thomas Gaudy', whose name appears in a Latin note on f.1 may be Thomas Gawdy of Snitterton, Norfolk. Inside the upper cover is the bookplate of Watkin Williams of Penbedw (d.1808). Penbedw was a Flintshire library of renown, which included an impressive collection of books from the library of Sir Kenelm Digby, acquired through marriage (initially through the marriage of Digby's granddaughter with Sir Richard Mostyn). Through the same channels, marriage, the Penbedw library was absorbed into the Peniarth library, which accounts for the paper label pasted on to the spine of this volume bearing the press-mark 'Peniarth M. SS No:38'. It was from Peniarth that the Davies sisters of Gregynog bought the volume for presentation to the National Library.

Although leather was adopted as a more durable covering from the 15th century onwards, textile bindings, including embroidered silk, remained popular for presentation copies. A Book of Common Prayer and New Testament bound *dos-à-dos* was a common gift at christenings and confirmations. One of the most charming in the Library is a 17th-century set, embroidered with the figure of Charles I on the upper cover and that of Henrietta Maria on the lower. Characteristically, the deterioration of the silk has been aggravated by tarnished silver thread.

Amongst the special collections of early books in the Department of Printed Books are Incunabula, Books printed in the British Isles 1500-1700,

Foreign Books 1500-1650 and a Euclid collection. They have been acquired from sundry sources. The Euclid collection was purchased by the Library in 1927. It was amassed by Sir Charles Thomas-Stanford, who published a bibliography of early editions as a Bibliographical Society Monograph in 1926. Another fine acquisition was the Romance collection of F. W. Bourdillon, purchased in 1922. A particularly generous donor of incunabula was A. R. Llewellin-Taylour, who made regular presentations of valuable books in memory of his wife.

Most of the incunabula, although often repaired, retain their original covers, displaying the distinctive characteristics of 15th and 16th-century binding styles in England, France, Germany, Italy and the Netherlands. The unprecedented increase in book production occasioned by the invention of printing by moveable type obviously benefited bookbinders. But just as the demands of printing could not be adequately met by the existing supply of parchment, resulting in texts being printed on paper, likewise did binders have to modify their techniques and materials to cope with the burgeoning trade. Clasps became ornamental rather than functional, for paper is not as volatile as parchment. Wooden boards were gradually displaced by cheaper pasteboards. Leather was recognized as the most durable material for book-covers, but to the medieval stamps used for tooling were added rolls and panels. Considerable artistry is displayed in the design of rolls, which incorporate heraldic symbols, flowers and small animals and even hunting scenes. The entrepreneur bindery-owners were emancipated from medieval anonymity. Some would incorporate their initials into their design, as did Nicholas Spierinck and Garrett Godfrey (16th-century binders from the Low Countries who settled in Cambridge). Bindings can usually be linked with binderies through their distinctive tools, as is the case with *The Book of fayttes of armes and of chivalrye* of 1489 from the Caxton bindery. Fragments of manuscripts used as spine-linings, joint-reinforcements or end-papers can also be revealing. Mr Graham Pollard was able to place a binder known as the 'Half-stamp Binder' firmly in Oxford rather than in London when he discovered that the pasteboards of the Library's copy of *Compendium iuris canonici* (Strasbourg, 1499) were made up of the 15th-century pledge-chest records of John Moore, an Oxford stationer.[5]

Leather had by this time been adopted as the favoured medium of book-covering, but while calf was most popular in England and both calf and sheep were used in the Netherlands, pigskin as well as calf may be found in Germany and morocco in Italy. White pigskin could be effectively blind-tooled and is particularly hard-wearing; examples in the Euclid collection are in excellent condition. The German panels and rolls were a curious mixture of gothic and Renaissance symbolism. It was not unusual for some binders, like Jacob Fritzsch, to incorporate into the rolls their own initials or those of whoever commissioned the binding. The advantages of pigskin were to be outweighed, however, by its unsuitability for gold-tooling.

Gold-tooling enhanced the aesthetic appeal of bookbindings. Morocco was eminently suitable for gold-tooling and certain 16th-century Italian books in the Library have an elegance which transcends any deficiencies of a technique still in its infancy. Edge-gilding had been practised in Italy from the end of the 15th century and was swiftly accompanied by gauffering, the decorating of gilt edges with heated finishing tools. As books were shelved with fore-edge facing outwards, the decoration of edges with painted heraldic or symbolic images was not uncommon in medieval times, but edge-gilding and gauffering elevated fore-edge decoration to the realms of art.

Gold-tooling was rare in England until the latter half of the 16th century, even though it was known to be practised from *c.*1519. The National Library has a specimen of gold-tooling pre-dating the annulment of the marriage of Henry VIII and Catherine of Aragon in 1532. The book is a 14th-century vellum Book of Hours, rebound in the 19th century with the sides of an earlier Tudor binding mounted onto the covers.[6] In a somewhat crudely executed centre panel are two shields, bearing the arms of Henry VIII and Catherine of Aragon respectively. The gilding on the upper cover has virtually disappeared, but enough remains on the lower cover to indicate that the panel was once blocked in gold. Presumably the gold did not stick because no heat could have been used on a block made of wood. The Kalendar of the Book of Hours has four entries relating to Wales and the manuscript is believed to have been written at Llanbeblig, the parish church of Caernarfon, for Isabella Godynogh, whose obit on 23 April 1413 has been added to the Kalendar in a later hand. Few illuminated manuscripts can confidently be associated with Wales and so the seven full-page miniatures, the decorated initials and the borders in this Book of Hours are of far greater interest than their artistic merit would justify. Howard Nixon postulated that the binding was also executed in Wales;[7] the roll is not recorded in J. B. Oldham's *English blind-stamped bindings* (Cambridge, 1952) and the panel-engraving lacks finesse. The volume was purchased by the Library at the Sotheby sale of the Dyson Perrins library on 29 November 1960. It was previously sold at Sotheby's on 10 May 1907 at the sale of the library of W. Bromley Davenport of Capesthorne, Chelford, Chester.

A glance at chronologically arranged early printed books reveals not only an obvious increase in book-production in succeeding decades but also a diminution in the size of volumes. The smaller format was better suited to the needs of the swelling ranks of personal collectors, as Aldus Manutius realized when he marketed his pocket-size classics.

Book collectors were proud of their collections and signalled their pride by having their coats of arms, ciphers or monograms gold-tooled on the covers or on the spines, for by the 18th century books were commonly shelved with the spines facing outwards. It was tempting to aim at uniformity in a purpose-built country house library by placing the owner's crest on the spines. One cannot but wonder at the vagaries of fate which brought by diverse means to Aberystwyth emblazoned volumes from the libraries of ecclesiastical dignitaries, royalty, the nobility and obsessive bibliophiles of many lands and many eras. Easily identifiable are items bound for Cardinal Colonna; Henry, Cardinal York; John Williams, Archbishop of York; Catherine de Medici, Marie de Medici, Anne of Austria, Jacques-Auguste de Thou, Lord Herbert of Cherbury, Elias Ashmole, Michael Wodhull, Thomas Pennant and William Beckford, to name but a few. The covers of *Horae ad usum Romanum* (Paris, 1549) have the cipher of Henri II and the bow of Diane de Poitiers. The royal arms of England appear on presentation copies, and there are long runs of morocco-bound English almanacks embellished with the royal cipher, a common practice for distribution to civil servants. One of the Library's few Spanish bindings is a 17th-century armorial binding, showing the arms of Felipe Ramirez de Guzman, Duke of Medina de las Tores, Marquis of Torres (dexter), and the arms of Anna Caraffa, Duchess of Sabbioneta, Mandragone and Trajetto, Princess of Stigliano (sinister).

Gold-tooling was slow in gaining acceptance in France, but once it became fashionable, the gilders ran riot and it is sometimes difficult to identify what kind of leather lay hidden under a mass of tooling, including *pointillé*, in which craftsmanship was not always accompanied by artistry. English bindings of the 17th century tended to be a more harmonious blend of art and craft. Morocco or russia leather was gold-tooled with a distinctive 'cottage-style' design and subtle use was made of coloured leather inlays and onlays. The tulip features prominently amongst the florets, for tulipomania was rife. When the occasion demanded less ostentation, as when black 'sombre' bindings were produced for funerals, considerable artistic effect could be achieved with patterned blind-tooling.

England's foremost native binders of the period, Samuel and Charles Mearne, are represented in the Library. The Library also possesses one of five known copies of an idiosyncratic 'backless' binding executed by Richard Balley, who is reputed to have been trained at the Mearne bindery. Like two of the other copies, the Library's example is a Book of Common Prayer. It bears the date 1701, but since the prayers for the Royal Family contain references to Queen Anne, it was actually published after 8 March 1702. The black morocco covers have an oriental-style rectangular panel containing a citron centrepiece, which is surrounded by a border of elaborately gold-tooled leafy sprays and floral tools, with tulips and roses inlaid in gold and citron. The most striking feature is that the book has no spine. The folded edges of the sections have been cut and the separate leaves are held together by cords or thongs of twisted vellum laced through holes stabbed through the inner margin and fastened to each board. All four edges are gilt and gauffered with a continuous design of a large tulip alternating with and joined by a stem to a large flower. The pink of the flowers and the green of the stem have now faded. The copy once belonged to 'The Honourable Mad^m Diana Blacket', whose date of birth (1703) appears in the manuscript notes on the flyleaves, which also contain particulars of the family of her second husband, Thomas Wetenhall, Rector of Walthamstow.

Classical restraint is the hallmark of 18th-century bindings. Unfortunately, the Library's holdings of the greatest of 18th-century English binders, Roger Payne, do not do him justice, not even the book once in the possession of the discriminating Beckford.[8] Likewise, there are no spectacular Irish bindings, and the Scottish 'wheel' and 'herring-bone' examples are by no means the best of their kind. There are better testimonies to the skills of the German immigrant binders, John Baumgarten, Henry Walther and Christian Kalthoeber. Well represented is the illustrious firm of Edwards, always referred to as 'Edwards of Halifax' despite the fact that three sons of the founder, William Edwards (1722-1808), moved to London.

The Edwards family is associated with 'Etruscan' calf bindings (entirely in keeping with the classical revival of the time), the popularization of fore-edge paintings and under-painted vellum bindings. James Edwards in 1785 took out a patent for rendering vellum transparent by soaking it in pearly ash. In 1977 a *de luxe* edition of the 1770 *Llyfr Gweddi Gyffredin* was purchased from the late Sir Ben Bowen Thomas (fig.2). The vellum binding is not signed but the outer Greek key-board roll in green and gilt and the inner border of stained terracotta classical palmettes on a black background blaze the house-style of the Edwards bindery. On the upper cover is an oval grey wash biblical scene, depicting Elijah confounding the prophets of Baal by calling on God to send fire down to consume the sacrifice on his stone altar. Edwards usually combined a biblical scene on the upper cover with a landscape or country seat on the lower cover, but in this case the oval centrepiece of the lower cover is an impressive black and white portrait on a blue background of the Reverend John Lloyd of Caerwys (1733-93), fellow antiquary and friend of Thomas Pennant. It is based on an engraving by Peter Mazell of a portrait by Pennant's chief illustrator, Moses Griffith. Inside the upper cover is a narrow strip of paper on which is printed 'Lloyd of Cwm Bychan.' On the flyleaf is the book-plate of Llewelyn Lloyd, on which has been written in ink 'M. A., J. P. Flints/ Great grandson of John Lloyd.' On the following leaf is a note written in an obviously elderly hand 'This Blessed Book, was given to/ my Father by Lady Egerton/ Grandmother to the present/ Lord Westminster – she and/ Syr Thomas Egerton, were/ great friends, and admirers/ of my dear: Father: A. Lh: – 1866/ Syr Thomas Egerton/ was created/ Earl of Wilton.' A. Lh. was Angharad Lhwyd, daughter of John Lloyd and a respected antiquary in her own right.

Edwards of Halifax also popularized the depiction of landscapes or estates or romantic ruins on fore-edge paintings, thereby displacing the floral designs or crucifixions favoured hitherto. Fore-edge painting was a sheer indulgence, since books were by this time all shelved with spines

Fig.2. Llyfr Gweddi Gyffredin (Caer-grawnt, 1770), bound by Edwards of Halifax. Reproduced by kind permission of the National Library of Wales.

facing outwards and since in any case the fore-edge painting is invisible under the gilding until the pages are fanned out. Fore-edge paintings are continually coming to light in the Library.[9] Amongst those already unearthed are four 19th-century depictions of recognizable Welsh places (Bangor and Bangor Cathedral, Barmouth, Neath Abbey and Conway) and one 18th-century fore-edge painting on an Edwards of Halifax binding identified in a pencil note as 'View in Wales'. Artistically, the finest fore-edge painting is a panoramic view of Conway Castle, the town walls and Thomas Telford's suspension bridge. This little masterpiece graces an otherwise unprepossessing duodecimo volume of *The Poetical Works of John Cunningham* (London, 1795), bound in straight-grained red morocco with no decoration other than a gilt border on each cover, gold-tooled turn-ins, and a gold-tooled spine. There is no hint as to who bound the book, or for whom, or who was responsible for the painting. A pencil note on the flyleaf merely confuses the issue with its misleading information: 'Edwards of Halifax the artist 1795. Fore-edge painting of Menai Bridge Bangor Ferry — N. Wales £20.' It appears in Hodgson's sale catalogue of 18-19 March 1948 (item 241), where the scene is correctly identified as Conway.

The Library has few striking German bindings post-dating the ones in the Euclid collection and, apart from a small collection of ecclesiastical armorial bindings, comparatively few Italian ones after 1700. In contrast, its holdings of French bookbindings are formidable. A number of books in the Bourdillon collection were bound or rebound in the 18th and 19th centuries by eminent French binders and gilded by famous gilders (in 1686 French gilders formed an association separate from the guild of French binders). Fortunately, their names are usually gold-tooled on turn-ins and credit may therefore be given where due to the families of Padeloup, Simier, le Monnier, Derome and Marius-Michel, to Rouseller, Purgold, Thouvenin, Thompson, Luc-Antoine Boyet, Niedrée, Lortic, Delanoe, to the firms of Chambolle-Duru, Thibaron-Joly and Trautz-Bauzonnet. Sometimes, these French bindings have to be opened to be fully appreciated: an austere outer cover gives no hint of the inner splendour of extravagantly gold-tooled doublures.

'Ruban, Marius Michel and Meunier form the triumvirate standing unchallenged at the head of the modern art-binding movement.' This was the opinion of a fellow-countryman, Octave Uzanne, writing in 1899.[10] At a Sotheby Parke Bernet Monaco S.A. sale in 1981, the Library bought bindings by Charles Meunier (1865-1940)[11] and Pétrus Ruban (1851-1929).[12] Meunier's binding has a geometrical simplicity, but it is firmly linked with the artistic trends of the turn of the century through turn-ins suggestive of Art Nouveau delicacy and the use of Japanese pattern endpapers. Ruban's design is unmistakably Art Nouveau, a style he abandoned in 1905. The binding is dated 1901 and his use of coloured onlays on a blue background to depict a fuchsia is deceptively simple. Both binders exemplify the contemporary stress on good craftsmanship; bookbinding was an ideal medium for protagonists of the Arts and Crafts movement.

Before the advent of the Arts and Crafts Movement in England, bookbinding had been radically affected during the 19th century by the introduction of a variety of materials and by unparalleled technical developments. Cloth was increasingly used for book-covering from the 1820s and a succession of mechanical innovations enabled multiple copies to be bound cheaply at unprecedented speed. As the afore-mentioned *Reports by the Juries* remarked, 'the production of books greatly exceeds that of any former period, and has caused the application of so much machinery to bookbinding, that it may fairly be said to have become a manufacturing business.'[13] Books were destined to reach the customer already bound and large binderies were established to fulfil orders for publishers, who no longer found it economical to run their own binding services. There was, however, still enough private patronage for talented binders of the calibre of Charles Hering, Charles Lewis and Francis Bedford. Also, commercial firms like Zaehnsdorf and Rivière were by no means denuded of skilled craftsmen and could oblige with special bindings when commissioned. 'One-off' bindings of this period may be found in special collections throughout the Library and others are being purchased for the Fine Bindings collection. Amongst the latter is a signed Zaehnsdorf binding, on No.56 of the 120 copies in a large-paper edition of *The Works of Thomas Campion*, privately printed at the Chiswick Press in 1889. Bound in a rich red straight-grained morocco, it is gold-tooled with maroon, green and citron onlays, with the spine being more ornate than the covers. The lavish gold-tooling of the turn-ins is shown to good advantage against maroon end-papers. The lower turn-in of the upper cover is tooled 'BOUND BY ZAEHNSDORF' and at the base of the end-paper inside the lower cover is a gold stamp depicting a medieval apprentice seated at a sewing-frame, the firm's quality mark used on superior bindings. Pasted inside the upper cover is the bookplate of Francis E. Bliss.

There were two categories of commercial binding: the limited editions of prestigious bindings intended as collectors' items and the mass-produced bindings. The former category gave free rein to Victorian ingenuity and examples abound in the Library of experimentation with a variety of materials: papier-mâché, ivory, tortoiseshell, imitation tortoiseshell, velvet, silk, vellum, various kinds of wood and silver. Papier-mâché bindings were expensive to produce and a run of a thousand was the average to offset the initial cost. Henry Noel Humphreys is the name most frequently associated with their design, the binders were the Leightons of London and the manufacturers of the boards usually Messrs. Jackson & Son. Of the many papier-mâché bindings in the Library, now safely removed from the general stock to the Fine Bindings collection, the most typical of Humphreys's heavy gothic style is *A Record of the Black Prince* (London, 1849). The design is based on a compartment of the Prince's tomb at Canterbury and the thick black, moulded covers are pierced to show a backing of crimson paper.

A London Welshman, Owen Jones (1809-74), was appointed Superintendent of the Works of the Great Exhibition of 1851. His influence on all aspects of Victorian design was prodigious and not surprisingly his services as designer were welcomed by contemporary binding firms. For Thomas de la Rue & Co. he actually designed binding tools. Amongst his innovations were heavily moulded and embossed leather 'relievo' bindings, usually executed by Remnant & Edmonds, an example being M. A. Bacon's *Winged thoughts* (Longman, 1851). He was also responsible for the design of the covers of *The Preacher* (Longman, 1849) for Remnant & Edmonds, one version of which was 'the application of carved wood to binding, by the patent mode of burning in the pattern.'[14]

Ironically, innovative bindings produced in limited numbers often proved less durable than commercial bindings. It seemed that they were designed to be looked at rather than to be handled, and, as any craft binder would predict, materials and techniques not tried and tested by time can fail to survive. Conservation problems arising from the decline in the quality of paper from the 19th century onwards have been compounded by the built-in obsolescence of gimmicky binding materials.

Run-of-the-mill bindings could fare better. The introduction of blocking-presses allowed scope for the imaginative decoration of cloth covers with scenes or artefacts apposite to the contents, blocked in black, gilt or silver (i.e. aluminium) or in colour or in a mixture of two or more. The Library's classified shelves are bedecked with countless Victorian books on all subjects, with covers still in excellent condition. They include books published in Wales, for the major Welsh publishers were finding it commercially advantageous to despatch consignments of their publications to the large commercial binderies in London.

Good commercial binderies were also flourishing in the provinces and binders' tickets from most major towns are regularly found inside the covers of volumes donated or purchased over the years. In order to have an insight into the administration of a provincial bindery, the National Library bought in 1980 part of the archive of a Northampton bindery, that of the Birdsall family, supplementing it a few years later with the purchase of further photographs, rubbings, sketches, tool-trials and lay-out boards. The Birdsall firm was a family business from 1792 until 1961. Richard Birdsall, who was in partnership with his father Anthony from c.1865, had been a keen photographer, and he photographed not only his own works but also the historic bindings which were restored at the bindery. An account of the firm in *The British Bookmaker*, December 1890, states that 'Everything in bookbinding from the goodly *reliure de luxe* to the cheap cloth-cased primer is executed on the premises.' The Library managed to purchase one such *reliure de luxe*, a large-paper copy of Milton's *Paradise Lost* (London, 1873) bound in skilfully gold-tooled crimson crushed morocco and signed

'BIRDSALL & SON NORTHAMPTON.' The Library is justifiably proud of its acquisition of the Birdsall Archive. Together with the binding manuals and technical encyclopaedias beloved of the Victorian age, it throws light on the business aspect of bookbinding.

Little reference has been made in this article to Welsh bookbinding. The Welsh, unlike the Scots and Irish, did not develop a tradition of fine binding.[15] Bookbinders had made a living in Wales before the advent of commercial printing in 1718 and their services were in increasing demand thereafter. Bookbinders were sometimes attached to a printing establishment, but more often they were freelance binders, who fulfilled commissions for the trade or for book collectors, working on site in country houses if need be. Eighteenth-century Welsh bindings are noteworthy for their durability rather than their artistry, being sturdily bound in leather (often sheep) with crude blind tooling. The accolade given by the antiquary Thomas Pennant was rare: 'I am fortunate in having in Thomas Roden of Denbigh, a most admirable binder: and so extremely elegant in his trade, that excepting a few of the most capital, unequalled by any in London.'[16] The volumes bound for Pennant, usually in vellum, were well executed, but they cannot qualify as 'fine bindings'. The only contemporary binding in that category which may have been done in Wales is the Alltyrodin commonplace book of 1770.[17] It belonged to David Lloyd of Alltyrodin, a Cardiganshire country seat, and it is bound in beautifully gold-tooled morocco. The ornaments are identical with those used on the binding of a copy of a Welsh Bible, with commentary by Peter Williams, printed in Carmarthen in 1770. The volume had remained in the hands of descendants of the Williams family until it was acquired by Principal J. H. Davies (d.1926), whose collection in due course came to the National Library. There was greater variety in style in the 19th century and greater sophistication in execution, but it is fair to state that ancillary material relating to Welsh bookbinders tends to be far more interesting than the end-products; diaries and account-books, advertisements and letters, wills and inventories are of inestimable value.

Dotted amongst the Welsh and Celtic collections in the Library are distinctive half-leather bindings which bear on the flyleaf a stamp 'BOUND BY BLACKWELL.' Henry Blackwell (1851-1928), born in Liverpool of a Welsh mother, emigrated to New York in 1877 and achieved renown as a bookseller, bookbinder, book collector and bibliographer, with a special interest in Welsh Americana. His bindings are generally sturdy but unremarkable and were it not for the fact that he donated to the National Library in October 1923 a copy of Max O'Rell's *Her Royal Highness, Woman* (New York etc., 1901), which has the manuscript inscription 'sample of my binding/ Henry Blackwell' on the flyleaf, his considerable talent as a fine binder might have gone unrecognized in the land of his ancestors. A drab slipcase gives no hint of what it protects. The actual volume is bound in navy-blue levant morocco, gold-tooled with green, blue, ivory, crimson and brown onlays, with both covers linked across the spine by a floral pattern. On the upper cover, a naked woman raises her head and arms to a star, while the lower cover shows a spider trapped in a web. Ornate leather doublures offer further testimony to the binder's consummate skills and embossed silk end-papers contribute a final touch of opulence.

In view of strong links between the north Welsh and Irish book trade, the paucity of Irish bindings in the Library is somewhat surprising. The finest examples are comparatively recent purchases. There is a set of volumes bound by the early 19th-century Dublin binder, George Mullen, and a small volume, Roger Hutchinson's *The Image of God* (London, 1560), bound by the bibliophile Sir Edward Sullivan (1852-1928). 'Bound by' is not entirely accurate, for it was Sir Edward's practice to decorate books already bound or to have books bound for him to decorate. The above volume, bearing the binder's customary signature 'E. S. AURIFEX', is bound in blue morocco, barely visible under a welter of crimson, purple, citron and green onlays and lavish gold-tooling. The tooling lacks a certain finesse but the total effect is pleasing in its exuberance. Sir Edward exhibited his bindings in the 1895 exhibition organized by the Arts and Crafts Society of Ireland. He defended bookbinding as an art in an address to Ye Sette of Odd Volumes in 1911, stating that 'Bookbinding in its highest forms . . . are in no sense inferior to the finest work we know in pottery, wood-carving, metal-chasing, or any of the textile crafts whose very excellence makes it a matter of extreme difficulty to determine the boundary line which really separates Craft from Art.'[18]

The first exhibition of the Arts and Craft Society in England was held in London in 1888. With protagonists such as William Morris, Walter and T. J. Cobden-Sanderson, the tenets of the Arts and Crafts Movement soon permeated the book world, affecting printing, illustration and binding, as the Library's comprehensive collection of private press books testifies. A bookseller, Frank Karslake, was fired by zeal for hand-craftsmanship and was the driving force behind the formation in 1898 of two shortlived but important ventures, the Hampstead Bindery and the Guild of Women Binders. The Hampstead Bindery is represented in the Library by one work: No.36 of an edition of 100 of A. M. F. Robinson's *An Italian garden* (Portland, Maine: printed for Thomas B. Mosher, 1897). Bound in green morocco and decorated in art nouveau style, with *pointillé* tooling and small gilt hearts and crimson onlays depicting petals, it is signed on the lower turn-in of the upper cover 'THE HAMPSTEAD BINDERY'. A book-plate dated 1894 pasted inside the upper cover reveals that a former owner was John Morgan, Rubshaw House, Aberdeen, architect and surveyor.

The Guild of Women Binders was a loosely-knit federation of binders who claimed in their advertisements that their work was 'entirely handwork aided by no mechanical devices whatsoever'. Of the examples in the Library, the nicest comes from the Gregynog Library Collection, a collection of private press books and fine bindings deposited in the National Library when the Gregynog Press ceased operating. A copy of Edward Garnett's *An Imaged world* (London, 1894) has been bound in green goatskin, elegantly gold-tooled with the delicate undulating lines associated with Art Nouveau. As was the case with the Hampstead Bindery, the signature does not identify the binder but is the modest 'GUILD OF WOMEN-BINDERS'. One of its members was Gwladys Edwards and the same collection has a striking example of her work. A copy of *Twenty Chinese Poems, paraphrased by Clifford Bax* (London, 1910), is bound in chestnut goatskin, blind-tooled with an intricate interlacing strapwork design against a stippled background. Tiny turquoise-green circular onlays are used to good effect, the turquoise being highlighted by matching coloured edges.

The Arts and Crafts movement brought in its wake a gracefulness which tempered the florid excesses of the Victorian era. Its proponents revitalized commercial book-production as well as the private press. Prominent artists were commissioned as illustrators and as designers of bindings. Covers displaying the unmistakable artistic styles of Dante Gabriel Rossetti, Aubrey Beardsley, Charles Ricketts, Laurence Housman and Walter Crane are as likely to be found gracing the shelves of the English Literature section as the Library's Private Presses collection. Morley of Oxford produced tasteful designs for the trade, several examples of which may be found in the Library, together with a few specimens of his special bindings, the most flamboyant being *The Book of Ceylon* by Henry W. Cave (London, 1912), which is bound in purple morocco and gold-tooled in a scintillating display of decoration and craftsmanship. The prestigious firm of Sangorski and Sutcliffe bound Sir Thomas Browne's *Urne buriall . . . With drawings by Paul Nash* (London, 1932) to a design by the illustrator.

As a result of the Arts and Crafts Movement, Wales entered the arena of fine binding. Inspired by its ideals, the Misses Gwendoline and Margaret Davies set up in 1922 at their Montgomeryshire country seat the Gregynog Press, with Dr Thomas Jones (then Deputy Secretary to the Cabinet) as its driving force. George Fisher, who joined the Press in 1924, conceived the idea of issuing 15 to 20 copies of every edition printed at the Press in special bindings. The National Library has a complete set of Gregynog books, in special and ordinary bindings. Fisher, although he could and did design bindings, was primarily a craftsman and was happy to execute the designs of R. A. Maynard, H. W. Bray and Blair Hughes-Stanton.[19] He was a perfectionist, whose exacting standards are recalled with awe by one of his apprentices, John Ewart Bowen.[20]

John Bowen, on finishing his apprenticeship in 1940, joined the Army and found on his return that the Gregynog Press had failed to survive the exigencies of the War. He entered the Binding and Conservation Section of the National Library of Wales. The demands of his post in the National Library, especially when he became head of department, meant that there were few opportunities for giving full rein to his talents as a fine binder. Consequently, the few examples of his work in the Fine Bindings Collection

Fig.3. The History of Merioneth, volume I, by E. G. Bowen and C. A. Gresham (Dolgellau, 1967), bound by John E. Bowen. Reproduced by kind permission of the National Library of Wales.

are greatly treasured. A particularly effective specimen is the binding of *The History of Merioneth*, volume I, by E. G. Bowen and C. A. Gresham (Dolgellau, 1967), in which black lines and onlays are subtly used to depict a menhir against a mountainous background (fig.3).

In 1970, the tradition of fine book production at Gregynog was revived by the setting up of Gwasg Gregynog.[21] Once again, a certain number of copies of each edition are issued in special bindings and once again the National Library has a complete set. Special bindings of Kate Roberts's *Two Old Men*, illustrated by Kyffin Williams (1981), were bound by Desmond Shaw to the artist's landscape design. Other 'specials' were done by James Brockman, Sally Lou Smith and Julian Thomas, all Fellows of Designer Bookbinders. The skills of other Fellows can be admired at the Library — Bernard Middleton, Elizabeth Greenhill, Jeff Clements, Edward Gray, Francis Womersley, Arthur Johnson and Paul Delrue.

Julian Thomas is currently Head of Binding and Conservation at the Library. Trained by John Bowen, he has benefited from the tradition of craftsmanship passed down from George Fisher. All members of the department undergo a rigorous training in binding and conservation and, remarkably, every member of staff has proved capable of producing fine bindings to exhibition standard. Julian Thomas has won several prizes in competitions set by Designer Bookbinders, the Society of Bookbinders and Book-restorers and the National Library of Scotland. He was invited 'as one of the finest binders capable of working in this medium' to bind and tool one of 30 copies of Bernard C. Middleton's *Recollections* for the Bird & Bull Press. Art and craft may be admired throughout the collections in the National Library of Wales, but nowhere are they more impressively united than in the living tradition manifest in the Binding and Conservation Section.

References

I am deeply indebted to the staff of the Binding and Conservation Section in the National Library of Wales for their help with descriptions of bindings. A series of short articles on 'Bookbindings in the National Library of Wales', written by Eiluned Rees, John E. Bowen and Julian Thomas, appeared in issues of *The National Library of Wales Journal* between 1985 and 1988.

1. *Exhibition of the Works of Industry of all Nations, 1851. Reports by the Juries . . . Vol.III* (London, 1852), p.928.
2. W. Ll. Davies, *The National Library of Wales: a survey of its history, its contents and its activities* (Aberystwyth, 1937).
3. Details of Sir John Williams's Library may be found in the Sir John Williams Centenary Number of *The National Library of Wales Journal*, 1 (1940), pp.173-232.
4. D. Huws, 'The making of Liber Landavensis', in *The National Library of Wales Journal*, 25 (1987), pp.133-60, with an Appendix 'The gilt-bronze Christ in Majesty' by Neil Stratford. I acknowledge the generous help given to me by Mr Huws in identifying and describing all

medieval bindings in the National Library as well as in allowing me to quote extensively from this article.

5. Personal discussions with the late G. Pollard.
6. National Library of Wales Add MS 17520A.
7. Personal discussions with the late H. Nixon.
8. *Selecti Dionysii Halicarnassensis de Prisis Scriptoribus Tractatus, Graece et Latine . . . Editio altera* (London, 1778).
9. A forthcoming article by John Holmes will discuss fore-edge paintings in the National Library of Wales.
10. Octave Uzanne, 'French bookbindings', in *The Studio* (1899), p.64.
11. G. Flaubert, *Salammbô* (Paris, 1900).
12. F. Coppée, *Le Passant* (Paris, 1897).
13. *Exhibition of the Works of Industry of all Nations, 1851. Reports by the Juries . . . Vol.III*, p.929. For further information see the article by Esther Potter in this volume.
14. *Ibid.*, p.930.
15. E. Rees, 'Bookbinding in 18th-century Wales', in *Journal of the Welsh Bibliographical Society*, 12 (1983-4), pp.51-66.
16. Manuscript version of Thomas Pennant's *Literary Life*, National Library of Wales Add MS 12706E.
17. National Library of Wales Add MS 14990F.
18. Reprinted in *Quarterly Bulletin of the Irish Georgian Society*, 17, no.3-4 (1974).
19. D. Harrop, *A History of the Gregynog Press* (Pinner: Private Libraries Association, 1980).
20. It was John Bowen who inspired my interest in bookbinding and who taught me how to appreciate the art and craft of bookbinding through the ages. I can never thank him enough for doing so, as the interest enriched the years I spent in the National Library of Wales.
21. D. Esslemont and G. Tegai Hughes, *Gwasg Gregynog: a descriptive catalogue of printing at Gregynog 1970-1990* (Newtown, Powys: Gwasg Gregynog, 1990).

Memoir of Robin Myers

MANY PEOPLE reading this book will have heard of Robin Myers; and many will be friends of hers, because Robin has an enormous capacity for friendship. These readers will recognize much in the reminiscences that follow, and maybe even find out something new about her; while for those who have never met Robin, or never encountered her in autobiographical mood, the official life reads something like this.

Robin was born in Cambridge, and educated at the Perse School for Girls and Lady Margaret Hall, Oxford, where she read English. After going down she became a schoolmistress, and then publicity officer for the Cambridge bookseller Bowes & Bowes, before teaching English as a foreign language in Cambridge, London and Madrid. After a brief spell running a children's bookshop in Kensington, she became Librarian of the National Book League and — from 1970 — taught English and Spanish at the North London Collegiate School, as well as running their archives. She became Archivist of the Stationers' Company in 1978, editing the 115-reel microfilm edition for the publishers Chadwyck-Healey in 1986 and publishing an index to them in 1990; and, together with Michael Harris, she founded the annual conferences on book trade history held by the Centre for Extra-Mural Studies at Birkbeck College, London. In 1996 she became the first woman President of the Bibliographical Society.

This is a varied curriculum vitae, and helps to explain why Robin has inspired a few apocryphal tales in her time. At the North London Collegiate School, where I first met her, she combined the roles of English and Spanish mistress and archivist, and was different from most teachers. It was vaguely known that she was an author, and we were in awe of this. Garbled versions of her other lives got out, satirized in a sketch about the staff in an end-of-term revue where one of the characters said breathlessly, 'Apparently she works in a stationers' shop'. She approached me first when I was a sixth-former, having heard that I collected books, and in parting, she said cheerfully, 'It's nice to meet a fellow enthusiast'. I think I remember this because it could serve as an epigraph for Robin's career.

This is not intended to be a formal biographical memoir. We felt that a montage was more appropriate, as a recognition of Robin's versatility and astonishingly various life, and have commissioned photographers from some of her milieux, though undoubtedly not all: a mixture of official poses and informal snapshots. Despite Robin's well-known dislike of being photographed, we hope she will forgive our temerity; at least all the likenesses are taken by friends.

ALISON SHELL

In the beginning

When Robin has visited me in Wiltshire over the years, she has come bearing gifts: home-made biscuits from her mother, and, invariably, some recent article that she herself has written. One particularly valued item, entitled 'The pleasures and pitfalls of bibliography—a personal reminiscence' (see Bibliography), gives a clue as to how that initial spark was ignited that has fired Robin's lifelong enthusiasm for this subject.

In the 1950s, Robin and I worked together at Bowes & Bowes in Cambridge: she doing the publicity, and I running the antiquarian book department. One day I happened to mention McKerrow's *Introduction to Bibliography*, and was most surprised at the degree of her enthusiasm for the book. Not only had she read it, but she seemed to have digested it as well. Robin was already on track! It was only later, when I came to read 'Pleasures and pitfalls of bibliography', that I realized why the mention of McKerrow had elicited such a keen response. By quoting from the article, I will let Robin speak for herself about those early influences which led her to think of bibliography as her business.

The start is way back . . . while I was still an undergraduate at Oxford. Three men introduced me to bibliography and stirred my imagination for what many find a dry field. . . . By a coincidence, two of them were running or had run the Clarendon Press in Oxford; all three were 'Press authors'. Kenneth Sisam . . . employed me to do a vacation job on the addenda to the Little Oxford Dictionary. . . . My ignorance was astounding, I now think, even for the very young, and he sought to extend my education in two ways unconnected with the task he set me. He put me before a typewriter . . . and he put into my hands his copy of R. B. McKerrow's *Introduction to bibliography for literary students*. I have it still, with my name written on the flyleaf in my best attempt at Elizabethan secretary hand, for which McKerrow gives the alphabet in the appendix. Counselled to read and digest, I soon became enthralled, even though I found it quite hard going without previous training. I suppose I should have fallen a casualty on the bibliographical battlefield if the volume had been Professor Bowers's *Principles of bibliographical description* instead, which was just then creating such a furore in Oxford. . . . The following term I attended a seminar on textual criticism given by R. W. Chapman, Mr Sisam's predecessor as Press Secretary. . . . I struggled through *Cancels* and read what Chapman had to say about the textual editing of Dr Johnson and Jane Austen, and no doubt the accounts made more impact for my being able to catch tones of voice in the printed words. The third man to influence me in a bibliographical way (to crib a phrase from Professor Bowers) was David Nichol Smith, by then professor emeritus. . . . He introduced me to historical bibliography. . . . He gave us an inspiring series of lectures on the development of the novel and the growth of the reading public. I at once fell in love with the history of the book trade, although I did not know it could ever become my business as well as my pleasure.

NEST DAVIES

The Stationers' Company

Robin Myers has been Honorary Archivist of the Stationers' and Newspaper Makers' Company since May 1979. It has been her achievement, with little assistance, to sort, rearrange and list the archives of the Company systematically; to supervise their transfer to a new Muniment Room near the Company's Library; to arrange better storage of loose items; and to carry out a methodical programme of restoration and conservation of many of the bound books in the archives. In addition, Robin arranged for the microfilm edition of the archival records to be published by Chadwyck-Healey in 1986, a development that has aided scholars throughout the world and saved wear and tear on the original items. The royalties on sales of the microfilm have benefited the Company in general and the archives in particular, and continue to do so. Robin's great work, *The Stationers' Company Archive 1554-1984*, a catalogue of the archival records with valuable commentaries, exemplifies her achievement. Within the last few years, Robin has taken the initiative in founding a society of City archivists – a very successful innovation.

Through all her work on the archives and her skill in encouraging others to use them, Robin has effectively made the Company's Muniment Room and Library at Stationers' Hall a small research centre. Visiting academics – from Britain and abroad – can study the microfilm or the original records in the Library, which contains, *inter alia*, general reference works of use to historians and bibliographers. The Library of the Bibliographical Society, of which Robin is Honorary Librarian, is housed in a room adjoining the Company's Library and complements it. Robin, indeed, has been tireless in the help she has given researchers, and has also good-humouredly answered many questions from people seeking, for example, information about forbears connected with the Company or its associated trades. My cousin, the late Charles Rivington, was a co-founder of the Company's Library, which was opened in 1978. He did much work at Stationers' Hall in arranging the Library and assisting Robin in some archival work. Robin and Charles became close friends and he would have been delighted to know that this festschrift was being published.

Today Robin Myers has almost certainly a better knowledge of the history of the Stationers' and Newspaper Makers' Company than anyone else, and she is currently editing a new history of the Company in the 19th and 20th centuries. Robin is widely respected within the Company, and many Liverymen value her friendship and helpful advice. She has succeeded in making most members of the Company appreciate that the archives are the jewel in the crown of its possessions, a significant change in outlook.

CHRISTOPHER RIVINGTON
Liveryman, Worshipful Company of Stationers and Newspaper Makers

The Bibliographical Society

When Robin Myers joined the Bibliographical Society in 1975 she was no stranger to its meetings, having previously come to the lectures using the institutional membership of the National Book League. One of the most regular attenders, enjoying the company over tea as well as the intellectual entertainment, she soon became a well-known feature, usually seated at the right-hand side of the second row, commenting pertinently on links with the Stationers' Company or testing the speaker with questions, frequently relating to the book trade.

Nor did her contributions remain purely intellectual. Great physical effort was expended in moving the Society's library, which for some time had been deteriorating slowly in the bowels of the Watson Library at University College, London, to its new home at Stationers' Hall. Robin had just been appointed the Society's archivist and librarian, and as no money was available for this move, she organized it herself. Together with the Secretary, her husband and a bevy of Robin's inexhaustible supply of useful young men, she dismantled and collected the shelving from the Robinson brothers, hired a van, packed, moved and unpacked the books and papers. After a long weekend of back-breaking work, the library was housed in the room adjacent to that occupied by the Stationers' Company library. Bringing these two libraries together was a splendid idea, and greatly improved the accessibility of the Society's library and archive. Now properly arranged, they provided most of the exhibits for the Society's centenary show at the London antiquarian book fair in 1992. Together with the Secretary, Robin chose the material, wrote the publicity leaflet and the labels and mounted this exhibition. The links between the Society and the Stationers' Company, visible throughout the former's history, became stronger and more apparent. The Society's grand centenary dinner took place in Stationers' Hall, an occasion that owed much of its success to the Archivist's persuasive powers and never-failing attention to domestic and decorative detail.

Being a convivial person with a natural inclination to dispense hospitality, Robin volunteered to relieve the Society's Secretary of the chore of organizing the twice-yearly dinners of the Colophon Club. Since 1986, first with the help of Jenny Stratford, then single-handedly, Robin has ordered food and wine for the Council and their guests, persuading a variety of restaurants and catering managers to ever-better bargains.

In October 1987 she was elected a Vice-President of the Society and nine years later she has become its first woman President.

MIRJAM FOOT
formerly Secretary to the Bibliographical Society

The Book Trade History Conferences

When I first had the idea of a regular conference on book trade history my first task was to identify someone who could become closely involved in the construction and direction of events. It had to be someone with a clear and widely acknowledged reputation in the field, with a broadly based experience in teaching and lecturing and, at the same time, someone who could put up with the tiresome activities which have become known as marketing. There was only one person whose range of interests and expertise in book trade history fitted those demanding requirements; and it was, of course, Robin Myers.

I had known Robin slightly for some time before 1978 when the plot was hatched, and was well aware of her range of interests and achievements: worn lightly, but with some appearance of severity. It was a great relief when, after a short discussion, she agreed to become involved in what, at the time, seemed a pretty short-term venture. Thanks to Robin, this has proved to be far from the case. The book trade conferences are continuing even now, and have become part of the calendar of activities which provide a focus for a subject which is generally under-represented in the academic system. The most recent, in 1996, was held at Stationers' Hall.

From the first, Robin has been closely involved in orchestrating the event. This has partly been through her effective chairing of the sessions, with rigorous attention to timing, as well as through the brilliant and soundly based material presented through her own contributions. However, in some respects, the keynote of her contribution has been her gift for friendship, and for initiating and sustaining relationships with people of all ages and backgrounds working in the field.

The proceedings of the conference have been published in book form since 1981, currently under the imprint of St Paul's Bibliographies, and the quality and range of the contributors is in itself a striking tribute to Robin's circle of personal contacts. Her combination of academic rigour, persistence and personal warmth have underpinned the conferences and are also reflected in the range of people, listed in each of the volumes, who have become a regular part of the audience. I am personally delighted to have the chance to acknowledge my own debt of support and friendship.

MICHAEL HARRIS

A bookseller's tale
The bookseller E. P. Goldschmidt had an ideal of the perfect customer as someone living a good way off, who occasionally sent a postcard ordering something expensive. This vision probably still holds good for many of his profession, even if the postcard might nowadays seem a little quaint. However, even the most obdurately misanthropic bibliopole could hardly fail to be charmed by an early evening invitation to Robin Myers's Islington home, there to sip a sherry *à l'Écosse* (thistle-shaped glass) or a g & t *à l'Anglais* (*sans glace*) while she inspects a selection of items from a recent catalogue. Whether or not one leaves noticeably richer or with a bag noticeably lighter is as irrelevant as looking to see whether or not a Zen archer has hit the target.

In the beginning, Robin was, for me, almost as chimaerical a figure as Goldschmidt's preferred client. 'Robin Myers' was a name bandied about with ubiquity, but there was an elusive, almost pseudonymous quality about it. For reasons unfathomable, I had envisaged the author of *The British Book Trade* as large and chaotic, maybe a cat-lover but most certainly a *man*.

Not everyone will have or have seen either or both of Robin's catalogues, so not everyone will be aware of her brief previous incarnation as a bookseller. The knowledge that Robin had, in truth, been the *éminence grise* behind MI5 for the last couple of decades, or was venerated as the leading lion-tamer of her day, somehow seems more credible than imagining her ever a bookseller; without the documentary evidence of a brace of RM catalogues before me, I would dismiss the notion with derision. Quite why the idea seems so implausible is hard to pinpoint, but doubtless she possesses subtle qualities not traced in a merchant of books. Whatever, the loss to our profession has been to the gain of bookworld scholarship. Unquestionably the ever-increasing interest in one of the serious books-about-books person's biggest dates in the calendar, the annual two-day conference on book-trade history, is in a great part due to her discrimination and energy. It would be pleasant to imagine that the antiquarian book world was full of international variations on a theme of Robin Myers, but sadly it isn't; she is indeed a rare tome, probably unique, and as such she is both valued and cherished.

JOHN WALWYN JONES
Questor Rare Books

North London Collegiate School
I am probably in the unique position of having known Robin first as a schoolteacher, then as a colleague and fellow archivist.

Her knowledge and her scholarship were her great strengths as an A-level teacher of English Literature. As her pupils we were amused to perceive that her choice of texts was governed as much by her love of the past as by her love of literature. Shakespeare and Milton were acceptable, but Sheridan was as close as she would get to the 20th century. Our interest was stimulated by her showing us some contemporary manuscripts, and at the end of the course we were touched to be invited for tea, strawberries and cream at her flat in Islington – it was small but elegant, its book-lined walls giving us a glimpse of her other life.

When I returned to NLCS to teach English I learned more about Robin's 'other life'. Her conversation was enlivened by her disarming habit of referring to historical figures by their Christian names only, as though they were old friends. We all also experienced her gracious hospitality, this time at her house in Islington – much larger, spread over five floors, but still full of books. Who could forget Robin's delicious summer pudding or the 'tipsy cake', when she always confessed to having 'overdone it' with the sherry?

As our school archivist, Robin's contacts and her knowledge of the relevant systems and skills were invaluable. She devoted many hours to setting up exhibitions, and it is to her dedication that we owe the beautiful enlarged photographs of Canons in the 1930s which are now permanently mounted around the school. Robin could also be remarkably forward-thinking: for someone who refused to have a television and could say 'Who is Ian Botham?' with all the hauteur of a high court judge, she was nevertheless eager to embrace computers and could often be seen with her trusty 'lap-top'. We have greatly benefited from Robin's company, scholarship and hospitality during her time at North London, and we still enjoy our occasional meetings: I look forward to many more.

HELEN TURNER
Ex-pupil, now Head of English Department,
North London Collegiate School

Mentoring
When I first limped into Robin's life (I had recently fallen downstairs when engaged on some sordid household task) I was a rootless temporary secretary with excellent office skills, an indifferent first degree and aspirations to become an archivist. Some ten years later my life has been transformed. I am now wife, mother and — thanks in large part to her help, encouragement and specialist training — archivist at the Fawcett Library and All Hallows by the Tower.

Robin also introduced me to the discipline of historical bibliography — or bibliographical history — through her Camden Local Authority evening class on book collecting, which she ran for almost 20 years. How I wish I had taken better notes. Many of the people who first met Robin at her class became lifelong friends, while others were birds of passage, but we all remember her perched on the teacher's desk in a most informal manner while delivering extremely solid and impressive lectures on aspects of the book. Sometimes we were allowed to bring our own treasures to pass round and discuss — which we all loved because other people do collect such strange things — sometimes Robin would have arranged a visit by an expert, or we would go on excursions. Such times! Thank you, Robin, for all your hard work and kindness.

I would recommend everybody to acquire a Robin, but sadly there are not many to the square mile and those of us who are privileged to know one are extremely fortunate.

ANNA GREENING

Then and now
Robin and I became friends at Lady Margaret Hall, when we both embarked on research. Her interest was in 18th-century learned ladies. Looking back, I see her full of optimism, flinging herself dauntlessly at the task before her. On holiday she would have no truck with maps, always sure

that, if she got lost, some white knight would come to her rescue. Her abiding optimism has almost always been justified. Undismayed by large undertakings, she has had the determination to see them through. On her own, she has made her name in the exacting field of bibliography.

Robin is proud of her Jewish stock, and especially of her gifted mother, whose indomitable spirit she has inherited. She is, as her mother was, elegant. Even in our early days, when clothes were rationed, holiday snaps show her attractively and stylishly dressed. She likes to have beautiful things about her, books handsomely bound.

Her wide circle of friends, of diverse ages, nationalities and interests, reflects not only her varied activities, but also her capacity to engage and retain the interest and affection of all sorts of people, and to share with them her pleasures. Always hospitable and sociable, Robin never seems to get older. Retirement is not for her. This is an occasion for celebrating the happy continuance of her bibliographical researches and her enjoyment of good fellowship.

CELIA SISAM

Published works of Robin Myers, 1954-1996

COMPILED BY ARNOLD HUNT

1954
'Bowes & Bowes, 1581-1945', *Antiquarian Booksellers' Journal*.

1962
'Miss Elizabeth Garrett [obituary]', *The Persean*, 54 (December 1962), 2-3.

1965
'English Books in Spain', *Books: the Journal of the National Book League*, 358 (March–April 1965), 62-5.

1967
Handlist of books and periodicals on British book design since the war. (12pp. pamphlet issued to accompany the Galley Club exhibition of Book Design 1945-66, held 4-7 April 1967 at Collins, 15 St James's Place, London SW1.)

1968
'The N.B.L. Library of Books about Books: its resources and the service it offers to book collectors', *Books: the Journal of the National Book League*, 374 (Summer 1968), 39-40.

1970
A Dictionary of Literature in the English Language, from Chaucer to 1940. Compiled and edited by Robin Myers for the National Book League. 2 volumes (vol.1: Dictionary; vol.2: Title-Author Index). Oxford: Pergamon Press. (See RM's article 'The Pleasures and Pitfalls of Bibliography' (1980) for an account of the publication of this work.)

1972
Robin Myers Catalogue 1 (Mainly Egyptology). (A catalogue of secondhand books, undated but *c.*1972.)

1973
The British Book Trade from Caxton to the Present Day: a bibliographical guide based on the libraries of the National Book League and St Bride Institute. André Deutsch in association with the National Book League. (See RM's article 'The Pleasures and Pitfalls of Bibliography' (1980) for an account of the publication of this work.) Reviewed: *The Library*, 5th ser., 33: 2 (David McKitterick).

Robin Myers Catalogue 2 (Mainly History, Topography and Travel). (A catalogue of secondhand books, undated but *c.*1973.)

'George Henry Robins (1778-1847): Strawberry Hill Auctioneer', *The Printing Art*, 1: 1 (Spring 1973), 2-10.

1974
Aids in the Selection of British Books: an annotated and classified guide to book selection for the use of booksellers, librarians and other bookbuyers. (60pp. bibliography published by the British Council and the National Book League, intended 'to help users to discover what books are published in Britain and how to obtain them'.)

'George Robins in Person: the Man and the Myth', *Printing Art Annual* (1974), 9-17. (On portraits and caricatures of Robins.)

1975

'John Watson (1914-1975)', *ABMR*, 2: 12, p.33.

1976

'The Quincentenary of William Caxton (1422?-1491)', *ABMR*, 3: 5/6 (June-July 1976), 158-61.

Caxtoniana, or the progress of Caxton studies from the earliest times to 1976. (16pp. catalogue issued to accompany exhibition at the St Bride Printing Library, 20 September-29 October 1976.)

'William Caxton: master mercer, printer, publisher, editor, translator . . .' (review of books on Caxton by G. D. Painter, N. F. Blake and Richard Deacon), *ABMR*, 3: 10 (October 1976), 296-8.

1977

'The Bibliomites (1950-)', *ABMR* 4: 9 (September 1977), 368-9.

'Key Works in Bibliography: 1. Michael Sadleir: the book collector as bibliographer', *ABMR*, 4: 10 (October 1977), 394-8.

1978

A Dictionary of Literature in the English Language from 1940 to 1970: complete with alphabetical title-author index and a geographical-chronological index to authors. Compiled and edited by Robin Myers. Oxford: Pergamon Press. (A sequel to the 1970 *Dictionary.*)

'Key Works in Bibliography: 2. R. B. McKerrow, *An Introduction to Bibliography*, a study in analytical and critical bibliography', *ABMR*, 5: 1 (January 1978), 8-11.

'Key Works in Bibliography: 3. W. W. Greg, A Bibliography of the English Printed Drama to the Restoration, descriptive bibliography and bibliographical theory', *ABMR*, 5: 3 (March 1978), 98-102.

'Gregynog: the Aberystwyth Bibliographical Group Residential Weekend Symposium on Book Collecting', *ABMR*, 5: 10 (October 1978), pp.444-5.

'A Meeting of the Printing Historical Society on Five Hundred Years of Printing at Oxford; held in Keble College, Oxford, 29th-30th September 1978', *ABMR*, 5: 11 (November 1978), 494.

'William Blades's Debt to Henry Bradshaw and G. I. F. Tupper in his Caxton Studies: a Further Look at Unpublished Documents', *The Library*, 5th ser., 33: 4 (December 1978), 265-83.

'George Isaac Frederick Tupper, Facsimilist 'whose ability in this description of work is beyond praise' (1820?-1911)', *Transactions of the Cambridge Bibliographical Society*, 7 (1978), 113-34.

Review of Ian Maxted, *The London Book Trade 1775-1800*, *The Library*, 5th ser., 33: 4 (December 1978), 338-40.

1979

'The First Fifty Years of the Bibliographical Society, 1892-1942' (no.4 in the series 'Key Works in Bibliography'), *ABMR*, 6: 4 (April 1979), 148-53.

'Key Works in Bibliography: 5. Percy Simpson: historical and analytical bibliography', *ABMR*, 6: 7 (July 1979), 286-9.

'Key Works in Bibliography: 7. Fredson Bowers: descriptive bibliography', *ABMR*, 6: 9 (September 1979), 362-7.

'A Forgotten Manuscript at Stationers' Hall', *British Book News* (September 1979), 709-10.

'A Manual of Printing as Bibliographical Tool: Joseph Moxon' (no.7 in the series 'Key Works in Bibliography'), *ABMR*, 6: 11 (November 1979), 476-9.

'Bibliographica: Papers on Books, their History and Art 1895-1897', *The Private Library*, 3rd ser., 2: 3 (Autumn 1979), 86-94.

'The Library of Waddesdon Manor', *The Private Library*, 3rd ser., 2: 3 (Autumn 1979), 115-20.

'Work in progress: and could be all according to Cocker', *The Stationer & Newspaper Maker*, 20 (Autumn 1979), 13.

1980

'The Pleasures and Pitfalls of Bibliography: a Personal Reminiscence', *Kentucky Review*, vol.2, no.1, pp.37-51.

'Had Slides—Did Travel', *The Stationer & Newspaper Maker*, 23 (Autumn 1980), 31.

1981

Development of the English Book Trade, 1700-1899. Edited by Robin Myers and Michael Harris. Oxford: Oxford Polytechnic Press. Reviewed: *The Library*, 6th ser., 5: 1 (Elizabeth James), *Notes & Queries*, 229: 1 (J. D. Fleeman), *TLS*, 2 April 1982 (Pat Rogers).

'Top Edge Guilt: John Carter and Graham Pollard, *An Enquiry into the Nature of Certain Nineteenth Century Pamphlets*', *ABMR*, 8: 1 (January 1981), 4-9 and 8: 2 (February 1981), 52-7.

'William Blades (1824-1890), *The Life and Typography of William Caxton* (2 vols. 1861-3)', *ABMR*, 8: 4 (April 1981), 130-6.

'In his own Write' (review of Peter Beal, *Index of English Literary Manuscripts*, vol.1, parts 1 and 2), *ABMR*, 8: 4 (April 1981), 140-3.

'The Hinman Collator: a new way of looking at Shakespeare First Folios', *ABMR*, 8: 6 (June 1981), 219-23.

'Natural Historians' (review of Gavin D. R. Bridson, Valerie C. Phillips and Anthony P. Harvey, *Natural History Manuscript Resources in the British Isles*), *ABMR*, 8: 11 (November 1981), 433-4.

'The Work of the Honorary Archivist', *The Stationer & Newspaper Maker*, 26 (Autumn 1981), 48, and 27 (Spring 1982), 52.

1982

Sale and Distribution of Books from 1700. Edited by Robin Myers and Michael Harris. Oxford: Oxford Polytechnic Press. RM contributes an article: 'Sale by Auction: the Rise of Auctioneering Exemplified in the Firm of Christopher Cock, the Langfords, and Henry, John and George Robins (c.1720-1847)', 126-63. Reviewed: *The Library*, 6th ser., 6: 2 (M. J. Crump), *Notes & Queries*, 229: 1 (J. D. Fleeman), *ABMR*, 10: 7 (D. J. Hall).

'It is hard to know whom the Union Catalogue is meant to serve' (review of F. J. G. Robinson *et al.*, *Eighteenth Century British Books: an Author Union Catalogue*), *ABMR*, 9: 4 (April 1982), 150.

'Fragments preserved' (review of Jenny Stratford, *Catalogue of the Jackson Collection of Manuscript Fragments in the Royal Library, Windsor Castle*), *ABMR*, 9: 11 (November 1982), 429.

'The whereabouts of manuscripts' (review of Barbara Rosenbaum and Pamela White, *Index of English Literary Manuscripts*, vol.4, part 1), *ABMR*, 9: 12 (December 1982), 474.

'Vita Humana Bulla Est: Human Life's a Bubble: Richard Johnson (1757-1793)', *The Stationer & Newspaper Maker*, 28 (Summer 1982), 61, and 29 (Autumn 1982), 71.

1983

Author/Publisher Relations during the Eighteenth and Nineteenth Centuries. Edited by Robin Myers and Michael Harris. Oxford: Oxford Polytechnic Press. RM contributes an article: 'Writing for Booksellers in the Early Nineteenth Century: a case study' (on the author Joseph Timothy Haydn), 119-55.

The English Stock of the Stationers' Company. Privately printed for the Wynkyn de Worde Society. (11pp. pamphlet based on a lecture delivered at Stationers' Hall on 23 September 1982, with a handlist of the accompanying exhibition.) Reprinted in *The Stationer & Newspaper Maker*, 34 (Summer 1984), 31-2, with a photograph of the author and her assistant in the muniment room at Stationers' Hall.

'The Records of the Worshipful Company of Stationers and Newspaper Makers 1554-1912', *Archives*, 16 (April 1983), 28-38; reprinted with additions and corrections in *Publishing History*, 13 (1983), 89-104.

'Maintaining a Specialist Archive in the Location that engendered it', *Society of Archivists Specialist Repositories Group, Occasional Papers*, 1 (1983), 17-21.

'Report of the Hon. Archivist for period 10 June 1982 to 10 January 1983', *The Stationer & Newspaper Maker*, 31 (Summer 1983), 15.

'Unique Copy of a Broadside Summons of 1762', *The Stationer & Newspaper Maker*, 32 (Autumn 1983), 19-20.

1984

Maps and Prints: Aspects of the English Book Trade. Edited by Robin Myers and Michael Harris. Oxford: Oxford Polytechnic Press. Reviewed: *British Book News*, 1985 (David McKitterick).

'Entered at Stationers' Hall'. An exhibition demonstrating the role of the Stationers' Company in the printing and publishing industries from 1554 to the present day. By Robin Myers and Herbert Smart. (4pp. leaflet issued to accompany exhibition at the Science Museum, South Kensington.)

'The Wise File – A Detective Story' (review of Nicolas Barker and John Collins, *A Sequel to an Enquiry*), *ABMR*, 11: 1 (January 1984), 20-1.

'A Rare Stationers' Company Broadside Summons', *Factotum*, 18 (March 1984), 14-15.

'Globetrotting: Robin Myers at Gregynog', *ABMR*, 11: 11 (November 1984), 453-4.

1985

Economics of the British Booktrade 1605-1939. Edited by Robin Myers and Michael Harris. Cambridge: Chadwyck-Healey. Publishing History Occasional Series no.1. (Prepared for publication by Oxford Polytechnic Press, but 'as a consequence of radical reorganisation of the publishing programme at Oxford Polytechnic' published instead by Chadwyck-Healey as 'the first volume in an occasional series to accompany the journal *Publishing History*'.) RM contributes an article: 'The Financial Records of the Stationers' Company, 1605-1811', 1-31. Reviewed: *British Journal for Eighteenth-Century Studies*, 11: 2 (David Pearson), *English Historical Review*, 104: 1 (Julian Roberts).

Canons: Drawings and Photographs of the North London Collegiate School. Compiled by Moy Keightley. Edgware: Chandos Press. RM contributes two historical notes: 'The Buildings', p.9, and 'The Grounds', p.45.

1986

Bibliophily. Edited by Robin Myers and Michael Harris. Cambridge: Chadwyck-Healey. Publishing History Occasional Series no.2. RM contributes an article: 'The Caxton Celebration of 1877: a Landmark in Bibliophily', 138-63. Reviewed: *ABMR*, 15: 5 (Giles Mandelbrote).

1987

The Records of the Stationers' Company 1554-1920. 115 reels of microfilm, with finding-list. Cambridge: Chadwyck-Healey. RM's finding-list was reprinted in *Book Trade History Group Newsletter*, 6 (February 1988), 18-42.

Robert William Buss: Painter in Oil and Lecturer in Art. Founder's Day exhibition of his life and work, from the School archives augmented by loan items. (12pp. catalogue issued to accompany exhibition held at North London Collegiate School, 31 March–3 April 1987.)

Aspects of Printing from 1600. Edited by Robin Myers and Michael Harris. Oxford: Oxford Polytechnic Press. RM contributes a note: 'Workshop Reports: Printing in the 19th Century', 171. Reviewed: *Libraries & Culture*, 25: 4 (Sidney E. Berger).

The Library and Archives Trust of the Worshipful Company of Stationers and Newspaper Makers. (8pp. pamphlet describing the library and archives at Stationers' Hall, published August 1987.)

1988

Pioneers in Bibliography. Edited by Robin Myers and Michael Harris. Winchester: St Paul's Bibliographies. RM contributes an article: 'Stationers' Company Bibliographers: the First Hundred Years: Ames to Arber', 40-57. Reviewed: *Libraries & Culture*, 25: 2 (Sidney E. Berger), *TLS*, 31 March 1989 (Robin Alston).

'One Author's Association with Pergamon', in *Robert Maxwell and Pergamon Press: 40 Years' Service in Science, Technology and Education* (Oxford: Pergamon Press), 713-15.

1989

Fakes and Frauds: Varieties of Deception in Print and Manuscript. Edited by Robin Myers and Michael Harris. Winchester: St Paul's Bibliographies; and Detroit: Omnigraphics Inc. Reviewed: *The Library*, 6th ser., 12: 4 (John Hewish), *Libraries & Culture*, 27: 1 (Sidney E. Berger).

'Samuel Richardson (1689-1761): Why should we celebrate him?', *The Stationer & Newspaper Maker*, 48 (Summer 1989), 121-2.

1990

The Stationers' Company Archive: an Account of the Records 1554-1984. Winchester: St Paul's Bibliographies; and Detroit: Omnigraphics Inc. Reviewed: *Publishing History*, 30 (Christine Ferdinand), *Eighteenth-Century Studies*, 27: 1 (William Proctor Williams), *Journal of the Society of Archivists*, 13: 1 (Arnold Hunt), *Printing Historical Society Bulletin*, 32 (Giles Mandelbrote), *Times Higher Educational Supplement*, 30 Nov. 1990 (Alison Shell), *TLS*, 1 May 1992 (T. A. Birrell).

Spreading the Word: the Distribution Networks of Print, 1550-1850. Edited by Robin Myers and Michael Harris. Winchester: St Paul's Bibliographies; and Detroit: Omnigraphics Inc. Reviewed: *The Library*, 6th ser., 16: 4 (Joad Raymond), *Library Association Record*, 93 (David Pearson).

Concentric Circles: Miss Buss and the Women's Movement. (17pp. catalogue issued to accompany exhibition held at North London Collegiate School, 31 March-5 April 1990.)

1991

The auto-biography of Luke Hansard, written in 1817. Edited with an introduction and notes by Robin Myers, and wood-engraved illustrations by John Lawrence. Wakefield: Fleece Press. Limited edition of 250 copies. Reprinted as *The auto-biography of Luke Hansard, Printer to the House, 1752-1828.* London: Printing Historical Society. Reviewed: *Printing Historical Society Bulletin*, 31 (David McKitterick), *The Library*, 6th ser., 18: 4 (Kevin L. Cope).

Property of a Gentleman: The formation, organisation and dispersal of the private library 1620-1920. Edited by Robin Myers and Michael Harris. Winchester: St Paul's Bibliographies. RM contributes an article: 'William Herbert: his library and his friends', 133-58. Reviewed: *Libraries & Culture*, 28: 1 (Alan Gribben).

Cannons through Eight Centuries. (15pp. catalogue issued to accompany exhibition held at North London Collegiate School, 21-27 March 1991.)

1992

Censorship and the Control of Print in England and France 1600-1910. Edited by Robin Myers and Michael Harris. Winchester: St Paul's Bibliographies. Reviewed: *PBSA*, 87: 3 (Maureen Bell), *Rare Books Newsletter*, 44 (Murray Simpson).

Journal of the Printing Historical Society, 21 (1992). RM edited this issue of the *Journal*, and also contributes an article: 'Searching the Stationers' Company Records for Printing History', 5-12.

'Stationers' Company bibliography, 1892-1992', *The Book Encompassed: Studies in Twentieth-Century Bibliography*, ed. Peter Davison, 116-21. Cambridge: Cambridge University Press.

A Hundred Years of Cambridge: a centenary exhibition of embroidery, photographs and artefacts illustrating the life and times of Clare Myers, Cambridge Townswoman, 1892-1990. (12pp. pamphlet issued to accompany an exhibition at Cambridge Central Library, 2-16 May 1992.)

Review of *Table Manners for Children: Stans puer ad mensam* by John Lydgate, translated with an introduction by Nicholas Orme and a foreword by Lotte Hellinga, *The Library*, 6th ser., 14: 1 (March 1992), 65-6.

Review of W. H. Bond, *Thomas Hollis of Lincoln's Inn, a Whig and his Books, Printing Historical Society Bulletin*, 32 (Summer 1992), pp.10-11.

1993

Serials and their Readers 1620-1914. Edited by Robin Myers and Michael Harris. Winchester: St Paul's Bibliographies: and Delaware: Oak Knoll Press.

Review of *The Bowyer Ledgers*, edited by Keith Maslen and John Lancaster, *Printing Historical Society Bulletin*, 34 (Spring 1993), p.12.

1994

A Millennium of the Book: Production, Design and Illustration in Manuscript and Print 900-1900. Edited by Robin Myers and Michael Harris. Winchester: St Paul's Bibliographies; and Delaware: Oak Knoll Press.

Reviews of Keith Maslen, *An Early London Printing House at Work: Studies in the Bowyer Ledgers*, and Charles A. Rivington, *Pepys and the Booksellers, Printing Historical Society Bulletin*, 38 (Winter 1994), pp.31-2.

1995

A Genius for Letters: Booksellers and Bookselling from the 16th to the 20th Century. Edited by Robin Myers and Michael Harris. Winchester: St Paul's Bibliographies; and Delaware: Oak Knoll Press.

1996

Antiquaries, Book Collectors and the Circles of Learning. Edited by Robin Myers and Michael Harris. Winchester: St Paul's Bibliographies; and Delaware: Oak Knoll Press. RM contributes an article: 'Dr Andrew Coltée Ducarel (1713-1785): pioneer of Anglo-Norman studies', 45-70.

Index